EXPLAINING EVIL

EXPLAINING EVIL

VOLUME 1
Definitions and Development

J. Harold Ellens, Editor

Psychology, Religion, and Spirituality

 PRAEGER

AN IMPRINT OF ABC-CLIO, LLC
Santa Barbara, California • Denver, Colorado • Oxford, England

Library of Congress Cataloging-in-Publication Data
Explaining evil / J. Harold Ellens, editor.
    p. cm.
    Includes bibliographical references and index.
    ISBN 978-0-313-38715-9 (hard copy : alk. paper) — ISBN 978-0-313-38716-6
(ebook)
    1. Good and evil. I. Ellens, J. Harold, 1932–
    BJ1401.E97   2011
    214—dc22   2010041383

ISBN: 978-0-313-38715-9
EISBN: 978-0-313-38716-6

15   14   13   12   11   1   2   3   4   5

This book is also available on the World Wide Web as an eBook.
Visit www.abc-clio.com for details.

Praeger
An Imprint of ABC-CLIO, LLC

ABC-CLIO, LLC
130 Cremona Drive, P.O. Box 1911
Santa Barbara, California 93116-1911

This book is printed on acid-free paper ∞

Manufactured in the United States of America

*These volumes are dedicated to three gentlemen
who constructively influenced my life in very substantial ways.*

*Professor Henry J. Stob of Calvin College inspired me to think creatively despite
the crimped and doctrinaire community from which
both of us derived.*

*Professor Seward Hiltner taught me how to savor the flavor of freedom,
in the thoughtful quest for truth, the careful cherishing of people
and an honest pastoral passion for those in need.*

*Dr. Jeffrey Zaks of Providence Medical Center
Department of Cardiology
saved my life repeatedly; and gave me reason to believe
that after four heart attacks, two open heart surgeries,
and two minor strokes,
life was still worth while and still held great possibilities.*

All of my significant published scholarship came about after that.

These men not only cared for me. They loved me and I loved them.

Contents

SERIES FOREWORD

The interface between psychology, religion, and spirituality has been of great interest to scholars for a century. In the last three decades a broad popular appetite has developed for books which make practical sense out of the sophisticated research on these three subjects. Freud expressed an essentially deconstructive perspective on this matter and indicated that he saw the relationship between human psychology and religion to be a destructive interaction. Jung, on the other hand, was quite sure that these three aspects of the human spirit, psychology, religion, and spirituality, were constructively and inextricably linked.

Anton Boisen and Seward Hiltner derived much insight from both Freud and Jung, as well as from Adler and Reik, while pressing the matter forward with ingenious skill and illumination. Boisen and Hiltner fashioned a framework within which the quest for a sound and sensible definition of the interface between psychology, religion, and spirituality might best be described or expressed.[1] We are in their debt.

This series of general interest books, so wisely urged by Praeger Publishers and vigorously sought after by its editor Deborah Carvalko, intends to define the terms and explore the interface of psychology, religion, and spirituality at the operational level of daily human experience. Each volume of the series identifies, analyzes, describes, and evaluates the full range of issues, of both popular and professional interest, that deal with the psychological factors at play (1) in the way religion takes shape and is expressed, (2) in the way spirituality functions within human persons and shapes both religious formation and expression, and (3) in the ways that spirituality is

shaped and expressed by religion. The interest is psycho-spiritual. In terms
of the rubrics of the disciplines and the science of psychology and spirituality this series of volumes investigates the *operational dynamics* of religion and
spirituality.

The verbs "shape" and "express" in the above paragraph refer to the forces
which prompt and form religion in persons and communities, as well as to
the manifestations of religious behavior (1) in personal forms of spirituality,
(2) in acts of spiritually motivated care for society, and (3) in ritual behaviors
such as liturgies of worship. In these various aspects of human function the
psychological and/or spiritual drivers are identified, isolated, and described
in terms of the way in which they unconsciously and consciously operate in
religion, thought, and behavior.

The books in this series are written for the general reader, the local library,
and the undergraduate university student. They are also of significant interest to the informed professional, particularly in fields corollary to his or her
primary interest. The volumes in this series have great value for pastoral settings in congregational ministry, in clinical settings, and in the development
of treatment models, as well.

This series editor has spent his professional lifetime focused specifically
upon research into the interface of psychology in religion and spirituality. This
present set of three volumes, entitled *Explaining Evil*, is an urgently needed
and timely work, the motivation for which is surely endorsed enthusiastically by the entire religious world today, as the international community
searches for strategies that will afford us better and deeper spiritual self-
understanding as individuals and communities as we struggle with palpable
forms of violent evil in our world.

This project addresses the deep psychosocial, psychospiritual, and biological sources of human nature which shape and drive our psychology and
spirituality. Careful strategies of empirical, heuristic, and phenomenological
research have been employed to give this work a solid scientific foundation
and formation. Never before has such wise analysis been brought to bear
upon the dynamic linkage between human physiology, psychology, and spirituality in an effort to understand the irrepressible and universal human quest
for meaning, which this work defines as spirituality.

For 50 years such organizations as the Christian Association for Psychological Studies and such graduate departments of psychology as those at
Boston College, Fuller Graduate School of Psychology, Rosemead Graduate
School of Psychology, Harvard, George Fox, Princeton, Emory, and the like,
have been publishing important building blocks of research on issues dealing
with psycho-spirituality. In this present project the insights generated by such
patient and careful research are explored in three categories. The first volume
treats evil itself while the second volume describes its role and dynamics in
the church and society, and the third volume addresses the psychodynamics

at play in countering evil and the psychosocial efforts to contain, control, and cure it in persons and society so as to guarantee or facilitate healthy social psychology and religion, thus affording us wholesome psycho-spirituality. These volumes employ an objective and experience-based approach to our spiritual life and growth as we pursue the quest for explaining evil.

Some of the influences of religion upon persons and society, now and throughout history, have been negative. In 2004 we published in this series four volumes entitled *The Destructive Power of Religion*. That set of volumes analyzed the biblical metaphors which infect our psychological archetypes with destructive forces that prompt humans to utilize our capacity for violence in the name of God. Such biblical metaphors as a cosmic conflict in which God is a warrior in mortal competition with the power of evil, and God's inclination to solve his ultimate problems with ultimate violence, prompt humans to behave in the same way. Such pathogenically evil images of idealized divine and human behavior are reprehensible and must be done away with. Those biblical myths have wreaked havoc upon our world for 3,000 years or more. Surely that must end now.

On the other hand, much of the impact of the great religions upon human life and culture has been profoundly redemptive and generative of great good. It is urgent, therefore, that we discover and understand better what the psychological and spiritual forces are which empower people of faith and genuine spirituality to open their lives to the transcendent connection and give themselves to all the creative and constructive enterprises that, throughout the centuries, have made human life the humane, ordered, prosperous, and aesthetic experience it can be at its best. Surely the forces for good in both psychology and spirituality far exceed the powers and proclivities toward evil.

These volumes are dedicated to the greater understanding of *Psychology, Religion, and Spirituality*, and thus to the profound understanding and empowerment of those psycho-spiritual drivers which can help us (1) transcend the malignancy of our earthly pilgrimage, (2) open our spirits to the divine spirit, (3) enhance the humaneness and majesty of the human spirit, (4) empower our potential for magnificence in human life, and (5) illumine us with an understanding of the problem of the evil with which we contend.

J. Harold Ellens
Series Editor

NOTE

1. L. Aden and J. H. Ellens, *Turning Points in Pastoral Care: The Legacy of Anton Boisen and Seward Hiltner* (Grand Rapids, MI: Baker, 1990).

CHAPTER 1

INTRODUCTION: SETTING THE COURSE

J. Harold Ellens

Donald Meekhof and I were the first two babies baptized by the Reverend John L. Shaver in the Lucas Christian Reformed Church, three miles outside of the little village of McBain, Michigan. It was July 1932. They tell me Don was first and I was second. Apparently that was the sort of thing to remember in that little Dutch-German immigrant community in those days. I do not remember it. There were lots of babies then, and they were all baptized as soon after birth as possible. I do remember rather vividly, however, two things about baptism from witnessing many other children baptized in my childhood years. First, the rather long and stuffy baptismal liturgy covered the theological waterfront with all the biblical and quasi-biblical ideas you could stuff into a 20- or 30-minute read. Second, there was one great line that stuck with me to this day, and probably saved my sanity many times over.

At the point that the liturgy tried to signify the particular meaning of baptizing infants (who would never remember a thing of it, of course), the preacher read that infant baptism was a sign on the child's forehead that God covenanted with that child "to avert all evil or turn it to our profit." That sounded like a good deal. I latched onto that assurance very early—long before I was 5 years old, as I recall. I fervently hoped it was true. I have spent the rest of my life trying to figure out just in what way that great line is operationally real and authentic.

I grew up in a grateful, pious family and community in a time of great suffering. The Great Depression and World War II shaped my formative socialization, intellectual development, and spirituality. Moreover, it was a time when children were dying all around me: two Warsen girls, the Sheppers twins, my very best friend Esther just across the country road, my brother Gordon Henry, my sister Fenne, a Scholten boy, the Sickema son, the Owinga child, and a veritable host of others. Talk about evil! I was quite sure it was all around me, and God did not seem to be averting it from a lot of little baptized kids. Moreover, once they were dead, how could God turn it to their profit? Each time another child died, evil seemed to be sneaking up on me and getting too close for comfort!

"God will avert all evil or turn it to our profit." So what the hell is evil, then? I would not say my life has been exactly preoccupied with evil, but I have always been consciously curious about its nature and source. I suppose this is an enigma in the mind of every thoughtful human being. I believe I came rather early to wondering whether evil is an abstract force or personified agent, something cosmic or of this world, anonymous, abstract, or personal. I remember John Kromminga, my church history professor in seminary, saying that pastors should be well acquainted with evil but not participate in it. I thought that was as enigmatic and mysterious as the line from the baptismal liturgy.

The *Encyclopedia Britannica* declared confidently that evil is "a theological problem that arises for any philosophical or religious view that affirms the following three propositions: (a) God is almighty, (b) God is perfectly good, and (c) evil exists. If evil exists, it seems either that God wants to obliterate evil and is not able to—and thus his omnipotence is denied—or that God is able to obliterate evil but does not want to—and thus his goodness is denied" ("The Problem of Evil," 1974, p. 1017). I was sure from the outset that God wanted to avert all evil or turn it to our profit, and that the matter was much more complicated than the rather slick statement in the encyclopedia seemed to suggest.

Of course, some faith traditions such as Vedanta Hinduism, Christian Science, and Greco-Roman Stoicism tried to craft their systems of thought in terms of the denial that evil exists at all. We only imagine it—or, to put it more accurately, evil is just a semantic construct, a set of words, that we make up in our heads. William James, the famous psychologist and philosopher of the late 19th and early 20th centuries, solved the enigma by denying that God is omnipotent. He was sure God is genuinely good but has limited power. Mainstream Judaism, Christianity, and Islam have tended to live precariously with the tension between the goodness of an omnipotent God and the fact that evil not only exists but also often seems rampant in the world. Leibnitz, a 17th-century German philosopher, said that God can only do what is logical, and the illogical always exists in the best of all possible worlds—and that is evil.

Aurelius Augustine, a Christian theologian who lived in the late fourth and early fifth centuries, had a greater influence upon shaping all subsequent Western thought about evil than anyone else, except perhaps Thomas

Aquinas. St. Augustine (1948) was sure that evil does not exist as a cosmic force or agent, or as an objective entity in this world. He argued that evil is only the absence of the good (Vol. 1, pp. 100–104). That sounds nicely benign and definitive, but as soon as you ask him what he means by that, things get complicated. Did he mean merely what Edmund Burke is reported to have said, "The only thing that is necessary for evil to triumph, is that good men do nothing"? Thus, if we do not act for good we create a vacuum that is evil or that propagates evil. That still leaves us wondering what that is that gets in the cracks where we are not doing good. It also leaves us as mystified as before about where it comes from and how it operates.

An entire chapter is devoted later in this work to Aquinas's view of evil. His view is treated there at length by Dr. Eppens. So I will only allude to it here. Aquinas was the greatest medieval theologian and philosopher. He treats the problem of evil at length in the second volume of his *Summa* (1945, Vol. 2, pp. 9–25). He argues relatively clearly that, as Augustine had contended, and contrary to Aristotle, evil is the unintentional consequence of a good act that proves inadequate or incomplete. Evil is that lack of the good, and the consequence that arises because of that deficit.

Evil has no essential existence, according to Aquinas, and is not an objective force that acts in time and space, much less an ontological agent, that is, an evil being. Evil is what we experience when we do some good but do an inadequate degree of good in the world. Gilson puts it precisely: "What is called an evil in the substance of a thing is only a lack of some quality which ought naturally to be there. . . . Evil is . . . negation. . . . It is not an essence, not a reality. . . . Evil is not a being" (156). Jacques Maritain, with Gilson one of the greatest modern scholars of medieval theology and philosophy and a stellar Aquinas interpreter, holds for essentially the same perspective on evil throughout his book on Aquinas's view of the problem of evil.

Samuel Johnson laid the foundation for modern research regarding evil in his *Free Inquiry Into the Nature and Origin of Evil*. He debated the view that has become the theological perspective of evangelical Christianity in the last two centuries since its development out of the philosophy and psychology of Jonathan Edwards. Johnson generally disagreed with the notion that evil is a force in life and history that derives from the actions of an evil agent, such as Satan, who opposes God and his intentions for this world.

Evangelicalism and fundamentalism are strongly persuaded that the Bible requires such a worldview. This outlook is essentially a heretical idea borrowed from Zoroastrianism by the Jews in exile in Babylon during the sixth century BCE. It was then developed elaborately in Second Temple Judaisms that proliferated during the five centuries between the exile and the births of Jesus, Philo, Josephus, and Paul. Those apocalyptic forms of Judaism included the theology of the Essenes, an extreme form of which characterized the people of the Dead Sea Scrolls at Qumran. Much of Christian orthodox theology has been tempted to follow that line ever since, deriving its unbiblical theology of providence and evil from Essene determinism. It supposes that evil is the product of a rebellion in heaven that set Lucifer or Satan against God in a cosmic war, the battlegrounds of which are history and the human heart. In the chapters in these present volumes that treat evil in the Hebrew Bible and in the New Testament (NT), this issue will be explicated in detail.

Much of Christian thought to the contrary throughout the last 17 centuries, as well as my position explicated in these volumes and in many of my earlier publications, is a broadside critique of that fundamentalist evangelical way of interpreting the Bible. There is no empirical, phenomenological, heuristic, biblical, or rational data or human experience on the basis of which to conclude that God is up against a challenging adversary in a cosmic battle, the outcome of which, at history's end, remains to be seen. That is a Zoroastrian notion and neither Judaic nor Christian. Not all the contributors to this three-volume work will work from the same perspective as I. This project on *Explaining Evil* is intended to bring to the issue many different outlooks and worldviews for the better illumination and informed reflection of the seriously interested reader.

It will be my intention in the chapters I write to develop the claim that evil is not an objective force and that the evil we experience in life has no cosmic source. There is nothing "out there" in the otherworldly realm except God, the God of providence and grace. God's grace is unconditional, radical, and universal. No devil or satanic agent is lurking around the corner of anyone's life, or beyond the screen between time and eternity. There is no such thing as devils, fallen angels, hell, or ultimate alienation from God. As John's gospel makes eminently clear, God intends to save all humanity and, indeed, all creation—"the world"—and God's purposes will not fail.

Of course, there are those who will immediately raise the question as to how to explain the problem of pain and suffering, the curse of evil human deeds, and the references in the Bible to "sheep and goats," "Gehenna," "being cast into outer darkness," and even Jesus's own references to hell. To raise such questions is legitimate, honest, and important. Providing definitive answers in each case is imperative. Let me attempt to do just that.

There is no reference in the Hebrew Bible to a place called hell. There are references to the afterlife, but those always use the Hebrew word, Sheol. "Sheol" is a term that refers to an undifferentiated state after death that is very much like that in Greek mythological references to Hades, the underworld. Neither Greek, nor Roman, nor Hebrew tradition invests the terms "Hades" or "Sheol" with any indication that it is a place of punishment of the wicked or blessed reward of the righteous. It is simply a shadowy place of undifferentiated existence of the good, the bad, and the ugly.

It is interesting that in both Greek and Israelite traditions, in the millennium before the birth of Jesus, Josephus, and Philo Judaeus, there was some reflection or speculation about the possibility of heroic persons of special quality being delivered from Sheol or Hades and somehow absorbed into the world of the gods. Hercules (Herakles in Greek) was a character in Greek mythology who perpetrated terribly evil deeds in his youth and was cursed by the gods to a destiny of hard labor. This was his punishment to compensate for his early murderous behavior toward his family. Hercules rose to the occasion, accomplished all the labors assigned him, and so sufficiently justified himself as heroically obedient to the gods that at his death he was delivered from Hades and turned into a deity.

In a certain sense a similar moment of exalting expectation is evident in the life of David, at least in his hope for the ultimate outcome of his afterlife. In Psalm 18:4–6, David imagines himself in Sheol, entangled in the "snares of death" or the "cords of Hades," from which he cried out for divine rescue. Psalm 116:8 seems a kind of follow-up on this anguish for it celebrates God's deliverance from Sheol, and in Psalm 16:9–11 David thanks God that God will not leave his holy ones in Sheol, or in the metaphoric equivalent of the city cesspool or dump—the Pit. These sentiments of the Psalmist are referenced in Acts 2:27 and 2:31, applying them to the resurrection of Jesus, the Christ:

> Thou wilt not abandon my soul to Hades,
> Nor let thy Holy One see corruption.

The Hebrew Bible, also known as the Old Testament (OT), does not know an afterlife of torture of the wicked and blessing of the righteous, except that some special holy ones may be taken up into the realm of deity or into the bosom of Abraham or of God. Nor does the Hebrew Bible know of a devil or a satanic counterforce to God. Satan is referred to in Job 1–3, but in that narrative he is one of God's cabinet ministers with a high level of esteem and responsibility, probably what today we would call God's chief of staff or secretary of state. He is a comrade of God and is referred to as one of a number of the lesser gods, "Elohim," who provide God (El) with counsel and guidance.

Even in Genesis 6, where evil in the world is explained by angels cohabiting with women and producing a generation of rather rambunctious giants, the angels are not referred to as "fallen." They are described as perhaps having made a mistake, but an understandable one considering the seductive force of sexuality—presumably a new experiment for those unfortunately deprived residents of heaven. In any case, it is not the angels who raise hell on earth, but the giants. Moreover, throughout, the angels are referred to as "sons of God," a term meaning "righteous persons" in Hebrew tradition. Besides, this entire story is merely a rewrite of an old myth borrowed from Mesopotamian lore, or perhaps Zoroastrian sources.

When the Israelites were exiled in Babylon, they had it so good there that when Cyrus the Great turned them loose to return to Palestine in 537 BCE, only about 10% of them wanted to leave Babylon. There they lived in a sophisticated suburb especially set up for them. They were on a rather luxuriant royal dole, and they had the status of counselors to the king himself, as in the case of Daniel and his friends. They had it made, and all the moaning about this exile was mainly typical self-pity on the part of those who thought they were "the chosen of God" who deserved special treatment, and were now being put through the discomfort of moving from their middle-class life in stuffy and irrelevant Jerusalem to first-class life in the capital of the empire. Bitching and moaning are just the style of some people.

Upon being rather well established in Babylon, the Israelites produced a prodigious amount of scholarly work, mostly devoted to their national tradition. This led them to incorporate into their master story a lot of material borrowed from Mesopotamian mythology and Zoroastrian theology. They believed they had relatively good memory of the roots of the people who became the Israelites. They remembered their traditions back to Abraham, and they had some records from Moses, the conquest of Palestine, their genocide of the Canaanites under Joshua, and the annals of the kings for about 500 years. What apparently perplexed them was the absence of any story that led back from Abraham to the creation of the world. That is, they could put together fairly well everything from Genesis 12 forward, but they had to make up the stories of Genesis 1–11.

They took the easy way out. They copied existing Babylonian, Chaldean, and Zoroastrian legends, myths, and religious explanations of Creation (Gen 1 and 2), the Fall (Gen 3), Cain and Abel (Gen 4), Seth to Methuselah (Gen 5), the sons of God cohabiting with women and producing giants and causing evil (Gen 6), the flood (Gen 7–10), and the Tower of Babel creating the various nations of the earth (Gen 11). Thereafter, the Hebrew Bible focuses on the nation of Israel.

While they were busy with all this interesting leisure activity and living luxuriantly off the royal dole, they got heavily into Zoroastrian explanations of the problem of evil as well. They not only devised the sexy story in Genesis 6 but also brought in the Zoroastrian dualism that gave rise to notions about a cosmic conflict between the good God, whom they called Yahweh, and an evil god they called the "prince of darkness" or the like. From there, such Zoroastrian influences sneaked into the New Testament.

The main theological problem the Israelites pondered in Babylon was how they, the special people of God, could have lost the dominant role in Palestine and in the western Fertile Crescent that they had during David's kingdom. How could God have allowed some pagan nation to overrun them? How was God in history—particularly in their history? What was the relationship between their suffering and their failures as the people of God? Zoroastrianism had an entire system that provided ready answers.

Zoroastrianism worshipped Ahura-Mazda, the god of light. It proposed that all of reality is divided into the dualism between the kingdom of light and the kingdom of darkness. On one side was the god of light, and the god of darkness was on the other. They had two competing and approximately equivalent gods. So the forces in history were god and devil, good and evil, light and darkness, righteous and unrighteous. The cosmic battle between these two kingdoms is ongoing and fought out on the battlegrounds of human history and the human heart. The job of humans is to make sure on which side we stand. This line of thought heavily influenced the Jewish answer to their central questions.

It is interesting how that happened. As a result of the rich ferment in the scholarly Jewish community in Babylon, a great variety of Judaisms developed during the 500 years between the exile and the birth of Jesus. Some strains of those Judaisms developed along a line of rather rationalistic philosophy and theology, not heavily influenced by Zoroastrianism. That school of thought eventually produced the Sadducees and Pharisees of whom we read in the NT. By the time of the establishment of the official Christian Church in the fourth century CE, that form of Judaism produced the Babylonian Talmud and what we now know as Rabbinic Judaism. That line of Judaism insists that it follows the original traditions that go back to Moses and Abraham. Perhaps in some ways and to some degree, that is so!

However, a host of other Judaisms proliferated after the exile, during the time between the end of the OT and the beginning of the NT. Josephus mentions a number of them. They include the Maccabees, the Essenes, the Zealots, the people of the Dead Sea Scrolls from Qumran, and apparently many others. Most of these were apocalyptic sects of one sort or another. They believed that evil was a cosmic force that would eventually pitch a huge catastrophic war with God and his minions. That war would end in a cataclysmic termination of history. When that happened, if God were lucky, he would win and exterminate all the wicked and all the cosmic forces of darkness, and gather into his kingdom all the righteous.

This solved a central problem for the Israelites who followed this trajectory. It meant that the good God, Yahweh, is justified in causing or allowing Israelites to be exiled and their kingdom reduced to irrelevance. They were unrighteous, and so they had to live with the consequence of that. They had found themselves on the wrong side of the cosmic battle.

However, that immediately gave rise to another central problem. How did they get on the wrong side, because they had always been sure they were the special people of Yahweh, the only true and living God? They dreamed up many different answers. Some Jews, like the Essenes of Qumran, were sure that God had decided before creation which group of humans would be the company of the righteous, escaping Sheol at death, and destined for eternal bliss with God. God had decided at the same time which crowd of humans would be unrighteous, perhaps escaping Sheol but condemned to eternal Zoroastrian torture in the kingdom of darkness.

If you asked what you could do to make sure you were in the company of the righteous in the end, the answer was enigmatic. Some said you could not do anything about that. You were stuck with what God had decreed before all time. Others said you could try to live the life of the righteous, and if it worked for you that probably meant you were among those elected for righteousness. If it did not work, you were stuck with the destiny of eternal damnation. Still others said that the door was not slammed that tightly shut. You could affect your ultimate destiny by working hard to be righteous, because the divine decision is taking place in time all the time. On the other hand, there were those who held to the original position that God had made the decision before time began, but those whom God foreknew would try to be righteous he decided to elect to the company of the saved. Those he foreknew would not choose to try for righteousness, God chose to damn.

It was this great variety of apocalyptic Judaisms that created the culture out of which came Jesus, the Jesus movement, and the NT writings. Consequently, because Jesus was a real man, whatever else the NT claimed him to be, he was ensconced in the culture, language, and metaphors of his day. He was an apocalyptic Jew, as the gospels clearly indicate. He spoke the language of the common people, with the common people, in the word pictures that were common to them.

Thus we have Jesus using such words as "the righteous and unrighteous"; those who are "sheep or goats"; those who suffer "Gehenna, where their worm never dies and their fire is never quenched"; and those who are "children of the light" and in God's company, *versus* those who are "children of darkness" and who find themselves in "outer darkness." These are, of course, not terms taken from what was the Bible in Jesus's day (i.e., the Hebrew OT). They are not OT religious language and proper Judaic ideology. They really have nothing to do with what would have been biblical tradition for Jesus. These are all from Zoroastrian religious language and ideology.

If you are familiar with the King James Version of the NT, or even some of the modern versions, you will have noted that the gospels report Jesus, on one occasion, telling a story about a rich man who was in hell and who requested that Lazarus, whom he had abused in life, come to put a drop of water on his tongue. Bible readers readily conclude that Jesus believed there was such a place as hell. There are two problems with this. The first problem is that the story is only a metaphoric story that does not prove that Jesus believed in the kind of three-story universe that is depicted in that parable.

However, the second factor is even more telling. The word in the original Greek language of that parable does not say the rich man is in hell. It says he is in Hades, Sheol, the undifferentiated underworld that is life after death—a world of shades and shadowy existence that is not quite life and not quite extermination. We know that no such place as the Greek underworld exists. Nobody proposes such a theology today.

The Bible nowhere uses the word "hell" or ever refers to a place called "hell," or an afterlife of eternal punishment and torment. Some passages in that very strange book of the Apocalypse of St. John might be cited as an exception; however, the entire book is such a wild and churned set of ethereal metaphors that nothing ontologically substantive can honestly be derived from it. Unfortunately, the King James Version, which has so heavily influenced English culture since 1611 CE, translated the Hebrew Sheol and Greek Hades as hell in nearly every case at which they appear in scripture. From that came the erroneous English Puritan and American fundamentalist evangelical claims that there is a place called hell and that the unrighteous are damned to that eternal place of punishment, down there in some ethereal netherworld. That is a completely unbiblical notion, a heresy.

Now, someone will raise the point that Jesus used all those Zoroastrian apocalyptic terms listed above, which seem to hint at a place for the wicked that is separated from God. Look at those texts more carefully. When Jesus speaks of the goats, those in outer darkness, those in Gehenna where their suffering is like a worm that never dies or a fire that is never quenched, he never once speaks of those terms as substantives. They are always terms that describe contingent states. Those are things people suffer who are not yet in full communion with God and are not consoled and forgiven by accepting God's grace. They are in a state of having fallen short until now, missed the mark, and not yet attained communion with God's saving grace. That is the reason for the gut ache that feels like a fire that will not go out, and the anxiety eating out their insides like a worm that will not die.

On the other hand, when Jesus and Paul refer to heaven, they always speak of it as a substantive reality, an actual state of being that is an experience of "going to the Father," or "going to be with the Lord." Moreover, Paul repeatedly says throughout his epistles that in the end, presumably in the moment of transition from this life to eternal life, "every eye shall see God, every knee shall bow before him, and every tongue shall affirm the embrace of God's grace, to the glory of God."

This conforms with John's gospel, the last word written in the NT. John's gospel declares that God will save the entire world (Jn 3:13–18), and that the judgment day took place before history when God judged that he would save the whole world. John's gospel, in consequence, has no second coming, no return on the clouds with the angelic host, no judgment day, no cataclysmic extermination of the ungodly or special treatment of the godly, and no end to history.

Instead, John proclaims that Jesus simply went to heaven where he belongs. He eliminated all the unrighteous from history by forgiving them all in advance, before they were born—before creation. Neither Jesus nor

God will judge anyone negatively or witness against us, no matter how much evil we perpetrate. If we feel under judgment, it is merely our own consciences correctly or incorrectly judging ourselves (Jn 3:18–21; 5:27–47). In the NT, there is no hell except the anguish we suffer here and now from our fear, guilt, and shame, even though God has thoroughly removed it from the equation of our relationship with God. There is no cosmic evil and no divine threat hanging over the world or our personal lives. There is no devil out there, only the God of grace and acceptance of us.

There is no biblical, rational, empirical, phenomenological, or heuristic basis for any notion of a cosmic battle with evil in this world, or for the devil, demons, or hell. That leaves us with a rather simple and concrete question about the nature of evil. The question is best formulated in this way. Because evil is confined to the experience humans have of undesirable or uncomfortable aspects of this world of time and space, how shall we define "evil," and what is its scope? A summary statement is sufficient here. The rest of these three volumes elaborate most of the important detailed aspects and implications of the matter.

There are only two kinds of evil: those destructive things that we do to each other, ourselves, or God's created world, by our bad will and bad intention; and that which we do to ourselves, each other, and the universe by ignorance and neglect. Those destructive things we do by bad will and intention fall into two categories also: those that are a result of unnecessary calculated intention to do harm, and those we do because of psychopathology. Of the former, we are morally and ethically culpable. Of the latter, we are not but should do our best to get help. The destructive things we do from ignorance and neglect fall into two categories: the actions of which we could have been informed and responsible, and those of which we had no way of being informed and hence responsible. Of the former, we are culpable. Of the latter, we are not culpable, but we should make ourselves as informed and responsible as we possibly can. These volumes address all the various sides of these issues.

One final matter remains to be addressed here. Someone will surely ask, "What of God's responsibility for the evil of deadly natural disasters?" Why does he allow or cause mudslides that wipe out Colombian villages, volcanoes that destroy Pompeii and Herculaneum, earthquakes that wreck entire civilizations or spoil the aesthetic artifacts that creative humans have devised, and tsunamis that wreak havoc over wide sections of our planet, at great cost of life and treasure? Why does a microbe infect a cow's milk and kill children in India?

God has designed and created this world in such a manner that everything functions with a total freedom within the confines of its own nature. That is true of inorganic as well as organic reality. It is equally true of the electron in orbit in the atom as it is true of a wife choosing to cherish or abuse her husband. The natural order has its own structure and patterns, and each element is free to conform to that pattern or fly out of it and wreak havoc. When a cell chooses to go wrong, we have cancer. When an electron chooses to leave its orbit, it creates another kind of molecule that may be constructive or destructive. When a human chooses good or ill, it has consequences. Regardless of the developments in any of these areas, God does not intervene to pay his world off every Saturday night, nor does he straighten us out every week.

The reason for God to allow this freedom to percolate along according to the inherent nature of things, even when humans make bad choices, is because God takes the natural cause-and-effect processes in the universe so seriously, and he takes the developmental dynamics of our growing personalities so seriously, that he will not intervene. God will not compromise the freedom for growth and constructive change that he has built into the created universe. Now, in such a world of total freedom, if there are no mistakes, destructive inadvertencies, and errors, there is not freedom. God has not created a clockwork orange, as we all know.

When mountains erupt volcanically, mudslides kill people, and earthquakes destroy, God does not prevent that. If Colombians are not to be killed by mudslides, we need to take responsibility for informing them of the danger, persuading them to place their villages on safer ground, and helping them when we can. The Pompeians knew that Vesuvius erupts every 1,000 years. They should have taken account of that when they built their village. At least they should have placed it on the typical upwind side of the mountain. Those destructive events are not evil.

We call them "evil" only because we have a kind of imperial attitude that assumes everything in the world is supposed to operate in a way that is comfortable and congenial to human beings. When Vesuvius, Mount St. Helens, or the Icelandic volcano erupts, that is a highly successful achievement for the natural forces in the tectonic plates and the quite amazing dynamics of the planet's crust. In our imperialist attitude, we sometimes call this evil and a destructive act of God. It is not so. We say that only because it makes us uncomfortable to have airline flights cancelled, stranding many humans in our busy pursuits. We are inconvenienced, and so we call it evil. That is really quite ridiculous.

Similarly, when a microbe hatches in the soil, climbs up a blade of grass to have its lunch, is inadvertently ingested by a cow that decided to have that blade of grass for its lunch, and then sets up housekeeping in the fermenting big paradise in the ruminating cow's stomachs, that entire enterprise is a great achievement for the microbe. Now, if it is a parasitic microbe that has evolved especially for this very scenario, because it is designed to attach itself to the stomach lining of the cow and infect the entire organism, including the cow's milk, that is a great victory for this particularly little bug.

When a child drinks that milk, is infected by that bug's numerous progeny, and dies, we call it evil. Surely it is a tragedy for us humans. It is a great sorrow, loss, grief, discomfort, and inconvenience for the persons affected. But it is not evil. It is the natural life of the microbe, following the freedom and necessity of its own destiny. If we do not like it, we must do something terrible to the microbe. Is that less evil than what the microbe does to us? It is interesting that Albert Schweitzer got to that point at his hospital in Lambaréné, Gabon, Africa. He was totally ambivalent about that point—almost to the point of being unable to act against the tropical diseases he confronted. He was not sure humans had any more right to kill bugs than the bug has to kill people. He saw it as a natural contest of life.

Once when I was an army officer overseas, a number of officers in my hospital unit prepared a ship full of medical supplies and antibiotics to send to Schweitzer's hospital in Lambaréné. Schweitzer refused to accept the medical supplies and medicine. He had come to the point of believing in and using only natural processes for the treatment of diseases. That meant that if the natural process meant that the bug was stronger than the patient, the patient died. If the patient was stronger than the source of the disease, the patient lived and the bug died or was accommodated somehow. The physician's task was to enhance the patient's ability to triumph over the bug.

There is no such thing as natural evil in this world. The only evil that exists in the world is the damage that humans do to each other. We surely do not need to make up myths about demons and devils causing evil in God's world. We are all perfectly capable of creating more than enough of it on our own. That is what these volumes are about, and they are about what to do with all this evil humans instigated, and with the pain and suffering we inflict upon each other.

BIBLIOGRAPHY

Aquinas, T. (1945). *Basic writings of St. Thomas Aquinas* (Ed. Anton C. Pegis, 2 vols.). New York: Random House.

Augustine, A. (1948). *Basic writings of St. Augustine* (Ed. Whitney J. Oates, 2 vols.). New York: Random House.

Gilson, E. (1956). *The Christian philosophy of St. Thomas Aquinas.* Notre Dame, IN: University of Notre Dame Press.

Johnson, S. (1757). *Free inquiry into the nature and origin of evil, a critical review in literary magazine of Soames Jenyns' book by that title.* Cambridge: Cambridge University Press.

Maritain, J. (1942). *St. Thomas and the problem of evil.* Milwaukee, WI: Marquette University Press.

The problem of evil. (1974). S.v. in *Encyclopaedia Britannica, Micropedia* (15th ed.). Chicago: Helen Hemingway Benton.

CHAPTER 2

THE PSYCHOLOGY OF EVIL

Ralph W. Hood Jr.

I shall die, but that is all I shall do for death.

—Edna St. Vincent Millay

It is perhaps more a mark of hubris than anything else to claim to write of *the* psychology of anything, much less than of such a powerful topic as evil. With some postmodern sympathies, *the* smacks of a totalization that is at best premature and at worst impossible. Better is to claim to write *a* psychology of evil, but even here the preliminary problems are immense. It may be that, as Belzen (2010) has said of religion, evil is not a psychological but is rather a cultural phenomenon. However, evil is surely experienced as a malevolent force acting intentionally to inflict pain on a human being. In many cultures this force is personified and evil becomes (D)evil. We concur with Russell (1977) that the existence of evil requires no further proof. "I am; therefore I suffer evil" (p. 17).

Psychologically, the phenomenology of evil must be noted lest we flounder in attempting a too restrictive definition of evil. "Evil is grasped by the mind immediately and felt by the emotions; it is sensed as hurt deliberately inflicted" (Russell, 1977, p. 1). If we accept this elegantly simply reflection, we need not try to unpack definitions that would endlessly relativize evil, making one person's or culture's evil another person's or culture's good. This is the error of psychologists who would assert the "myth of pure evil" (Baumeister, 1997, pp. 60–96). We accept that no person is purely evil.

Thus, the myth of pure evil balances another myth, that of pure innocence. There are no pure innocents either. This is part of the reason why the major historian of evil, Russell, finds Jungian psychology so congenial to his understanding of evil personified or the D(evil). Individuals, like Jung's God, must gradually differentiate evil and good in the process of development. To deny one's evil nature can easily lead to repression, causing the growth of one's shadow, often projected onto another and providing the psychological mechanism for the myths of pure evil and innocence. However, if the Jungian process of individuation is completed, good and evil are both recognized and held in balance. Jung's speculative views have a depth that challenges Christianity Trinitarian views with a Quaternitarian view in which the Devil emerges into bright light as but the shadow of God exposed and acknowledged. This development of the imago of God we shall discuss below.

Our task in this chapter is not to seek a metaphysical domain for evil or to tackle the considerable theological issues involved with seeking a justification for evil given an omnipotent God (theodicy), or to explore theological traditions in which independent forces of evil contest those of good. This would be to tackle problems that psychology can only acknowledge but not provide satisfactory answers for. What shall be our task in this chapter is to provide a theory of evil, psychologically based in a distinction that denies that one must define evil by content or belief but instead defines evil by the process by which beliefs are held. Thus, our focus is not upon *what* is evil, but rather *how* is evil possible at all.

THREE SOCIAL SCIENTIFIC MODELS OF (D)EVIL

It is to social scientific models that we shall turn for our initial exploration of (D)evil. We shall seek not simply a psychological but a social psychological explanation for (D)evil. Social psychology is crucial for it is a discipline situated at the intersection between two sister disciplines, psychology and sociology. Ironically, the efforts to create this hybrid discipline began with the most widely adopted social psychology textbook of the 1960s, which teamed a psychologist (Paul F. Secord) and a sociologist (Carl W. Backman). They tried to create an interdisciplinary social psychology, noting that "social psychology can no longer be adequately surveyed by a person trained in only one of its parent disciplines" (Secord & Backman, 1964, p. vii). Often, the parent disciplines had been pitted against one another, with psychologists arguing for intrapsychic determinants of behavior while sociologists argued for situational and interpersonal determinants of behavior. In terms of the intention to inflict pain upon another, social psychologists seek to navigate between the Scylla of a purely psychological explanation of (D)evil and the Charybdis of a purely sociological explanation of (D)evil. The path is as difficult for contemporary social psychologists as it was for Homer's *Ulysses*.

A schematic illustration of the options can be illustrated in the simplified schema in Table 2.1. P stands for person, S for situation, and yes or no indicates the presence or absence of D(evil). The first option attributes (D)evil to intrapsychic factors, locating evil within the person. The second option attributes (D)evil to situational factors, locating evil in social or cultural factors. The third is a social psychological option in which individuals interact with situations to produce (D)evil.

In these options, the psychology of (D)evil (1) is indicated by person 1 being evil in both situations 1 and 2, so the (D) evil overrides situational determinants. Likewise, person 2 is not (D) evil, regardless of situation. Here the major determinant is the person, and the assumption is that only evil persons do evil deeds.

The second model is situational: Both persons do not do evil in situation 1, but both do evil in situation 2. Hence, situational factors rather than personality factors produce evil. Although many who work outside of the field of psychology assume individuals to be responsible for acts of evil, social psychologists refer to this as a fundamental attribution error (FAE) (Ross, 1977; Ross & Nisbett, 1988). The error is based upon studies indicating that individuals tend to underestimate the influence of situational factors and to overestimate the influence of personality in behavior. In the situational model, evil deeds are not produced by evil persons, but rather by persons who do evil in a particular situation.

In option 3, we have a truly interactive model. Person 1 is (D)evil in situation 1 but not 2, whereas person 2 is (D)evil is situation 2 but not 1. In the interactional model evil persons produce evil deeds only under specified situations. Furthermore, the specified conditions may vary for different individuals. Hence, personality and situations interact to produce evil; neither alone is sufficient.

The three models are more ideal types than isolated empirical realities. What is important is the relative weight given to personality and situational factors in producing evil. Because we are concerned with a social psychology of evil in this chapter, our emphasis will be upon models 2 and 3. Model 1 essentially reduces to a model of psychopathology in which (D)evil deeds are done by (D)evil persons. Insofar as the researcher focuses exclusively upon genetic, physiological, or psychological factors, the preferred term is "psychopath," but nevertheless the traits and behaviors that describe (D)evil deeds are identical even if the deeds themselves lead some to label the doer a

Table 2.1. Three Models of Evil: (D)evil (Yes or No)

	1. Personal			2. Situational			3. Interactional	
	S1	S2		S1	S2		S1	S2
P1	Yes	Yes	P1	No	Yes	P1	No	Yes
P2	No	No	P2	No	Yes	P2	Yes	No

"sociopath" (Tangney & Stuewig, 2004, p. 327). Our concern in this chapter is not to be concerned with (D)evil as psychopathology because that denies the intentionality and commonality of (D)evil that we wish to explore. Simply put, we deny that pathology is itself capable of (D)evil just as natural occurrences cannot appropriately be conceived as producing evil. Thus, in what follows we can simply indicate (D)evil as evil, with the reader aware that evil is always an intentional act of a person, not an unfortunate occurrence that simply happens.

Nazi Germany as an Exemplar

In order to focus upon the situational and interactional models of evil, we will use as a reference point Nazi Germany. There are several reasons to do this. First, the Holocaust is a fairly recent historical event for which there is extensive documentation. It occurred in an advanced culture, the seat of great art, music, literature, and science. Although Nazi Germany is not the only genocidal culture (one can document mass murders in many advanced cultures), few would deny that genocide and mass murder deserve to be identified as evil regardless of the culture in which they occur. Nazi Germany is simply a more recent historical example of the historical and cultural expression of the existence of evil that we agree with Russell requires no further justification.

Second, the Holocaust sanctioned by Nazi Germany has spawned arguably the two most intense and extensive research traditions in American social psychology. First is that identified as the *authoritarian personality* tradition associated with the classic book by that title (Adorno, Frenkel-Brunswik, Levinson, & Sanford, 1950). The second are the famous obedience experiments associated with the programmatic research of Stanley Milgram (1963, 1974).

The Authoritarian Personality Tradition

The authoritarian personality tradition is important for the psychology of evil for it is the strongest candidate for an interactional model of evil. However, it is usually presented as a purely psychological model in which evil is a personal attribute, as in model 1. It is closely related to two of the four root causes of evil identified by Baumeister, idealism and threatened egoism (Baumeister, 1977; Baumeister & Vohs, 2004). Furthermore, idealism can be linked with another root cause of evil, instrumentality or the means–end distinction we explore more fully in this chapter. However, the focus on root causes should not be personal, as in model 1 above. Perhaps only sadism, the final root cause of evil identified by Baumeister, is appropriately linked to model 1. However, sadism is less an act of evil than a pathological expression lacking the crucial element of conscious intent that we identify with evil, as noted above. The authoritarian personality tradition thesis is best identified with our model 3. Here, as we shall see, idealism is linked to threatened egoism influenced heavily by classical Freudian theory. However, for now it is only important to note that this authoritarian research tradition began as an explicit response to the Holocaust, when members of the American Jewish Committee teamed up with scholars at the University of California–Berkeley to attempt to understand how the Holocaust happened. Equally important, this research program desired to understand if it could occur again in other cultures with others as the targets for extermination.

The literature on authoritarianism runs to thousands of studies, and the initial book summarizing research findings was itself a focus of an entire volume dedicated to methodological critiques of the research (Christie & Jahoda, 1954). However, our concern is not with the minutiae of detail, but with robust findings that have both survived criticism and proven to be replicable by other researchers in a research tradition that is now over a half century old.

The model proposed by the authoritarian personality researchers was simple. First a measure of anti-Semitism was devised based upon Nazi propaganda. Included in this measure were five subscales referencing the intrusive and exclusive nature of Jews, their presumed defective nature deemed offensive to culture, and generalized negative attitudes toward Jews. These subscales clustered together suggesting that anti-Semitism was an ideology or an organized system of beliefs. Further scale development focused upon other social groups common in the United States but excluding Jews. This resulted in a measure of ethnocentrism that included subscales measuring negative attitudes toward blacks ("Negroes" in the original), women, and other minority groups. It also contained what would prove to be a controversial subscale, one to assess patriotism. The ethnocentrism scale correlated with the anti-Semitism scale, broadening the claim that prejudice is ideological. The patriotism subscale correlated with other subscales, suggesting that patriotism was a specific expression of a more general ethnocentrism consisting of a heightened acceptance of one's own group combined with a heightened rejection of others. This led to a measure of political and economic conservatism considered as a single measure indicating a commitment to conservative economic and cultural values combined with a resistance to radical social change. With some methodological caveats we can ignore here, the conservatism measured correlated with both ethnocentrisms and anti-Semitism, completing the empirical claim that anti-Semitism is not simply opposition to Jews but also part of a larger ideological cluster in which others different from oneself are stereotyped as different and rejected. The question then became "What type of person would accept such an ideology?"

The crux of this research tradition was the development of a personality measure, the *California F Scale*. It became widely referred to as the "Fascism" scale, although that term was never used by the original researchers. The personality measure was heavily influenced by classical Freudian theory and essentially identified nine subscales, of which three survived as the now standard measure of authoritarianism: authoritarian aggression, authoritarian submission, and conventionalism (Altemeyer, 1981, 1988, 1996).

The identification of a personality type, the authoritarian personality, was crucial for three reasons. First, both survey research using the various measures noted above, and in-depth clinical interviews with those scoring high and low on the *California F Scale*, supported the claim that it was authoritarian personalities who were accepting of an ideologically based prejudice. Second, demographic data and survey results using the various measures, combined with clinical interview data, indicated that authoritarian persons were likely to be less intelligent, less educated, from lower socioeconomic situations, and, crucially, politically and economically conservative. Indeed, the persistent claim is that there is no general measure of authoritarianism, but rather authoritarianism is a "right-wing" phenomenon (Altemeyer, 1981). Finally, a model of the development of prejudicial attitudes was developed in which psychodynamically understood children raised in difficult circumstances, likely by authoritarian parents who lack both education and intelligence, respond to authoritarian parenting styles (including physical punishment) by uncritically submitting to authority and seeking to relieve their frustrations by scapegoating others. Hence authoritarian submission fuels aggression toward others, especially minorities and those who tend to oppose the conservatism of the culture. Thus, the authoritarian tradition returned to the initial concern, how to explain the Holocaust. The answer is as elegant as it is limited.

Prejudice is a matter of belief, not behavior. It is an ideology that justifies discrimination. Discrimination is the actual differential treatment of others requiring situational or cultural support. Prejudices are beliefs held by persons whose own psychodynamically understood deficiencies lead them to stereotype, demonize, and demean others. However, whether they will act on such beliefs is largely situational. Nazi Germany simply fueled the fires of anti-Semitism, long a part of European culture, and the rise of Hitler finally allowed individuals to express their prejudices in ultimate acts of discrimination. Thus within a decade, millions of Jews and perhaps an equal number of other demonized individuals were exterminated. And, of course, it could occur again given the model noted above. Anti-Semitism is not about Jews; it is about those who hate Jews as an expression of their own inadequacies. Such hatred can be triggered into action (discrimination) by appropriate situational, cultural, and historical conditions.

There is much to criticize in this theory, but for now we need note only one major concern before moving on to Milgram's obedience experiments.

The concern will be the basis for our own model of evil, to be discussed at the end of this chapter.

Our concern is the claim that inevitable belief content follows from a presumed psychological process. In other words, the demonization and denigration of outsiders (the basis of scapegoating) occur only among authoritarians, who, as noted above, are "right wing." The claim that there is no authoritarianism of the left is more than a little suspicious. In fact, insofar as prejudice is partly demonizing and demeaning others seen as distant from one's own self, it is perhaps more than a little curious that researchers who are highly educated, intelligent, and often rooted in liberal political and economic philosophies found the problem of evil to be situated in the less educated and intelligent who adhere to political and economic conservatism! We shall return to this issue when we develop a theory of evil that does not exclude the possibility that the political left can be as evil as the political right. Outside of World War II, there have been at least as many mass murders from Mao's Cultural Revolution and the Stalinist purges as occurred in the Holocaust of Nazi Germany (Baumeister & Vohs, 2004, pp. 93–94).

The Milgram Obedience Experiments

In 1963 a mere eight-page article, perhaps the most influential article in American social psychology, was published in the *Journal of Abnormal and Social Psychology*. The initial article had not only been rejected by the journal in which it was eventually published but also had been rejected by the more prestigious *Journal of Personality and Social Psychology*. The study itself was part of a programmatic research effort, eventually including almost 20 studies summarized in Milgram's *Obedience to Authority: An Experimental View* (1974). Strictly speaking, Milgram's research program was not experimental, and no statistical analyses were conducted (Burger, 2009; Hood, 1987). Furthermore, the immediate ethical critiques of Milgram's research continue to be discussed by social psychologists and have resulted in the likelihood that Milgram's research will never be permitted again, surely not in any research institute that follows the American Psychological Association's ethical guidelines for research with human participants (Baumrind, 1964; Burger, 2009; Hood, 1987; Milgram, 1964). As with the *authoritarian personality* research, Milgram's research resulted in a critical text, part of which was devoted to a methodological critique of Milgram's research program to explore obedience in a laboratory context (Miller, 1986). However, unlike the Christie and Jahoda volume critical of the research methodology of *The Authoritarian Personality*, Miller's volume was largely laudatory of Milgram's methodology.

What links Milgram's obedience experiments to the authoritarian personality tradition is the immediate discussion of the presumed relevance of Milgram's research to the Holocaust. Milgram explicitly suggested this linkage in his original article and in subsequent publications. Furthermore, in a television interview summarizing his programmatic research on obedience, Milgram responded to Mr. Sacer's reference to the Holocaust and the possibility of its occurrence in the United States as follows:

> I would say, on the basis of having observed a thousand people in the experiment and having my own intuition shaped and informed by these experiments, that if a system of death camps were set up in the United States of the sort we have seen in Nazi Germany, one would be able to find sufficient personnel for these camps in any medium-size American town. (CBS News, *Sixty Minutes*, March 31, 1979, as quoted in Blass, 1999, pp. 955–956)

However, the explanation offered for the Holocaust is not the same proposed by the authors of *The Authoritarian Personality*. It is our model 2, noted above. Milgram was later to explicitly acknowledge that the evil done as an act of obedience is almost entirely situational. Evil persons do not do evil deeds under specific historical or situational conditions; rather, evil deeds occur from simple acts of obedience, when a person in authority orders another to harm a third person. It is just this simple!

Hannah Arendt published her influential work *Eichmann in Jerusalem: A Report on the Banality of Evil* in the same year (1963) that Milgram published his initial study. The banality of evil echoed the situational model and asserted, against the psychopathological or personal model (model 1) noted above, the simple fact that Eichmann and others like him "were neither perverted nor sadistic, that they were, and still are, terribly and terrifying[ly] normal" (Arendt, 1963, p. 276). In the book-length summary of his own programmatic work, which went on to be published in 11 languages, Milgram (1974) adopted the situationist view and explicitly referred to Arendt's thesis: "I must conclude that Arendt's conception of the *banality of evil* comes closer to the truth than one may dare imagine" (p. 6, emphasis in original).

The scope and breadth of Milgram's research are impressive. A single research paradigm was employed for almost a decade. Over 1,000 participants participated in just under 20 different studies all focused on conditions of obedience. Milgram had been a student of Solomon Asch and modified his work on conformity to include conformity to instructions to harm another. His concern was to focus on the process of obedience *to* authority and not on the content of what the authority required.

Despite minor variations, the basic scenario of Milgram's obedience studies is simple, and various summaries are readily available (Burger, 2009, p. 1; Hood, 1987, pp. 841–842; Milgram, 1974; Miller, 2004, p. 195). A participant and a confederate of the experiment were told that they were to be involved in a paired association task when the "learner" was to be punished with electric shock for any errors made. In an elaborate staging, a rigged drawing was staged so that the "teacher" was always the real subject, whereas the "learner" was always the confederate.

The participants were shown an elaborate shock generator with 30 switches clearly labeled by 15 volt increments (15 to 450 volts). The "teacher" was to administer the lowest level of shock for the first wrong answer, and move up by 15 volt increments for each subsequent error. The teacher was administered a 45 volt shock as a demonstration before the actual study began.

In reality the learner, sitting in another room and responding (in most versions) via intercom, received no real shocks for the numerous scripted errors made. Enough errors were made to allow all 30 switches to be used. At the 150 volt level, the confederate emitted cries of protest and claimed to be experiencing excessive pain, to have a heart problem, and to desire to quit the study. From that point on (until 330 volts), each time the confederate was shocked he yelled in pain and requested the study to be discontinued. After the 330 volt level, the confederate no longer responded. The experimenter, near by the "teacher," encouraged with four specific sequenced prods for the "teacher" to continue the experiment and to administer the next level of shock.

The actual study was intended to explore disobedience by identifying the level at which participants would refuse to obey and to continue to administer shock to a person in pain and requesting to exit the study. The results, however, surprised many. Overall, over 60% of the participants continued to administer shock until the last switch was administered, presumably 450 volts. Most persons do not ever disobey.

In all studies, there was what Burger (2009, p. 2) has called the 150 volt solution. This is the crucial point when the confederate acknowledges pain and asks to be excused from the experiment. In almost all cases, the true participant pauses and looks to the experimenter for guidance. This is when the experimenter responds with the first of four verbal prods, all essentially asking in varying degrees of explicitness that the "teacher" should continue the experiment.

Milgram ran his studies with sets of 40 true participants and simply indicated the number who stopped at various voltage levels. The most consistent generalization is that a bit more than 10% of the true participants (6 or 7) stop at or before 150 volts. Of those who continued past 150 volts, a similar percentage drops out at various levels before 450 volts. However, approximately 80% who continue past 150 volts administer all possible levels of shock. These data are from experiment 5, but similar variations occur across most studies. Thus, in the recent only partial replication of Milgram's obedience scenario, Burger (2009) was able to obtain permission to study individuals under the condition that if, at the 150 volt level, the participant wished to continue even after all four prods, when he or she used the next switch the experimenter stopped the experiment.

Burger could then use the 150 volt criterion and compare this with
Milgram's data while apparently avoiding the more serious ethical considerations associated with administering higher levels of shock. Overall Burger's
results parallel closely Milgram's, suggesting a positive answer to the sub-
title of his article, "Would People Still Obey Today?"

It is important to note that Milgram's situational explanation for obedience is made in the absence of any personality assessment of participants.
Milgram focused almost entirely on the situation. In his summary text, he
argued that obedience is a fundamental psychological process in which a person told by legitimate authority to harm another individual simply obeys.
He never assessed individuals on any personality dimensions. He did explore
gender differences (as have others) and found none (Blass, 1999, pp. 967–969).
He then explicitly linked his obedience paradigm to Nazi Germany. "The situation confronted both our experimental subjects and the German subject and
evoked in each a set of parallel psychological adjustment" (Milgram, 1974, p. 177,
emphasis mine). The situationist perspective, along with Arendt's banality
of evil thesis, spawned a massive literature on the willingness of Germans
to simply be obedient and hence to be merely following orders even if they
meant the extermination of millions (Goldhagen, 1996; Sandley, 1998).

As we did with the *authoritarian personality* tradition above, we shall not
indulge methodological critiques of the obedience experiments. Suffice it to
say that there are critical dissenters who refuse to use the obedience experiments to explain the Holocaust (Berkowitz, 1999; Fenigstein, 1998; Hood,
1987). Furthermore, if no assessment is made of personality, then the interaction model is not given a fair test. All we know is that, ignoring personality factors, certain situations produce obedience. However, as Berkowitz
(1999) has emphasized, evil is more than banal; it is seldom simply obedience. Obedience is accentuated when the target is stereotyped, demeaned,
and demonized. Similarly, Fenigstein (1998) has noted that although we may
be disappointed by the outcome of the obedience studies, the parallel to the
Holocaust is unwarranted. The Holocaust was preceded by a long tradition
of demonizing and demeaning Jews, and the terms that suggest the evil of
the Holocaust are not captured by terms such as "banality" but terms such
as "atrocity" and" inhumanity" (Fenigstein, 1998, p. 7). Milgram ignored the
insights of the authoritarian personality research tradition in his obedience
studies and the fact that their explanations for the Holocaust were more
complementary than competing.

TOWARD AN INTERACTIONIST MODEL OF EVIL: THE INCONGRUITY OF MEANS AND ENDS

We suggest that one can no more ignore the situation within which a
person exists than one can ignore that a person is in a given situation. Thus,

an interactionist model of evil is intuitively credible. We shall present such a model by an appeal to what we suggested is an apparent bias implicit in the authoritarian personality research. By unmasking this bias, we shall then propose a model of evil that identifies the basic psychological process that sustains evil to be identified as all-pervasive and the recognition of which suggests a way out of the situationist dilemma.

Rokeach and the Shift to Dogmatism

Milton Rokeach (1960) was among the most vocal social psychologists to argue that authoritarianism may characterize the left as well as the right. The error as he saw it of research on authoritarianism is that it confused the *content* of belief with the *process* of belief. Thus, in Rokeach's model, knowing the content of belief gives us no sure information regarding prejudice. The issue is *how* one believes. Rokeach dropped the term "authoritarianism" in favor of "dogmatism." Dogmatism is identified by the acceptance of absolute authority often sustained by a sacred text that is self-authenticating. This is the basis of the *intratextual* model of fundamentalism we have recently developed (Hood, Hill, & Williamson, 2005). However, dogmatism is more than simply intratextual; it is also connected with the conditional rejection of others based upon belief incongruity. The fact of belief incongruity rather than ethnicity is the ideological basis of prejudice. In this sense, prejudice can be prescribed by submission to an absolute authority that provides a meaningful frame for the denigration of others, as with some fundamentalist religious groups.

The Dogmatism Scale functions much like measures of authoritarianism on the political right, but uniquely identify similar processes on the political left (Vacchiano, Strauss, & Hochman, 1969). Not surprisingly, academics have challenged Rokeach as he, so to speak, tars them with their own brush. Although the political left may not be authoritarian, they can be dogmatic. Here we are not concerned to develop further Rokeach's theory but only to point out that it assumes what we think is crucial for any understanding of evil: that it can be omnipresent, that it does not privilege one particular social group, and that it is not absent in the intelligent and highly educated. Furthermore, it privileges the process of belief over the content of belief, a position consistent with our intratextual view of fundamentalism (Hood et al., 2005; Kirkpatrick, Hood, & Hartz, 1991) The advantage of this is that we can look to the process of acquiring evil beliefs and the conditions under which such beliefs can be acted upon, in an interactional model.

Means and Ends

If we now focus upon process rather than content, we can define "evil" as a disjunction between means and ends. There is a long tradition in the psychology of religion in which Allport made the theoretical distinction between two types of religiosity based upon the motivation for, rather than the content of, belief. One, extrinsic religiosity, uses religion as a means to achieve something else desired. The other, intrinsic religiosity, has no ulterior motive. Religion is an end itself, not a means. A scale to measure these differing motivations, the Religious Orientation Scale, has generated a massive and contentious literature too extensive to review here (Allport & Ross, 1967; Hood, Hill, & Spilka, 2009; Krauss & Hood, in press). However, the important theoretical issue is that intrinsic religious orientations do not support prejudices as do external religious orientations (Krauss & Hood, in press). And thus one can argue that psychological processes not based upon deficiency motivations or dependent upon psychological defense mechanisms (as in both authoritarian and dogmatic research traditions) do not lead to belief content that demeans, demonizes, or requires conditional acceptance based upon belief. These caveats will now allow us to explicitly develop our model of evil.

If we return to our definition of evil as acting intentionally to inflict pain on a human being, we see that evil is inherently entangled with violence. Psychologists are more likely to speak of aggression than violence, and theories of aggression abound. Within the authoritarian tradition, aggression is a secondary response to frustration, elicited when the submission to authority belies frustration and anger than are transposed toward others who are scapegoats. Although some psychologists have argued that the proximate cause of evil is the failure of self-control of aggressive impulses (Baumeister & Vohs, 2004), evolutionary psychologists tend to find violence as having adaptive value (Duntley & Buss, 2004). This would make aggressive evil a means to survival, something our model of evil opposes. Integral to our concern is that there can be no distinction between means and ends. Our model places nonviolence at the core of opposition to evil, and it thus must have some evolutionary support.

Evolutionary Nonviolence

In an often reported *Los Angeles Times* article, an epidemiologist (Scott Layne) and a political scientist (Michael Sommer) emphasized that that humankind now possesses the power to produce its own extinction at a cheap cost. What have been called "weapons of mass destruction" include any and all means to produce evil insofar as the intentional destruction of large segments of humanity is prima facie evidence of evil. The ability to produce weapons of mass destruction is made more widespread with the movement from nuclear weapons (estimated to cost $1 million for each person killed) to chemical weapons (estimated to cost $1,000 for each person killed) to a mere $1.00 per person killed by biological weapons. Miles's (2004) quip regarding this article is precisely on target: "As $1 million shrinks to $1.00, the means for Armageddon are miniaturized and democratized" (p. 134). The task for eradicating this evil potential (and a potential often historically actualized) must be a commitment to nonviolence. Further, there is an evolutionary base to this if we considered what evolutionary psychologists have referred to as "evolutionary preadaptation."

Evolutionary preadaptation is expressed in faith traditions that model nonviolence. In the Western Judeo-Christian tradition, this is associated with the Marcion heresy integral to Jung's (1973) analysis of the Book of Job. In his analysis of Job, Jung develops what has become in purely psychology terms the empathy-induced altruism hypothesis (Batson, Ahmad, & Stocks, 2004). The essence of the Marcion heresy is that the Christian Bible forced the merger of two gods, the Jewish god, a warrior god demanding the obedience and worship of his people, and the Christian god, remarkable in his refusal to endorse violence and in his willingness to die for humankind's salvation. Jung's analysis suggests that as the answer to Job, Christ is the self-realization of the Jewish god from whom Job demanded justice while affirming unconditional love. Job's innocence in the sense of not deserving pain and suffering from God is mirrored when god as Christ (truly innocent) can understand via empathy Job's own experience. In Miles's (2004, p. 138) own similar view and response to Marcion, there are not two gods, but one God that has repented and changed. Although Jung's and Miles's analyses are not without controversy, they are supported by a masterful reading of scripture, partly through the lens of evolutionary theory. As Miles (2004) noted, "Or, as we may now choose to put it, God adapted" (p. 134).

The key exemplars that Miles notes are the contrast between the Jewish God's actions in 2 Kings 1 and those of Jesus in Luke 9:54–56 (Miles, 2004, p. 126). I will use the same examples as Miles but quote from the King James Bible. Responding to King Ahaziah's appeal to a rival god, Beelzebub, Yahweh sends his prophet Elijah to rebuke Ahaziah. In the process, Elijah confronts Ahaziah's army:

> And Elijah answered and said unto them, if I *be* a man of God, let fire come down from heaven, and consume thee and thy fifty. And the fire of God came down from heaven, and consumed him and his fifty. (2 Kings 1:12)

In Luke, Jesus responds to his disciples (James and John) who ask Jesus in the face of religious opponents if they should follow Elijah's precedent:

> And when his disciples James and John saw *this*, they said, Lord, wilt thou that we command fire to come down from heaven, and consume them, even as Elias did? (Luke 9:54)

However, God has changed. Yahweh is now the Son of Man, who denies violence:

> But he turned, and rebuked them, and said, Ye know not what manner of spirit ye are of. For the Son of man is not come to destroy men's lives, but to save *them*. And they went to another village. (Luke 9:55–56)

If insight into nonviolence, modeled in the Christian tradition by Yahweh's transformation, is acknowledged, it can be seen as an example of preadaptive evolution. The pivotal issue is that evolutionary preadaptive traits developed in one environment prove to be adaptive in unanticipated future environments. Although we are not exclusively committed to an evolutionary model, it is useful in that it highlights that nonviolence may be a necessary adaptation for humankind's survival. If nonviolence is seen as preadaptive, we can seek exemplars in modern history in such figures as Mahatma Gandhi and Martin Luther King Jr. Both actively opposed evil, and each demanded the use of nonviolence, refusing to make a distinction between the means used to eradicate evil and evil itself. Perhaps this is most evident in Gandhi's commitment to *satyagraha*, a concept with no easy English equivalent but one perhaps best summarized as the force of nonviolence. Hence, *satyagraha* is far from passive, seeking to eradicate evil by means that themselves are not tainted with evil (Bondurant, 1965). Perhaps in Western Christianity, the Quakers have most expressed this view. It is over 300 years since the Quakers declared to Charles II of England, "We utterly deny all outward wars and strife, and fighting with outward weapons, for any end, or under any pretense whatever; this is our testimony to the whole world" (quoted in Olson & Christiansen, 1966, p. 141). The commitment to nonviolence as an evolutionary preadaption whose time has perhaps not quite yet come can be illustrated by a simple empirical study in which we contrasted American college students' evaluations of two cultural icons of the American civil rights movement, Martin Luther King Jr. and Malcolm X (Hood, Morris, Hickman, & Watson, 1995).

Martin and Malcolm as Cultural Icons

The simplest contrast between Martin Luther King Jr. and Malcolm X is distilled in Malcolm's phrase, "by any means necessary." Whereas Martin's commitment to nonviolence was unflinching, Malcolm argued that one could, if need be, use violence to achieve the goals of the civil rights movement. The assumption, implicit in most conflict resolution, is that among those committed to justice and the eradication of evil, the claim is that use of violence may be both necessary and justified. Hence, evil (violence) can be used to eradicate evil (violence), a contradiction that believers committed to nonviolence refuse to accept. Our suspicion is that among individuals actually opposed to civil rights, Martin's nonviolence was preferable to Malcolm's willingness to use violence precisely because of the assumption that nonviolence is a tool of the weak and incapable of succeeding in the face of superior force. Our use of the phrase *cultural icon* is meant to suggest a subjective reaction to culturally influential public figures that is less grounded in explicit ideological terms than in the affectively shaded meanings that such figures have for individuals.

To test our hunches, we established the reliability of two rating scales used in an empirical study. One was an evaluative scale, and the other was a scale as to assess potency or power. Our hypothesis was that both African American males and White males would rate Malcolm as more potent or powerful than Martin. This was indeed the case. However, we also predicted that White males would rate Martin more positively than Malcolm precisely because his nonviolence was presumed to be indicative of a lack of threat. On the other hand, we predicted that African American males would rate Malcolm more positively precisely because his willingness to use violence made him a great threat to the establishment. Our point here is simply that the use of violence is perceived by many to be effective in achieving ends that nonviolence presumably cannot. As the United States once again is at war as this chapter is written, it is perhaps ironic that in his acceptance speech upon receiving the Nobel Peace Prize, the first U.S. president of color acknowledged Martin while siding with Malcolm.

How Noble a Prize Is Peace?

Our discussion of Martin and Malcolm is paralleled by recent events. President Barack Obama was for many a surprise recipient of the Nobel Peace Prize. In his acceptance speech he made explicit reference to Martin Luther King Jr.'s own Nobel Peace Prize acceptance speech, delivered December 10, 1964. A day before his acceptance lecture, Martin explicitly acknowledged that the Nobel Peace Prize "is a profound recognition that nonviolence is the answer to the crucial political and moral question of our time—the need for man to overcome oppression and violence without resorting to violence and oppression" (King, 1964, p. 1). President Obama ignored King's acceptance speech but referenced his Nobel acceptance lecture several times. President Obama acknowledged Gandhi's and King's commitment to nonviolence but argued, "There will be times when nations—acting individually or in concert—will find the use of force not only necessary but morally justified" (Obama, 2009, p. 4). The irony of President Obama echoing Malcolm X in praise of Martin Luther King Jr. repeats what many accept as the common sense of historical reality: Violence is necessary under certain conditions to fight evil. The means justify the end. To quote President Obama once more, "For make no mistake: evil does exist in this world. A non-violent movement could not have halted Hitler's armies" (Obama, 2009, p. 4). Such a statement seems obvious but perhaps masks a counterintuitive claim.

Is Obedience Really Counterintuitive?

Martin Luther King Jr. received the Nobel Peace Prize one year after Milgram published his first study of obedience and a decade and a half after the publication of *The Authoritarian Personality*. Both these studies were motivated by an effort to understand the Holocaust and both offered limited explanations, each assuming that psychological processes and situational contexts could elicit a willingness to harm others. Commenters on Milgram's research have made much of the counterintuitive nature of his research, noting that even 40 psychiatrists had assured Milgram that virtually none would exhaust all the shock options and leading Milgram to comment in a letter to H. P. Hollander in September 24, 1962, "The psychiatrists—although they expressed great certainty in the accuracy of their predictions—were wrong by a factor of 500" (quoted in Blass, 1999, pp. 963–964). Blass argued that it is this counterintuitive fact of underestimation of actual rates of obedience that accounts for the influence of Milgram's research. However, as Mixon (1971, p. 28) has noted, the dominant methodology of American social psychology has been to create a unique situation to produce unknown outcomes. Social scientists gain reputations by demonstrating phenomena that are counterintuitive. Milgram's obedience experiments are a perfect exemplar of this phenomenon. Mixon's use of role playing rather than deception has demonstrated that with proper descriptions, role-playing schemes can uncover the determining features of a situation whose outcome is known in advance. Thus, persons should be able, given the proper description, to predict what others see as counterintuitive; Mixon (1972) replicated Milgram's 1963 study with a careful description of the procedures employed and found that 50% of his participants correctly predicted perfect obedience. Likewise, in a second scenario parallel to one of Milgram's later studies, Mixon demonstrated that when the experimenter was described as having increased levels of agitation and worry as additional shock were administered, participants correctly predicted lower obedience rates. Thus, either in actual experimental studies or in role-playing analogues, conditions that alter obedience can be correctly predicted. Perhaps participants in a scientific experiment approved by a prestigious American university simply do not believe the cover story that is the basis of the obedience paradigm.

CONCLUDING COMMENTS ON THE MEANS–END INTERACTIONAL MODEL OF EVIL

Our interactive nonviolent model of evil makes a first step at identifying a universal dimension to evil—that it is present whenever means and ends are disjunctive. If one accepts that evil is the intentional act of harming, maiming, or killing another, no act using violence is free from evil. The recognition of this is a first step toward empirical work isolating the conditions under which violence can be refused. We know many of these conditions already from both the authoritarian and obedience research traditions. Hitler's armies could have been stopped, and in some conditions were. There are good studies of nonviolent resistance to Nazism in such countries as Norway and Holland (Schwartz, 1959). Likewise, Evelyn Wilcock (2005) documented that nonviolent dissent rescued Jews in the Holocaust, and she provided her own counterintuitive claim that Jews and the Holocaust in no sense provide evidence to the impossibility of nonviolence even in the face of horrendous evil.

Thus, although we claim no current programmatic research tradition to support our model, we do insist that the first step in exploration is to unmask the myth of evil. That violent means can be used to eradicate evil assumes that the use of evil itself can eradicate evil. If we deny this, we can begin to seek to explore psychological processes and situational contexts in which evil is denied its dominance. Many of these conditions are already known— the research traditions surrounding authoritarianism and dogmatism have unmasked the conditions that foster degradation and demonization of others in which violence begets violence. A rich conceptual debate continues on the obedience experiments and why so few refuse to be disobedient. Fundamental issues of the disjunction between means and ends in the very methods used in social psychology have been raised since Mixon's (1972) role-playing alternatives to Milgram's actual deception, and are integral to most experimental social psychological research placing the distinction between ends and means at the very heart of methods that would seek to understand evil that itself is a disjunction between means and ends. The first step in any future programmatic research strategy ought to be to find means to study evil that are not tainted with evil and to note that the conditions that produce persons susceptible to evil and the situations known to produce evil are themselves possible of eradication. To know what end is desired may require refusal of any means that are incongruent if we are to understand, much less eradicate, evil. The personal dimension to evil, (D)evil, identifies all of us that use means that deny the ends we seek to achieve.

A PARTING THOUGHT ON NONVIOLENCE

To question the efficacy of nonviolence by an appeal to the necessity of violence in the face of great evil is to fail to treat nonviolence as a genuine empirical option. In the Quaker-sponsored experiment in nonviolent civilian national defense, the authors of *Thirty-One Hours: The Grindstone Experiment* placed as a colophon to the print edition the following quotation from an

American Friends Service Committee document: "Is there a method for dealing with conflict that does not involve us in the betrayal of our OWN beliefs,
either through acquiescence to our opponent's will or through resorting to
evil means to resist him?" (Olson & Christiansen, 1966, p. 141, emphasis in
the original). The answer for Quakers is in the effectiveness of love as an
alternative to evil, not simply as an end but as the means by which evil is, if
not overcome, at least held at bay. It is a hopeful sign that social scientists
have begun to study this alternative to evil under the rubric of godly love
(Lee & Poloma, 2009; Poloma & Hood, 2008). Perhaps the poetic refusal to
do nothing more for death is a prolegomenon for future social scientific work
not trying to elicit violence in staged situations, but trying to actually eliminate it from human history.

REFERENCES

Adorno, T. W., Frenkel-Brunswik, E., Levinson, D. J., & Sanford, R. N. (1950). *The
    authoritarian personality.* New York: Harper & Row.
Allport, G. W., & Ross, J. M. (1967). Personal religious orientation and prejudice.
    Journal of Personality and Social Psychology, 5, 432–443.
Altemeyer, B. (1981). *Right-wing authoritarianism.* Winnipeg: University of Manitoba
    Press.
Altemeyer, B. (1988). *Enemies of freedom: Understanding right-wing authoritarianism.*
    San Francisco: Jossey-Bass.
Altemeyer, B. (1996). *The authoritarian specter.* Cambridge, MA: Harvard University
    Press.
Arendt, H. (1963). *Eichmann in Jerusalem: A report on the banality of evil.* New York:
    Viking Press.
Batson, C. D., Ahmad, N., & Stocks, E. L. (2004). Benefits and liabilities of empathy-
    induced altruism. In A. G. Miller (Ed.), *The social psychology of good and evil* (pp.
    359–385). New York: Guilford.
Baumeister, R. F. (1997). *Evil: Inside human violence and cruelty.* New York:
    Freeman.
Baumeister, R. F., & Vohs, K. D. (2004). Four roots of evil. In A. G. Miller (Ed.), *The
    social psychology of good and evil* (pp. 85–101). New York: Guilford.
Baumrind, D. (1964). Some thoughts on the ethics of research: After read-
    ing Milgram's "behavioral study of obedience." *American Psychologist, 19,*
    421–433.
Belzen, J. A. (2010). *Towards a cultural psychology of religion: Principles, approaches, and
    applications.* New York: Springer.
Berkowitz, L. (1999). Evil is more than banal: Situationism and the concept of evil.
    Personality and Social Psychology Review, 3, 246–253.
Blass, T. (1999). The Milgram paradigm after 35 years: Some things we know about
    obedience to authority. *Journal of Applied Social Psychology, 29,* 955–978.
Bondurant, J. V. (1965). *Conquest of violence: The Gandhian philosophy of conflict.*
    Berkeley: University of California Press. (Originally published in 1958)

Burger, J. M. (2009). Replicating Milgram: Would people still obey today? *American Psychologist, 64*, 1–11.

Christie, R., & Jahoda, M. (Eds). (1954). *Studies in the scope and methods of the authoritarian personality.* Glencoe, IL: Free Press.

Duntley, J. D., & Buss, D. M. (2004). The evolution of evil. In A. G. Miller (Ed.), *The social psychology of good and evil* (pp. 102–123). New York: Guilford.

Fenigstein, A. (1998). Were obedience pressures a factor in the Holocaust? *Analyse & Kritik, 20*, 1–20.

Goldhagen, D. (1996). *Hitler's willing executioners: Ordinary Germans and the Holocaust.* New York: Knopf.

Hood, R. W., Jr. (1987). Review of A. G. Miller, the obedience experiments: A case study of controversy in social science. *Educational and Psychological Measurement, 37*, 840–845.

Hood, R. W., Jr., Hill, P. C., & Spilka, B. (2009). *The psychology of religion: An empirical approach* (4th ed.). New York: Guilford.

Hood, R. W., Jr., Hill, P. C., & Williamson, W. P. (2005). *The psychology of religious fundamentalism.* New York: Guilford.

Hood, R. W., Jr., Morris, R. J., Hickman, S. E., & Watson, P. J. (1995). Martin and Malcolm as cultural icons: An empirical study comparing lower class African American and white males. *Review of Religious Research, 36*, 382–388.

Jung, C. G. (1973). *Answer to Job.* In *Collected works* (Trans. R. F. C. Hull, Vol. 11). Princeton, NJ: Bollingen.

King, M. L., Jr. (1964). Noble Peace Prize acceptance speech. Retrieved from http://nobelprize.org/nobel_prizes/peace/laureates/1964/king-acceptance.html

Kirkpatrick, L. A., Hood, R. W., Jr., & Hartz, G. W. (1991). Fundamentalist religion conceptualized in terms of Rokeach's theory of the open and closed mind: New perspectives on some old ideas. In M. L. Lynn & D. O. Moberg (Eds.), *Research in the social scientific study of religion* (Vol. 3, pp. 157–179). Greenwich, CT: JAI Press.

Krauss, S., & Hood, R. W., Jr. (In press). *A new approach to religious orientation: The commitment-reflectivity circumplex.* New York: Rodopi.

Lee, M. T., Poloma, & M. M. (2009). *A sociological study of the great commandment in Pentecostalism: The practice of godly love as benevolent servitude.* Lewiston: Edwin Mellon Press.

Miles, J. (2004). The disbarment of God. In J. H. Ellens (Ed.), *The destructive power or religion: Violence in Judaism, Christianity and Islam: Vol. 1. Sacred scriptures, ideology and violence* (pp. 123–167). Westport, CT: Praeger.

Milgram, S. (1963). Behavioral study of obedience. *Journal of Abnormal and Social Psychology, 67*, 371–378.

Milgram, S. (1964). Issue in the study of obedience: A reply to Baumrind. *American Psychologist, 19*, 848–852.

Milgram, S. (1974). *Obedience to authority: An experimental view.* New York: Harper & Row.

Miller, A. G. (1986). *The obedience experiments: A case study of controversy in social science.* New York: Praeger.

Miller, A. G. (2004). What can the obedience experiments tell us about the Holocaust? Generalizing from the social psychology laboratory. In A. G. Miller (Ed.), *The social psychology of good and evil* (pp. 240–268). New York: Guilford.

Mixon, D. (1971). Behaviour analysis treating subjects as actors rather than organ-
    isms. *Journal for the Theory of Social Behaviour, 1*, 19–31.
Mixon, D. (1972). Instead of deception. *Journal for the Theory of Social Behaviour, 2*,
    145–177.
Obama, B. H. (2009). Nobel Prize acceptance lecture. Retrieved from http://latimes-
    blogs.latimes.com/washOlson, T. &U Christoington/2009/12/barack-obama-
    peace-prize-speech
Olson, T., & Christiansen. G. (1966). *Thirty-one hours: The Grindstone experiment.*
    Toronto: American Friends Service Committee. Retrieved from http://www.
    civilresistance.info/grindstone.
Poloma, M., & Hood, R. W., Jr. (2008). *Blood and fire: Godly love in a Pentecostal emerg-
    ing church.* New York: New York University Press.
Rokeach, M. (1960). *The open and closed mind.* New York: Basic Books.
Ross, L. D. (1977). The intuitive psychologist and his shortcomings. In L. Berkowitz
    (Ed.), *Advances in experimental social psychology* (Vol. 10, pp. 173–220). New York:
    Academic Press.
Ross, L. D., & Nisbett, R. E. (1988). *The person and the situation: Perspectives of social
    psychology.* New York: McGraw Hill.
Russell, J. B. (1977). *The devil: Perceptions of evil from antiquity to primitive Christianity.*
    Ithaca, NY: Cornell University Press.
Sandley, R. R. (1998). *Unwilling Germans? The Goldhagen debate.* Minneapolis: Uni-
    versity of Minnesota Press.
Schwartz, E. (1959). *Paths to freedom through nonviolence.* Vienna: SensenVerrlag.
Secord, P. F., & Backman, C. W. (1964). *Social psychology.* New York: McGraw-Hill.
Tangney, J. P., & Stuewig, J. (2004). A moral-emotional perspective on evil persons
    and evil deeds. In A. G. Miller (Ed.), *The social psychology of good and evil* (pp.
    327–355). New York: Guilford.
Vacchiano, R. B., Strauss, P. S., & Hochman, L. (1969). The open and closed mind: A
    review of dogmatism. *Psychological Bulletin, 71*, 261–273.
Wilcock, E. (2005). Impossible pacifism: Jews the Holocaust and nonviolence. In
    R. L. Holmes & B. L. Gan (Eds.), *Nonviolence in theory and practice* (2nd ed., pp.
    194–204). Long Grove, IL: Waveland Press.w

CHAPTER 3

THE SOCIOLOGY OF EVIL: A COMPARISON OF MODERN AND ANCIENT SOCIETIES

Richard K. Fenn

In this chapter, I intend to arrive at a notion of evil that fits a world in which contingency and temporariness become the media in which people live and move and have their own being. What can we learn about evil from sources that assumed that evil was part of the created order, however much it remained an invisible or unexamined part of human nature? What can we learn from antiquity, where evil resulted in and emanated from the most illicit forms of coupling between men and women? What can we learn about evil from a world that believed, as we do, that the passage of time could lead to the fall of great cities and the raising up of those that previously had been of no account, but that also regarded history as a source of providential responses to primitive forms of desire and aggression?

The passage of time, with all the changes and uncertainties that it brings, used to be an expression of providential disdain for the evil that causes wars and the destruction of great cities such as Troy. In discussing Herodotus as a writer within the Hellenistic wisdom tradition, the historians Marek Wecowski and Benedetto Bravo allow that Herodotus criticizes literal-minded or simplistic accounts of wars that find their source in violence against women. However, Herodotus does not dismiss, for instance, the idea that the Trojan War originated in the rape of Helen but finds in that rape an offense against the Creator of the world: an offense that over time could only be punished. His argument, then, is fundamentally theological. Time undermines what was formerly great, and brings to prominence what previously was of little account: an idea that finds important echoes in the biblical tradition about the relation of the first to the last (Bravo & Wecowski, 2004, p. 155). It is in that same framework, then, that we are to understand that the passage of time is in itself a fate that reflects the consequences of illicit or illegitimate forms of coupling.

What form, then, can evil take in a world in which the passage of time, with its continuous changeability and frequent crises, its constant alteration of fates and transformations of both individuals and the social order, is taken as routine? Even in early modern England, it was understood that it is in the midst of flux, of changes over time, of innovations and the violation of the social order, that time asserts itself as the medium though which evil and providential punishments of human vanity assert themselves. In the midst of the conspiracies and threats of the early 17th century, the English aristocracy was reading the classical Stoics; they would understand Herodotus's insight that history and the passage of time itself, by raising up things that were small and making small things that once were great, are providential expressions of judgment on evil. Cromwell often spoke of the special blessings that his armies received from a providential God who had no trouble discerning who was on His side.

Others found it difficult to know precisely on whose side anyone might be and that time was not always on the side of the good, or the good themselves immune from evil influences. Lord Essex, writing in a time of Jacobean intrigue, may have been the author of a document that cited an ancient authority on evil thus:

> In Galba thou mayest learn that a good prince governed by evil ministers is as dangerous as if he were evil himself; by Otho that the fortune of a vain man is torrenti similis, which rises at an instant and falls in a moment; by Vitellius that he that hath no virtue can never be happy, for by his own baseness [he] will lose all which either fortune or other men's labors cast upon him; by Vespasian that in civil tumults an advised patience, and opportunity well taken, are the only weapons of advantage. In them all, and in the state of Rome under them, thou mayest see the calamities that follow civil wars, where laws lie asleep and all things judged by the sword. (Salmon, 1989, p. 210)

Where temporality is accepted as the medium in which alone we live and move and have our being, what possibility is there that, by coupling oneself to the eternal, one can avoid a fate so common as to be universal? It is not only wars and unscrupulous civil servants who may alter the fate of the great and bring them low; evil has more indirect but equally divisive and disturbing outlets in revealed religion. Like civil wars and insurrections, the claims of a new revelation may introduce distinctions between the self and the social order, between individual and social status, between appearance and reality: distinctions that undermine faith that the individual's being is grounded in a sacred order that, in its turn, is deeply rooted in the cosmos itself. Special revelations, like violence itself, may dissolve conventional boundaries between significance and insignificance, the sacred and the mundane, the specialized and the ordinary. The loss of these boundaries creates a demand for the very teachings and reassurances offered by much of the Wisdom tradition and by Stoicism: a demand for a notion of reason that transcends both the self and any particular social order. Both found evil in a sense of absence and of emptiness, of mourning for a lost connection with the source or guarantor of one's own being; and, secondly, in terror of a power that undertakes to destroy the people and places, objects and symbols that have seemed necessary for one's own being.

In a complex, constantly changing modern society, in which individuals are also constantly revising not only how they present themselves to others but also how they sense and define their own selves, what resonance will there be for an antique notion of evil as representing a threat to their very being? In modern societies, the psyche of the individual is more or less differentiated from that of any social order, although perhaps least so from the most intimate and enduring of relationships. Although apocalypticism is alive and well in modern societies, its threat more often translated to the existential and perennial. That is, demonic expressions of aggression and desire, whether or not they are acted out in rape or incest, are pervasive, perennial aspects of human nature. Still invisible though they may be, these sources or aspects of evil are as ordinary as the human unconscious. The demonic is simple human nature, whether in the form of existential doubts about one's place in the universe, psychic doubts about the strength of one's most important and intimate connections, or tendencies toward aggressive and dismissive emotions such as jealousy, envy, and anger.

In antiquity, where no clear line was drawn between corporate and personal psyches, what afflicted groups and communities, even peoples and nations, could also undermine the very being of the individual. Entire communities devoted themselves to warding off the threat, for instance, of a terrifying absence, emptiness, or darkness, in which the individual's psyche is no longer able to maintain itself and simply dissolves or evaporates. Buddhist communities exhaustively dug out caves, for instance, in which the figure of the Buddha emerges momentarily only once a year in the light from the sun at the winter solstice; this would be a site in which this particular threat of nonbeing would be overcome, as would burial chambers created in Neolithic societies, into which the light of the sun at the winter solstice finally penetrates, if only for a moment on one day of the year.

This is not to say that in antiquity, there was no awareness of evil as inhabiting the inner recesses of the human psyche. Rather than a loss of a sense of one's own being coming from exposure to nothingness, individuals may find themselves being destroyed from within by spiritual forces. As Loren Stuckenbruck points out in his superb contribution to this volume of

essays, in first-century CE Israel, some individuals and communities understood themselves to be living in danger of being inhabited by such spirits,
and the devout commentaries on the life of Jesus presented him as one who
could restore individuals to themselves. As Loren Stuckenbruck reminds us,
evil is very hard to domesticate; demons turn the house of one's own psyche
or soul into their own dwelling place. What is at stake is the recovery of one's
own being in time.

Evil, as Stuckenbruck wisely points out, is "ongoing and cannot be wished
away." But communities could mount defenses for the individual psyche by
relocating evil outside the social order; it could be wished upon others. An
entire society could pray that the angel of death would destroy the firstborn
of the Egyptians; they might also have seemed better for an evil spirit to
destroy the swine of the Gadarenes, even though the relief would only be temporary, and the final destruction of evil would have to await the end of time.
It would be difficult to distinguish between psychic and ethnic cleansing.

If Stuckenbruck is right about demons, then, variability is built into the
nature of evil itself. Evil is a socially constructed variable that may take a wide
variety of forms under an even wider variety of conditions and be understood
in even more various ways according to the ideas, symbols, and traditions
available in any particular culture. Some demons cause afflictions but do not
cause the soul to lose the ground of its own being; that is, they have to do
with the way the person exists in this world, with more or less affliction and
suffering. Other demons, however, have to do with the way in which a person
loses touch with the ground of his or her own being; they take over the soul,
and make it their own dwelling place. The demon can speak of the person's
soul as "my house."

Despite these more obvious differences between ancient and modern societies, there are sources in antiquity that suggest that evil is somehow part of
human nature, and not merely of the human condition; the demonic is utterly
human. Take, for example, a verse from a sixth-century poem attributed to
Columbanus:

> Our first two parents having been assailed and led astray,\the devil falls
> a second time, together with his retinue,\by the horror of whose faces
> and the sound of whose flying\frail men might be dismayed, stricken with
> fear, unable to gaze with their bodily eyes on those\who are now bound
> in bundles in the bonds of their prisons.\Driven out from the midst, he
> was thrust down by the Lord;\the space of air is choked by a wild mass\
> of his attendants, invisible\lest, tainted by their wicked examples and
> their crimes\—no fences or walls ever concealing them—\folk should sin
> openly, before the eyes of all. (*Altus Prosator* Stanzas G and H, in Clancy &
> Markus, 1995, p. 47)

To imitate the hitherto invisible demonic spirits is to become more like them than we already are. The choice is one's own, and the question is how to choose the object of one's own passions. Even in the sixth century, then, the miracle of being left humans with a sense of their own contingency. Not only did their being depend on the participation in the created order, but also who they were to become depended on their own will; they could express, choose, imitate, and thus couple with the demonic, or like the angels they could give "thanks to the Lord\not by any endowment of nature, but out of love and choice" (*Altus Prosator* Stanzas G and H, in Clancy & Markus, 1995, p. 47).

The question of evil, then, turns out to be a question of the fundamental tendency in the soul; however, that fundamental tendency is not one with which we are endowed by nature or the Creator; it turns out to be a matter of choice, driven by the passions associated with the demonic or by love itself. To understand Columbanus's viewpoint, we might turn to a recent treatment of German philosophy: Fred Dallmayr's discussion of Schelling and Heidegger.

> In Schelling's treatise (as well as in Heidegger's commentary), the transition from capability to living reality is guided neither by arbitrary whim nor by external compulsion but by a kind of inclination or bent (Hang) inclining human conduct in one way or another. (Dallmayr, 2006, p. 180)

God is driven by love and choice, too, in a desire to couple with humanity, and thus God implants in human nature a desire for coupling with the divine. However, humans cannot be counted on always and everywhere to ground their being in the cosmos in and through a love of God. Their desire to protect themselves from the terrors of nonbeing may lead them to couple themselves with others in ways that have demonic consequences. That is, they may couple with other humans as demons do, whether through seeking possession of others' beings, through aggressive actions that cause affliction to others, or through both affliction and possession.

There is nothing uniquely Christian or biblical about such a sense that coupling lies at the heart of what is both good and evil in human history, and that both kinds of coupling have their origins in a created order: one kind of coupling being demonic in its consequences and an offense against the creation itself, and the other kind of coupling being out of love and choice.

Sociologists do try to understand the world through the eyes and hearts of those whom they are studying, but it is very hard for them to diagnose the underlying tendency or direction of a person, or of a society's being. In the case of people along the Mediterranean, the very innermost being of humans, the soul, was miraculous. As Cicero put it,

[I]t is when the body sleeps that the soul most clearly manifests its divine nature; for when it is unfettered and free it sees many things that are to come. Hence we know what the soul's future state will be when it has been wholly released from the shackles of the flesh. Wherefore, if what I said be true, cherish me as you would a god. ("De Senectute," xxii.81, in Henderson, 1923, p. 89)

Of course, not all beings were equally miraculous. The nobility, as Weber reminded us, tended to be regarded as having beings that were underived and hence not conditional on anyone's favor. Lesser beings perhaps took part in mystery rites in order to possess, like a seed that they would hold up at the end of the rite, a sense of their own being as inherently miraculous and a vital presence.

Others sensed their being as miraculous because they lived in a world contested between good and evil spirits, where the soul was the site of spiritual struggle between invisible forces, with Satan ranged on one side, and the company of heaven on the other. As we have seen, Columbanus found a parallel universe inhabited by Satan and his retinue of the demonic. That is, the creation itself harbors terror; in its midst there is a presence that is in itself terrifying, and it can provoke individuals to a kind of fury, a madness, as they stare into the presence of evil. The questions were, then, "Whose side are you on? What is your inner direction, your basic intention?"

In modern societies, that question is sometimes framed in terms of the unconscious: the hidden, motivating, often dominating, and occasionally terrifying presence as unseen and unbeknownst to the individual as Columbanus's demonic presences. If the unconscious were to be directly encountered, it could drive one mad, in the sense that one would lose a sense of one's own being and be consumed by its passions. That is why demonic spirits, to quote Columbanus once more, "are invisible lest\—no fences or walls ever concealing them—\folk should sin openly, before the eyes of all." There is simply no doubt that evil was part of the created order, and that humans, if they were not protected from them by their own ignorance, might all the more willingly make common cause with evil spirits. The question, then, was whether one would live out of anxieties and passions, the longings and the drives characteristic of the demonic—or whether one would, like the angels, live out of love and choice.

The last-ditch defense against evil still takes place in the soul, which is at once most vulnerable to terror and the passage of time, and yet the only place where transcendence may be sought over terror. As Cicero proclaimed,

Nor indeed would the fame of illustrious men survive their death if the souls of those very men did not cause us to retain their memory longer . . . the soul alone remains unseen, both when it is present and when it departs. ("De Senectute," xxi. 78 ff., xxii 81 ff., in Henderson, 1923, pp. 91, 93)

Thus, in reassuring us that the soul of the illustrious and venerable dead remains present to the living, he is reconnecting the living with the dead, the extraordinary with the ordinary, the sacred with the mundane. He is closing the gaps into which terror seeps, along with the flood of time, into the inner reaches of the individual psyche. He is recoupling presence with absence, the human with the superhuman, the natural with the supernatural. In reaffirming the importance of sacred people and objects, who embody what they express and convey, and who, like the divine soul that permeates the cosmos, synthesize agency with presence, Cicero is answering the question of what side he is on, and what should be the underlying and central tendency of our beings.

We therefore live in the face of threats to our own being, threats that arise from our own existence: death and destruction, the loss of our inner wholeness and vitality, a sense of being dominated by spiritual forces beyond our ken and control, suffering and anguish beyond the point of human bearing, and a sense of loss of our own being in the absence of any other being whose presence is vital to and can confirm our own. From Stuckenbruck, I take the point that the question of demonic possession and evil is far too important to be left to discussions of apocalypticism or to dogmatic reflections on the Incarnation. Evil is too mundane for such talk; besides, as Stuckenbruck points out, some demons are more evil than others. Evil is thus what sociologists would call a *variable*. New Testament narratives are therefore best understood when translated outside of their original mythological language into the existential concerns of ordinary speech or the parlance of secular humanists who think that evil may be a social construction or that the Sabbath, too, may have been made for man.

Some demons may be more like the Stoic god whose presence permeates the entire cosmos and makes happen everything that does happen. Such a god can only be opposed by an evil whose presence and effectiveness are commensurate with the divine. Demons, as we have noted, may be more or less evil, of course: The more evil they are, the more able they are to be effective by their mere presence, and the more they permeate the cosmos. Other demons, therefore, may be less capable of causing affliction by their mere presence: less capable of possessing the psyche from within. They have to act upon the human soul from without. That is, it is in the nature of the created order to suffer a split between presence and activity, between possession of the ground of one's own being and the experience of being subject to contingency, to the resistance of others and of objects, and to the passage of time itself.

Demons are thus notably not self-possessed. They seek to couple with others, to take possession of others, precisely because they are not fully grounded in their own beings. They seek a ground for their being, just as humans do who try to anchor their beings in the cosmos by building circles out of stones that embody the passage of time or, conversely, stop time in its tracks. Demons are as unsure of the ground of their own being as are humans who seek that ground by entering into covenants with a God who prefers them to others, or by following a law that has been revealed to have its source in the divine, by building one temple after another, or by taking possession of a land that they believe to have been promised to them from the beginning. Speaking of this inclination to ground one's being as a source of evil, Fred Dallmayr wrote,

> In the case of evil, Schelling traces this bent to a "contraction of the ground" (Anziehen des Grundes), that is, to a self-enclosure of particularity which terminates indecision, but in such a way as to provoke divisiveness and disjuncture. On the other hand, goodness follows the attraction of spirit or existence, which in its most genuine form is the attraction of eros or love (Liebe). "Love," Heidegger states, "is the original union of elements of which each might exist separately and yet does not so exist and cannot really be without the other." However, love is not simply unity or identity but rather a unity in difference or a unity that lets otherness be . . . including the contraction of the ground and the resulting disjuncture. As he adds: "Love must condone the will of the ground, because otherwise love would annihilate itself. Only by letting the ground operate, love has that foil in or against which it can manifest its supremacy." (Dallmayr, 2006, p. 180)

Evil, then, is the desire to seek a ground for one's own being at the expense of other's being able freely and completely to ground their own being outside the sphere of one's own psyche. It is the primordial attempt to couple the psyche to the cosmos, to bind the temporal aspects of the self to what is everlasting. Evil underlies the formation of the sacred: the coupling of the passage of time in rock that endures while yet embodying the flow of time itself. It is evil that underlies the search for transcendence and the couplings of heaven and earth, of the temporal with the eternal, that are the perennial forms of the sacred. No wonder Columba rejoices that demons live in the world of the invisible; otherwise, as he points out, we might imitate them.

I am grateful to Stuckenbruck for another insight. He is careful to remind us that, despite the apocalyptic language of the passages concerning evil spirits and the danger of demonic possession, the threat is ubiquitous and in a sense quite ordinary. In much the same way, Stuckenbruck points out that the miraculous nature of the exorcisms attributed to Jesus may serve, for the devout, to emphasize his extraordinary powers. I infer Stuckenbruck to be saying that for any original audience these accounts, one's own being, as part of what Stuckenbruck calls "the created order," is in itself something of a miracle. That awareness opens the door to acute forms of existential anxiety as well as to a primitive joy: anxiety that one's own being may be snuffed out or taken away by passions, or demons, beyond one's awareness or control; joy that one's being is sustained in the face of invisible forces.

I have suggested that the sheer existence of the human being, as part of "the created order," was itself miraculous, if only because each soul, created in the divine image, might never have been and at any time might not be. Such an understanding of the human being as essentially miraculous carries with it, however, the awareness that one's own being is utterly vulnerable to nonbeing. Emptiness and absence, darkness and the unknown, may swallow up the soul; so may demonic presences that inhabit and may destroy the psyche. The popular vision of everyday life was, as Berger put it some years ago, "precarious"; their universe, in Weberian terms, was all the more precarious for being enchanted. Therefore people needed powerful friends, like Jesus, whose spiritual strength was more than sufficient to offset even the most evil of spirits.

Such a sense of being, even human being, as miraculous may have been lost in a modernity that considers selfhood to be achieved despite being neurologically and sociologically conditioned. However, it is not clear that individuals in modern societies are any less aware of their vulnerability and mortality; the threat of evil is still widespread. If it were not for religion, therefore, we would not have any clear notion of evil and we might have terror without being terrified by something, such as evil, which we imagine to have a uniquely, even supernaturally, potent and destructive form of presence and agency. Religion creates the conditions for evil by tying together, or binding, the various forms of reality, both the sacred and the profane, the significant and insignificant, the interpretation of signs by specialists from the reality that is open to inspection by ordinary people. Religion integrates particular times and places within the sacred calendar with times and places that are clearly profane. The ethic of the sanctuary and of the marketplace is articulated in religious law; priesthoods instruct on ritual performance as well as on times and places for getting and spending, working and resting, playing and celebrating; religious elites distinguish between the significant and the insignificant, the *adiaphora*; and religious prophets and mystics discern the distinction between appearance and reality.

In the interests of full disclosure, of course, I must say that none of this seems to be anything other than ordinary Christian insight about the nature of evil as being a side effect of religion and the sacred. As I have noted, it was Jesus, after all, who urged his followers not to resist evil. After all, he had dispensed with the sacred by announcing that the Sabbath was made for man, and he was at liberty to heal the sick, forgive sins, and feed his disciples however and whenever he wished to. He even refused to sacralize himself, by saying that there is no one good but the Father. As for religion, he had several ways of dispensing with it by announcing a new dispensation. He urged his followers to forget what Moses had said and to listen to him; he told them that God could raise up children from Abraham out of the stones of the streets; and as for the temple, he could make a new one without lifting a finger. If even a sparrow did not fall without the careful oversight of the deity, who needed a covenantal history, a revealed law, or a temple to anchor their beings in the cosmos? If his followers were afraid of enemies who might destroy them, they should be more afraid of harming the soul of the least powerful and significant, the "little ones." It would be better for them that they be subject to eternal torment than to be the source of harm to a vulnerable soul. Evil itself was both quotidian and mundane, unless one happened to be the source of it oneself. Its effects on one's own soul would be everlasting.

Of course, not all forms of contemporary religion fit this description. Various kinds of fundamentalism mount a rear guard attempt to hold on to the more particular, specific, and local forms of loyalty, attachment, and belonging that are undermined in complex societies and replaced by more abstract and generalized beliefs and values. Talcott Parsons used to speak of the need to control the "motivational commitments" of individuals, by replacing these local loyalties and attachments with more abstract and generalized ones (e.g., professionalization). But there abstractions offered little in the way of assurance that the soul was anchored to the cosmos: little defense against either existential terror or the fear of mortal adversaries. Similarly, apocalypticism seeks to recouple the earthly with the heavenly, the natural and the social with the supernatural, and the individual with the cosmos. Both apocalypticism and fundamentalism know evil, even when they do not see it (Fenn, 2009, pp. 87–88).

In modern societies, individuals are to be held responsible for their own psyches, albeit on occasion with therapeutic or analytic help in demystifying the unconscious, making it more visible, and enabling the individual, out of love and choice, to decide whether to imitate these hitherto unconscious passions or to ground his or her own being in the cosmos in some other way.

Although people seek religion and the sacred as defenses against evil or as cures for it, they inevitably cause or intensify apprehension that evil may afflict or even dispossess and destroy the soul. That is, religion and the sacred may seem to offer guarantees for the agency of the human soul, for its vital connections, or for a presence that will undergird the soul's sense of its own being, but they also pose a threat to personal agency, to a sense of connection with others, and to the soul's sense of its own being. This threat may materialize in at least two ways. On the one hand, the very coupling of the soul of the individual to a person or power of superhuman or divine power may be tenuous, unreliable, disappointing, and a source of anxiety; the devout still pray that their God will not leave them. However, the fact that Alcoholics Anonymous seeks to couple each soul with a higher power as the beginning of personal transformation is enough of an indicator that such coupling is still an essential aspect of human well-being in modern societies, and those who inhibit or destroy that coupling are the source of untold agony.

On the other hand, the very presence of such a divine power or agency may undermine the individual's confidence in his or her own being. Furthermore, religious institutions and movements often attack the people, the places, the objects, and the practices that have given individuals in the past some sense of their own being and their connection with reassuringly vital and effective presences. A sacred history, a religious "narrative of progress," can undermine "the sureness of living people's own powers" by attributing true agency to God, if the narrative of progress is religious, or if it is secular, to "false gods" or idols. Indeed, religious ideologies that stress conversion and a rejection of the past, like modernizing ideologies, can make people distrust—even fear as evil—their own language and tradition, or to reject objects to which they have become attached; their own practices and traditions can be made to seem to undermine their own agency and presence. By distinguishing appearance from reality, or accident from substance, religion may attack such objects and practices by revealing them as agents of some evil presence like Satan, who will in the end deprive the individual of his or her own soul (Keane, 2007, p. 134). Consider the case of reformist iconoclasm, in which religious movements destroy objects and symbols that, because they are sacred, seem to endow individuals with an enhanced sense of their own agency (Keane, 2007, p. 135). Evil may thus be practices stigmatized by any religion interested in offering protection from them or even a cure through the assistance of more or less divine, supernatural, or charismatic helpers.

By exploiting the difference between accident and substance, appearance and reality, however, religion may be doing something more than conjuring up an evil from which it can then offer rescue and protection. That is, these distinctions may inhere in the sacred itself. Take, for example, the sacrament of the Eucharist, which in some Christian traditions offers the substance of divinity under the accident of bread and wine, or the reality of the Christ's presence under the appearance of a wafer and a chalice filled with wine. The fleeting and the insubstantial are thus indissolubly coupled with the enduring and the solid: very much in the same way that for Neolithic peoples, the sacred can be found in rocks whose solidity and shape reflect the effects of water over time. Just as Christians have sacralized water poured into a hollowed-out stone to make a cure for sin and mortality, Neolithic peoples coupled water and rock, the fluid and the substantial, the fleeting and the enduring, in ways that promise a coupling of the living with the dead, and of time with the eternal.

If it were not for the sacred, then, there would be no threat to be encountered from the uncoupling of water and rock: no evil force that could allow the waters to issue forth from the mountains and engulf the world; no destructive power that could destroy the ground of our being; no uncoupling of the solid and enduring from the transient that could, at the very least, undermine the soul by creating an empty space or a darkness devoid of any presence in relation to whom the soul could be sure of its own. Without the sacred there would be no demonic embodiment of the destructive but invisible passions that, were they to become visible, might inspire humans to imitate them. Without taboos there would be no passions that, as Freud pointed out, not only attract people but also threaten to destroy those who approach them carelessly or too closely.

To put it another way, were there no resistance to evil in the form of the sacred, there would be no evil to resist. Evil comes from the partial, incomplete, ambiguous differentiation of time from space, the living from the dead, the conscious from the unconscious, the human from the superhuman or the subhuman, the heavenly from the earthly, and the present from the absent. Thus, as Freud pointed out on the subject of taboos, even by making something or someone sacred, one can only be partially removed or protected from the danger. Taboos only partly disguise the unconscious motives underlying the prohibition of close encounters between powerful figures like chieftains and their followers. Because the powerful and the relatively weak still pose a danger to each other even when authority is sacralized, dangers still arise from the passions underlying the taboo. The connection between the weak and the powerful is not strong or trustworthy enough to make certain that the passions that bring them together, like desire and anger, *Eros* and *Thanatos*, will not be sufficiently inhibited or safely expressed. The same caveat applies to prohibitions on private encounters between older men and their young female relatives.

Granted that something as sacred as a taboo is indebted to be unconditional and therefore timeless, its very existence suggests that something sufficiently momentous may happen that will undermine its claim to timelessness. Like the Christian cross, which "towers over the wrecks of time," the sacred also marks a moment that radically changes the passage of time itself. To paraphrase a remark attributed to Anatole France: Lovers may seek to pack all of eternity into a kiss, but they love all the more intensely because they know that death will part them. Coupling is never perfect enough, never sufficiently complete, to avoid the trauma of time. Passions may erupt that destroy the allegiance of the people to the king or the devotion of followers to their leader. The sacred, being perennially true, present, effective, and therefore beyond and above the passage of time, is always marked by time itself. Like the waterstones that mark sacred Neolithic sites, the stones themselves have been marked by the passage of water over many centuries. The stones therefore either seek to freeze the passage of time or to carve time in, well, stone.

Take, for example, Steve Vinson's (2004) account of "the commemoration of the return of morality and proper order to ancient Egypt." In an article aptly entitled "The Accent's on Evil," Vinson describes a monument celebrating "the restoration by Tutankhamen of legitimate rule" after an insurrection that had interrupted the cult of Amun in Egypt. A timeless order had been broken into by time itself. After the restoration of legitimate rule, Tutankhamen raised the Restoration Stela, which, according to Vinson, lifted the historical event entirely outside of the passage of time.

> Although often treated as a historical text . . . that is, as a witness to the historical fact that the cult of Amun was restored some point early in the reign of Tutankhamun . . . the Restoration Stela is in fact pure topos. It is almost completely devoid of any specifics or any chronological references, and instead describes the events of the Amarna period in the same timeless terms as any other example of pessimistic literature, from the Prophecy of Neferti . . . down to the Lamb of Bocchoris . . . and even the Hermetic Asklepios. (Vinson, 2004, p. 33)

The restoration becomes a return to timelessness as if the taboo against timelessness had never been broken, but marks a moment that interrupts a timeless order. In the case of an insurrection, we meet the several faces of evil. A taboo has been broken, and the flood of time begins again to wash away an order once thought to have been coupled with the cosmos. Order has been destroyed by desire and aggression: by the desire of unmediated and total access to the sources of life and power, and aggression toward the institution that stands in the way of such immediacy.

However, what gave evil its opportunity was the sacralization of a social order: a sacralization renewed or recreated by Tutankhamen in the Restoration Stela. Without such a claim neither the intrusion of the temporal nor the desires and aggressiveness that violated the sanctity of the old order would bear the taint of evil, however disturbing they may have been. Nonetheless, we also have to allow for the experience of the ordinary person, who may or may not have viewed the social order as sacred, but who in the midst of the insurrection and its aftermath may well have experienced terror. That is, even for Columbanus, a universe that bears the imprint and carries the presence of divinity also harbors the seeds of apocalypse and the last judgment. Terror is always a possibility, even in the heart of a created order.

Modernity and the more abstract, generalized forms of religion in complex societies, as well as missionary forms of religion in colonial societies, increase the terror of individuals by depriving them of a sense of their own autonomous and effective presence. Many occupations, for instance, require high levels of inner, subjective, and emotional participation of their workers; stewards and stewardesses, waiters and waitresses, actors and actresses are required to perform themselves within their roles on behalf of their customers, clients, or audiences, regardless of the reality and promptings

of their own inner beings. The priesthood of all believers makes it legitimate for employers to require that their employees regard their jobs as their
vocations, at the same time as the social contract between employers and
employees has become increasingly temporary and contingent on a variety
of factors. Employees are increasingly encouraged to regard themselves as
responsible for their own professional development and future employment.
On the one hand, they are subjectively at the disposal of their employers; if
they are an effective presence, it is only within the guidelines of the occu-
pational role in question. On the other hand, they are relatively defenseless
against downgrading and downsizing and exposed to the market both for
their level of compensation and for the future of their own employment. In
this sense, they are exposed to influences that Stuckenbruck has identified as
demonic: Some deprive the psyche of effective presence, and others cause a
variety of job-related afflictions.

Both religion and the secular thus make existential terror more mundane
by undermining the sacrality of the immediate, local, particular forms of social
life in which the individuals seek certainty and security and in which they
live, move, and have their being. Secularization is often described as a process
that undermines a society's capacity for sustaining fundamental or primitive
sources of personal agency and identity, as well as the continuity, renewal,
and transformation of communities and entire societies. Roles supply limited
opportunities for individual initiative and personal responsibility; communities
are undermined by mobility as unfamiliar people move in and friends, family,
and neighbors move out or around. The sectors of life, such as work and play,
family and community, and the public and private, become increasingly separated from each other; bureaucracies replace more personal forms of administration and problem solving with policies and procedures. Laws get in the
way of customary or personal notions of what is fair or just, right and wrong.
Religion loses touch with the demands and circumstances of everyday life.

Professionalized versions of religious belief and practice compete with
and may trump or even supplant the traditional or ordinary devotions of
individuals and communities. Traditions and popular culture give way to
official or institutionalized beliefs and practices. The past becomes a matter
of record rather than of living memory, a source of legal precedent rather
than a model for heroism or justice, and the future becomes a matter far more
of projection and prediction based on extrapolations from present trends
rather than a time or place nourished with opportunities and dangers by a
lively cultural imagination. Scenarios replace utopias and apocalyptic visions.
The present goes on and on into an infinite number of moments without any
natural, organic, essential, spiritual, or moral connection with each other.
You might say that the way people live, the conditions in which they become
human or experience their own humanity, become increasingly separated
from the grounds of their being.

There is something very modern about Columbanus's insight that, if we should discover demonic presences, we might start imitating them. The crowds in Munich saluting Hitler by torchlight come to mind; so do legions of priests whose superiors collude with them in avoiding disclosure and punishment for the sexual abuse of children. The very ground of our being is sustained by a cosmos that conspires to keep us from knowing ourselves too deeply. To put it another way, were we to see the demonic realm that surrounds us, we might become like it and so fulfill a potential that is already embedded within our own psyches and could become our own central tendency, our bent or *Hang*. Otherwise, why would Columbanus himself fight off his own desires, his own tendencies to envy and anger, with such rigorously ascetic self-discipline? Evil is sustained by any social context that conspires to keep us from knowing ourselves too deeply.

The question of our underlying, central tendency has been raised for modern societies by no one more pointedly than Freud. He argued that to know our central tendency, we would have to lift the veil of repression of the unconscious, and we might indeed be alarmed by what we see there. It is repression that deprives us of a sense of our being, and so causes us to couple ourselves with others from whom we can acquire vicariously a sense of our being, our own presence, and our own vitality. In such coupling we avoid experiencing existential terror at the prospect of our own nonbeing. In order to avoid anxiety, frustration, or despair, we seek to immerse ourselves in another's being and thus fulfill the desire for fusion and the end of the boundaries that separate our being from the world around us. However, we also make ourselves vulnerable to doubts about the depth and permanence of our connection with the other with whom we are most deeply coupled, and to the anger we may feel at even a momentary frustration of our desire for unconditional and continuous connection. Such forms of coupling are like the demonic possessions of which we read in the New Testament, where the evil spirit seeks to domesticate and possess the soul of another.

What we have lost in modern societies is a sense of the miraculous nature of all being, including our own. It is a sense that can be acquired, however, only in the face of the terror of nonbeing and of the knowledge, therefore, that we might never have been, might not be now, and will someday die. Given a sense of our radical contingency and dependence, a sense of the possibility that our being may or may not survive the presence of emptiness and darkness, we may yet live like one of Columbanus's angels: out of love and choice.

In antiquity, as in Freud's notion of the Oedipus complex, it is unconscious forms of illicit coupling that underlie evil and cause a plague to destroy the city. It is, furthermore, those least aware of their own tendencies, the most "innocent," who are the most destructive, whether they are calling out a plague on the enemies of the people of God, the Islamicists and the feminists, the gays and the civil libertarians, the detractors of the clergy and the papacy, or whether they are the rivals of the king of Thebes. Indeed, if there is a modern metaphor for evil that unites us with antiquity, it is the plague. Like the one that afflicted the people of Thebes in Sophocles's drama *Oedipus Rex*, the plague is invisible, pervasive, wantonly and indiscriminately destructive, part of the natural and created order, and capable of exposing the inner direction and underlying tendency of the individual soul.

Such a form of evil, under modern conditions, appears in Camus' novel *The Plague*. Camus' character of the doctor, like one of Columbanus's angels, lived each day in a city filled with radical and fatal contagion, without self-protection and without illusions of safety, but chose for the sake of love to care for those afflicted with the plague. In choosing that exposure without seeking to gloss it with ultimate meaning or self-justification, he is contrasted with the demonic figure of Camus' priest, who insisted that people continue, as children lay dying, to praise God not out of love or choice but from obedience and fear. To the view of this priest, and of those countless clerics who have protected the Church from accusations of abuse, we might oppose the work of psychiatrists who have written extensively of what they call "soul murder": the abuse that places some part of the child's soul permanently beyond recovery. As one writer puts it, of her long experience as an educator of young children, "I pray unendingly for the children I know. In an environment that satisfies their natural drive for growth and change, they will become transfigured. . . . Depriving a child of the miracle of his or her own being is the closest thing to evil that I know."[1]

NOTE

1. In the interest of full disclosure, I wish to add that these words are part of a manuscript in preparation for eventual publication by my wife, Juliana McIntyre, for many years an educator of young children in the Princeton, New Jersey, area.

REFERENCES

Bravo, B., & Wecowski, M. (2004). The hedgehog and the fox: Form and meaning in the prologue of Herodotus. *Journal of Hellenic Studies, 124,* 143–164.

Burkett, W. (1983). *Homo Necans: The anthropology of ancient Greek sacrificial ritual and myth* (Trans. Peter Bing). Berkeley: University of California Press.

Clancy, T. O., & Markus, G. (1995). *Iona: The earliest poetry of a Celtic monastery.* Edinburgh: Edinburgh University Press.

Dallmayr, F. (2006). An end to evil? Philosophical and political reflections. *International Journal for Philosophy of Religion, 60*(1–3), 169–186.

Douglas, M. (1960). *Purity and danger.* New York: Praeger.

Douglas, M. (1973). *Natural symbols.* New York: Random House.

Fenn, R. (2009). *Key thinkers in the sociology of religion.* New York: Continuum.

Henderson, J. (Ed.). (1923). *Cicero on old age; on friendship; on divination* (Trans. W. A. Falconer) (Loeb Classical Library, Cicero XX). Cambridge, MA: Harvard University Press.

Keane, W. (2007). *Christian moderns: Freedom and fetish in the mission encounter.* Berkeley: University of California Press.

Salmon, J. H. M. (1989). Stoicism and Roman example: Seneca and Tacitus in Jacobean England. *Journal of the History of Ideas, 50* (2), 199–225.

Vinson, S. (2004). The accent's on evil: Ancient Egyptian "melodrama" and the problem of genre. *Journal of the American Research Center in Egypt, 41,* 33.

CHAPTER 4

DEPERSONALIZATION AND THE PSYCHOBIOLOGY OF EVIL

Patrick McNamara and
Paul M. Butler

INTRODUCTION

Theologically, the problem of evil in the world (theodicy) has traditionally been addressed in one of the following forms: (a) self- and soul-construction, (b) libertarian free will, (c) and natural law. The theodicy of type (a) attempts to explain and justify (given the assumption of a just and loving God) the existence of evil in the world as a character-building locomotive force (Hick, 1966/1978). From this perspective, spiritual growth occurs when one attains the moral goodness required to resist temptations by habitual navigation of difficult circumstances or proper handling of evil influences or events when they come. Under this interpretation, a supernatural agent (usually a supreme god) designed our nature and environment to include evil for the ultimate purpose of human moral growth and achievement.

Several iterations of type (b) theodicy exist. One common instantiation suggests that human free will, unfettered by the influences of metaphysical agents, furnishes the best of all possible worlds. A physical world filled with biological automata acting out predestined behavioral responses precludes the possibility for true spiritual depth and greatness (Lewis, 1940/1996; Plantinga, 1974). Free will provides humankind with the constant, recurring occasion to choose to either increase pain, suffering, and evil in the world or attempt to seek that which is true, good, and praiseworthy. Besides libertarian human will and choice, other sources of evil include natural processes like earthquakes or immaterial sources, such as immoral supernatural beings. Another common theodicy, type (c), propounds that evil is an emergent property of the entities that exist in the natural world. Whether by the intentional design of a god-creator or fine-tuner of physical constants, a blind watchmaker, or simply abstract selective forces, the natural world we inhabit obeys immutable and fundamental natural laws. Natural laws provide the constancy for stable processes to emerge, and evil is either a by-product or a necessary shaping force of the physical entities filling this space–time continuum.

In this chapter on the biology of evil, we will take our cue from type (c) theodicy—natural law but with an awareness of the crucial role that free will (types a and b) plays in the generation of evil and good. As scientists, we approach the issue of evil as methodological materialists. With the tools of modern neuroscience and evolutionary theory, we address proximal causes of moral impulses and evil choices as constrained by the biology of human nature and social interaction. The neurophysiologist, chemist, and physicist might well extend our proximate explanations with distal biophysical explanations of evil including discussions on subatomic forces, chemical interactions, forces of natural disaster, probabilities of imminent earthly demise by meteor showers, imploding stars or universes, pluriverses, or entropy and the laws of thermodynamics.

Attempts to understand proximate and distal biophysical causation are intended to deepen rather than constrain the ineluctable intuitions that human beings experience through the metaphysical or ontological imagination. In addressing the biology of evil, surely a topic deserving a several-volume series in its own respect, we constrict our attention within the biological sciences to the neuroscience and psychology of human morality and potential for evil. We then turn our discussion toward a human psychobiological process, termed *deindividuation* or *depersonalization*, which we suggest to be a major source of evil.

THE NEUROSCIENCE OF MORALITY AND THE SELF

A fundamental tenet of jurisprudence is that criminal acts do not necessarily define guilt, but the intention-system produced by the mind-brain must also be guilty. We pardon unintentional or accidental harms and proscribe failed attempts to harm. A wrongdoer or evil power is one that *intends* to do harm to another. This is assumed to be intuitively true by virtually all; a universal moral sense founded on implicit abilities to cognize intention, motivation, and action is, albeit conditioned by local mores and cultural practice, inextricable from the biology of human nature (Abarbanell & Hauser, 2010; Hauser, 2006; Nisbett & Cohen, 1996).

Understanding intentions, attributing mental states to others, and presuming motivations are distinctly human abilities quickly becoming elucidated by social and cognitive neuroscience. Evil acts, whether perceived by a given culture as minor peccadilloes or monstrous atrocities, presume that (1) a distinct "self" agent exists separately in intention, motivation, and action from other selves; (2) this self perceives itself as a moral agent; and (3) this self exists in a social space with great capacity for social attachment or aversion. Human moral cognition is about an intuitive sense of fairness, concern for others, and observance of cultural norms. Moral sentiments run the gamut of deeply felt visceral reactions to propositions resultant from ratiocinations divorced from context or felt emotional reaction. If we take evolutionary theory as the probable force that shaped our biology, then our brains make possible moral cognition because a strong adaptive element for social cohesion and cooperation was selected for in the environment of evolutionary adaptation (Darwin, 1871/1977).

Prerequisite to any moral sentiment is the presence of a distinct "self" set off from other agents aware of its own behavior as the author of this behavior. *Sense of agency*, or the subjective experience of being the cause of our own actions or attributing agency to the actions of others, is deeply bound to the human moral experience (Moll et al., 2007). Sense of agency is fundamental to the human experience of intentionality, perspective taking, and feeling personal responsibility for one's actions. Although humans share basic emotions with some mammalian species, the panoply of moral emotions is most expansive in our species, including guilt, anger, regret, indignation, shame, contempt, awe, jealousy, rage, embarrassment, pride, and gratitude (de Wall, 1998; Haidt, 2001; Moll et al., 2007). For instance, one can feel a sense of pride following an impressive public demonstration of some skill or talent, namely, because that individual experienced a felt sense of agency as the author of his or her actions, an understood sense of how other agents in the public domain appreciated or neglected the show of skill, and a subsequent linking up of the perceived response of other agents with one's sense of agency in the form of felt pride.

Agency cannot be reduced, however, to the simple linking up of embodied emotions with a given self-generated experience. Sense of agency can be constructed at varying cognitive and neural levels (Damasio, 1994, 2003; Decety & Sommerville, 2003). A widely distributed brain network undergirds moral sentiments: sections of the prefrontal cortex (PFC), such as the orbitofrontal cortex (OFC) and anterior PFC, anterior temporal poles, superior temporal sulcus (STS), temporo-parietal junction (TPJ), and limbic-subcortical structures, such as the hypothalamus, basal forebrain, and ventral striatum (Moll, Oliveira-Souza, & Eslinger, 2003; Moll, Zahn, Oliveira-Souza, Krueger, & Grafman, 2005; Young et al., 2010; Young, Camprodon, Hauser, Pascual-Leone, & Saxe, 2010). Strikingly, neuroimaging studies that identify brain activation patterns during tasks that probe agency and intentionality recruit an overlapping brain network with regions responsible for moral cognition (Blakemore & Frith, 2004; Frith & Frith, 2005). A recent study by Moll et al.

(2007) teased apart the varying neuroanatomical and functional activation of emotions, sense of agency, social agency, and intentionality. Agency- and intentionality-based tasks were primarily mediated by frontotemporal networks (PFC and STS, and TPJ), whereas emotional and motivational aspects involved limbic and paralimbic structures in conjunction with anterior PFC and anterior temporal cortices.

Social attachment and affiliative behaviors for prosocial emotions and empathy activate the basal forebrain, ventral striatum, medial OFC, and subgenual area, whereas aversive emotions and aggression are mediated by the amygdala, dorsal anterior cingulate cortex, and lateral OFC (Kringelbach & Rolls, 2004; O'Doherty, Kringelbach, Rolls, Hornak, & Andrews, 2001). The role of evolutionarily ancient brain systems of motivation and emotion is fundamental to human moral sentiments. Ancient limbic-neurohumoral systems are more than evolutionary remnants or functionless "vestigial tails" for the purpose of human moral cognition. Rather, these systems that govern affiliation versus detachment from a social group are tightly intertwined with cortical and neocortical (evolutionarily modern) brain systems (Moll & Schulkin, 2009). Attachment and affiliation promote parent–offspring care, cooperation amongst asymmetrically related kin, social reciprocity, and altruism. The other pole of the neurohumoral motivation–emotion axis is aversion, which engenders blame, group fragmentation, and prejudice against outgroup members. A critical developmental step in the evolution of the human moral brain was likely the linking up and/or parallel coactivation of the more ancient neurohumoral attachment–aversion systems (deep-brain subcortical and hypothalamic structures) with the newly evolved neocortical systems that facilitate social cognition, larger semantic memory for symbols and abstract concept manipulation, and cultural learning (Han & Northoff, 2008; MacLean, 1990; Moll & de Oliveira-Souza, 2008; Moll & Schulkin, 2009).

Moral cognition can powerfully activate and dictate human behavior. Moral sentiments can lead groups to enact punishment on noncooperators, free riders, or other saprophytic members of a group strong in affiliative connection. Many lines of evidence within the emerging neuroscience of morality, social psychology, and anthropology demonstrate that groups can drive the behavior of their constituents along the attachment–aversion continuum with minimal ratiocinative justification (Bechara, Tranel, & Damasi, 2000; De Quervain et al., 2004). That is, taking on the moral ideology or behavior of a given group or role can powerfully draw out either a "Jekyll or Hyde" from within (Haney, Banks, & Zimbardo, 1973; Zimbardo, 2007).

Rational moral judgment and decision can often dissociate with actual behavior in the case of both normal people and patients with brain lesions or psychiatric disturbance. This can result from a disconnection of the autonomic nervous system (e.g., the stress-mobilizing "fight or flight" branch of the nervous system) from moral cognitive decision networks or from emotional processing in general (Cima, Tonnaer, & Hauser, 2010; Damasio, 1994; Eslinger & Damasio, 1985). Deep-visceral experiences, such as disgust or profound embarrassment, shape moral cognition and behavior, but calm emotional detachment can often be the case during moral judgments.

As previously mentioned, at the center of all of these neurobiologic contributors to the moral sense is the Self. The Self, of course, is yet another complex, socially constructed, but biologically constrained entity. The Self is defined by sense of agency, intentionality, and decision-making processes. The sense of Self as "agent" appears to draw on several psychological and neuropsychological domains such as autobiographical memory, emotional and evaluative systems, self-monitoring, bodily awareness, subjectivity or perspectivalness in perception, and so on. But the two processes most implicated in agency per se is Will or the sense of being the cause of some action, and goal-directed choice or the sense of choosing among alternatives and aiming for one of those alternatives. These two processes, will and goal-directedness, lie at the heart of the historical-philosophical problem of free will.

The conscious experience of "free will" undergirds our conceptions of the dignity and autonomy of the human personality as well as the responsibility of each person as he or she interacts with and affects, for better or ill, the lives of others. Depersonalization, on the other hand, is a state that indicates loss of personal autonomy and choice. Slaves are depersonalized by their slave owners, and enemies are depersonalized by combatants. We now turn our attention to the process of depersonalization. The importance of the issue of free will is acknowledged by most philosophers, theologians, and scientists, but there has been a consistent thread of "free will skepticism" that has run through the intellectual history of reflection on this phenomenon. The skeptical vein of thought has only intensified in the modern age as science has increasingly led to skeptical pronouncements on the issue of free will. But if we equate free will with a strong executive self or agent, then the skeptical stance is less necessary as there is plenty of scientific evidence concerning this executive self.

BIOLOGICAL AND COGNITIVE ROOTS OF THE EXECUTIVE SELF

The "executive self" (McNamara, 2010) refers to the ability to facultatively inhibit powerful impulsive and related free rider behavioral strategies when seeking to cooperate with, or become a member of, a particular group or association. It follows that the human mind-brain had to develop powerful inhibitory capacities around the suite of impulsive appetitive behaviors that motivate the free rider behavioral strategy. This inhibitory capacity is precisely one of the best-established and major functions of the anterior temporal and frontal lobes. The content and experience of this central executive self are manifested as *free will*, which *is* the control we have over our own acts, plans, and thoughts. The experience of Self and agency underwrites the experience of free will. Even when we do not move a muscle in our body, but instead inwardly give a nod of assent to a proposition or some other image or idea, the feeling of agency still obtains and is fundamental to the cognitive moment of assent. Although the experience of the Self underlies will and assent, it itself is both a biological and a social entity.

The Self is embedded within a social group, and the interaction of the Self with the social group is the process where all kinds of evil phenomena, including the process of depersonalization, emerge. It is to that interaction we turn next.

One of the major sources of evil in the world is the lack of empathy for another's suffering. Whence comes that lack of empathy? A minority of the population, so-called sociopaths or psychopaths, do not experience empathy as easily as most of us do. These psychopaths exhibit muted autonomic nervous system (ANS) responses when they witness the sufferings of others. Some psychopaths appear to have brain abnormalities in the orbitofrontal cortex—an area of the brain that regulates the ANS as well as emotional responses. Perhaps this brain disorder contributes to psychopathic inability to experience empathy for others. How else can we explain the cold-blooded murder of innocents? Psychopathic murderers are known to kill not out of hate, passion, impulsivity, or criminality. Often they kill merely for convenience's sake or because there is something fascinating for them in the act itself.

Many psychopaths prey on people who cannot effectively fight back (i.e., women, children, and the elderly). This is not due solely to cowardice. Instead, it again is due to convenience. To have to engage in a struggle would detract from the intellectual satisfaction of the kill. These psychopaths, however, represent only a tiny percentage of the population. It would be absurd to think that they are a major source of the world's evil. Their basic inability to experience empathy for others, however, can give us a clue as to a major source of the world's evil: deindividuation.

Depersonalization is the loss of individual awareness, autonomy, and self-control and the transference of basic functions of the Self, such as empathy and intercourse with others, over to a group. In short, there is a reduction in self-awareness and an increase in group or social identity. Typically the transfer of Self is to a group that the individual identifies with. It is, to use a technical term, a highly *entitative* group. The group carries much of the individual's identity such that the individual is comfortable adopting the group's actions as his or her own. If the group stigmatizes some other outgroup as noxious, so too will the individual once deindividuation occurs. If the group acts with a kind of herd mentality, moving with fads or waves of irrational attachments to various salient "ideas," so too will the individual once depersonalization occurs. If the group decides that violent elimination of other groups or of selected individuals is necessary, the individual member of the group will produce rationales to justify the violence—once depersonalization occurs.

How, then, does depersonalization occur? This is where psychobiology can make a contribution to the theory of evil. Before detailing the process of depersonalization and its capacity to engender evil, we will first briefly consider the neuroscientific and psychological structure of the distinctly human magnitude for moral sentiments.

THE PROCESS OF DEPERSONALIZATION

Depersonalization is the loss of individuality via the transferral of the Self and its functions over to a group entity. Of course, that transfer is always temporary. No one can function for long in a completely deindividuated state. But regular or frequent collapses into a depersonalized state are likely for most people. Once depersonalization occurs, once that transfer of Self from the individual to the group is made, serious evil becomes possible.

Social psychologists have made significant contributions to our understanding of the process of depersonalization. Deindividuation, as distinct from depersonalization, is commonly understood to involve a reduction in self-awareness and a resultant social *anonymity* such that responsibility for behavioral acts is diffused throughout the group (e.g., Zimbardo, 1969). Unlike the case of depersonalization, however, deindividuation may not be associated with a concomitant increase in social identity. Instead of a merging of Self with the group, the individual who is deindividuated seems to just drift or to become powerless. Whereas both deindividuation and depersonalization harm the individual psychically, depersonalization is fraught with greater potential for evil, and that is because depersonalization involves not just a decrease in personal awareness but also a replacement of personal identity with a group identity—a merging of the Self with the group. Instead of a person we get a group entity, a kind of machine. Now the person functions not in pursuit of his own aims but in pursuit of the group aim. The group calls the shots, and the individual loses self-control and personal autonomy as well as his capacity to feel the suffering of others. At the basis of the biology of evil, therefore, lies the phenomenon of the group.

GOOD AND BAD GROUPS

The reason why evil becomes possible with depersonalization is because only an individual can experience empathy for the suffering of another individual. The infliction of suffering on a person or persons is more likely to stop if someone present at the event can feel the suffering that the person is undergoing. Groups cannot do that. They act only to increase their weight, density, influence, and power. Now it should be noted that there are two major forms of groups: "civil" and "enterprise" associations (Oakeshott, 1975/1991). In civil associations, individuals rule, under some agreed upon law or contract. In enterprise associations, managers rule and individuals exist for the purpose of the enterprise, whatever it is.

Of course, there is a place for both types of groups, and both types of groups can harm people in various ways, but enterprise associations are by far more dangerous in terms of potential for evil. It should now be clear why that is the case: Enterprise associations are highly entitative groups that demand surrender of individual aims and identities so that the group purpose can be accomplished. Every human group varies in the extent to which it is civil or enterprise. Religions and political entities tend to be enterprise associations and thus fraught with high potential for evil. Religions in particular exhibit both tendencies. On the one hand, most religions encourage personal growth and transformation as well as self-control and individual autonomy. On the other hand, many religions also emphasize ethnic and group allegiances that tend to demand a sacrifice of personal autonomy.

Military groups exhibit a similar dichotomy. On the one hand, obedience and discipline are required to win battles, but, on the other hand, the history of warfare has repeatedly demonstrated that slavish and blind obedience loses battles (witness the Persians versus the Greek hoplites) and individual initiative and courage give an army the edge in certain types of battle. In short, the story is complex, but it seems safe to say that depersonalization in the context of highly entitative "enterprise associations" carries the greatest potential for evil.

In *The Bacchae*, the great tragedian Euripides seemed to intuit this potential for evil. The play begins with reports that the Bacchae, the female worshippers of Dionysus, the god of wine and ecstasy, are acting up again. They have been appearing in public with snakes in their hair, and suckling wild wolves and gazelles. The women rove in bands, and one band of drunken or crazed women descended on a herd of cows, ripping them to shreds with their bare hands. Thus the bizarre conduct of the cult's members has led to destruction of property, and the king must act. King Pentheus appears, therefore, to be acting reasonably when trying to rein in the maenads' destructive practices. But the god Dionysus refuses to see his cult suppressed, and he lays a plot to destroy Pentheus. So he goes to Pentheus in disguise and talks Pentheus into self-destruction. The god knows that Pentheus is secretly fascinated with these ecstatic rites. The stories he is told about the women involved seem fantastic. His own mother, Queen Agave, is a devotee of Dionysus and apparently participates in the maenads' frenzied rites. Even Pentheus's grandfather, Cadmus, speaks enthusiastically about the cult.

Thus the god disguised as a stranger bringing news of the maenads' ecstatic practices uses Pentheus's curiosity and deep desire to see the ecstatic women to lead Pentheus to his own self-destruction.

Once he has Pentheus identified with this self-destructive desire to see and perhaps participate in the cultic rites, the god then proceeds to systematically strip the king of dignity and rationality. The god decides to humiliate Pentheus by having him dress as a woman. He convinces the king to dress as a female maenad to avoid detection by the other maenads and thus be able to observe the rites without molestation. Dionysus balks at this further humiliation: "Nay; am I a woman, then, And no man more?" Dionysus points out that if he is seen by the maenads to be a man, they will kill him: "Would ye have them slay thee dead? No man may see their mysteries" . . . and live. Pentheus then consents to being dressed as a woman and a maenad, and in doing so is led inexorably to his own destruction. The king is depersonalized and then begins the process of submerging his identity with that of the group. We will see that this will lead to his personal destruction. Dionysus dresses Pentheus as a woman and gives him a thyrsus and fawn skins, then leads him out into the streets to be mocked. Pentheus begins to see double, and then hallucinates two bulls (Dionysus often took the form of a bull) leading him. The scene switches back to the palace, where a messenger reports to Cadmus that Pentheus has been killed. He recounts the story of what happened to the tragic king: When the stranger and the king reached Cithaeron, the site where the rites were underway, the blond stranger helped the king climb atop a tree to view the rites. Then the stranger manifested as the god in all his glory, and Dionysus called out to his followers that a man was watching them. This, of course, drove the maenads wild with rage, and they pulled down the trapped Pentheus and ripped his body to pieces.

After the messenger has relayed this grievous news to Cadmus, Agave arrives carrying the head of her son. She thinks that the head is the head of a mountain lion. She had killed the "lion," she boasts, with her bare hands and pulled his head off. Then, in the most macabre and tragic scene imaginable, she proudly displays her son's head to her father Cadmus, the grandfather of the slain son, believing it to be a hunting trophy. She is confused when Cadmus does not delight in her "success" and hunting prowess. By that time, however, Dionysus's possession of Agave is beginning to wear off, and as Cadmus reels from the horror of his grandson's grisly death at the hands of his own mother, Agave slowly realizes what she has done, and then she is destroyed as well.

WHAT WE CAN LEARN FROM THE BACCHAE

First the play tells us that to the degree the sense of personal agency is impaired, the individual is in danger of submerging his identity into that of the group, and if that occurs destruction follows (assuming the group is cultic like an enterprise association). The emotion of ecstasy is a key component of ecstatic cults and very often involves bloodcurdling destructive acts like those engaged in by the maenads. Ecstasy, when it occurs in the context of a religion that is seeking to promote self-control and self-transformation into a saintly or even a godlike state, is a good. In that case, ecstasy leads to a self-transcendence into something larger, better, and paradoxically more individual. When, however, ecstasy leads to a self-transcendence into something that is lower, smaller, less individual, less unique, and more group-like, with less individual autonomy and self-control, then it is an evil.

The Bacchae also suggests that evil can be studied as a phenomenon of inheritance or an intergenerational transmission of proclivities, behaviors, and "sins." Generation 1, represented by Cadmus the grandfather, is fascinated with the maenads and their rites. Generation 2, represented by Agave, actually participates in the rites. Generation 3, represented by Pentheus, pays the price of that participation. Pentheus is even more fascinated with the rites than is Cadmus, but Pentheus becomes the sacrificial victim to the rites. Inheritance can be construed as a group phenomenon like any other. If the family line is considered something better than an individual's autonomy, then it will function like a highly entitative group with all the destructive consequences that follow.

In summary, depersonalization in the context of highly entitative, enterprise-type associations or groups carries great potential for evil. What, then, in biological terms leads to depersonalization and fusion into the group?

THE BIOLOGY OF DEPERSONALIZATION

Depersonalized states have long been associated with temporal lobe lesions, but when one examines the cases that describe depersonalized states, it soon becomes clear that what is being described here is really deindividuation rather than depersonalization. The individual loses personal awareness but does not become fused with a highly entitative group. When, however, depersonalization moves toward the experience of self-transcendence, we get closer to depersonalization and fusion into the group entity.

A recent paper by Cosimo Urgesi, Salvatore M. Aglioti, Miran Skrap, and Franco Fabbro (2010) described a group of patients who underwent surgical procedures to control brain cancer. Patients with selective damage to left and right inferior posterior parietal regions induced an increase in self-report scores on the Self-Transcendence (ST) scale of the Temperament and Character Inventory (TCI). Self-Transcendence scores measure the extent to which subjects feel connected to or drawn toward an experience beyond their individual lives. People with high levels of self-transcendence often report frequent feelings of "boundlessness" or the loss of awareness of themselves as separate beings. Urgesi et al. (2010) looked for brain correlates for changes in the felt experience of ST by studying scores obtained before and after surgery to remove brain gliomas (a type of cancer affecting neural brain tissue) using advanced lesion-mapping procedures. The authors asked what happens to self-reports of ST before and soon after surgical ablation of tissue in specific brain regions. They predicted that "selective damage to frontal and temporoparietal areas decreased and increased ST, respectively," and that is what they found.

The results showed that both anterior and posterior lesions had effects, and those effects were opposite, with anterior lesions decreasing ST and posterior lesions increasing ST; however, the posterior lesions had the most pronounced effects overall. ST scores in patients with meningioma involving the anterior or posterior areas revealed no significant effect. The analysis of a set of recurrent glioma patients who had undergone previous operations several months before testing showed that enhanced ST induced by posterior cortical ablation persisted.

Voxel analysis revealed that the main sites responsible for effects on ST were located in the left inferior parietal lobe and in the right angular gyrus whose damage was associated with a significant ST increase. Presurgical interviews with patients, furthermore, revealed that a greater number of patients with posterior than anterior lesions judged themselves as being religious persons. The 59 patients who judged themselves as religious also showed higher ST scores before surgery.

In sum, these results demonstrate pretty clearly that ablation of two sites within posterior cortical regions (the inferior parietal lobe and the angular gyrus) has an enhancing effect on the subjective experience of self-transcendence.

Why should that be?

Certainly nonspecific effects of the surgery itself (craniotomy) can be ruled out, as no changes in ST were associated with meningioma surgery itself. Could some cognitive or emotional effect associated with the surgery be driving the results? The authors claim that this is not the case, as neuropsychological scores did not change in association with surgery except in expected ways. They also argue against the influence of mood as the TCI scales of harm avoidance and self-directedness (which are altered in cases of depression) were not altered by the surgery. This, however, is not an entirely satisfactory explanation. The authors should have assessed mood directly instead of relying on the TCI. In any case, the authors rule out mood and cognitive changes as inducers of the enhanced ST effect.

So what is driving the enhanced ST after removal of tissue in the parietal lobes?

Urgesi et al. (2010) argued "that interindividual differences in spirituality may reflect differences in the ability to transcend the spatiotemporal constraints of the physical body" and that "dysfunctional parietal neural activity may underpin altered spiritual and religious attitudes and behaviors." They noted that lesions in parietal lobes are associated with distortions of bodily awareness and that dysfunction in parietal lobes may plausibly also alter self-awareness and self–world boundaries. Although this explanation is certainly plausible, the authors did not adequately address the rest of their data. Perusal of their tables shows a consistent diminution of ST scores in the anterior group. Although the effects are not large, they are consistent across patient groups. Lesions in the anterior cortex produce a diminution of ST.

Now, when you combine this fact with the other finding of lesions in posterior regions producing an increase in ST, you get what appears to be a kind of double dissociation: Lesions in area x produce a decrease in behavior a, and lesions in area y produce an increase in behavior a. Now couple this consideration with the spate of functional neuroimaging studies on religious practices, most of which converge on the finding that religious practices are associated with activation in the ventral prefrontal cortex, among other brain sites. All of these data taken together suggest that the crucial site for support of religious experiences and practices is the prefrontal cortex. The authors do not endorse this conclusion, but it is a reasonable one.

So why does ablation of the parietal cortex induce enhanced ST?

It has long been known that the parietal lobes are in mutual inhibitory balance with the frontal lobes—when you lesion one, you release the other from inhibition and then the behavior you see is behavior mediated solely by that "released" region. So when you lesion the parietal cortex, you get disinhibition of frontally mediated behaviors. Among those frontally mediated behaviors, it now appears, is self-transcendence. In short, personal autonomy is a product of the mutual inhibitory interplay of the anterior prefrontal cortex with posterior parietal cortex. When this balance is destroyed via surgical intervention or injury in either site, personal autonomy is compromised.

We suggest that something similar happens functionally speaking with the fusion of self into a highly entitative group. The mutual inhibitory balance between anterior and posterior brain sites is impaired, thus making dissolution of the self and the merging of the individual into the group entity more likely. This conclusion implies that anything we can do to improve prefrontal functions and to more generally improve the sense of an executive Self or the sense of agency will strengthen the individual's ability to resist the lure of the group.

REFERENCES

Abarbanell, L., & Hauser, M. D. (2010). Mayan morality: An exploration of permissible harms. *Cognition, 115*, 207–224.

Bechara, A., Tranel, D., & Damasi, H. (2000). Characterization of the decision-making deficit of patients with ventromedial prefrontal cortex lesions. *Brain, 123* (Pt. 11), 2189–2202.

Blakemore, S. J., & Frith, U. (2004). How does the brain deal with the social world? *NeuroReport, 15,* 119–128.

Cima, M., Tonnaer, F., & Hauser, M. D. (2010). Psychopaths know right from wrong but don't care. *Scan, 5,* 59–67.

Damasio, A. (1994). *Descartes' error: Emotion, reason, and the human brain.* London: Papermac.

Damasio, A. (2003) *Looking for Spinoza: Joy, sorrow, and the feeling brain.* New York: Harcourt.

Darwin, C. (1977). *The origin of species* and *The descent of man.* New York: Modern Library. (Original work published in 1871)

Decety, J., & Sommerville, J. A. (2003). Shared representations between self and other: A social cognitive neuroscience view. *Trends in Cognitive Sciences, 7,* 527–533.

De Quervain, D.J-F., Fischbacher, U., Treyer, V., Schellhammer, M., Schnyder, U., Buck, A., et al. (2004). The neural basis of altruistic punishment. *Science, 305* (5688), 1254–1258.

de Wall, F. (1998). *Chimpanzee politics: Power and sex among apes.* Baltimore: Johns Hopkins University Press.

Eslinger, P. J., & Damasio, A. R. (1985). Severe disturbance of higher cognition after bilateral frontal lobe ablation: Patient EVR. *Neurology, 35* (12), 1731–1741.

Frith, C., & Frith, U. (2005). Theory of mind. *Current Biology, 15,* R644–R646.

Haidt, J. (2001). The emotional dog and its rational tail: A social intuitionist approach to moral judgment. *Psychological Review, 108,* 814–834.

Han, S., & Northoff, G. (2008). Reading direction and culture. *Nature Reviews Neuroscience, 9* (12), 965.

Haney, C., Banks, W. C., & Zimbardo, P. G. (1973). Interpersonal dynamics in a simulated prison. *International Journal of Criminology and Penology, 1,* 69–97.

Hauser, M. D. (2006). *Moral minds: How nature designed our sense of right and wrong.* New York: Ecco/HarperCollins.

Hick, J. (1978). *Evil and the god of love.* New York: Harper & Row. (Original work published in 1966).

Kringelbach, M. L., & Rolls, E. T. (2004). The functional neuroanatomy of human orbitofrontal cortex: Evidence from neuroimaging and neuropsychology. *Progress in Neurobiology, 72,* 341–372.

Lewis, C. S. (1996). *The problem of pain.* San Francisco: HarperCollins. (Original work published in 1940).

MacLean, P. D. (1990). *The triune brain in evolution: Role in paleocerebral functions.* New York: Plenum Press.

McNamara, P. (2010). *The neuroscience of religious experience.* Cambridge: Cambridge University Press.

Moll, J., & de Oliveira-Souza, R. (2008). Extended attachment and the human brain: Internalized cultural values and evolutionary implications. In J. Braeckman, J. Verplaetse, & J. De Schrijver (Eds.), *The moral brain: Essays on the evolutionary and neuroscientific aspects of morality.* New York: Springer Scientific.

Moll, J., de Oliveira-Souza, R., & Eslinger, P. J. (2003). Morals and the human brain: A working model. *NeuroReport, 14* (3), 299–304.

Moll, J., de Oliveira-Souza, R., Garrido, G. J., Bramati, I. E., Caparelli-Daquer, E. M. A., Paiva, M. L. M. F., et al. (2007). The self as a moral agent: Linking the neural bases of social agency and moral sensitivity. *Social Neuroscience, 2* (3–4), 336–352.

Moll, J., & Schulkin, J. (2009). Social attachment and aversion in human moral cognition. *Neuroscience and Biobehavioral Reviews, 33,* 456–465.

Moll, J., Zahn, R., de Oliveira-Souza, R., Krueger, K., & Grafman, J. (2005). The neural basis of human moral cognition. *Nature Reviews Neuroscience, 6,* 799–809.

Nisbett, R. E., & Cohen, D. (1996). *Culture of honor: The psychology of violence in the South.* Boulder, CO: Westview Press.

Oakeshott, M. (1991). *On human conduct.* New York: Oxford University Press. (Original work published in 1975).

O'Doherty, J., Kringelbach, M. L., Rolls, E. T., Hornak, J., & Andrews, C. (2001). Abstract reward and punishment representations in the human orbitofrontal cortex. *Nature Neuroscience, 4,* 95–102.

Plantinga, A. (1974). *God, freedom, and evil.* New York: Harper and Collins.

Urgesi, C., Aglioti, S., Skrap, M., & Fabbro, F. (2010). The spiritual brain: Selective cortical lesions modulate human self transcendence. *Neuron, 65* (3), 309.

Young, L., Bechara, A., Tranel, D., Damasio, H., Hauser, M., & Damasio, A. (2010). Damage to ventromedial prefrontal cortex impairs judgment of harmful intent. *Neuron, 65,* 845–851.

Young, L., Camprodon, J. A., Hauser, M., Pascual-Leone, A., & Saxe, R. (2010). Disruption of the right temporoparietal junction with transcranial magnetic stimulation reduces the role of beliefs in moral judgments. *Proceedings for the National Academy of Science.* Retrieved from http://www.pnas.org/cgi/doi/10.1073/pnas.0914826107.

Zimbardo, P. G. (1969). The human choice: Individuation, reason, and order versus deindividuation, impulse, and chaos. *Nebraska Symposium on Motivation, 17,* 237–307.

Zimbardo, P. G. (2007). *The Lucifer effect: Understanding how good people turn evil.* New York: Random House.

CHAPTER 5

Evil Experienced by One Who Was There: Exodus—From Bondage to Deliverance and the Promised Land

Virginia Ingram

This chapter is a personal odyssey. My story is best seen through the biblical lens of the Exodus narrative, and the biblical Exodus narrative is best understood when seen through the lens of such real-life experiences as mine. The Exodus story is so much a part of the bloodstream of Western culture as it has unfolded over the last 3 millennia that it shapes and illumines the sense of self and destiny for all individuals and communities of faith, quite regardless of whether or not we are consciously aware of it. Exodus is not just an archetypal story in an ancient book. It is the real-life story of each of us every day. We rehearse it in all our fears and hopes and celebrate it in the symbols of the sacraments. If we miss its relevance to our daily experience, we miss the opportunity for understanding the entire essential biblical message of the Old Testament and the New, and we miss the meaning of our own personal odysseys.

Growing up, I had a belief in God that was not fostered in a faith community. Consequently, my understanding of religion and spirituality was confused. I thought of God as an uncompromising disciplinarian whose control I did not welcome. However, the father motif was so important to me, as a child from a broken home, that I persisted in trying to establish a relationship with the God of my youthful misinterpretation.

In my rebellious years I sought an independence from God, which I will later argue is a path to death and destruction; and broke as many rules as I could, trying all of the things I was told to stay away from. Unfortunately one of these things was heroin. I was easily seduced by the good feelings it gave me, even though I realized they were manufactured and there was a price to pay.

I soon developed an addiction and lived a desperate life with my partner, who eventually hung himself in a time of great hopelessness. When I discovered his body hanging in the garage, the overwhelming feeling I had was of intense fear. I could sense an oppressive evil in the air, and I believed that if I stayed in the house overnight I would be at risk of taking my own life.

The following personal narrative is about the psychospiritual journey of a person captured by evil. *Psychology* is traditionally defined as a behavioral science that studies the functions of the human mind as it relates to the world. The term was originally translated from Greek to indicate the investigation of the psyche or spirit. As too readily happens with the sciences, we can divorce the spiritual aspect from the original perspective that is an inherent part of the function of the psyche.

It is my perspective that psychology is a holistic study that must incorporate the understanding of the human spirit as it is expressed physically and mentally. In reference to the following story, I hope to show the correlation of the spirit–body–mind function in a unique setting that was my own life course. More saliently, I have chosen not to shear off the spiritual aspect of my life from the mental and physical, but to integrate all in that illumining place where we meet God and the divine spirit. Spirituality, as I see it, is the universal irrepressible human hunger for that illumining experience with the divine spirit (Ellens, 2008, p. 1; see also Ellens, 2009, p. xvi). This is in line with Gerken (1984), who presented psychology and spirituality as the two universes of discourse, perspectives, and quest trajectories for dealing with the same domain, the living human document (p. 20).

In retrospect, I suspect I was so shocked by the realization that Ray had freely made the decision to end his life that I could only process the event as an oppressive agent that forced him to commit suicide. Now, I know it is not uncommon for evil to give off an aura that pervades a space; however, that aura is a by-product, and not the cause, of evil actions (J. Harold Ellens, e-mail correspondence to Virginia Ingram, April 12, 2010).

Seeking safety I went to stay with my father and his partner, who urged me to "get off" heroin. My father's partner is a deeply religious man who stuck an icon of St. George on the wall of their spare room, and prayed next to the bed as I tried to withstand the pains of withdrawal. I did not understand what he was trying to achieve at the time, yet I found myself entering into it and can conclusively say that something happened to me in that room, though I cannot articulate the experience. All I can say is that I know it was the prelude to and preparation for my confession of discipleship; and the beginning of my conversion experience, whereby I was taught how to identify evil, and the means I would have to take to thwart it.

Sadly the pains of withdrawal were too great for me, and I went back to my life, defeated yet armed. Before I left, my father and his partner gave me a crucifix on a rope, which I accepted and wore around my neck. It was one of the few possessions I had when I was captured a few months later, and incredibly it is still with me.

The Bible has few explicit references to addiction. In the letters of Titus and Timothy, we are told a bishop should not be addicted to wine (Tim 3:3; Tit 1:7), which would indicate addiction is not close to godliness, although we are not told why. It is only later in Titus (2:3) where we find the answer. Addiction makes a person a slave to the object of the disorder, and if "No one can serve two masters" (Matthew 6:24), then the addicted person cannot put God in his rightful place, and is a slave to evil instead.

In terms of addiction, it is difficult to speak of choice. The addict is certainly free to choose before the addiction takes hold, yet after that time any choice is suspended until the addict reaches "rock bottom." When that time comes, the addict is moved to either choose death or cry "life" with a full heart.

Little did I know my lowest point would arrive shortly after leaving my father's house. I began living on the streets, and did whatever I had to in order to sustain my addiction, including acts of prostitution. One day, when I was very desperate for heroin, I was approached by a woman who told me she could take me to a place where I would be given drugs, as long as I promised to work in a brothel that evening and pay off the money in the morning. I said I would do it.

The place she took me to was a factory in an industrial area that had been barely converted for prostitution. There were no rooms to speak of, only partitioned areas with beds. My instincts told me this was not a place I wanted to be, but I felt the pains of withdrawal starting and I decided I would take the drugs that were offered, pay off the money that was due, and leave as soon as I could.

My first impression of Tony, the man who would come to shape the next few years of my life, was of a man who understood the evil effects of addiction and who was consciously prepared to exploit those effects for his own personal gain. Yet, this was not unfamiliar. He just fit the drug-dealing stereotype. He gave me the drugs I needed, and then sent me out with the other girls to work on the street as a gang of young boys supervised us in bringing the men back into the factory.

After working the agreed 18-hour shift, I was told it would be OK if I slept on one of the beds until I wanted to leave. I was very tired and accepted the offer, yet I was intent on leaving when I awoke. Here I am reminded of Bonhoeffer's (2001) statement that "evil can be disguised as light"; because although I felt it was a kind offer, my sleep was interrupted by Tony coming into the room, raping me and telling me I was now his girlfriend. My choice to say no and assert my will had been ignored; and I found myself in a situation where my body had been taken by the evil intent of another.

Yet, Tony's act of rape was not only a violation of my physical, emotional, and spiritual well-being, but also a direct affront to God's self-giving creative energy. This sex was not creative of love and unity but rather a violent expression of degradation and ownership: violence and violation (Ellens, 2006, p. 142). Evil is intimately concerned with submitting the beauty of life to the utmost degradation and perversion.

Unfortunately, our sexuality, which is at the core of our spiritual life force (Ellens, 2006, p. 142), is left vulnerable to fiendish people. We find that, historically, sex has been used as a tool to oppress, violate, and humiliate. We are all too familiar with the dehumanizing acts of sexual torture that were committed at the Abu Ghraib detention center, precisely typical of the horrible abuses that have characterized brutality, apparently since time began.

Tragically the powers that oppose God almost won in demonizing sex, or rather infecting societal conscience. When we consider the story of Sodom and Gomorrah, a story of the violation of the ancient law of hospitality, we are confronting a story that also includes depredation and violent sexual intent; yet the ongoing evil effect rendered by the misinterpretation of this narrative is judgment against homosexuality, and the vilification of homosexual persons. What is more beautiful than people seeking enmeshing sexual relations, creative of love and unity, regardless of their gender, as determined by God's own gift of inborn orientation and design? Frighteningly, this illustrates that the effects of evil can be felt by large groups of people far removed by thousands of years from the initial act of degradation and violence in the biblical narrative and its misinterpretation (Ellens, 2006, pp. 103–106).

Yet evil and its effects will not go away of their own accord. Evil is capable of adversely affecting a person years after an event, and can have a generational impact, when family patterns of abuse are repeated. However, the grace of God is unending, and not only heals the effects of evil but also can transform the most brutal situation into a place of great beauty.

When I heard him leave the building, I dressed to go. Yet, as I did I was confronted by one of the gang members, who seemed to be guarding the front door and said, "You can't leave; you're Tony's girlfriend now." A more accurate understanding of this expression would be "You can't leave, because Tony wants you as his possession." Suddenly I realized there was a life on the other side of the door that was being taken away from me.

In retrospect, I believe I had abandoned the world on the other side years earlier; and the evils of drug addiction that had enslaved me subjectively were about to have an objective force, whereby my life was to be lived out in the confinement of pure objective evil.

This may seem to be a strong thing to say, but when one is contending with group dynamics and a hierarchy of evil control, an intensity of evil is easy to develop. Robert J. Lifton described a phenomenon he called "doubling" in relation to mob mentality and the officers at Auschwitz. He posited that many of the officers were caring and upstanding men when they were at

home with their families, and seemed to turn into monsters only when they
were in the camp (Lifton, 1986).

Strikingly, I was told by one of the gang members there was something
about the factory that turned men evil, and in his experience this change
occurred as soon as a person walked over the threshold. I view this less as the
phenomenon of a double self and prefer the work of Lars Svendsen, whereby
he identified only a single self that interprets itself differently within the
prison and outside (Svendsen, 2010, p. 163). Yet, I struggle with this proposition also. From my experience, although the girls who were captive did not
create a loving bond and pitted themselves against each other for favors from
the gang leaders, this was purely an instinctive reaction and I could not have
imagined one of the girls holding a gun to the head of another purely for
pleasure; as the gang members did.

Thereby, I am less inclined to represent my captors and their gang members as men who were themselves of a demonic evil that possessed them
and took away their choice and control. This is a misunderstanding of evil.
Rather, they were men who had permission to commit evil within the factory
and not outside. This is somewhat akin to a brutal person who abuses his or
her family behind closed doors, yet abides by societal norms otherwise, even
being a prominent leader and exemplar in church and society. The factory
became a place where they sought to go, because they wished to be evil.

I cite the example of the volunteer brigade, Police Battalion 101, who
viciously murdered 38,000 Jews. Astoundingly, the men were told they might
withdraw from the operation with impunity after they were informed they
were required to kill men, women, and children at close quarters and in mass
numbers; and, indeed, a small percentage of the men did. However, the majority took part in the massacre of their own free will; and as time went by and
the permission to commit evil was well known, there were more volunteers
for Police Battalion 101 than were needed for the operation. These men are
widely thought of as ordinary men (Browning, 1998).

In one way, it can be seen as a sad indictment on the human condition
that these men can be called ordinary, a keen reminder that we must always
strive to be extraordinary. However, from another perspective the statement
is revealing of the sobering truth that evil comes from within us. Evil does
not have an external ontology that overtakes those who are unlucky. If that
is the case, it is not something to be overly worried about; after all, I do not
know of anybody personally who has been possessed by a demon, and it was
not Tony's legal defense (Svendsen, 2010).

Yet, this primitive symbolic understanding of evil seems to be the overriding view of evil. Too frightening is it for us to think evil is a possibility that
lies not only in our own heart but also in our spouse, our neighbor, and our
government. When we understand evil in this way and not as a personified

creature that in no way resembles us, the dimensions and implications are terrifying.

Identifying the genesis of evil is the first step in establishing responsibility. So when John said to me that as soon as a person walked across the threshold of the factory they became an "asshole," I believe that was the truth; however, he was intimating that there was some kind of absolved responsibility and they were powerless to the evil surroundings. I posit that they came to the factory because in the factory existed the opportunity to do evil without reproach. I cite the case of John as evidence for their free will.

John had told me he was a family man, teacher, and soccer coach in Lebanon when the civil war struck. He said that the village knew an attack was imminent and that the men of the village would practice warfare in preparation, although inside themselves they never really thought it would eventuate. The symbol that realized all of their fears was of the priest handing machine guns to 14-year-old boys. He said they knew there was no escaping the horror then because the most peace-loving man in the village had resigned himself to the bloodshed. Tragically, John witnessed his soccer team and his 5-year-old child being killed.

Tony was John's cousin, who assisted John to come to the safety of Australia and looked after him with the proceeds of the factory. He reasoned to John that although he was participating in sexual slavery and widespread drug dealing, it was all for the greater good, as he was sending some of the proceeds to a guerrilla group in Lebanon. John doubted Tony's motive and maintained Tony was there to serve his evil heart. As a result, John not only left the factory but also left the country to put as much distance between Tony and himself as he could.

The reason I have devoted so much space in telling John's story is because it demonstrates that although there was an oppressive feeling of evil in the factory, it did not take away the will of those who walked into it; and furthermore, the reason the men became evil as soon as they walked through the door was of their own desire. Although John participated in some of the activity at the factory, he realized it was wrong and walked away. What if all of them had realized it was wrong and walked away? What if none of the men of Police Battalion 101 could have pulled the trigger? Then they would have become heroic and their lives would have had meaning.

There was a thick malevolent feeling in the factory, as it took on the form of a place that was personified with evil. It was the place where evil was acted out, and evil intentions and desires became concrete realities. Therefore, in the factory these men were completely personified by evil, and the auras that surrounded them were so pervasive they seeped out of their bodies and filled the space around them (J. Harold Ellens, e-mail correspondence to Virginia Ingram, April 12, 2010).

I find it interesting to note that the Bible represents an evil that is so concentrated and intense as Satan (Hebrew for adversary); and I am starkly reminded of Tony's catchcry, "Fuck God—I am God." From a psychological perspective, this statement is the mark of a man with a grandiosity indicative of a borderline personality; theologically speaking, it is also the expression of Satan, who seeks to do battle with God and take over his power.

Tragically, people who channel a satanic energy do it because they seek an ultimate power with which to serve themselves. The only power that is independent of God is that which harms others and leads to tendentious or absolute destruction. Paradoxically Tony attributed destructive power to creative energy, and the more he destroyed the more he felt a heroic self-image. Yet, his broken victims are a constant reminder of the destruction wrought by the evil that came from him and worked through him. In this way, the weak and powerless valiantly stand as the moral arbiters of the world calling for divine justice.

Moreover, earthly tyranny devoid of the sanctifying grace of God can only lead to death and finality. Yet, the evildoer is deceived into believing that evil acts grant the doer supreme freedom. There is no absolute freedom in the temporal world. The only act of absolute freedom was the singular event that brought forth the Creation. Furthermore, it is not possible to live an independent state of being, and when we speak of free will, it is only a freedom to choose right or wrong (Svendsen, 2010). The evildoer is never independent; he or she comes forth from the mother's womb and the Creator's handiwork, but, more strikingly, evil is distinctly relational in its desire to subvert the needs of another person or the bonds of Creation.

Yet, there is a spiritual freedom, which can never be taken away or imposed upon, and in situations of physical incarceration the spiritual dimension develops unconsciously (Simon, 1979, p. 46). The Bible recounts numerous examples of spiritual growth in times of physical restriction. In the Exodus account, it is the Hebrews' "groanings" that create the necessity of God's response; also the Babylonian exile engenders spiritual creativity. New Testament accounts are equally plentiful, most saliently in the Passion of the cross, as Christ is completely immobilized and nailed to a tree.

My lack of freedom turned me to God, because I needed some softness in a world that was hard. However, the first thing I had to do was reassess my vision of God. The God of my youth could not help me in this situation, and I was forced to radically trust in the *benevolence* of God for the first time.

Yet I had always trusted in the power of good to triumph over evil, and I sincerely believe an encounter with evil can never be ambivalent. Evil entreats a person to either choose destruction or choose life. This is the point of the Book of Job. If we are to abandon God, what is the alternative? It can only be to embrace destruction. So no matter how much pain and suffering we go through, we must still have faith in God, because when God tells Satan to spare Job his life (Job 2:6), we know when we are contending with the "satans" of the world, they cannot steal our eternal existence.

Like Job's friends, one of the gang members grabbed me and shook me when he caught me praying, and yelled, "Where is your God? Your life is shit." At the time, I responded by merely saying God was in my life; but if I were asked now, I would borrow my friend Harold's line and say, "God is going to turn that horse manure into fertilizer, and beautiful flowers are going to grow."

Looking back, I am shocked at how devoted I was. I think because of my lack of formal religious education I felt as though my understanding of God was poor. Yet, I remember in the early mornings just before we were about to go to sleep, I would pray next to my bed in the silence, and cry myself to sleep with the cross pressed against my face. I know my prayers were the girls' prayers, because the lack of privacy ensured that we shared the brutality, the degradation, and the humiliation and became in some ways a single unit of pain and suffering.

The day of the murder was particularly ominous. I was extremely agitated, and I believe I had sensed I was on the precipice of death. When one of the gang members came into the factory vacant and bloodied, my fear intensified. Yet, in the midst of my extreme anxiety I distinctly remember a feeling of awesome calmness and the awareness of a protecting presence. This phenomenon of a sensed presence in extreme and unusual environments is not uncommon, and is ordinarily attributed to a "religious figure, friend, acquaintance or relative" (Suedfeld & Geiger, 2008), yet I would suggest that regardless of the projected image, any of these helpers manifest themselves from the divine spirit within us.

The afternoon moved slowly, until all the gang members arrived at the factory with guns and machetes. The rival gang arrived with premeditated intent and began by opening fire on the factory before they made their way in. Together they were a wall of evil, and I knew somebody was going to die that afternoon. I thought it might be Tony as he struggled to keep another man with a gun away from him. Yet, in the office which was next to me, I saw where the fever pitch of evil had situated itself.

The shooter Joe (who was a young gang member) had an expressionless face with eyes focused on death. I have heard soldiers recount of knowing the intent to kill by the look in a person's eyes. It is a reflection of fierce, uncompromising determination, and the response can only be one of resignation. Then in the space of a minute, he had fired the gun and murdered a man.

As I sat in the recess with my arms wrapped around my legs, with bullets flying around me and a man who had been shot lying on the office floor, I was instantly and instinctively thrown into prayer. I remember saying to God, "If you save my life, I will give my life to your service." This is in fact a rather common form of bargaining that people resort to in the face of impending death. Yet, at the time I felt it was quite a bargain, because I could not think of anything worse than living the religious life.

However, as the shooter paced up and down surveying his destruction and me, his only witness, there was never a moment I sought to reason with him; he had seemed so intent on living out his violent fantasy. Thereby, the only other avenue available to me was to pray constantly to God, as a declaration of my choice to live, regardless of the shooter's will. When we call on God, we call on eternal life, and evil knows it is thwarted.

Yet, the thing I find interesting about Joe is that before the shooting he looked somewhat possessed by evil, and I do not mean he looked like a man who was taken over by evil, but a man who had given himself completely to this evil desire. His mind appeared to be so fixed on murder, and as he pointed the gun at Stephen and pulled the trigger, it was almost as if the taking of Stephen's life was a huge release of demonic energy. Afterward he did not appear to be a smooth calculated killer, but maybe an ordinary man who regretted what he had done.

I do not know why Tony didn't shoot me; there would be too many variables to consider, and in terms of my confession of faith to God this is irrelevant anyway. My conversion was not based on a belief that God granted my wish. That would ignore the depth of communion I felt at that time. Otherwise, how would I know? It could have been just a coincidence.

Yet, the strength of the moment for me was stripped of any distractions, I was in absolute destitution and poverty with no personal freedom, living dangerously on the precipice of finality, where there is only one choice to make: Do you want to live or die? At that moment my mind, my will, and my heart turned to the source of all life, and even if I had been shot dead in that moment, I would have commended myself to God's eternal Spirit. This was the moment in my life when I really turned to God, and said, "I am with you." My cry was the cry of life and discipleship, in stark contrast to Tony's, which was a call for death and dominance.

I think the fundamental spiritual question for a person who is under the control of evil forces is not what is the nature of evil, but what shall I do about it? If we cannot overcome it by force and free ourselves from its grasp, the only solution is to accept it. Yet, accepting evil on the face of it is a difficult thing to do, and can result in the victim joining the ranks of evil in order to give some purpose to the trials. When we accept the reality of suffering as a part of life that we can get through with faith, then it ceases to be able to own and destroy us.

Furthermore, these moments in time that mark our lives become sacred moments, but not other-worldly. They are humanizing times because they are the cries through which we can experience divine and sustaining grace-if we have the eyes to see and the ears to hear.

When we commit ourselves to God in faith, our life story is not only punctuated by evil and suffering, but also enveloped in eternal glory; this means we still feel the pain of our mortal lives, but we interpret it in our eternal existence. Thereby, stories of martyrs and confessors who feel no pain whilst being tortured and murdered can only be seen as mythological. If this were not the case, we would have to imagine Christ felt no pain on the cross, and if that were so we would have to think God was cheating us and taking the easy way out. To be truly human is to feel pain and suffering and also to experience profound grace. The biblical model and the psychological authenticity require that we face the reality of suffering head-on and honestly if we are to find the grace in it.

I was not tortured, and only a victim of physical violence a minority of the time because I learned to "behave" in order not to be harmed. Yet, I was the victim of extreme degradation and humiliation that affected me for years to come. In a medical and psychological report done close to the time, the conditions from which I was suffering were a direct result of the harm that I endured. According to confidential medical and psychological reports, I was diagnosed with epileptic seizures, "fearfulness, anxiety, insomnia, agitation, restlessness, a sense of depersonalisation, panic, sense of loss of self, depression, agro-phobia, rumination, low self-esteem, insecurity, and hyper-vigilance." Today this would be described as a complex type of PTSD. Yet, wonderfully in the psychological report, it is also written, "Virginia experiences a sense of surreal calmness when she feels exposed to danger."

As I stated earlier, I sensed this calmness on the day of the murder, which I directly attribute to a sensed presence of God. Yet, God did not remove my pain; to do that would have been artificial, and a denial of my human experience. God affirms my humanity by allowing me to be human, and by being with me in my time of trial; and in knowing God is with me, I feel comforted.

I am comforted by God, in the knowledge of a man who was full of the Holy Spirit enduring unspeakable pain and suffering. Thereby, as God walks with us He knows our suffering and comforts us, but he also orients us to our own resurrection and the life eternal. Had it not been for my circumstances, I may not have come to God as conclusively as I did. Yet, the majesty of God determines that all roads lead to Him eventually, as God is both omnipotent and merciful. St. Paul declares that every eye shall see him, every knee bow, and every tongue profess this one day (Rom. 14:11).

When we speak of Jesus Christ, it is important to emphasize he was a person, and a person not unlike ourselves. He shared our bodily existence and everything that entails. He would have coughed and blown his nose, and like us he would have had to eat and drink. Very much like my friends and me, he was at times accused of being a drunkard and a glutton (Matt 11:19). He would also have felt pain and suffering, as is clearly evident in his profound expression of grief alongside Lazarus's dead body (John 11:35).

Yet, we are sometimes told that Jesus's thoughts and feelings are not important, and we must seek the spiritual message from the Gospel rather than the historical figure. However, we deceive ourselves in doing so, because it is in Jesus's ordinariness that he helps us. He was an exceptional human being, but an ordinary one at that. In being the ordinary person, he becomes the perfect counter for the ordinary person who commits evil. It is not God's intention that we follow Jesus in dispassionate awe, but that we realize the possibilities that lie within us, by Jesus's example, and we follow him in emulation and transformation. It is our responsibility to acknowledge Jesus was like us.

However, it is all too easy for us to set Jesus apart as the divine man, rather than a man who was not only full of the Holy Spirit but also possessing of a Spirit that poured out of him into the entire world for all time.

In the first instance, we interpret Jesus as someone so unlike us that there is no point even trying to be like him. Why should we? We are not God, so it is a futile exercise, we may say. Furthermore, we believe in Christ so we are saved; thereby, we do not have to do anything else. If he is the divine man, why do we not just sit back and adore him? The reason we cannot view Jesus in this way is because it is idolatrous. It is even anti-creational in some regards, because it means we deny the Creation as a dynamic work of art. Why worship the Creator, and deny the artist's expression of himself as is put forth in the Creation? To deny the possibilities of ourselves is to deny God.

To affirm God is to trust in the goodness within ourselves; and the power of grace to assist and transform us until we are so graced it spills forth into the lives of the people we encounter. There is no great secret: God is transparent. We do not even have to ask for grace, and it is given to us; but if we do ask, it is never refused. Furthermore, God gives love freely, so it is never a burden to ask.

When Joe walked out of the factory, I screamed Stephen's name at the top of my lungs, and there was a moment of silence before the shooters ran out of the factory. I then walked into the office with another girl, and we agreed Stephen had gone to a better place. There is no other thought to have when confronted with a dead body: the empty shell of a person and the absence of a life force to ignite the imagination.

A poetic account I wrote closer to the time spoke of God crying because it was raining the day Stephen was murdered. There is no sense in this, but it contrasted starkly with the reality of myself and the other girls, who were beaten by Tony if we cried in his presence. Thereby, our time in his company was completely manipulated, right down to the expression of our emotions.

Given this, it is not difficult for me to see how I had become a psychological captive of Tony's evil.

After some time in absolute captivity, we were granted a degree of freedom. I remember taking Tony's German shepherd, who guarded the factory, for a walk around the block on some occasions and going to the local shops. This "freedom" is always a curse for victims, and becomes the greatest source of shame and guilt when the question arises, "Why did you not just run away?" Without going into psychological models such as the Stockholm syndrome, which does not adequately describe my case, I think it can easily be said, after being a victim of and witnessing such violence, that even the thought of Tony could control me from afar. His criminal network was wide, and in the end it became enough for him just to threaten me with murder if I left. Thereby evil plays on itself, and can control the victim with the revelation of the possibility of evil of unimaginable proportions. The only foreseeable way I could ever leave the factory, Tony, and his gang members was if I was physically extricated. By the grace of God, that happened.

After the murder, Tony was arrested in his car with drugs and a handgun. He informed us there would come a point where we were going to be interviewed by the police, and he told us what we should say; yet when the time came for us to sit in the witness box, and swear to the tell the truth on a Bible in the presence of God, all our fear had lifted, and Tony's reign of evil was exposed passionately.

As my time in the factory drew to a close, I began to bond with the gang member who had asked me where God was. He was very different from the others, and never participated in the heavy violence. One day he came to the factory, grabbed me, and told me to get into his car. I did not know what was happening, but I felt I could trust him.

He told me that Tony was planning to kill me and he was protecting my life. I cannot help but think it is ironic he questioned the whereabouts of God to me earlier when he had shown himself to be an agent of God in this world, risking his life to care for others. We did not talk a great deal, but at one point he turned to me and without further explanation said, "It is a war on drugs." It must be a war if evil is an adversary. He then asked me where my life would be if I had never touched drugs.

His nature was very determined as he took me to a house where he said I would be safe, and gave me some money to look after myself. I never saw him again, and I am forbidden to mention his name, but I did track down his phone number and made a nervous phone call to say thank you. He sighed, was silent, and then hung up.

As the court trial loomed, feelings of extreme anxiety and fear began to surface. It was brought to my attention that Tony and his gang had most probably been involved in the murder of four sex workers in the area, and that bugging devices had caught them devising a plan to murder me so I would not testify. It is a sickening feeling to know somebody is actively trying to kill you, and I was staving off having a complete mental and physical breakdown, as I was told I would only be safe once they were all behind bars permanently.

The 2 years waiting for the trial were almost as bad as the 18 months I spent at the factory, and a team of people including a doctor and a psychologist were assigned to me to ensure I could cope with the task. In that time, one of the girls was found dead of an overdose at the house of one of the gangsters.

There was only one sanctuary for me, and that was the Anglican Cathedral in Sydney. I did not understand the differences between Christian denominations at that time; it was just in a convenient location and a beautiful building. As soon as I walked into the cathedral, I was overcome with a pervasive sense of peace and joy and knew nobody would hurt me there; so I spent most of the days waiting for the trial sitting in the church talking to God.

I did not know how to pray, but I started by saying, "So here I am," and the conversation just flowed by the grace of the divine spirit. Those conversations (although I don't remember much of the content) remain very dear to me, because God became my friend, and I began to enjoy going to the cathedral to be with my friend, although I felt a little bit self-conscious when the priest asked me if I needed to talk. I would always tell him I did not want to talk, so he would ask me if I would mind if he prayed next to me. Then one day as I left, he gave me a Bible.

Throughout this time, I gave evidence in a few different court cases that resulted from my time in the factory, until the day came when all of the gang members were behind bars. Tony, the ringleader, received two life sentences, which was a record sentence for these offenses in New South Wales (NSW), and the judge in her submission wrote,

I accept the Crown's submissions that his conduct in the commission of these offenses involved wickedness of the highest order and that there is no better expression of the misery and depredation inflicted upon human life by the illicit trade in hard drugs. (Confidential Sentencing Report, NSW District Court)

Life then became somewhat normal. I stopped going to the cathedral, but I decided I would read the Bible. It was a labor of love and I did not understand it at the time, yet after further reading I decided to enter into full communion with God and be baptised. Much has happened since my baptism; most noticeably, I have moved to the other side of the country and am seeking ordination in the care of St. George's Anglican Cathedral in Perth.

However, there would be a problem with ending the story here. The difficulty with situations of great evil and brutality is finding a space for forgiveness. There is a challenge which comes with being a victim, and that is to see the perpetrator as deserving of God's love. If we do not, we bring hate into our lives and into the world. For when we can love the person who has harmed us the most, we can love anybody and everybody; this is God's will.

St. John of the Cross says, "where there is no love, put love and there will be love."

In conclusion, it's too easy to say, "The things that happened in the past make me what I am today, and I do not regret a thing." I regret a lot, and if I had a magic wand I would erase not only the experience of this tragedy but also its perpetual presence in my life story. Yet, this is not the case, so the only option I have is to keep reconsidering the events, gleaning them for meaning.

The meaning I find is that I am a human being in an Exodus odyssey, and a human being who longs for God in all of that. Therefore, I am not unlike everybody else struggling to find their way in the world, but like everybody else I am also unique. My life is not perfect like a Hollywood script played by flawless actors. It is challenging and more like the biblical story. Like the story of the Exodus, it is an iconic narrative of all of Christian life and liturgy.

God heard my groanings, and like the ancient Israelites came to me in the aid of heroic people who were prepared to help me on my way. It lifts that ancient story out of its ancient setting and places it firmly in this moment for this person. As I was waiting for the trial, I complained endlessly in the wilderness of my quandary. Yet the people around me who were working with God's love kept drawing me forward despite my protestations; and this is still the case today as I seek ordination. At first, I was sure I could never get over this horrific trauma. Now I am discovering that it is true. I can never get over it, but I have discovered that I do not need to get over it. I am able to live with it by the grace of God, and it is becoming my Exodus odyssey. It is seasoning me, as I am being teased forward toward the Promised Land of ministry.

REFERENCES

Bonhoeffer, D. (2001). *Discipleship*. Minneapolis, MN: Fortress.

Browning, C. R. (1998). *Ordinary men: Police Reserve Battalion 101 and the Final Solution in Poland*. New York: HarperCollins.

Ellens, J. H. (2006). *Sex in the Bible*. Westport, CT: Praeger.

Ellens, J. H. (2008). *Understanding religious experience: What the bible says about spirituality*. Westport, CT: Praeger.

Ellens, J. H. (2009). *The spirituality of sex*. Westport, CT: Praeger.

Gerken, C. V. (1984). *The living human document: Re-visioning pastoral counselling in a hermeneutic mode*. Nashville, TN: Abingdon.

Haaretz.com. (2010, May 21). Pope Benedict XVI. Retrieved from www.Haaretz.com.

Lifton, R. J. (1986). *The Nazi doctors: Medical killing and the psychology of genocide*. New York: Basic Books.

Simon, U. (1979). *A theology of evil*. Atlanta, GA: John Knox Press.

Suedfeld, P., & Geiger, J. (2008). The sensed presence as a coping resource in extreme
    environments. In J. H. Ellens (Ed.), *Miracles: God, science, and psychology in the para-
    normal* (3 vols.). Westport, CT: Praeger.
Svendsen, L. (2010). *A philosophy of evil* (Trans. Kerri A. Pierce). London: Dalkey
    Archive Press.

CHAPTER 6

A BIBLICAL THEOLOGY OF EVIL

J. Harold Ellens

The ancient Israelites, who present themselves as the core of the biblical narrative, arose as a self-conscious people around the middle of the second millennium (1500) BCE. Their story continues as the story of the Hebrew Bible until 500 BCE. For that 1,000 years, they seem to have had little interest in devising an explanation about how evil got into the world. Not until they encountered Babylonian and Zoroastrian mythic philosophy about such issues as creation and the problem of evil did they attempt to add such accounts to their literary heritage. Then they borrowed their explanations from Mesopotamian myths and rewrote them into stories in which their own God, Yahweh or Elohim, figured as the primary mover and shaker. That all happened as they were trying to formulate the legends that explained their concept of history from Abraham back to the beginning of the world.

Thus, during their sojourn in Babylon during the sixth century BCE, they began to work out these kinds of problems and record them near the beginning of their sacred scriptures. Before 500 BCE, they seemed to have had some kind of code for their behavior but no formal explanation of evil. They certainly noticed that some people did not follow the established or idealized code of conduct for Israelites, but that really only prompted them to scold each other a lot. The kings scolded the people, and the people scolded each other and the kings when they thought they could get away with it. The prophets scolded everything that moved, so to speak, and they kept right on doing it until the Lord shut their mouths about 500 BCE. Moreover, prophets were constantly scolding each other; and everybody who was scolding anybody constantly appealed to God as their judge; and if we can take the prophets at their word, God was scolding everybody who did not seem to be getting enough scolding already. Sometimes God outright threatened the daylights out of people who were thought to be misbehaving.

Sometime at or after the turn into the fifth century BCE, as they developed their proliferating notions of apocalyptic Judaism, the Jewish scholars made a couple of early attempts to explain the theology of evil. Both proved in the end to be false starts, but they remained in the official canon of sacred scripture nonetheless. As intimated in Chapter 1, the earliest one appears in Genesis 6 and is an old legend that appeared in many forms and places in the ancient Mesopotamian world. The second one to be developed is placed earlier in the Bible, in Genesis 3. It too is simply copied from an ancient fertility cult story and turned into the explanation of how things got wicked in God's good world.

It is interesting that God's people needed to borrow some pagan stories to solve the problem of the source of evil. The first story blames God, and the second story blames humans. That is probably why there are two. There were two different general strains of apocalyptic theology developing in Second Temple Judaism in the fifth century, and they both wanted to get their oar in on this exciting speculation about the origin of evil.

That first story, in Genesis 6, claims that evil came into this world, rather benignly, from the heavenly realm. The Elohim—that is, demigods or angels—descended to earth, saw how beautiful and sexy human women are, and took them as wives. Seems like a rather natural thing to do. The result was pregnancy and the birth of a race of giants who taught men how to devise implements of agriculture and war, while teaching women the use of cosmetics so as to be even more seductive. This apparently produced a great deal of conflict and turbulence on earth. God was so upset by all this that eventually the answer was to kill a lot of people with the flood.

Analyzing this explanation of evil gives the impression that there were two issues that turned a rather understandable drama into a source of evil. First, the heavenly beings apparently lusted after the women, that is, there is something about sex that can get you into trouble. Second, the heavenly beings crossed a boundary that is supposed to be inviolable (i.e., the boundary between things divine and things human, the heavenly and the earthly). In any case, it is clear that the humans are essentially without fault and not the source of evil. Evil comes from a decision and act of God's heavenly agents according to this line of thought. They fouled up this planet with their lust and irresponsibility. God and his minions are to blame for evil. That is the full explanation and that is all there is to it, according to Genesis 6.

Obviously, there were those Jewish scholars at and after 500 BCE who were inclined to defend God against this accusation. They wanted to protect God at all cost, sort of like an abused child wants to protect the parent at all cost, because if the parent is bad what does the child have left? That means that where he or she is plugged into the universe, things are flawed. Hence, it shapes the child's own image of self. The scholars trying to protect God wanted to write a theodicy that kept God pristine and perfect, even if they needed to blame humans, indeed themselves, for the rise of evil in this world. So they found an old fertility myth in Babylon and turned it into the fall story in Genesis 3.

What a really dumb idea, because that does not get God off the hook. Either the omnipotent, omniscient, and omnipresent God, who is the creator and cause behind everything, caused evil or he let it happen. He willed it or did not will its prevention. He permitted it, at least. There are no other options. In either case the issue goes all the way back to God. As President Harry Truman said, "The buck stops with the big guy."

The mythic story of the fall of human beings into the prideful sin of disobedience, presented by the Hebrew Scriptures in Genesis 3, is intensely intriguing from many points of view. Whether it is understood literally, metaphorically, mythically, or symbolically, the story provokes a spontaneous and universal sense of its authenticity. It is one of those stories that carries with it such archetypal quality that we sense at once how it touches at the center, a generic truth of obvious humanness and of vital personal experience. It speaks of the radical and tragic distance between what we can imagine as our finest potential as persons, and what we know as our often defeating and dissonant experiences in real life. The story says we are broken, and life's experience makes that seem like a deep and central truth, whether God caused it or God permitted it, or our willful pursuit of bad courses of action is just typical of us apparently flawed humans.

One reason this story is always intriguing arises from the way the archaic Mesopotamian sources of this legend are woven into a narrative about Israel's God. The formal elements present here, derived as they are from the much more ancient primordial myth, include the role of the virgin, the tree, the fruit, the phallic serpent as tempter, and the like. These are all imported with little alteration from ancient fertility literature. Though the story is not explicitly sexual, as we find it in the Hebrew Bible, it is the story of a contest between two potential lovers for the allegiance of the virgin: God and God's Adversary. Thus we have a double seduction. The phallic serpent seduces Eve, and Eve seduces Adam. This framework for the story carries the sexual overtones of the original story in Genesis 1:27 over into Genesis 2–3. In Genesis 3, of course, the narrative includes the response of guilt and shame regarding sexual vulnerability.

The story is equally intriguing for the manner in which the Hebrew editors attempted to adapt it for use in their religion. Their key difference from the Mesopotamian myth is the obvious literary effort invested here to make the story fit into Israelite theological ideology, and to make it reveal something essential about the manner in which Israel's God, Yahweh, relates to the impaired universe and the fractured human community.

THE FUNCTION OF THE STORY

Related to this is the implication in the story of the general problem of evil. Clearly, this foreign literary material is inserted into the fabric of the Hebrew scripture to service Israel's theology. It establishes a baseline for dealing with the problem of evil as humans suffer it. The claim is unquestionably made here that a hubristic egotism led humans beyond their appropriate domain and landed them in such an erroneous perspective that God's design for nature, for our sense of the presence of God, and for interpersonal relationships seemed seriously disturbed. The flowering shrubs began to look like thorn bushes, the walks with God began to look dangerous and something to hide from, and the complexity of human relationships began to look like thickets of unsortable confusion and pain.

The fall story tries hard to account for the problem of human pain and universal disorder in the world. It attempts to explain why humans can conceive of aesthetic ideals but can hardly create them, can long for a perfect world but not fashion one, can hope for genuine love but seldom express or experience it, and can remember and anticipate paradise yet sense that it always eludes us.

This is an intensely pathetic story of loss, grief, guilt, and shame. The pathos of the story is significant in revealing the essential nature of the universal human predicament, whether the story is understood as history or as myth. The literary characteristics clearly establish, of course, that it should be viewed as a mythical section of the Bible. It is so invested with confessional theological content that it is profoundly true in what it says about our fractured humanness. Myth is a confessional statement that is usually truer than mere historical reporting could ever possibly be. The truth it articulates is that of the general state of the flawedness and incompleteness of human nature and the material world. It describes the sense of the wrongness of things within and between us as humans. We all experience this. It is expressed in the pervading dysfunction and anxiety that afflict us all.

So the story is a theological myth, imported into the sacred canon from pagan sources by the Hebrew believers, for the purpose of describing the psychological state of affairs they perceived to afflict humanity. They saw themselves and the human race as alienated, orphaned, and diseased. They were, of course, quite correct. St. Paul described it succinctly: "We have all sinned and fallen short of the glory of God" (Rom 3:23).

The story depicts a cosmic paradigm for general human psychological development. It describes a crucial stage in human growth from the childlikeness of Eden to mature work in building God's reign of love and grace in this world. This narrative represents the adolescent move from human naïveté to humans taking social and cultural responsibility in God's world. It is not a story about a fall down, but of humans stumbling up the stairs to a new level of maturation and functionality. In that growth process, the story describes, for the human race, the development equivalent to the individual growth process of birth and adolescent disengagement. It tells us how humankind decided to grow up, from the cradle of the Garden, to move forward to building the Holy City.

The personal separation experiences of birth and adolescence are normally fraught with a good deal of anxiety. That anxiety is also evident in the story of the fall, as we observe the reaction of Adam and Eve. There is significant anxiety there, regarding the presence of the forbidden tree, the perception of the possibility of making a wrong decision, the appearance of the sexual symbol of the tempting serpent, the offer of the seduction of Eve, her offer of seduction to Adam, the threat of death, and the guilt and shame of cutting loose from God. The whole fabric is expressive of intense adolescent anxiety.

In fact, the most interesting element is the plain implication of an important and dangerous state of anxiety existing in the life and spirit of Adam and Eve before the fall, when paradise was presumably still intact. The recognition of significant anxiety before the fall is crucial for insight into essential human nature as seen by the ancient Hebrews. It implies the need in Adam, as he was created, for an anxiety reduction mechanism that would make it possible for him to cope and to open up the door of his primitive and childlike life to real growth. He experienced this need in terms of his growth-oriented nature and destiny.

As soon as God announced the presence and import of the forbidden tree, a state of anxiety existed in terms of Adam's perception that his potential destiny was open-ended and required decision making by him and Eve. He recognized that he possessed the potential for change and for negative or positive growth. The anxiety increased in intensity as the story recounts Adam and Eve struggling with the essential decision about their unknown and challenging future. Moreover, the pressure of that anxiety is further increased as they contemplate, quite correctly, the possibility of being like God, knowing both good and evil.

It should not surprise us that the story describes Eden as anxiety laden. Nor should we shrink from the implied fact that anxiety is not a part of our brokenness but an essential element of our natures, and of the fact that we are not fully evolved. Thus, the problem of evil becomes significantly more complex. Stress in the pre-fall state, as described in this theological myth, is already evident much earlier. Adam is described as finding himself alone in the garden in a state of sufficient disequilibrium that he looked for a mate or companion among the animals. He found none adequate or appropriate. God noted the stress and anxiety, and intervened by creating Eve as a help appropriate to his neediness. Obviously, that means that she filled out some condition of lack and anguish in Adam and thereby reduced his stress and anxiety.

One can imagine that Adam had considerable stress from numerous directions in Eden: from the pressure of responsibility to keep the garden, to find companionship that was appropriate, to name the animals, and to fashion a meaningful relationship with his wife, who ultimately chose a liberation course of independence from him and then seduced him into following her, presumably lest he lose her. Then he had anxiety about his responsibility to obey and love God in a world where the manner of doing that held considerable ambiguity. So what is the source of evil? If it is the evil that humans do to each other, is it not preset by the way God fashioned humans and their world?

The man was under pressure. His anxiety is not a consequence of his sin. It is clearly the consequence of his being a person with unexplored potentials and possibilities. It is inherent to his nature and all human nature. It is inevitable to human existence, because of the nature of the potential for growth, and of the unfolding unknown that is inherent to growth. The Hebrews saw that and related it to the potential in the world for the problem of evil. So they told the old Mesopotamian story in a new way and captured so precisely a truth generic to our existence that when we read the story 5,000 or 6,000 years later, we find it touching the center of our predicament in some fundamental ways.

The story urges that all this stress and anxiety that Adam experienced were finally culminated in the enigma of what to do about the possibility of being like God. The story of the fall, as the Hebrews understood it, describes the event and the decision as Adam's anxiety reduction move, designed to free his psyche for further function, coping, and growth. The critical question, therefore, must be raised as to whether the event was a constructive or destructive anxiety reduction procedure for Adam and the human race, as the Hebrews saw it. How does that relate to the onset of the problem of evil? Is evil merely human dysfunction, and does that arise exclusively out of the choices we make in reducing the stress of life?

We ask the same question when we consider whether the painful process of birth and adolescent disengagement is a constructive or destructive anxiety reduction experience. It is important because it will give us some clues as to whether we are to look at human alienation, pain, and anxiety and their consequences as difficult but inevitable stages in the evolution of persons and the human race, or as an unfortunate aberration of a sinful, destructive type of behavior, and the source of the problem of evil, as the Hebrews suggested.

SAYING NO AND YES TO GOD

I am persuaded that the story of the fall is a metaphor of the human process of maturing to individuality and responsible agency as individuated persons. The story is a report on the human psychological process of asserting the will of the human person against the will of God. To do so is a necessary act for humans because saying "yes" to God has no meaning or content if it is impossible to say "no" to God. To be a committed biblical believer and a builder of God's kind of world, one needs to be an independent agent who can commit to that kind of vocation. It is no different for the human race than it is for a child moving through adolescence in relationship to his or her parents. Adolescence is supposed to be a time for individuation from parents, disengagement from dependency, and assertion of one's own ego, so as to test and find one's own authentic identity and personal style.

Maturity for humans requires the ego strength and will that forge the power to disengage from authority, in order to give significance to the intent and behavior of commitment to freely chosen relationships. The story of the fall in Genesis 2–3 assumes that adolescent disengagement requires a willful aggressive act, testing one's own strength over against one's parents, against general authority, against God's requirements, or against any pressures toward conformity. This is necessary so that the person can authentically choose, as an independent agent, to conform willingly to God's will and way. Without this adolescent disengagement, there can be no growth and no later adult refusion with parents or authorities as friends, peers, colleagues, or compatriots. This is as true in our relationship with God as it is with our parents.

Childhood is a stage of fusion with parents. It moves progressively toward differentiation of individual persons, and moves toward that contest and contrast in adolescence. Once the differentiation is successfully established and genuine individuality is achieved, there follows a process of return toward union, commitment, cherishing, and a new kind of fusion. In this sense, the myth of the fall represents a growth step of such disengagement, in preparation for devoted commitment to godliness. It is of great interest that the ancient Hebrews saw this transitional process as a very precarious stage in which the act or the style of the act could produce the problem of evil and alienation from God and the good. If Adam and Eve were not wrong in declaring their independence, they were wrong in doing it as a revolution rather than as a maturing evolution, the Hebrews thought. So also with adolescents in our human processes!

Thus, it is not quite clear whether the story of the fall is intended to describe a step taken in the best possible manner, even if it was a necessary step. Human development, individually and communally, is a continuum of evolutionary process and progress. What are usually thought to be negative aspects of human development are often constructive stages of maturing. In this perspective, the fall story can be seen for just what it is: a mythic or analogic story. Although it comments in interesting and entertaining metaphors upon glitches in the evolutionary process of maturation, it does not comment in any meaningful way upon the real steps of that human process. What it does say is that the human odyssey is a tragic adventure and the source or matrix for the problem of evil.

In this model, humans move more or less consistently along the growth line from primitivity, or childhood, to maturity, without the sort of negative psychological and historical discontinuity that the fall story is usually taken to represent. It is depicted as a revolutionary break from our divinely intended style and destiny. The admittedly painful adolescent disengagement is inherently necessary to achieving responsible individual agency. That is how persons take constructive action in life. The fall was not down, but upward to the status of builders of culture, history, and a godly world. This myth moves the process of this planet from a nursery in the mythic garden of Eden to the achievement of the Holy City, a myth about the maturation of the historical process.

It is useful, nonetheless, to ask whether, as a character in a mythic story, Adam might have done it in a better way. Was his anxiety reduction process really constructive or destructive, pragmatically considered? Does humanity, or do persons, need to express so much disjunction and experience so much alienation and loss in order to achieve personhood and growth—a sense of our true selves? Or does this inevitably produce the problem of evil and human suffering as its consequence?

It is tempting to say that Adam chose the best course and, in view of his limited knowledge and experience, the only one he really had available. If this produced a problem of evil or suffering, it was simply inherent and inevitable to the natural process. Agreed. That is a way of saying that the loss and alienation we all experience in the expulsion from the womb and in adolescent individuation are virtually inevitable. Its problems and pain are built into the system. That suggests that the consequent internal and social distortions these bring, which drive our sickness and our sin, are not wholly avoidable in real life.

As we grow, we have limited knowledge, inadequate experience, and immature levels of wisdom. These frequently cause us to choose painful and alienating courses. Our decisions often alienate us from others, from God, and from our own clear sense of our selves. So our dysfunction and the interpersonal or social damage it brings are part of the process of growth in a world that God created free. That suggests that God is not the cause or the problem of evil, but that the evil humans do to each other is the price God was willing to pay to insure that the world was free to grow. Growth and change come mainly by exploration and experimentation. Where there is freedom, there will be errors. In a system where there are no errors, there is no freedom.

This model manages most of the real-life data rather well. It implies that humans are in the process of evolving. That implies that at any given

moment, we are inadequately evolved, individually and communally. Therefore, change is the objective toward which we drive. Change always brings
the pain of losing what was before. Hence, pain is inevitable. No alternative ever existed, nor can ever exist. The choice of being responsible agents,
shaping our own painful evolution, could not have been different for Adam
in the story and cannot be different for us today in real life. This is the best
of all worlds, because it is a world in which we are free to become our full
true selves. There is no other way out of our primitive childlike naïveté in
the Eden womb into the growth and maturation of whole personhood. Some
persons get stuck in the transitional alienation phase. This may result from
genetic, biochemical, or situational reasons. Such folks do a lot of damage to
the rest of us. Social psychology research on prison populations, for example,
demonstrated that 80% of the prisoners suffer from some form of genetically
inherited psychotic or schizoid disorder.

It is interesting, therefore, and very clear, that the formulators of the
ancient Hebrew story intended to explain the problem of evil and human
disorder by asserting that humanity made a bad choice in the Garden of
Eden. They were sure it had a permanent and pervasive effect. This does not
imply that some decisive act by Adam to move him from naïveté to maturity
was not necessary. Neither does it mean that nothing constructive toward
real growth came out of Adam's decision. It only contends that his decision
was a transitional act unnecessarily fraught with a self-defeating price: rebellion and alienation. The Hebrews saw it as a destructive anxiety reduction
mechanism, insofar as they sensed it in those terms.

One can posit the notion, as the ancient Hebrews did, that the fall story represents such a destructive move that paradigmatically explains the disorder
and alienation in humans. Then the story describes an essentially destructive
and self-defeating response to the generic anxiety of birth and differentiation. That would represent it as a dysfunctional response to our responsibility for choosing our personal destinies. Even so, that would not erase the
fact that the fall has constructive, freedom-affording results for humankind.
Similarly, adolescence may be handled unnecessarily rebelliously by some
teenagers but lead out to a growth process that results in profoundly healthy
relationships with parents, authorities, and traditions later on. Paul seems to
imply something of this regarding humanity when he ties the naïve primordial state of human bliss in Eden to a continuum that leads from paradise to
fallen humanity in Genesis 3, and then on to fruition in the believer as a new
person in Christ. Paul believed that to be the true destiny of all humanity.

The fall story represents one option for implementing the necessary
and inevitable differentiation process of self-actualization. If the Hebrews
thought of it as a destructive option and the source of evil in the world, the
implication is that Adam might have exercised an equally growth-inducing
act of will and ego strength had he chosen, for independent and personal

reasons, to affirm God's will and value system, and not eat of the tree of knowledge. Would that have been as initiatory, independent, and effectively disengaging an act toward growth as disobedience proved to be? Would it have had adequately self-affirming, though less self-defeating, consequences? If so, the paradigmatic import for human history is that the distortion, pain, alienation, and sickness with which humans have responded to our choice of destiny throughout history were not inevitable elements of the growth process of the race. That is apparently what the ancient Hebrews thought. However, what should this mythic figure, Adam, have done about the choice of facing the issues of both good and evil in life? Adam, of course, symbolizes each of us. How can we move beyond naïveté to face reality if we shut our eyes to the problem of evil? Adam marched forward boldly and took it on. Good for him.

Humans have made many bad decisions: in the way we have apprehended God's real disposition toward us, in the way we have responded to the quandary and ambiguity of life, and in the degree of finesse with which we have processed our own psychological dynamics, development, and destiny. The ancient Hebrews were claiming in their story that such decisions can be made more wisely, redemptively, and faithfully, and with healthier consequences. Evil is the damage we do to each other and ourselves by our distance from God's will and way. Perhaps so, but I think the pain of life is just an inevitable consequence of the experiment of human development in a system built on the grace of free choice.

Comparably, it is possible, I suppose, that the disengaging adolescent can achieve health and growth while choosing, as an independent act of will and ego, to affirm and follow the healthful values of parents, authority, and traditions toward constructive conformity. Indeed, that course, when expressing rather than compromising the child's own authenticity, may be far less self-defeating, inefficient, erosive of health, and painful than disengagement that strains relationships or maximizes confrontation, alienation, and griefloss. However, when I get a family into my clinic that has two children in midadolescence, and bitterly complains that one of the two is a troublesome child, self-defeating and disobedient, whereas the other one has always been a perfect child, the one I worry about most is the perfectionist child who is not engaging in the experiment of finding out who he or she is as an individual.

The story of the fall is theological mythology that confesses the meaning of human pain and disorder, as humanly induced, in the face of a gracious and provident God, who generously created and sustains us in freedom and forgiveness. However, our differentiation from a womblike relation with God is absolutely necessary. It appears that the Hebrews were correct in implying that the disengagement could be more or less self-defeating. The story suggests that such individuation could probably be done in a way that affirms the perspective and value system that heals. It need not be a decision that aggravates generic human anxiety and sickens us. However, it seems like those are more correctly on the right track who deemphasize the cataclysmic and alienating dimension of human fallenness while placing all the emphasis on the freedom for growth that humans as independent agents need and possess. Losing paradise in the ancient story freed Adam and Eve. They accepted the price they had to pay and the blessings that they earned: sexual awareness and fruitfulness, progeny, and generations of creative farmers and city builders.

That growth model handles the data of human perplexity in a way that implies that the fall story speaks of a *revolution* and that, however paradigmatic that may be of actual human experience, humankind always has the alternative option of an *evolutionary* growth response to our generic human anxiety. It is intriguing to consider the possibility of humanity in general, and our children in particular, developing through a peaceful adolescence, a relatively nonturbulent exploration of the possibilities of being like God or like parents, knowing good and evil.

My initial outlook in wrestling with the fall story was to conclude that Adam had no alternative. I was strongly inclined to the notion that a turbulent and alienating process is inherent to adolescence and its disengagement, as it is inherent to the rather violent and painful business of being born. However, I am indebted to many years in clinical work and pastoral care for being teased out into rethinking that. The fall story, as it stands, really does represent an unnecessarily self-destructive form of adolescent rebellion.

Presumably Adam's growth and differentiation could have developed tranquilly and evolved constructively to maturity, as in healthy and cherishing adolescents. That seems clearly to be what the authors of the myth intended to say. What urged me to take a new look at the matter was the increasing success I discern in some thoughtful and considerate adolescents who assiduously refuse to give up a course of evolutionary rather than revolutionary disengagement. It seems possible for them constructively to explore the growth and maturation process with a genius for humor and humaneness, even when their parents are, betimes, less than helpful to their wholesome development.

Disengagement by evolutionary and constructive anxiety reduction seems to work for them. It struck me in thinking of this that the odyssey of Jacques Cousteau's son seems to be a good illustration of this kind of growth. Instead of running away to sea, so to speak, literally or figuratively, as so many adolescents do, he "went down to the sea in ships" with his father and found wisdom and a beautiful new world. The metaphor is somewhat tortured by his untimely death in the ocean deep.

It is intriguing, in any case, to contemplate how things might have been in human history if the state of affairs in the human psyche and spirit were such as to permit and prompt a different mythic story in Genesis 3. What if the story could have represented humanity as reaching forward within the will of God, for individuality, maturity, and wisdom; and for knowledge of being like God in comprehending the world inside out, in knowing God as he now knows us? Cooperative growth with God and exploration of the possibilities of human destiny in tranquility do not comprise a story that rings true to the human experience of dissonance, alienation, and dis-ease. However, growth in joyful faith and trust suggests a redemptive alternate model that might have been from the beginning, if we were not so badly distorted by generic anxiety.

However, the human race was set upon the course of its experiment with destiny, without an adequate database, without adequate experience, and without a vote in the matter of our own existence in the first place. We did not choose to exist, or to launch ourselves in primitivity and ignorance, or to pursue our destiny without a light to see the next step. We did not choose to be inadequate to the responsibilities of life and the challenges of godliness.

THE IMAGE OF GOD IN FALLEN HUMANITY

If we think of the fall story and of human distortion as destructive anxiety reduction dynamics, a final significant question regarding human nature arises. In what sense do humans image God in choosing self-destructive or self-defeating courses? The human behavior of will and ego over against power and authority reflects and is possible because of an essential dimension of God's nature in humans: the function and attribute of being independent creators and independent agents of our own destiny. In the story of the fall and in the real human experience of pain, disorder, distortion, and disease, humans act as independent creators gone awry and as independent agents choosing self-defeating destinies. Those choices free us to be persons and to grow, but they decrease the focus, efficiency, and gratification of that freedom. They increase the dissonance, conflict, and erosive sense of alienation.

God, as independent agent, could also act in self-defeating ways but apparently does not because he decides not to do so. That is a credit to God's moral character as an independent moral being, not a result of his essential nature, as if he had no alternative. This reminds me of the cynic's joke: "Can God create a rock that is so heavy that God cannot lift it?" The joke has greatly entertained the superficial and cynical secularist and unduly troubled the Christian philosopher. It is to the credit of the superficial Christian and the secular philosopher, perhaps, that it troubles neither of them much, both thinking it quite absurd.

It is, however, a profound question. The answer is not the one that Christian philosophers have given, namely, that God cannot create a rock too heavy for God to lift, because that is out of keeping with God's true character. The answer, I judge, is rather that God can very well create such a rock. He can do anything like that, or any other sort of self-defeating thing, if he chooses to do so. Moreover, he can do it without ceasing to be God, contrary to the view of some Christian philosophers. He would, of course, turn out to be a bad God in the moral sense of that term as well as in the social sense of the term. But he would not be a bad God in the ontological sense. He would still be God, and that is all that counts ontologically. In that sense, it is not different for God than for humans who are bad morally and socially because they choose self-defeating behavior but remain humans in every ontological sense.

The crucial issue here, however, is that God has not created a rock too heavy for God to lift, so to speak, and has chosen not to engage in other self-defeating behavior because he has apparently chosen to behave with inviolate moral integrity. He has chosen to be true to his own nature and destiny. He is not merely locked into an inevitable moral quality because of his essence. He is free to choose, grow, explore, experiment, decide, and fail.

He has chosen not to do so, not because of his essence, but because of his moral integrity. Therefore, because all morality is ultimately aesthetics, he has made this choice because of his aesthetic integrity, and his sensitivity to what is beautiful, comporting well with authentic coherence in his world. Hence, God decides against self-defeating behavior. That is a matter of appropriateness and proportion. He is trustworthy, not merely as a being defined by logical or ontological inevitability, but by moral agency: a being who is psychologically committed to holiness in the sense of wholeness. The God of the Bible is not a Greek God in a pantheon of abstract qualities personified in archetypal figures, but a God who chooses, acts, could err as Jesus could have in the wilderness temptations, and decides not to do so. He decides to be moral, gracious, and aesthetically appropriate.

Humans reflect the image of God in our nature by the integrity of our choices. In that, we are independent choosers; we image God and reflect his nature and moral quality. We spoil the clear quality of that imaging process when we choose inappropriateness and disproportion, and when we defeat ourselves in our growth endeavors or needs by being aesthetically inappropriate.

Such was the case of Adam, as the Hebrews saw it and reported it in the myth of the fall. Such is the case in our daily failures to make sound, wholesome, and healing choices, when we have adequate information, ability, and genetic disposition to make such choices. When we make such good choices, we usually create good results. When we make bad choices because we have inadequate information, lack of ability, or genetically preset dysfunction, we are not evil, even if our choices create pain.

When we willfully inflict damage or pain while having adequate information, ability, and genetic health to prevent it, we are the sources of the only evil that happens in the world. Humans recapitulate the fall story daily.

That is undoubtedly why we so spontaneously perceive the authenticity of that ancient myth. God is not the source of evil just because God created a world that is free, intending human and animal experimentation to pursue our potential destinies.

CHAPTER 7

EVIL AS A PASTOR SEES IT

F. Morgan Roberts

It is only as a pastor that I can address the question of evil. Even though my seminary education acquainted me with the disciplines of theology and biblical scholarship, my more than half-century career in ministry was spent almost entirely in congregations and not as a teacher of theology or biblical studies. Even when, toward the end of my active ministry, I served on a seminary faculty, my work was focused upon congregational ministry. Thus, it is only within that context that I can discuss the subject of evil. So let me begin with words addressed to a congregation by the Apostle Paul.

Writing to the congregation of Christians at Rome, Paul offered them this audacious challenge: "Do not be overcome by evil, but overcome evil with good" (Romans 12:21). I believe that we can assume, without elaborate exegesis, that he was urging them to do something that he believed to be possible. My experience in the church, however, indicates that a majority of Christians have never believed in such a possibility. It took me many years to arrive fully at the realization of this fact; however, it did begin to dawn upon me by the time I was seven years into my journey in ministry. It was at this point that I began to realize that my ministry was being carried on in two very different churches within the same congregation, and that the radical difference between them was whether they believed that Paul's challenge to overcome evil was possible. One church believed that it was possible and was involved in making the possibility a reality. The "other church" did not believe that victory over evil could ever be conclusive. It may be helpful to label these two churches the *overcoming church* and the *surviving church*.

One part of the surviving church was doing its best to endure the "world, the flesh, and the devil," as it awaited its future life in heaven. Another constituency was watching as a guilty bystander, while still another was even aiding and abetting the victory of evil in the world. The lines between all of these distinctions were not clear; indeed, a pastor or church member can be living partially in both churches, or even in all four camps, without being aware of what is happening. I wish I could say that I made a clear choice to carry on my ministry in the overcoming church, but I now realize that it would take many years to realize all of what was involved in being a pastor in the overcoming church. Even then I realized that in every part of that mixed multitude that constitutes Christ's church in the world, there were always dear people who somehow lived closer to God than I did, despite the bad influence of the kind of church to which they belonged. So in what I will say as we talk about evil, I want to speak both with humility and gratitude to all those saintly souls who were always better than their church and so wonderfully kind to me along the way of my journey.

What I do remember is the day when I could begin to articulate the existence of these two radically different churches. It was in 1965 when I came upon these words:

> Within the strange, sprawling, quarrelling mass of the churches, within their stifling narrowness, their ignorance, their insensitivity, their stupidity, their fear of the senses and of the truth, I perceive another Church, one which really is Christ at work in the world. To this Church men seem to be admitted as much by a baptism of the heart as of the body, and they know more of intellectual charity, of vulnerability, of love, of joy, of peace, than most of the rest of us. They have learned to live with few defenses and so conquered the isolation that torments us. They do not judge, especially morally; their own relationships make it possible for others to grow. It does not matter what their circumstances are, what their physical and mental limitations are. They are really free men, the prisoners who have been released and who in turn can release others. (Furlong, 1965, p. 22)

By the time I reach the end of my sojourn in ministry, I hope that I will be able to say that I have given myself, heart and soul, to the service of such a church. Indeed, what a different world it would be if what Monica Furlong describes could be said of the entire church. Sadly, it is not, but I would like to begin by describing my vision of what just one congregation might be like if the pastor and the people sought to realize the overcoming reign of God in the world.

In my vision of a congregation that is alive with a spirit of goodness, I see a gathering of common people who live with a vibrant sense of personal, God-created worth. I see excitement in their experience of the Creator Spirit's ongoing work of creation in their lives as they engage in the realization of the unique possibilities that God intends for every life. This is not to be confused with fuzzy "possibility thinking" or the pop gospel of "be all you can." Their hope is not about getting anything as a reward for their faith, whether the reward is prosperity in this world or heaven in the world to come. In fact, "getting" is an entirely foreign word in the faith vocabulary of this congregation because of their realization of having already received more than an abundance of the spiritual health and wealth of God's radical grace.

Because of this, their worship service does not begin with the kind of general confession in which they bewail the past week's sins and the depraved, fallen condition of their sin-sick souls from which their daily sins supposedly arise. Concerning the obvious imperfection of human nature, they "prefer the theory that He is not done making it yet" (MacDonald, 1867, p. 32). They accept themselves as works in progress, knowing that a loving Heavenly Father shares their sadness when growth is slow, but also rejoices at their every little attempt to let the Spirit fill their lives to the full with the Divine Presence, just as that same Spirit filled the life of Jesus.

One glance at this congregation tells you that they practice radical hospitality. They welcome all persons, "regardless of race, ethnic origin, worldly condition, or any other circumstance not related to the profession of faith" (First Presbyterian Church, n.d.). Because of this, those attending worship will be dressed in various ways, reflecting individual taste or material condition. As a newcomer, you may notice these differing styles, but the members are hardly aware of such superficial differences of dress because they have learned to look beyond the *packaging* of every life. Sexual orientation does not exclude anyone from full participation in membership or leadership in the congregation, and special care assures that worship is accessible for those with handicaps or special needs. Newcomers will probably be puzzled at first in trying to categorize what kind of church this is because it will turn out to be neither a flocking together of predictably affluent, educated "culture vulture" liberals, nor will it look like "the Republican Party at prayer," a charge often leveled at traditional Presbyterian congregations. In other words, the members will draw their life justifying proof texts from neither the *New York Times* nor the *Wall Street Journal*.

Even the parking lot will look different to those coming to worship for the first time. There will be a conspicuous absence of new and expensive cars, a striking contrast to one of my former churches in which older members boasted of past times when a long line of chauffeured limousines lined the street during worship. The parking lot, instead, will reflect the simple lifestyle of the church's members, whose plain living and stern stewardship make possible the giving of unbelievable sums of money to support the mission outreach of this congregation. Even the location of the church facility will reflect such stewardship. The members will have chosen to build their church where it is accessible by bus to those who cannot afford cars, rejecting the policies of denominations that squander valuable resources upon developing new congregations in affluent suburbs or gated communities so as to acquire their market share of the new wealth, and also to insure that such isolated and insulated congregations need never fear that the penniless Nazarene and his little friends will ever disturb their suburban Sabbath solitude.

It will become obvious that the message from the pulpit plays a determining role in shaping the uniquely gracious atmosphere of this congregation, because every message will be steeped in the proclamation of God's radically universal, unconditional, inescapable, and unlimited grace. Never a Sunday will pass without the worshippers being reminded of that amazing grace that is greater than all our sin. This gospel of grace will be made operationally genuine by caring strategies in which both pastor and laity demonstrate the reality of Jesus's healing presence in our midst today.

This pulpit will not be preoccupied with defending such postbiblical doctrines as original sin, the infallibility of scripture, the virginal conception or birth, the substitutionary atonement, the bodily resurrection as the only possible interpretation of the Easter message, or the second coming of Christ, particularly as it has been hijacked by "rapture racketeers." In both preaching and teaching, no one will ever be asked to mouth creedal shibboleths that force upon the heart what no honest mind could ever affirm. Instead, the quality of the message from this pulpit will create a deep love and hunger for the grace-filled heart of scripture. People will be carrying their Bibles to worship on Sundays, no longer as repositories of proof texts, but because the pastor's penetrating preaching and informed teaching will have led them into an exciting rediscovery of the Bible and a rebaptism of their imagination.

This same fearlessness of the truth will guide the education of children and youth. Teaching materials will recognize that a rating system needs to govern the teaching of the Bible's story, especially for young children. "Strong content" and stories of violent, vengeful warfare will not be "colored friendly." Characters like Samson will not "make the cut," and the precious time of teachers and children will no longer be wasted upon making tedious models of the Tabernacle and explaining its sacrificial system, as though the killing of any animal should ever be made appealing to any child. Teachers will cease from "finding Christ" in Old Testament stories as though Hebrew scripture does not clearly, with careful interpretation, contain the prophetic proclamation of the God who "delights in steadfast love . . . and will cast all our sins into the depths of the sea" (cf. Micah 7:18, 19).

In both preaching and teaching, there will be no fear of the truth as though the minds of the laity are too fragile to wrestle with the questions raised by biblical scholarship. Likewise, there will be no fear of science, no attempt to place blinders on the minds of young people lest they be led astray by the "godless theory" of evolution. Regarding the origins of our world, the young will receive that gentle wisdom that Professor Bruce Metzger offered to his teenage son, "There had to be a push and a pull," thus stating that both God and nature were involved in the process (Metzger, 2003).

The same fearlessness will characterize the thinking and relationships of this congregation with persons of other faith traditions. Convinced that they can follow Jesus faithfully without rejecting the possibility of God's presence along other pathways, they will seek dialogue with other religious groups and engage in ways of working together for the health and welfare of their community and world. Following the way of Quaker George Fox, they will "walk cheerfully over the world, answering that of God in every one" (Jones, 1976).

Freed from all the fears that cripple heart and mind, these people will find ways to reach out to those whom others fear and neglect. Members of this church will find ways to visit prisoners and reach out to those migrant workers who are the victims of modern-day slavery in the United States. In the same spirit, they will find effective ways to speak out against injustice and oppression, and will reject all of the ways in which "the myth of redemptive violence" invades every level of our life from national policy to children's television (cf. Wink, 2007).

It will be clear that these people are determined to follow Jesus wherever they find his footprints in our world. When they celebrate the sacrament of baptism, they celebrate God's gracious acceptance of all the children of the world. At the Lord's Table, instead of looking backward upon a blood atonement, they look forward to the great banquet of the kingdom when people will come from east and west, north and south to sit at table in the kingdom of God. As they have learned from their pastor's sermons, they will talk much about Jesus, but speak seldom of Christ because, after all, neither did Jesus. For them, discipleship is not about believing, but about following, not about affirming creeds, but about abiding in the life-giving presence of Jesus. Perhaps in this sense, it may be helpful to think of the two different churches with which we began our discussion as the *following church* and the *believing church*. Instead of those church bulletin boards that define a church as a "Bible-believing church," this church will advertise itself as a "Jesus-following church."

After such a vision, some reader will surely wonder if such a church could ever become a reality. The truth is that such a church has, indeed, always been secretly present in our world. Indeed, the kinds of people described in my opening quotation who seem to "know more of intellectual charity, of vulnerability, of love, of joy, of peace, than most of the rest of us" have always been present in small numbers in all of my congregations.

Across the years, it has been my privilege to have known people who have followed Jesus in some rather radical ways. Women who might have remained in the comfort of their suburban homes have visited women in prison, cared for them lovingly upon their release, and hoped and believed in such outcasts despite the ways in which drugs and prostitution had destroyed their humanity. I have known a couple whose retirements from medicine and banking could have taken the usual course of world travel and leisure but who, instead, travelled to places of need, ministering to medical needs, and employing financial skills to raise millions of dollars for the rebuilding of hospitals and for raising venture capital that has enriched the lives of poor people who might otherwise have had a dismally deprived existence. All of these adventures were not my idea! I simply stood by and marveled, proud to be the pastor of such noble souls—and there are other pastors from other times and places who could also tell such stories.

What is even more intriguing is that such saintly souls, without the advantage of much biblical scholarship, seemed to know instinctively how to interpret scripture in a positively critical manner. They were somehow able to filter out of the gospels those harsh words placed upon Jesus's lips by a later generation that attributed to him their own apocalyptic nightmares, making Jesus seem delusional. Instead, these people seemed led by the Spirit to the Jesus of the Sermon on the Mount, the Jesus who made that longest of all journeys, across the doorsteps of the very poor in Galilee, the Jesus who promised to be incarnate in the sufferings of the least of his brothers and sisters.

It is because I have known such saints that I feel sure that my vision of a church that overcomes evil with good is a possibility. I believe that we can build again such a church because their lives demonstrated God's power to overcome the evils of ignorance, superstition, arrogance, greed, sexism, homophobia, injustice, disease, hunger, and violence.

DEFINING EVIL

The perceptive reader will surely by now have anticipated my definition of *evil*, the outlines of a theology of hope in the God who is overcoming evil, and the quality of a community of faith in which such healing of evil is operationally realized. Let me try a few simple sentences to express and enlarge upon my definition of evil:

- Evil is the bad stuff that people do to themselves and one another.
- Evil is the destructive manner in which people treat themselves and one another when they cannot trust in a benevolent God.
- Evil is overcome when people believe that their life is in good hands, so that they are empowered to bear not only their own burdens but also the burdens of others.
- Evil is overcome when people, believing in the kindness of God's providential care of their lives, begin treating themselves and one another with similar kindness.

In these simple definitions, it is obvious that I have not dealt with the problem of natural evil. How does a pastor deal with evil as people experience the destructive power of nature in storms, tornadoes, hurricanes, tsunamis, or epidemics that claim the lives of millions, or in the death of a child or the premature death of any loved one?

To address this question with thoroughness would require another entire chapter (or book?), so I can share only my experience of caring for those who have suffered from the destructive whims of nature, which include the inexplicable illnesses of our natural body. My experience is certainly not unique; almost every pastor is called upon to answer such questions as "Why did God create a world in which such destructive acts of nature can happen?" or "Why did this happen to our family?" There are, of course, no satisfying answers.

I think, however, that a faithful pastor will be careful to identify the wrong answers. In such harrowing situations, people need to know what is *not* happening to them. To do this, a pastor must state unequivocally that God does not send natural disasters or illness upon people as punishment for their supposed sins. To claim that the recent earthquake in Haiti was sent by God upon the people of that country for their alleged alliance with the devil is pastoral *malpractice* at a *theologically criminal* level. Likewise, to attribute such disasters to cosmic evil, suggesting that those who have suffered are helpless victims of a cosmic battle that is raging in the universe, in the course of which some are randomly chosen as victims by the devil and his minions, is to substitute biblically responsible pastoral practice with *superstitious gibberish*.

A responsible ministry will deal with the mysteries of natural disaster and unexplained illness ahead of time by a teaching ministry that prepares people to live with the inherent ambiguity of an uncertain world. Some of the subjects for discussion will include the following.

THE ESSENTIAL GOODNESS OF CREATION

The world as the creation of God is still to be celebrated as "very good." The natural order of events is, overall, reliable. The sun comes up every morning, and seedtime and harvest continue according to the ancient promise. Although some traffic accidents happen as a result of the law of gravity (e.g., cars careening off mountain highways), gravity is still a benevolent law of nature, insuring that things will remain in the place where I left them. Although a sudden rainstorm may spoil my daughter's outdoor wedding, the same rain will benefit the crops of many farmers, assuring our food supply. We cannot tame the earth, but we can learn to live prudently with its irregularities, building better houses that will withstand earthquakes or planning indoor weddings, as the wise and caring pastor will have counseled us to do anyway.

However, when our best planning cannot ward off the whims of natural disaster, such events are not evil, and to classify them as such is to deny the goodness of God's creation. As J. Harold Ellens has often declared,

> If a microbe sets up housekeeping on a leaf of grass, and a cow who eats that leaf contracts a serious disorder that infects its milk, and a baby drinks that milk and dies, it is not an evil inflicted by God upon us. It is an enormous grief, an overwhelming discomfort, a terrible inconvenience for us. It is a temporary illness for the cow. But it is a great achievement for that parasitic microbe. God has given us a world in which all things are totally free to act according to their own nature. That makes God's world a wonderful world for all things, as well as for us, though our freedom in life, growth, and development has a certain risk of which we do well to be as cautious as possible.

Beyond our best scientific knowledge, the earth may be caring for its health by tectonic shifts or changing temperatures, so let us treat it with reverence and common sense as the only Mother we have at present.

THE ESSENTIAL GOODNESS OF THE HUMAN BODY

Our bodies are remarkable creations. Even if I object to the teaching of intelligent design in science curriculums, the marvelous capacity and durability of my body and my mind are some of my strongest personal reasons for believing in God. Twenty years ago, when I was in my early 60s and still jogging, during a late afternoon run at a retreat center I came upon an abandoned steam locomotive on a country railroad siding. Fascinated with steam engines since my boyhood, when I listened to the haunting sounds of night trains from the tracks below our home, I climbed into the cab of the engine and discovered a rusted plate that identified the date when it was made. It emerged from a famous locomotive factory in Ohio and was put into service in 1928, the very year of my birth! Upon returning home, I went to a T-shirt store and had one made for me with lettering that stated, "Made in 1928, and still running." With all of the aches and pains of my aging body that keep me from running as fast as I could in my teens, God has still done a better job in making my body than the manufacturers of that abandoned locomotive.

Of course, it is not always so. The hardest task of any pastor is to minister to a family in which a child is dying prematurely of some ravaging disease. To endure the death of one's own child is the greatest test of faith that I can imagine. However, the physical suffering and untimely death of children are the exceptions, not the rule, of human experience. Despite the abuse that our bodies sustain from our own poor stewardship of our health, our bodies are remarkably durable, demonstrating what amazing creations they are.

Thus, I cannot think of my wrinkling skin and stiff joints at age 82 as evidence of the presence of any element of evil or flawed workmanship in God's good work of creation. It is not an evil thing that I am going to die someday. My body has served me more faithfully than I deserve, and I am hoping for something better anyway when, at last, my remains are scattered upon the earth from which I came.

Natural disasters and illnesses are not evidence of evil in the very good creation of God. Even if the worst natural disasters and illnesses should yet befall me, I can still believe in the possibility of a community of faith in which I will receive kindly support, and in which also real evil is being overcome by faith in a gracious and loving God. We can overcome evil with good.

GOD, PLEASE SAVE ME FROM YOUR FOLLOWERS!

Those were the words of a bumper sticker given to me by a friend who was dying of AIDS. When he ought to have received support from the church, what he received instead was the unhelpful harassment of true believers who pestered him with tracts proclaiming the plan of salvation by believing in which he would, at least, be saved from the eternal damnation to which his perverted sexuality had doomed him, in their view. Indeed, these were not followers of Jesus, but instead "believing Christians" for whom the Christian life bore more resemblance to the behavior of those who condemned and would have stoned the woman taken in adultery (Jn 8) than to the way of compassion demonstrated by Jesus's forgiveness of that woman and his embrace of outcast lepers.

What has hindered the church from becoming a community of radical grace in which people, believing in the kindness of their Heavenly Father's providential care, begin treating themselves and one another with kindness? Sadly, it is the church itself that has been the major roadblock in the realization of God's vision of the beloved community, of the One Body and the One Spirit. By its selective interpretation of scripture and the construction of its creeds, the church has replaced God's vision of the kingdom with the church's own controlling, imperial goals. By its doctrines of original sin and substitutionary atonement, the church has taken control of our salvation, proclaiming and pushing the church's version of a future heaven instead of God's vision of a kingdom of love and justice on earth. What a morbid mess confronts us when we review the prospectus of the church's insurance plan for our salvation. "In effect, the church has created the ultimate spiritual franchise, a kind of salvation monopoly. We are pronounced bad by birth and given only one possible cure by the same entity that provided the diagnosis" (Meyers, 2009, p. 97).

We are diagnosed as having been born with an incurable disease called sin that we inherited from our original parents in the Garden of Eden. Because of their alleged disobedience when tempted by the devil, disguised that day as a snake, God's wrath was kindled against them and all their descendants thereafter. Thus, even though we did not ask to be born, we were born guilty, incapable of pleasing God because of our flawed and sinful nature. The penalty for having been born is that, unless a way could be found to appease God's wrath, we would be sent to hell, the devil's headquarters, and tormented forever because of our spiritually useless condition.

Because it was unthinkable that those dying in infancy would be damned forever, one branch of the church invented a middle region for unbaptized infants called *limbo*. Being neither heaven nor hell, limbo gave relief to grieving parents who had lost a little one. But what slim comfort this must have been to bereaved relatives on the Roman Catholic side of my family; they would never see their baby in heaven, although that would be better than having it burning in hell.

If all of this sounds like spiritual nonsense, God's purported solution, as seen by such churches, becomes more mystifying. To relieve God's pent-up anger over the mess created by our bad decision to disobey one of the garden regulations (mind you, it was God's idea in the first place to make us creatures of choice), on one day when God just could not "hold it any longer," the decision was made that God would relieve his wrath by killing his own son as a substitute, even though God had previously outlawed the idea of child sacrifice. So Jesus died in our place for our sin so that, if we accept him as our savior and scapegoat, God will no longer be furiously mad at us, and we will be admitted to his heavenly mansions upon our death.

Lest this plan seem too simple, some other details of the plan need to be understood. In order to be a perfect sacrifice for our sin, Jesus had to be a sinless, sexless substitute. None of the angels could qualify for the job. Only Jesus, God's son, could do what needed to be done, the church claims. However, being human was not enough. He had to be born of a virgin so as to escape the contamination caused by sexual intercourse, a nasty compromising animal activity, in that view, created by God for the perpetuation of the human race.

In such a perspective, most of Jesus's life was spent waiting around to do his real job. Having been born of the Virgin Mary, there wasn't really much for him to do but await his confrontation with Pontius Pilate. What he did during some of those years of waiting was filled in by some of his friends, who told stories about his superhuman miracles and wise sayings. Those sayings, however, are seldom emphasized as being of the greatest importance. They are sure that "[t]he central thing is the Cross on the Hill rather than the Sermon on the Mount" (Manson, 1949, p. 9). They say that Jesus's real mission was that of being a blood sacrifice for our sins. Because of this, the main business of the church that he left behind has been that of getting people to buy into this insurance plan so that they can escape hell and gain admission to heaven. Additional wrinkles were added to the plan when some churches disagreed about certain details.

Some theologians argued that we actually never had a decision to make about the plan, but that God had decided ahead of time who would be saved and who would be lost. Others maintained that the decision was solely ours to make. A very few others, deemed by the church to be "crazies," said that none of the above was true, that the entire plan made no sense, that God did not need to kill anyone in order to forgive us, that God had decided to save all of us, and that Jesus's death was the ultimate demonstration of how nothing can change God's universally loving attitude toward all of his children, however bad, good, or imperfect they may be.

The "crazies" have always been a minority in the church; many of them are not even considered to be Christians, and some have even been driven out of the church. Thus, the no-choicers and the free-choicers have run the main insurance agencies for the plan of salvation. Despite their differences, however, they have agreed that, finally, time will run out and the window of opportunity for buying into the insurance plan will be closed. At some moment Jesus will return to earth, descending on the clouds, just as he ascended many years ago. Some say it cannot be known when, whereas others have set an exact date. The final whistle (Gabriel's horn) will sound and the game will be over, with the winners going to heaven and the losers heading into eternal torment.

There will be no final handshakes between the winners and the losers (nothing like the good sportsmanship during NCAA March Madness). No more Mr. Nice Guy stuff from Jesus. Shockingly, Jesus will have taken on some of his Father's meanness. Gone will be the humble donkey upon which he rode, mocking the pomp and pretense of Pilate. Instead, just like Pilate, he will now be riding a white war horse (Rev 19:11), judging and making war. The lowly Jesus will, strangely, have been Romanized! The kingdom vision of love and justice will have given way to the church's version of empire.

Please note that I do not single out the Roman Catholic Church as principal purveyor of this plan. It is peddled by all kinds of churches, denominational and nondenominational, although with slightly different add-ons. But let the buyer beware! In whatever form, it is the major hindrance to the creation of a church in which the good news of radical grace overcomes the power of evil.

THY KINGDOM COME, THY WILL BE DONE ON EARTH!

One of my morning prayers is that I may live more nearly as I pray. Would that it were so for the church that, while it has prayed for centuries for the coming of God's kingdom, has frittered away its life, for nearly 2 millennia, upon the careful management of its franchise as the sole purveyor of a cheap, otherworldly salvation. Ever since the fourth century, when the successors of an original band of unlettered but doctrinally unfettered fishermen became bishops, wining and dining at Constantine's table, the exhilaration of real discipleship has been lost. If this is all that the church has to offer, I am left asking, "Is this all there is?" The church's cherry-picking of scripture as the basis for its creedal formulations has left me with nothing that could excite a soul's highest aspirations. Instead, it has left me with:

A God I Cannot Love

How could I possibly enjoy a passionate, personal relationship with a God who is subject to fits of violent anger? A God whose anger for his errant children is so intense that it can be discharged only by killing his only son is a God who cannot be loved. Why would any decent person long to be in a heaven where the winners live with the knowledge that those who have not embraced the tenets of the Shorter Catechism are finally getting their just desserts, and where one of the principal forms of entertainment is that of looking down with delight from heaven's balcony upon the torments of the damned? How could I harp and hallelujah forever with people whose tastes for such exquisite violence exceeds the crudity of the Roman gladiatorial contests?

A Church I Cannot Respect

The need to be in constant control is an inherent element in the church's traditional plan of salvation. When salvation resides in the church's doctrinal monopoly, there must always be oversight, lest some newcomer opens a window by mistake, letting the uncontrollable winds of the Spirit blow all the carefully kept balance sheets off the table. Because the ongoing business of such a theology must always be that of reducing God to a manageable proposition, constant quality control must always be the order of the day. Nothing can be left to the free-flowing breezes of grace that waft in from Calvary. Temptations to absolute corruption by absolute power are constantly present, whatever the form of church government. Whether we have a church run by a bishop, presbyter, or televangelist, the need for control is written into the manual of operations.

A Jesus I Cannot Follow

A Jesus garbed in the church's garments of perfection is someone I cannot follow. We must admit that such a removal of Jesus from our common life begins in two of the gospels in which he is virginally conceived; from birth, he is already on the way to becoming a sinless, sexless Superman. For many modern believers, Jesus is none other than a biblicized version of Superman, actually the Gnostic Jesus whose humanity was only a temporary costume. His sinless divinity locates him beyond my limited humanity and places no demand upon me to let my humanity be filled with the presence of God as was his. His sexlessness offers a lesser level of discipleship to married disciples, elevates celibacy, and forever taints our sexuality with shame. I cannot possibly be like him, nor can I aspire as did the early martyrs to follow him even unto death. Because his death is an atoning death, it is a death that only he can die and becomes, therefore, my draft exemption from ever having to die in his service on any spiritual battlefield.

A Self I Cannot Value

What inducement for my personal growth can ever be derived from the dismal doctrine of original sin? What kind of joyful worship can follow a general confession in which we must confess that "there is no health in us"? I have often arrived at worship, having "won some and lost some" during the previous week, hoping for sermon or song in which I will be given a spiritual workout, only to be dragged down in a confession of sins that I did not commit.

Sometimes I want to return later that afternoon to place a quarantine sign on the door of such a church, warning others to stay away lest they be infected by such enervating worship. The church does us no service when, from the opening moment of worship, it treats us as invalids. Such a spirit can even infect preaching. I have not returned to worship at a particular church in which the preacher speaks to us as though our minds cannot process tough truths, and instead jollies us with *Readers Digest*-level humor, as though we are nursing home patients. Instead of speaking to me like someone on the edge of the grave, challenge me to climb steep mountains. Say to my soul,

> So let me draw you to the great forgiveness, not as one above who stoops to save you, not as one who stands aside with counsel. Nay! But as one who says, "I too was poisoned with the flowers that sting, but now, arisen, I am struggling up the path beside you. Rise, and let us face these heights together."

A Neighbor I Cannot Embrace

If the only business of the church is that of getting people to believe certain things so that they will escape hell and gain heaven, I cannot have a grace-filled relationship with my neighbor. When the mission of the church is reduced to such alternatives, I must size up every person as either saved or lost. How can I possibly sleep, knowing that my neighbor may slide into eternal torment during the still watches of the night? How can I have casual backyard conversations with someone who is living on the brink of hell? How can I enjoy a friendly cookout with lost souls? The church's bad news gospel forces me to divide my world up into black–white, yes–no, saved–lost, good guy–bad guy categories. Such a binary mind-set is destroying our world because it has no reality. The truth lies in an intriguing koan-like statement: "You see, dear, I think there are two types of people in the world. Those who divide the world up into two kinds of people . . . and those who don't" (Hendra, 2004, p. 190). Radical grace means that all of our neighbors are just people, people like ourselves, already loved, accepted, and justified by grace. My neighbor is already—and has always been—a child of God. My only mission is to embrace and love my neighbor into being what he or she already is.

A Future I Cannot Fathom

What helpful meaning can be derived from the apocalyptic promises in the Synoptic gospels of Jesus's coming again? Except for members of the Flat Earth Society, how can Christians in a post-Copernican world find meaning in the promise that Jesus will return upon the clouds so that "every eye shall see Him"? I have often wondered what nourishment for daily living can be taken away from worship services in which participants stand to affirm, "And he shall come again with glory to judge both the quick and the dead." Then, too, what additional complications have been festooned upon the doctrine of the Second Coming by those who have fastened upon a few words of Paul to the Thessalonians and, supplying some other unrelated texts, have pieced together an entire scenario to create the idea of the Rapture, a word never found in scripture?

How much confusion could the church have been spared if we had recognized that, whatever Paul may have meant by his words to the Thessalonians, he later abandoned such apocalyptic prophecies and saw instead that, for the Church as the Body of Christ, the future is always in the Eternal Now. Clearly, we must not

> fasten upon him [Paul] the eschatology of Thessalonians which he manifestly discarded and which was never more than a secondary and temporary element in his thinking. We must embrace the concept of the one Body and one Spirit by which he replaced that erroneous idea, and which is plainly his mature and dominant conviction. (Raven, 1961, p. 130)

When we read the last word from the early church upon this matter as it comes to us from the fourth and final Gospel of John, we notice that the risen

Jesus makes no promise of returning, but instead breathes upon his disciples the Holy Spirit, fulfilling his Maundy Thursday promise to send the Spirit to guide, teach, and equip all future followers for service in the world. How ironic that the church, stuck upon the apocalyptic visions of the Synoptics, has waited centuries for the return of One who is already vibrantly present and available. Jesus did not leave us to live as orphans in God's world. When he died saying, "It is finished," he meant exactly that—that God's judgment had been signed, sealed, and delivered—and the verdict is that God has decided to save the entire world (Jn 3:16–17)! And that, indeed, is the kind of good future that we *can* fathom.

PLEASE COME HOME—WE MISS YOU

I've been trying to come up with a sign to place on the front of the new church I wish we could build, one that would be inspired by God's vision for the church, a church that would no longer surrender to the evil that results when the church abandons its true message of radical grace. Maybe the one above this paragraph would work. I saw one like it on the outskirts of Toledo many years ago, inviting people to come home to St. Joseph's Roman Catholic Church. It would work as a good sign for any church that wants to embrace God's vision because I believe that all kinds of people are waiting to come home to the kind of church that grew out of that ragged band of men who followed Jesus.

If we kept the message simple, asking people not to *believe*, but to *follow* Jesus, I think we would be surprised by the kind of people who showed up. At first, the group would be small, but when the word got around it would be hard to keep people away from such a church. The attraction would *not* be that the real good news is easy. To be saved by grace is never easy. It means surrendering all my pride and pretense in the realization that I did not do anything to deserve God's acceptance. It means that I did not discover anything, but that I was found out by God—and still loved. We are all a bit uneasy about being found out; in every life there are buried secrets; but the good news is that we don't have to worry any longer because God has found us out and loved us anyway.

The tough part for all of us is "coming out," letting go, and realizing that we owe everyone in the entire world that same acceptance. That can fill every hour of every day for the rest of my life. It will demand my time and my money. It could even demand my life if I really let go; but I think that there are still people in the world looking for something not only to live for but also worth dying for. It is probably too late for me to talk with bravado about such heroic challenges. At age 82, I can promise to follow Jesus to the end of the world only if there are restrooms every 20 minutes along the way. However, I can hope that someone with a younger bladder will read these words and consider living, or maybe even dying, to make the church into what it is meant to be. I believe that there are people who are tired of a safe church that offers only a safe heaven.

Many years ago, I came upon an advertisement that the explorer Ernest Shackleton allegedly placed in the *London Times*, seeking recruits for his 1914 Antarctic Expedition. The ad read, "Men wanted for hazardous journey. Small wages, bitter cold, long months in complete darkness, constant danger, safe return doubtful." The response was overwhelming, with more applicants than needed. Maybe that is another good idea for my church sign: "Safe Return Doubtful." But what an adventure it would be to follow Jesus again as did those first fishermen who left their nets behind to follow the blood-stained footsteps of the Man of Nazareth. Any takers?

REFERENCES

First Presbyterian Church of Birmingham, Michigan. (N.d.) Inclusion policy statement. Birmingham, MI: Author.

Furlong, M. (1965). *With love to the church.* London: Hodder and Stoughton.

Hendra, T. (2004). *Father Joe: The man who saved my soul.* New York: Random House.

Jones, R. (Ed.). (1976). *The journal of George Fox.* Richmond, IN: Friends United Press.

MacDonald, G. (1876). *Annals of a quiet neighborhood.* New York: Harper & Brothers.

Manson, T. W. (1949). *The sayings of Jesus.* London: SCM Press.

Metzger, J. M. (2003, June 15). [Tribute to J. M. Metzger's father Bruce Manning Metzger, New Testament professor emeritus at Princeton Theological Seminary, presented during Dr. Metzger's 90th year]. *Princeton Seminary Bulletin.*

Meyers, R. (2009). *Saving Jesus from the church.* New York: HarperCollins.

Raven, Canon C. E. (1961). *St. Paul and the Gospel of Jesus.* London: SCM Press.

Wink, W. (2007). *The myth of redemptive violence.* In J. Harold Ellens (Ed.), *The destructive power of religion: Violence in Judaism, Christianity, and Islam* (pp. 161–179). Westport, CT: Praeger.

CHAPTER 8

ASSESSING EVIL: TWO CLINICAL CASES

Raymond J. Lawrence

Sometime in the early 1930s in Germany, a group of theologians was discussing the rise of Adolf Hitler and the question of whether he might qualify for the label of Anti-Christ. He was cruel, ruthless, and murderous, and he quickly consolidated political power in his own person. He was a tyrant who had gathered full political power in a short space of time. The discussion of Hitler's qualifications as Anti-Christ concluded with the judgment by Tillich that he did not qualify. According to Tillich, he lacked one essential characteristic: the appearance of goodness.

Neither the thinking nor the unthinking public in this mostly post-Christian world is seeking any Anti-Christ, except perhaps for a few fundamentalists. Nor was Tillich. Nevertheless, the discussion continues to be relevant, and the wisdom of Tillich needs to be remembered. He raises the bar of critical thinking on matters of good and evil. He promotes the importance of suspicion in ethical analysis and cautions against gullibility in relation to those who succeed in creating for themselves a benign public image.

Tillich's analysis of Hitler is an essential benchmark to keep in view whenever we attempt to measure good and evil. The essential principle is this: The most profound evil lies not with pickpockets, streetwalkers, and drunks, nor with persons who are otherwise easily associated with troublesomeness. More significant evil should be sought among the well-dressed, the reputable, and especially the seemingly beneficent. This means that assessing good and evil requires a suspicious and penetrating mind. The most powerful and effective perpetrators of evil will take measures to assure that they have a beneficent public image. In assessing data, a readiness to take the data at face value will not lead to a coherent or reliable analysis of good and evil.

I present two clinical cases in which a gullible acceptance of the superficial combined with a failure of suspicion resulted in serious misjudgment and consequently poor, even sadistic treatment of two medical patients. In each case, the misjudgment was a result of the wider public having been deceived by the appearance of goodness on the part of the decision makers.

THE CASE OF CARDINAL JACKSON

The medical ethics journal *Second Opinion* bills itself as Park Ridge Center's (located in Chicago) "journal of intelligent opinion." In April 1992, the journal published a case entitled, "House Calls to Cardinal Jackson." It was written by the patient's physician, David Schiedermayer, MD, associate professor of medicine and associate director of the Center for the Study of Bioethics at the Medical College of Wisconsin. This was part of a series of case studies edited by Stephen H. Mills and Kathryn Montgomery Hunter. Responses were provided by Stanley Hauerwas and Elizabeth M. Johnson.

Cardinal Jackson was the pseudonym of a 79-year-old African American woman who for 10 years had been lying in bed motionless and nonresponsive, a victim of dementia that was a consequence of Alzheimer's. Other than the fact that her eyes were open and that she sometimes seemed restless, she appeared to be in a prolonged persistent vegetative state. As her physician himself then reported, "The lights are on, but nobody's home."

Jackson was fed by a gastric tube. Her diapers were changed regularly. She was plagued with diarrhea. A catheter received her urine. She was regularly turned, wiped, and washed by family members. Her hair was often fixed for her, and she was consistently well cared for by family members and professional visitors. A visiting nurse came three times a week. Her physician made regular house calls. He notes in his write-up that he smelled the greens cooking in the kitchen as he gave Jackson his careful examinations. She was given Tylenol and other unspecified pain medication, potassium, antibiotics, and antidiarrheal medications. She was given annual flu shots. She was taken to the hospital about once a year for life-threatening pneumonia. (Pneumonia traditionally was called "the old man's friend" because it carried away those too debilitated to live a life worth living.)

Jackson's bed was situated in the living room, occupying a large part of the space. A sofa and the family television kept her company. Jackson's daughter, her son-in-law, and an unspecified number of grandchildren lived with her. The house was located on a well-cared-for block in an undesirable inner-city neighborhood where troublesome groups loitered at the corners, and near where prostitutes worked the traffic curbside.

Jackson's physician was deeply invested in her, he reports. He was also ambivalent. On the one hand, he described her predicament as "blessed." On the other hand, he suggested five times to the family that they consider stopping the feeding of the patient. The response from the family each time was a shocked and adamant refusal to consider such a thing.

Curiously, when the physician then presented the Jackson case to his medical ethics class for discussion, he defended the family's decision to keep her stable and living. He reported that he could not explain why. Perhaps, he said, it was all those years of knowing her. He felt perhaps that the race issue played a role here, with the generations of discrimination and abuse. Or, he confesses, he "can't stand to think of the fire dying in those green eyes." He was fixed on those eyes. They symbolized his urgency to keep her alive. They were as "wild as a girl's . . . green as a Georgia hill, humid, warm, smoky, full of wonder and mystery." They were as "full as the moon, luminous and sweet."

Elizabeth M. Johnson, a nurse and health educator in graduate school, was first respondent to the case. She expressed her approval of the physician's care. She hoped that someone like him would be around if she ever became demented and bedridden. She does have questions, too many questions. More than 50 of them. And some are pointed, such as the question of who is paying the bills here. She wonders about the impact of the class distinctions in this case, such as that between the family and the physician. She points out that Schiedermayer's driving around in a rusted, 15-year-old Dodge, wishing he had a new Toyota, does not resolve for Johnson the curious class distinctions in this case. It does seem to be a case of protesting too much when a physician and faculty member of a major medical center suggests he cannot afford a new Toyota. Maybe there is more here than meets the eye, and Johnson is correct to raise this question. But she does not follow through.

Johnson also expresses suspicion that gender or class bias might be at work in the case when Cardinal Jackson's granddaughter expresses her hopes to become a physician. Schiedermayer repeatedly emphasized to the granddaughter how hard both the study and the work are. Johnson questions whether he would have responded similarly had he been talking with a male or to a woman of the upper classes. The lower classes are typically quite accustomed to hard work and study if they are ambitious. Johnson's critique is potent but diffuse. She raises important questions, but she raises so many questions that it is impossible to see what she considered most important.

The second respondent was Stanley Hauerwas, a well-known and respected ethicist and professor at Duke University Divinity School. He has a reputation for pointed and significant observations and ethical assessments. In responding to this case, however, he was not in good form. The title of his response was "The Eyes Have It." He is approving of Schiedermayer's attention to Jackson's "wild, green eyes." He judges that the physician, in observing Jackson's eyes, has paid attention to details that give Jackson dignity. The patient's eyes, and the smell of greens cooking, are the kind of attention to details that keep the physician's work with this patient humane, according to Hauerwas. He applauds Schiedermayer for declining to be swayed by "medical ethics principles and the bureaucratic character of medical care."

Hauerwas seems to put the full weight of his ethical position on the lovely, wild, green eyes of Cardinal Jackson. But as far as anyone could tell, the patient was not even dimly conscious during the past decade. Both Schiedermayer and, to an even larger extent, Hauerwas were invested in their own dreamy projections about the patient, projections that do not seem even slightly rooted in fact or experience. This appears to be some sort of romanticism carried to bizarre extremes. It is understandable if the physician and family experience grief at the demise of an important and well-loved woman, but wishful thinking will not bring her back to life, or even bring her a minimal amount of consciousness. Neither Schiedermeyer nor Hauerwas ask hard questions. Each seems bereft of serious questions. Each is seemingly seduced by the appearance of extraordinary care given to a person who for all intents and purposes is now a dead body maintained in a vegetative state. After all, brain dead is really dead.

Perhaps Schiedermeyer and Hauerwas hold to the view, though they don't say so, that persons in a vegetative state must be maintained at all costs. If so, they should at least own up to the tremendous medical cost incurred while at the same time others in the neighborhood go without. They should at least question the motivation of the family, who may be exploiting a financial jackpot of government and insurance payments. The focus on Cardinal Jackson's wild green eyes as if she is a sensate human being is a kind of bizarre Gnosticism without a shred of data to support it. The entire critique is founded on the misguided assumption that the continuing care to this brain-dead old woman is a noble act. The aura of gracious and loving care masques what is likely a form of abuse that is disguised by wishful thinking. After all, what can be more noble than consistent, continuing care and attention to a sick old woman?

Some of the hard questions that were not pursued are as follows:

1. Is the 10 years of extensive care given to this brain-dead woman an appropriate use of scarce public resources, especially given the other needs in this slum community?
2. Is there a hidden agenda at work here, namely, is the family milking disability insurance and Social Security payments that will discontinue when the patient dies?
3. Is the physician's possible class guilt motivating him to drive an old wreck of a car and invest considerable time in house calls to a patient who arguably does not benefit from his care?

Two even more troubling questions are "Was Cardinal Jackson actually abused under the cover of loving care?" and "Was her treatment evil masquerading as good, the worst kind of evil, as Tillich would say?"

We should note that not one of the experts in the case asked the question of what *presumably* the patient might want in her dire circumstances. There was no clear attempt to imagine the patient's own desires. The physician comes close when he recommends the cessation of feeding, but he gives up quickly in the face of family objections. Cardinal Jackson has been lying motionless for a decade in that bed, unable to communicate in any way with the world around her. In spite of those "lovely green eyes," she has been unconscious as far as current medical examination can determine. But let's suppose those lovely green eyes *are* aware of her surroundings, even dimly. That would certainly account for the wild look in her lovely green eyes.

The most troubling ethical question in this case is whether and to what extent Cardinal Jackson may have been suffering what could be classified as torture. Torture under the guise of medical care is still torture. If she had been to any degree conscious those past 10 years, she must have become completely insane. Who would agree to a decade of lying immobile with a total inability to communicate? A truly chilling thought is that the wild look in those green eyes might have been the look of a woman who was trapped incommunicado for a decade and had consequently gone mad. Who could tolerate 10 years of the television with no ability to turn it off, and no ability to communicate in any respect whatsoever? If Cardinal Jackson were conscious to any degree, we have to conclude she had been subjected to 10 years of torture. In summary, neither the medical team nor the family nor the respondents were really identifying with the patient. They are focused principally on their own agenda.

A key principal of ethics in the Jewish, Muslim, and Christian traditions—the Abrahamic faiths—is the requirement to consider the plight of the other person. As Rabbi Hillel (30 BCE–9 CE) put it, "What is hateful to you, do not do to your neighbor." Jesus is remembered to have said about the same thing in Matthew 7:12 and Luke 6:31. What rational person would want to accept even one more day of Cardinal Jackson's predicament? Surely death is better than her recent decade of life.

Even more astonishing is the fact that a sophisticated medical ethics journal could publish such an article and in summary leave the impression that the care of Cardinal Jackson was on balance a humane example of medical care. In fact, the last 10 years of Cardinal Jackson's life were a violation of humane principles on several counts. The case is a stunning example of the failure to search for corruption hidden beneath an account that purports to be humane treatment. This is an example of what Tillich alluded to. Pickpockets, pimps, and hoodlums in the street are easy to label as evil. The care of Cardinal Jackson is a worse evil because it is able to parade under the presumption of great benevolence.

THE BUBBLE BOY CASE

The infamous Bubble Boy case was also a medical case with the aura of human benefaction that was in reality a story of evil, a second illustration of the axiom that the worst abuse parades as an act of benevolence.

I had some limited involvement personally in the Bubble Boy case. In addition to my own involvement, I became a close friend with the woman who was the Bubble Boy's most significant relationship.

I happened to be the director of pastoral care and education at St. Luke's–Texas Children's Hospital in the early 1970s. The so-called Bubble Boy was David Vetter, who was born in 1971 and lived for 12 and a half years, most of that time in Texas Children's Hospital (TCH).

The public media, informed by the hospital's public relations department and David's medical team, cultivated a misleading public picture of David. They implied, though not explicitly, that David was a boy who was saved from certain death by advanced medical science. This drew sympathy for David and approbation for the medical team. In fact, David was a terrible victim of modern science and medicine. The failure of serious thought and consultation on the part of the medical team led to the extraordinary abuse of a human being. David lived his entire life in what was essentially a large test tube, never able to have physical contact with any other living thing. And the medical team assessed this as his fate. He was the only human being in history who was bred to live his entire life in a laboratory, a true human guinea pig. Furthermore, the medical team considered his predicament limited and unfortunate but certainly tolerable. In fact, it was neither his fate, nor was it tolerable. This was a story of horrendous abuse parading as beneficence.

The story began with a scientific team of gnotobiologists in place at TCH in 1970. (Gnotobiology is the science of sterile conditions, and it was a new and arcane scientific discipline.) Naturally, the team was on the lookout for children needing its services. In the fall of 1970, an infant was admitted to TCH dying of severe combined immune deficiency syndrome (SCID). This meant the child was born with no functioning immune system. His name was David Vetter, the first of two David Vetters, and he died on November 21 of multiple infections against which his body had no defense. The gnotobiology team approached the Vetter couple and informed them of the possibility of treating any future child of theirs who may also carry the SCID syndrome. (The mother is the carrier of this inherited disease, and 50% of her male children will be symptomatic.)

One of the serendipitous aspects of this story is that the putative leader of the gnotobiology team was Rafael Wilson, who was not a medical doctor but a PhD, and also a Roman Catholic monk. The Vetters were conventional practicing Roman Catholics. The trust between the Vetters and Wilson was quick, deep, and long-lasting, mostly because of their mutual religious commitments.

The Vetters took up the offer and were carrying their next child barely a month after burying their only son, the first David. They were very eager to have a viable son. (They already had a daughter.) Later testing revealed that the embryo was male, though whether it was symptomatic with SCID was unknown during the pregnancy. Nevertheless, as a precaution, the second David Vetter was delivered September 22, 1971, by caesarian section directly into a newly constructed sterile chamber, an isolator popularly labeled the Bubble. The delivery itself was performed under the most severe sterile conditions possible. The physicians communicated with hand signals so as not to spew microorganisms into the air. From a scientific perspective, it was a great success. For 12-and-a-half years, David was free from the multitude of microorganisms that could kill him. A very few microorganisms did manage to enter the Bubble, but those that did were innocuous.

I personally did not have occasion to meet David until the fall of 1974, when he was 3 years old. I approached Wilson, who was the team leader of David's case, and Wilson graciously took me to visit David. He was a dark and beautiful boy, and related somewhat like an adult, which was understandable because his relationships were almost entirely with adults. I must say that I was deeply disturbed to observe another human being in such confinement, and never having physical contact with any living thing. My immediate thought was that this isolation could not be sustained indefinitely.

I did not express my personal reactions to Wilson. I did visit David several times subsequently. However, Wilson made it clear that he was David's religious adviser and was already teaching him religion. Though I thought this dual role of religious adviser and medical authority on the part of Wilson inadvisable, I knew I would not likely be effective should I voice such concerns.

That subsequent winter, the renowned ethicist Joseph Fletcher was spending several months in residence as a visiting consultant at Houston Medical Center's Institute of Religion. I approached both Wilson and David's primary physician, John Montgomery, MD, and asked if they might consider having me invite Fletcher in for an ethics consultation on David. They readily agreed, probably in part because never before had there been any multi-disciplinary ethical discussion on this case, and Fletcher was of course a big fish in the field. And he charged no fee for this.

The ethical case conference took place in February 1975. There were about 30 persons present: the two primary physicians, several nurses, social workers, chaplains, and public relations personnel. I chaired the meeting. Wilson opened with a long history of the case. In summary he presented a sanguine picture of a healthy, intelligent, lovable boy who was doing quite well in his confinement. Wilson raised no alarm, nor did he express any fears or concerns about David's future. The medical team was waiting for a well-matched bone marrow transplant to be made available that would provide

David with an immune system and permit him to leave the Bubble. For three years, none had been found. There was certainly no urgency expressed, and no estimate as to how long David may have to wait in confinement. In summary, Wilson's review of the case was upbeat, positive, and optimistic.

The chaplains under my direction had already discussed the case to some extent, and they, like me, had some serious questions about how long David could live in his sterile chamber. So after some general discussion, the chaplains raised the question directly to the medical team. Wilson was decisive and clear. David was well adjusted, had a good mind, and could live to be 80 in the sterile chamber if necessary. Chaplain Robert Main then boldly asked how the medical team would deal with puberty, and whether David might break out of the bubble when he became an adolescent. This question threw the meeting into some amount of chaos. Some of the women started crying. The physicians and Wilson became defensive. In fact, they were on the defensive. The chaplains predicted that David could not be sustained indefinitely in such isolation. Fletcher commented at the end that sometimes the flame is not worth the candle. The meeting broke up in some disarray. That is to say, there were some raw feelings all around. Six months later, I left the hospital.

By a peculiar twist of fate, the hospital electrician, Tom Langford, and I had invested in a small apartment building. He came to me shortly after I left the hospital, proposing that he sell his interest in the apartment building to a Mary Murphy. The exchange was made, and I met Mary, whom I did not know previously. However, to my surprise I found that she was then working with David, and that she had been in attendance at David's ethical case conference. She was a Ph.D. in psychology and a lecturer at Baylor College of Medicine, and had just been assigned to be David's psychologist. Subsequently, Mary and I became very good friends.

Mary first met David when he was three, about the same time I did, and during one of his brief times at home. She was sent to do a psychological workup on him. On that visit she brought a small cutting from a tree in the yard to show David a leaf close-up. She became for David from that point "the lady with the leaf." David had a duplicate sterile chamber at his family home in Conroe, some hour's drive north of Houston. A sterile transporter was created that fit in a van, and he was able to be moved. In his early years, he spent brief amounts of time at home. As he got older, his time at home was increased. Mary was on good terms with David's family, and she would typically spend Friday nights at the family home when David was in residence there.

The relationship between Mary and David evolved naturally from the psychological testing to become arguably the most important relationship in David's life. The relationship evolved serendipitously. Mary simply filled a staff vacuum, becoming David's "go-to" person. Soon after the lady with the leaf encounter, when David was back at the hospital, he was at one point being extremely uncooperative and the nurses were frustrated. At their wits' end, the nurses called for assistance from Mary as the psychologist. In response, Mary found a bowl of goldfish and took it to David for him to see. His misbehavior disappeared instantly. She had a facility for engaging him that was a special talent. Officially, Mary was never more than staff psychologist, but her unofficial role was that of "hospital mother and best friend." David spent more time with her than he did with his own mother.

One of the first initiatives Mary undertook was to call for privacy sheets to be hung in the Bubble. Up to then David did all his toileting in full view of whoever was in the area. She taught him modesty and privacy. For the rest of David's life, Mary was central to his existence. She dealt with his bad behavior. She comforted his fears. She explained the world to him. Mary was a divorcee with one grown child who lived in Asia. David became her surrogate child. She saw him several times every day. When he was fearful, she slept all night on a cot next to his bubble, embracing him through the plastic arms. In fact, Mary got criticized by some of the medical staff for getting too close to David. One of the physicians referred to her as "an old hen with one chick." It was a fairly accurate characterization, though Mary thought it was meant to be demeaning. She was old, and he was her one chick. Truth is that it would be hard to imagine how David would have survived as well as he did without some close and consistent attention from someone as caring and as wise—and available—as Mary was.

As David grew older, he became more of a companion to Mary. She shared with him her private life. He met her family and friends. They discussed her stocks and bonds. (She was and is financially well off.) Mary owned an apartment complex that she managed herself. By the time David became old enough to use the phone, a plastic insert was made in the Bubble that enabled David to use the telephone. He became Mary's apartment manager, taking calls from tenants and doing such chores as calling the plumber.

David was sometimes a prankster. When he got phone access, he was known to have made random calls to strangers announcing that he was the Bubble Boy, among other kinds of less cordial telephone pranks. That may have been his only creative means of preadolescent defiance, trapped as he was in his sterile chamber.

Though David had some visits from children his own age, he was barred from any significant peer relationships because of his physical isolation. At one point, he was connected by audiovisual technology to a school room at his grade level. Although this gave him some degree of peer connection, it also dramatized both the uniqueness and alienation of his predicament.

NASA built a space suit for him that enabled him, until he outgrew it, to take brief walks outside his Bubble. These were always grand events, with media people, staff, and family. In his last space suit walk, done at home in Conroe, he delighted in turning the garden hose on reporters and bystanders.

But the walks were also traumatic events. No one was more conscious of germs than David. The process of dressing in the space suit within the sterile chamber, with no one inside to help, was nerve-wracking. It was a major undertaking, and he only did a few "walks."

As the years passed, David became more starkly aware of his unique plight, and he became more and more troubled. He complained verbally that he was caged like a wild animal. By the time he was 8, he was exhibiting alarmingly erratic behavior. He picked sores on himself. He developed a tic. He stimulated himself sexually in view of others. He would sometimes beat on the walls of his Bubble as if to break out, though at the same time he was terribly frightened of the consequences of contact with the microorganisms outside that he clearly understood would kill him.

As the years passed, he increasingly resented both his confinement and his utter dependency on others. When he wanted or needed something, he must ask someone to fetch it for him. Then he would have to wait for it to be sterilized. He could of course not receive anything that could not be subjected to extreme sterilization processes. This took time, sometimes a couple of weeks. All his food had to be sterilized. Most of his life, he lived on baby food.

David's behavior deteriorated to the point where a child psychiatrist was called in for a consult "to find out what was bothering him." As if only a psychiatrist might know. David got word of this impending consult, and when the appointed time arrived he posted a sign on his isolator reading, "Get the Hell Out of Here!" David's mother came in from Conroe and forced him to apologize to the psychiatrist.

David developed some peculiar perceptual deficits as a result of his isolation. One of the most striking was his inability to conceive of the three-dimensional buildings that he could see out of his hospital suite window. He was convinced that they were simply two-dimensional. Nor could he visualize what was under the surface of the earth or under the surface of a body of water. Mary brought potted plants to demonstrate "underground." She pulled them out by the roots to demonstrate what is under the earth's surface, but he would not hear of it. A similar perceptual distortion occurred in one of his "space walks," the one at his home in Conroe. When he proposed to go from his own front yard to his backyard, he insisted that the direction was across the street.

By the time David was eight years old, the original medical team had left for other positions in distant cities, and a new set of physicians took over David's care. They quickly saw that David was going to be more and more of a problem to himself and others as he got older. They proposed that the wait for a perfect bone marrow transplant was unrealistic, and that the time had come to take some risks in order to get David out of the Bubble. The family objected. They contacted the original triumvirate of Wilson, Montgomery, and Mary Ann South, who, alarmed, came to Houston uninvited to confront the current medical team. It was a testy meeting. The original team accused the new team of endangering David's life. "Killing the patient is not an option," said Mary Ann South. The medical team backed down. For another year, the status quo held. Then the medical team decided that David had no need to live most of his time in the hospital. They ordered him sent home, reducing his time in the hospital to a regimen of twice a year for a week, for checkups. He went home August 1, 1981. He was almost 10. Mary saw much less of him during the next year and a half. She did have frequent phone contact and many Friday overnights at the Vetter home.

After a year and a half at home, David's family approached the medical team confessing that they too had reached the conclusion that David could not continue in his sterile chamber. They finally came around to the conclusion that the status quo was untenable. Something must be done. The medical team decided that the best—though long shot—option was to donate David's sister's bone marrow in an attempt to jump-start his own immune system. When David was 12, in the fall of 1983, he received by injection his sister's marrow. It contained a virus—mononucleosis—unbeknownst to the medical team, and by February David was dead.

In an ironic twist, some experts in the field have said that such a bone marrow transplant very early in David's life, when his system was malleable, would have cured him. This is assuming, of course, that no hidden viruses were transmitted.

As could be expected, following David's death there was little space for critique or dissident opinion. A year after David's death, I wrote a criticism of the case entitled "David, the Bubble Boy, and the Boundaries of the Human." It was published by the *Journal of the American Medical Association* (Lawrence, 1985). I was excoriated by the medical team and the family. Mary Murphy received permission to write her own decade-long saga with David, and was given permission to do so by both Baylor College of Medicine and the family. She wrote a true account from her perspective, warts and all. It was in fact a love story between an aging woman and a young boy. She felt she was fulfilling a promise she made to David. He had asked her to write "the story of their private world" after he died. It was to be, in his own words, the story of "the boy in the isolator and the woman who never touched him." It is a beautiful and touching account of a real love affair between the two. When the family saw the page proofs, they reacted with rage, threatened a lawsuit, and enticed Baylor to withdraw its permission for Mary to publish. So the account collects dust now, waiting someday to be published.

The evil in the case of David, the Bubble Boy, was the cavalier assumption that a person could live a full life physically separated from other human beings. The chaplains were correct in their prognosis, that it would become an intolerably dehumanizing burden. The medical team was blind to the ramifications of such isolation. They were partly informed, or misinformed, by Catholic notions of monasticism and the nobility of a life without sex. David was deprived of any opportunity for sexual experience, but more than that, he was deprived of any form of physical touch. It seemed that Wilson was creating his little monastery for David and saw no impediment to his potentially lifelong imprisonment. "He has a good mind," said Wilson at the ethics consultation, as if the mind matters and the body does not. Wilson also compared the Bubble to an iron lung, which was hardly apt, because iron lung patients can be touched and usually can leave the machine for certain periods of time.

What was done to David Vetter was evil, and it was the kind of evil that carried every appearance of good. The public and the media lauded the wonderful physicians who provided David with 12 years of life. They saw David as someone rescued from death by modern medical science. The public rejoiced at David's life and saw the medical team as benefactors. The truth was that medical science foisted a horrible injustice on David, something that should never have been done and should never be done again. David was the one and only human laboratory animal in history. It was a cruel burden to place on a human being.

REFERENCE

Lawrence, R. J. (1985). David, the Bubble Boy, and the boundaries of the human. *Journal of the American Medical Association, 253*, 74–76.

Schiedermayer, D. (1992, April). The case: House calls to Cardinal Jackson. *Second Opinion*, 35–40.

CHAPTER 9

DEMONIC BEINGS AND THE DEAD SEA SCROLLS

Loren T. Stuckenbruck

INTRODUCTION

This chapter is about demonic beings in the Dead Sea Scrolls. Although this may sound like a relatively small focus, the merits of the discussion are enhanced by the number of basic issues that come into focus. Any broad topical study of the Dead Sea Scrolls is not as straightforward as would have been assumed by many from the time of their discovery among 11 caves in 1947–1956 until the rapid publication of numerous materials during the last 20 years. Although many of the previously unknown Hebrew documents were often attributed by default to authorship related to a movement of "Essenes" thought to have settled at Khirbet Qumran, there is some recognition that some of these documents do not show telltale or obvious signs of such an origin.[1] This suggests, in turn, that the Dead Sea Scrolls, taken as a whole, preserve works that reflect traditions that circulated more broadly in Hebrew- and, of course, Aramaic-speaking Judaism of the Eastern Mediterranean world.

Lest one have the impression that the present topic is ubiquitous in the Scrolls, it is important to note from the start that many of the texts have little or nothing specifically to say about the demonic world. The absence of any explicit reference to demonic beings in the texts does not in each case have to be interpreted as an ideological avoidance of language when dealing with the question of evil. When demons are not mentioned, this may simply have to do with the genre of a given work or with the one-sided purposes of their composition—for example, a strict focus on topics such as heavenly liturgy (*Songs of the Sabbath Sacrifice*), wisdom instruction (e.g., *4QInstruction* and Ben Sira), halakhic instruction (e.g., *4QMiqṣeh Maʿaseh ha-Torah*), and interpretation and reconfiguration of sacred tradition (e.g., *Temple Scroll*, *Reworked Pentateuch*, Tanḥumim, and pesharim) and the calendrical texts (see, e.g., 4Q317, 319–326, 328–330, 334, 337).

In recognition of the complex nature of the Dead Sea materials, the following outline of the demonic world among the Scrolls will nevertheless attempt to be diachronic. I shall, where relevant, begin with what may be regarded as earlier, often Aramaic, traditions that show little sign of having been produced by the Qumran community (Ya'ad). A further group of texts, mostly in Hebrew, likewise cannot be assigned to the Qumran community but to varying degrees may anticipate ideas found among some of the more "sectarian" texts. Finally, the discussion will take up the Hebrew literature of the Ya'ad itself. At the risk of being overly confident at "knowing too much," such an approach may allow us to entertain possible lines of development in relation to ideas and practices without assuming that these developed in a linearly, traceable social continuum.

In anticipation of the discussion to follow, we should note several points about which to remain cautious. First, we may expect the texts, as a whole, to present us with a complex web of traditions that wove their way in and out of any number of pious Jewish groups whose relationship to each other sometimes cannot be easily discerned. Second, it should be clear that the developments or shifts one might trace should not be confused with what was going on in all parts of Judaism generally during the Second Temple period. The voices of each text need to be heard and not imposed onto other texts if connections with them are not evident. Third, it is possible, if not likely, that a number of logically incompatible ideas could have coexisted in a single, sociologically definable group. In other words, different ideas do not always have to be traced to different groups.

I am nevertheless convinced that certain developments regarding attitudes toward demonic powers can be upheld within the literature and that some of these attitudes can be associated with particular groups. One of the observable shifts in profile, for example, emerges between ideas and practices in unambiguous Ya'ad and less clearly non-Ya'ad texts. Moreover, to some degree, we shall notice a broad difference between traditions about demonic beings among the writings preserved in Aramaic, on the one hand, and those coming to us in Hebrew, on the other. The crucial period for these shifts will be the second century BCE, a period of major change not only in the way Jews were responding to incursions of Hellenistic culture under the Seleucids but also in the way Jewish groups began to form while openly staking out distinct religious claims in response to one another.

DEMONIC ORIGINS IN THE ENOCHIC TRADITION AND ITS EARLY INFLUENCE

In the present section, I can only briefly summarize what other publications have discussed in more detail; we note especially those of Philip Alexander

(1997; 1999, pp. 337–341), Esther Eshel (1999, pp. 10–90, "The Origin of the Evil Spirits"), Archie Wright (2005, esp. pp. 96–177), Kelly Coblentz Bautch (2007, 2009), and myself (2003, 2004). Also, see Collins (1997), Lyons and Reimer, (1998), and Kister (1999).

Fragmentary Aramaic texts recovered from the Dead Sea caves, such as those belonging to the Book of Watchers of *1 Enoch* and the very fragmentary *Book of Giants*, attribute the origin of evil to a club of rebellious angels and their offspring, the giants, who in these texts are held responsible for deteriorating conditions on earth before the Great Flood. The brief tradition from Genesis 6:1–4 is paralleled in the Enochic literature by a more elaborate scheme that blames fallen angels (and less so human beings, who are at most represented as complicit) for much of the sin and violence committed on the earth during antediluvian times. The Flood tradition, as well as internecine fighting amongst the giants, is then presented as a divine response to these catastrophic events (cf. *1 En.* 8:4–10:16; *Book of Giants* at 4Q530 4Q530 2 ii + 6–7 i + 8–12). The storyline of these early Enochic traditions not only is concerned with the very ancient past but also serves to explain what the writers wished to emphasize about the presence and effects of demonic evil in their own times (cf. *1 En.* 15:8–16:1).

At least two main purposes can be discerned in the telling of the story about fallen angels in *1 Enoch* chapters 6–16. First, the story functions as a way of condemning expressions of culture associated with foreign impositions, perhaps in the wake of the conquests of Alexander the Great and his successors.[2] Thus, the rebellious angels are said to have introduced to humanity the making of weaponry, jewelry, techniques of beautification, and all kinds of "magical" arts (*1 En.* 7:3–5, 8:3). The reprehensible practices and instructions in *1 Enoch* 7–8 can be traced back to a strand of tradition according to which 'Asa'el was the leading mutinous angel. Second, the story provides an etiology, or explanation, for the origin of demonic spirits (*1 En.* 15–16). This etiology focuses primarily on the giants, the offspring of the angels who have breached the cosmic order by mating with the daughters of humanity; this storyline was primarily associated with the angel Shemiazah. The deeds committed by the giants before the Flood include the agricultural enslavement of humanity to grow and produce food to satisfy their appetites, the killing of sea and land animals, the destruction of birds, and even cannibalism. Divine intervention against these giants comes about when (a) the giants turn against and kill one another; and (b), as apparently stressed in the *Book of Giants*, when they are destroyed by the Flood. Either way, it is significant that the giants are by nature half angel and half human, and as such are regarded as an illegitimate mixture of spheres that should have been kept separate (*1 En.* 15:8–16:1; cf. 10:9, where they are called "bastards"—Cod. Pan. μαζηρους = mamzerim). Divine punishment thus only brought them physical death, after which they continued to have a disembodied existence as spirits. We may infer that, being jealous of humanity who have survived the cataclysm with their bodies intact, these spirits instinctively attempt to reclaim a corporal existence that they once had and so are especially inclined to afflict by attacking or entering the bodies of humans (15:12). Although only a partial punishment of evil, the Flood's significance is clear: God's decisive intervention in the past against the angels and especially the giants demonstrates that powers of evil in all their forms are, in effect, already defeated and that their final annihilation is assured (16:1). The implication of this is that measures to be taken against them in the present, such as exorcism or other methods of warding and staving them off, are to be regarded as temporary expedients that portend God's ultimate triumph.

A number of traditions that survive from antiquity adapt this Enochic etiology (not least the exorcistic tradition preserved for us in Jesus's tradition), including several documents preserved among the Dead Sea Scrolls (see, e.g., Alexander, 1999; Wright, 2005). However, despite the influence of the Enochic accounts, the names of the chief angelic perpetrators of evil are conspicuously absent outside the Enoch tradition.[3] What does survive outside the Enoch tradition is a few references to the term *Nephilim*, a designation for the giants based on Genesis 6:4.[4] However, Nephilim, if a proper name, does not designate any of the giants individually, nor is there any mention of giants' names from the *Book of Giants* to be found elsewhere in Second Temple literature,[5] that is, until we get to the much later rabbinic, Manichaean, and medieval Jewish sources.

Nevertheless, the examples of Enochic influence on demonology among the Dead Sea texts are significant, not only in specific details but also in the overarching eschatological framework within which they negotiate the persistence of and triumph over evil. The fragmentary Hebrew document that has been given the title *"Songs of the Maskil"* (4Q510–511 and 4Q444) lists at several points a series of demonic beings called demons, Lilith, hyenas, howlers, jackals, and mamzerim (so 4Q510 1.4–8; 4Q511 10.1–4; 35.7; 48–49+51.2–3; 121; cf. 4Q444 2 i 4).[6] The last-mentioned mamzerim, which occurs in *1 Enoch* 10:9 (mentioned above), is a designation for the disembodied spirits of the giants. These beings, though considered operative during the present age (designated in *Songs of the Maskil* as "the age of the dominion of wickedness"),[7] can be managed in the present in anticipation of their final punishment. The tension in the Enochic tradition between God's triumph over evil in the past (i.e., during the time of the Great Flood) and the complete annihilation of evil in the future has contributed to at least some of this (see Stuckenbruck, 2007, pp. 94–95, which provides a comment on *1 En.* 93:4c and related texts). In addition, it is possible that one of the demonic beings denounced in an "in[]cantation" (laḥaš) is addressed directly in the second-person singular in 11Q11 and may be called "offspring from[] Adam and from the seed of the ho[ly one]s" (v 6) (for a discussion of the alternative reconstructions of the lacuna, see Wright, 2005, pp. 183–184 and n. 66). If this restoration of the text is correct, then it may be taken as a reference to a demonic being whose nature is ultimately a *mixtum compositum* (a hybrid—i.e., angelic and human—creature), as is the case with the Enochic giants.[8]

The only other obvious place where the tradition's impact within the Dead Sea Scrolls can be observed is the *Book of Jubilees*, originally composed in Hebrew. The evil spirits who afflict Noah's grandchildren following the Flood are identified as the spirits that emerged from the giants' bodies when they were destroyed (*Jub.* 10:5).[9] In *Jubilees* these spirits, however, come under the rule, not of one of the named fallen angels in the Book of Watchers (cf. *1 En.* 6:7) and *Book of Giants*, but under Mastema (see below), whose origin is not specified. As in the Enoch tradition, they are given temporary leave to afflict humanity, their ultimate destruction is assured, and measures given to Noah to neutralize some of their malevolent effects are temporary expedients (cf. *Jub.* 10:10–14).

"DEMONS," "SPIRITS," AND "ANGELS" IN THE DEAD SEA SCROLLS

It is outside the scope of the present discussion to discuss all demonic beings that are mentioned in the Dead Sea texts. Here we shall focus on several general designations applied to such entities that occur in both Aramaic and Hebrew texts. These are (a) šēd (i.e., "demon"), (b) ruaḥ (in this context, "spirit"), and (c) mal'ak ("angel").

"Demon" (šēd)

The word *demon* is preserved six times in the Hebrew texts. Four of these occurrences are found in the above-mentioned small text of 11Q11,[10] which, as noted, shows signs of having been influenced by the Enochic fallen angels tradition. In addition, there is one occurrence of the term in *Songs of the Maskil* (at 4Q510 1.5), where the plural form (šēdim) is placed within a list of malevolent beings that includes the "spirits of the mamzerim." As 11Q11, this document also shows signs of influence by the Enochic tradition. The only other reference to "demon" surfaces in a manuscript called *4QPseudo-Ezekiel* in 4Q386 1 iii 4, the context of which suggests that Babylon is being referred to as "a dwelling place of demons." The manuscript contains no language that is characteristic of either the Yaḥad or of a community that is precisely defined other than "the children of Israel" (4Q386 1 i 3).

With respect to the far less numerous Aramaic materials from the Dead Sea, the term *demon* is preserved eight times among fragments from three documents. In five cases, we have to do with the Book of Tobit (4Q196 14 i 5, 12; and 4Q197 4 i 13, ii 9 and 13). Each of these comes from Tobit chapter 6.

In one of these texts, the term occurs as part of a recipe for getting rid of a demon that probably circulated apart from the book and has been reproduced here (6:8) (as I have argued in Stuckenbruck, 2002). In the other four instances, the term directly refers to Asmodaeus (Tob. 6:15–17), who in the story attempts to prevent Sarah from marrying and threatens her divinely preordained marriage to Tobias. Significantly, in the later Testament of Solomon, Christian in its present form, Asmodaeus is identified as one of the giants, that is, as an offspring of a fallen angel and a human woman (*T. Sol.* 5:1–11, esp. v 3).

The second Aramaic document, which refers to *demons* in the plural (šedim), is designated *Pseudo-Daniel* in the overlapping texts of 4Q243 13.2 and 4Q244 12.2.[11] This overlapping text from two manuscripts claims that "the children of Israel chose their presence (i.e., the presence of other gods) more than [the presence of God and sacr]ificed their children to demons of error." By attributing such a practice to Jews, the text reflects an idea that is developed within the Enochic tradition and in the *Book of Jubilees* (see below in this section).

The term *demon* is not extant among the Dead Sea Scrolls Aramaic fragments corresponding to *1 Enoch*. However, in the Book of Watchers at 1 Enoch 19:1, we have a reference to people offering sacrifice "to demons as gods until the great day of judgment" (Cod. Pan.—τοις δαιμονιοις μεχρι της μεγαλης κρισεως). Significantly, this activity of sacrificing to demons is blamed on the fallen angels' spirits, which have led humans astray. This text, which may be a facile allusion to Gentile idolatry, influences the Epistle of Enoch at *1 Enoch* 99:7: The sinners "will worship evil spirits and demons and every (kind of) error" (so the Eth.; Grk. of the Chester-Beatty Michigan papyrus: "worship [phan]toms and demons [and abomina]tions and evi[l] spirits and all (kinds of) errors."[12] Here the motif of demon worship is more explicitly associated with idolatry. The text of the Epistle probably not only describes what Gentiles do but also has in mind those whom the writer regards as faithless Jews.

This association of "demons" with idolatry, of course, may have been shaped by texts such as Deuteronomy 32:16–17 and Psalm 96[95]:5 (where the Grk. δαιμονια corresponds to Heb. אלילים, "idols"). However, the accusation that other Jews are engaged in idol worship, as we find in *Pseudo-Daniel* and probably the Epistle of Enoch, is more developed than in the biblical texts. The *Book of Jubilees* deals with the motif in much the same way as the Epistle of Enoch: Because the Gentiles can be labeled as those who "offer their sacrifices to the dead, and . . . worship demons" (*Jub.* 22:17),[13] the force of attributing this to Jews who are disloyal to the covenant is not lost: God instructs Moses to write down the message of the book because, in the future, his posterity, as a consequence of serving the gods of the nations, will "sacrifice their children to demons and to every product (conceived by) their erring minds" (1:11). The influence of "demons" on Israel is otherwise seen in the immediate aftermath of the Flood, when Noah petitions that his grandchildren be delivered from the "demons" (in this case, the disembodied spirits of the dead giants) who are leading them astray (10:1–14). Unfortunately, none of these texts from Jubilees are preserved amongst the Hebrew Dead Sea fragments.

Keeping in mind that we do not have—and never will have—access to all the materials originally deposited in the Qumran caves, we can only observe that, for the most part (except for the identification of Babylon as a dwelling place for demons in *4QPseudo-Ezekiel*), those texts that refer to "demons" bear a certain affinity with different parts of the Enoch tradition. Furthermore, in no case does any document that uses the term for *demon* draw on language that is characteristic for the Yaḥad literature related to the Qumran community.

"Spirit" (ruaḥ)

Unlike the term for *demons*—which can operate as a category or classification of beings on its own—the term *spirit*, whether in the singular or plural, is never applied in the absolute sense; it is always qualified through the addition of a further word. In particular, the references to malevolent beings as "spirits" (the plural form, *ruḥot* or *ruḥim*) abound.

Here, something can be made of the distinction between Aramaic and Hebrew literature. In the Aramaic texts, the term *ruaḥ*, when it is applied to an evil being, occurs only eight times. In these cases, it is always in the singular:

> *Genesis Apocryphon* (1Q20 xx 16, 17, 20, 26, 28—the afflicting spirit sent by God against Pharaoh Zoan, king of Egypt)
> Tobit 6:8 (at 4Q197 4 i 13—"evil spirit" functions as a synonym for "demon")
> 4Q538 1+2.4 (the "evil [s]pirit")
> 4Q560 1 ii 5, 6 (the "spirit" that is adjured)

In the Hebrew materials, however, the term, when used for malevolent power, occurs mostly in the plural. These instances are itemized below:

> *Damascus Document* in CD xii 2 ("spirits of Belial" par. 4Q271 5 i 18)
> *Serek ha-Yaḥad* (*Community Rule*) in 1QS iii 18, 24 (spirits of the lot of the Angel of Darkness)
> *Serek ha-Milḥamah* (*War Rule*) in 1QM xiii 2 and 4 (spirits of the lot of Belial)
> 1QM xiii 11 (spirits of his [Belial's] lot, the angels of destruction)
> 1QM xv 14 (spirits of wick[edness])

Hodayot (*Thanksgiving Hymns*) in 1QHᵃ iv 23 (perverted spirit rules over a
    human being)
1QHᵃ xi 18 (spirits of the serpent)
1QHᵃ 5.4 (spirits of wickedness)
1QHᵃ 5.6 (spirits of iniquity that lay waste for mourning)
1Q36 (spirits of transgression)
4QCatena A (=4Q177) 1–4.7 (spirits of Belial)
4Q177 12–13 i 9 (God's great hand will help them from all the spirits of
    [Belial])
Songs of the Maskil in 4Q444 1–4 i+5.2 (spirits of dispute)
4Q444 1–4 i+5.4 (spirits of wickedness)
4Q444 1–4 i+5.8 ("spirits of the b]astards")
4Q449 1.3 (rule of the spirits of his [Belial's?] lot)
Serek ha-Milḥamah in 4Q491 14–15.10 (spirits of [his] lot; no par. in
    1QM)
Songs of the Maskil in 4Q510 1.5 (all the spirits of the angels of
    destruction)
Songs of the Maskil in 4Q510 1.5 (the spirits of the mamzerim, the demons,
    Lilith, the howlers, and the jackals)
Songs of the Maskil in 4Q511 1.6 (spirits of wickedness)
4Q511 15.5 (spirits of vanity-ḥebalim)
4Q511 35.7 (spirits of the mamzerim)
4Q511 43.6 (spirits of vanity-ḥebel)
4Q511 48–49+51.2–3 ("spirits of] the mamzerim)
4Q511 182.1 ("spirit]s of the mamzeri]m")
11Q11 ii 3 (*11QApocryphal Psalms*) ("sp]irits [ ] and demons")
11QMelchizedek (=11Q13) ii 12 (against Belial and the spirits of his lot);
    and 11Q13 ii 13 ("from the power of] Belial and from the power of all
    the s[pirits of his lot")

Although the examples listed here show an affinity with the Enochic
tradition (cf. "spirits" of the giants in *1 En.* 15:8–16:1; and recall the association of "spirits" in *Songs of the Maskil* with mamzerim and in 11Q11 with
demonic hybrid beings), they demonstrate a growing association of the
spirits with a figurehead called Belial who acts as their leader. Moreover, the
predominant occurrence of this connection in the *Damascus Document, Serek
ha-Yaḥad, Serek ha-Milḥamah, Hodayot,* and *4QCatena A* (4Q177) suggests
that this association with Belial flourished in a sectarian context,[14] whereas
the connection of "spirits" with mamzerim did not. Less clear is whether, as
Philip Alexander has argued, "the angels of destruction" refers to the fallen
angels and their association with the "spirits" under Belial, which amounts
to a demotion and subordination of them into a more clearly structured
hierarchy with only Belial at the top;[15] after all, like Belial, such spirits can
be said to "rule over" human beings (so the *Damascus Document* in CD xii 2
par. 4Q271 5 i 18).

Given the frequency of the plural form for *spirit* to denote evil beings in the Hebrew texts, it is instructive to note, in the Hebrew texts, how the singular form is used, including when it denotes single beings. To be sure, expressions like *spirit of perversity* (*ruaḥ 'awlah*), *promiscuous spirit* (*ruaḥ zanut*), *spirit of wickedness* (*ruaḥ reša'/riš'ah*), *spirit of impurity* (*ruaḥ niddah*), *spirit of error* (*ruaḥ ha-to'ah*), and *twisted spirit* (*ruaḥ na'awlah*) function less as references to invasive spirits than as ways of describing the human condition. There are, however, a few exceptions to this. First, in the Treatise on the Two Spirits (cf. 1QS iii 13 – iv 26), the phrase *the spirits of truth and of deceit* does not refer to two collectives of opposing spirits, but rather to the two contrasting beings, each of which is called, respectively, the Prince of Lights (1QS iii 20) and the Angel of Darkness (iii 20–21) and to which are assigned further cohorts that cause the children of light to stumble (iii 24). Second, in fragmentary text of *4QBerakot* (=4Q286), a curse is pronounced against "the ange⸍l of the pit and ⸢the⸣ spiri⸢t of destr⸣uction" (4Q286 7 ii 7), where the spirit stands at the head of the cohort of spirits just cursed in the text (4Q286 7 ii 3). Third, it is possible that in the *Songs of the Maskil* at 4Q444 1–4 I + 5.8, "the spirit of uncleanness" (*ruaḥ ha-ṭum'ah*) is listed alongside the mamzerim and thus is treated as a demonic being, perhaps even as a leading member of the fallen angels whose corruption of humanity (see *1 En.* 9:8; 15:4; and *Book of Giants* at 4Q531 1.1, "they [i.e. the fallen angels] defiled ⸢'aṭmyw⸣]") is represented by a more generic designation. Fourth, and following on the last example, the writer of a "Prayer of Deliverance" in 11Q5 petitions God, "⸢D⸣o not let Satan/a satan or a spirit of uncleanness (*ruaḥ ṭum'ah*) have authority over me" (xix 15). The coupling of this impure spirit with "satan" suggests that the spirit is being treated as an external power that threatens the human being. These exceptional occurrences of the singular "spirit" in the Hebrew texts are revealing. Apart from possibly *4QBerakot*, they are not found in an obviously Yaḥad or sectarian context; instead, they reflect more closely ideas that can be said to have developed out of the Enochic traditions.

In this connection, it is instructive to consider the *Book of Jubilees* in Ethiopic texts that probably derive from an originally lost Hebrew text that did not survive among the Dead Sea materials. In *Jubilees*, with the exception of two texts (cf. *Jub.* 2:2; 15:32), the term *spirits* occurs almost always in a negative sense; this holds, for example, in 10:3, 5, 8, 11, 13; 11:5; 12:20; and 15:31–32. The storyline makes clear that, as in the early Enochic traditions, these "spirits" represent the afterlife of the giants who rule over the Gentiles (15:31–32), on the one hand, and who plague Noah's offspring (chapters 10–11), on the other. In the book, they are subordinate to a chief being called Mastema (10:8). Alongside this, "spirit" (Eth. *manfas*) can apply to a top-ranked malevolent force. In his prayer near the beginning of the work, Moses petitions God not to let "the spirit of Belial" rule over Israel so as to bring charges against them (1:20). The reference to a single spirit at the top is, when compared with the Enochic traditions, innovative. The combination of "spirits" derived from the giants and "the spirit of Belial" within the narrative world of *Jubilees* anticipates what will develop within the sectarian literature into a lack of any specific mention of the giants' spirits as well as the use of *spirit*, as we have seen, in senses (e.g., the human condition, and spirits of Belial) that depart from the Enochic tradition.

"Angel" (mal'āk)

As with *spirit*, the term *angel*, when referring to an evil power, never occurs as an absolute noun unless it is combined with other words. For the malevolent use of this term, a similar picture emerges among the Hebrew texts that we have observed for *spirit*: the predominant usage is plural, most often in combinations such as *angels of enmity* or *angels of Mastema* (*mal'āke mastema/h*—*Pseudo-Jubilees* at 4Q225 2 ii 6 [*mal'āke ha-ma(s)temah*]; and *4QPseudo-Ezekiel* at 4Q387 2 iii 4, 4Q390 1.11 and 2 i 7 [*mal'āke ha-mastemut*]), *angels of destruction* (*mal'āke hebel*—CD ii 6; 1QS iv 12; 1QM xiii 11; 4Q495 2.4?; and 4Q510 1.5, *ruhe mal'eke hebel*), and *angels of his [Belial's] rule* (*mal'āke mamjalto*, 1QM i 15). In one text, the so-called Ages of Creation, the plural denotes the fallen angels who are mentioned together with 'Azaz'el as having sired giants (4Q180 1.7–8).

There are also several occurrences in the Hebrew texts of the singular "angel"; these are in the Treatise on the Two Spirits ("the Angel of Darkness," 1QS iii 20–21), *Damascus Document* ("the angel of enmity/Mastema," CD xvi 6 pars. 4Q270 6 ii 18, 4Q271 4 ii 6), and *Serek ha-Milḥamah* ("the angel of enmity/Mastema," 1QM xiii 11). Both the *Damascus Document* and *Serek ha-Milḥamah* use the plural and singular together in relation to the term *enmity* or *Mastema*. I will have more to say about Mastema in the "'Mastema' and 'Belial'" section of this chapter.

Before we turn our attention to "angel(s)" in the Aramaic texts, it is again instructive to look at the *Book of Jubilees*. Significantly, there is little general use of this term for malevolent beings; when referring to demonic beings, the term *spirit*, whether in the singular or plural, is the preferred designation. The term for *angel* (Eth. *malak*, Heb. *mal'āk*) is never employed in the singular for a being obedient to God. However, the plural *angels* (Eth. *malā'ekt*, Heb. *mal'ākim*) is made to designate the fallen angels twice. In *Jubilees* 4:15 they are called "the angels of the Lord" who "descended to earth to teach mankind and to do what is just and upright upon the earth," whereas in 5:1 they are called "his [i.e., God's] angels whom he had sent to the earth." In both these cases, the nomenclature reflects the tendency in *Jubilees* to apply the appellation to angels who are subordinate to God (which is expressly recognized as the fallen angels' original state). Within the Hebrew texts of the Dead Sea Scrolls, then, the introduction of the singular *angel* to designate an evil being is first preserved in proto-Yaḥad works such as the *Damascus Document* and perhaps within the editorial growth of *Serek ha-Milḥamah*.

Now the lean use of *angel* to designate an evil being in Jubilees is interesting when we note the complete absence of this among the preserved materials in Aramaic, where each interpretable context has in view "angels" or an "angel" subordinate to God or acting on God's behalf (*Genesis Apocryphon* at 1Q20 xv 14 and 4Q157 1 ii 3; Tobit at 4Q196 13.2, 17 i 5 and 4 i 5; *Aramaic Levi Document* at 4Q213a 2.18 and 4Q529 1.1, 4; *Book of Giants* at 4Q531 47.1; *Visions of Amram* at 4Q543 2a–b.4, 4Q545 1a i 9, 17; 4Q552 1.5; 4Q553 2 ii 1; and 4Q557 2; and *Targum Job* at 11Q10 xxx 5). In the Enochic Book of Watchers, no single fallen angel is actually referred to as an "angel," whereas the "sons of heaven" are collectively referred to as "angels" on a number of occasions (so *1 En.* 6:2, 8; 10:7; 19:1–2; 21:10; cf. Birth of Noah in *1 En.* 106:5–6, 12, though in the Epistle of Enoch of *1 En.* 92:1 5 | 93:11–105:2 there is no reference to these beings). Thus, in avoiding the term *angel* for a demonic being, *Jubilees* follows what we know from the early Enoch tradition. In introducing a single figure at the top of the malevolent hierarchy, *Jubilees* adopt other terminology (see below).

The main words used to designate the fallen angels in the Aramaic literature (including the Enoch texts) are, instead, "watcher(s)" (*'irin*—extant in *Genesis Apocryphon* 1Q20 ii 1, 16; Book of Watchers at 4Q202 1 iv 6 and 4Q204 1 vi 8; *Book of Giants* at 4Q203 7a.7, 7b i 4, 4Q531 1.1, 36.1?, and 4Q532 2.7; *Visions of Amram* at 4Q546 22.1) and, more rarely, "holy ones" (*qadišin*—so *Genesis Apocryphon* 1Q20 ii 1 and vi 20; and Book of Watchers at 4Q201 1 i 3). The term *watcher* (*'ir*) is picked up in *Jubilees* and several of the Hebrew Dead Sea texts (*Damascus Document* in CD ii 18 par. 4Q266 2 ii 18 and *Pseudo-Jubilees* at 4Q227 2.4, which probably echoes terminology of the now lost Hebrew portions of *Jubilees* [cf. 4:15, 22; 7:21; 8:3; and 10:5]). By contrast, the term *holy ones* is arguably only applied to the rebellious angels in 11Q11 v 6, a text that we have seen is influenced by the Enochic tradition.

CHIEF DEMONIC BEINGS

Over against the Enoch tradition that, in its early received form, presented both Shemiḥazah and 'Asa'el as leaders of rebellious angels, many of the writings among the Dead Sea Scrolls draw demonic forces together under a single figure. It is not clear how much the widely divergent texts allow us to infer that any of the writers identified a figure designated by one name with a figure designated by another. Moreover, we cannot assume that when single figures are referred to, their designations always function as proper names rather than as descriptions. In what follows, I briefly outline the material and organize my observations around the names or designations that actually occur in the texts. Here I focus on the five main ones: (a) Melki-reša', (b) "Angel of Darkness," (c) "S/satan," (d) Mastema, and (e) Belial.

Melki-reša'

This designation, which means "king of wickedness," occurs twice, once in an Aramaic source and once in a Hebrew text. In the Aramaic *Visions of Amram* (4Q544 2.13), Melki-reša' is mentioned as one of two angelic beings who strive against one another to have authority over the patriarch. His association in the passage with "darkness" and with its "deeds" is contrasted with the association of his counterpart (probably Melchizedek) with "light" (4Q544 2.13–16). The dualistic framework within which Melki-reša' participates is not one of predeterminism, as is found in the Treatise on the Two Spirits (cf. 1QS iii 13—iv 26).[16] Instead, it is the patriarch, Amram himself, who is asked to choose between these opposing angels and to decide which one may have authority over him (see "'Angel of Darkness' (*mal'āk ha-ḥošek*)," below). In the Hebrew text of 4QCurses (=4Q280) 1.2–7, Melki-reša' is expressly cursed in terms that are reminiscent of the denunciation in *Serek ha-Yaḥad* that is pronounced against "all the men of the lot of Belial" (1QS ii 5–9; see under "'Mastema' and 'Belial,'" below).

"Angel of Darkness" (mal'āk ha-ḥošek)

The scholarly attention devoted to this figure is disproportionate to the two times he is mentioned in the Dead Sea Scrolls. This is because this angel is presented as the negative counterpart to the Prince of Lights in the well-known Treatise on the Two Spirits (1QS iii 20, 21), which, in turn, has frequently, though misleadingly, been regarded as the core or pinnacle of the Qumran community's theological perspective.[17] As such, the Angel of Darkness is further identified as the "spirit . . . of deceit" (iii 18–19, *ruaḥ . . . ha-'awlah*), one of opposing "two spirits" placed within human beings until the eschatological time of visitation (iii 18). Parallels, of course, have been noted between the dualistic duo in the Treatise and that involving Melki-reša' in the *Visions of Amram*; for example, the opposition between the beings are expressed cosmologically in terms of darkness and light. Fuller comparison, however, cannot be undertaken due to the fragmentary text in *Visions of Amram*. Nevertheless, one difference does appear to lie in the existence, activities, and outcome of the activities of the "two spirits" in the Treatise; unlike the *Visions of Amram*, their influences on humanity are from the start predetermined by "the God of knowledge" and are unalterable (iii 13–16). The selection of one angel or another by the patriarch in *Visions of Amram* comes closer to the implicit exhortation underlying the description in the Treatise of the two ways in terms of virtues and vices correlated, respectively, to "the spirit of the sons of truth" (iv 2–8) and "the spirit of deceit" (iv 9–14, *ruaḥ 'awlah*).

Although the Angel of Darkness initially appears to be an external force under the auspices of God the creator of all, the association of the "spirit of deceit" in 1QS iv with vices for which human beings are held responsible suggests a close association between such a figure and a notion of theological anthropology that renders the angel's influence as part of the human condition. Until the eschatological visitation of God destroys all evil, it is taken for granted that an invasive force of evil within every human being will persist.

"Satan" (saṭan)

As is well known, the term *saṭan* means "accuser" or "one who brings charges against." There are five occurrence of the term in the Hebrew Dead Sea texts. In two, perhaps three, of these instances, the word is preceded by the adjective *all* or, with the negative, *any* (*kol saṭan*; cf. 1QH^a 4.6, 45.3; 1QSb i 8?). In this case, we do not have to do with "satan" as a proper name, but rather with a figure that could as well include a human as an angelic adversary. The same may also be inferred from the negative that precedes it in *Words of the Luminaries* at 4Q504 1–2 iv 12: "and there is no satan or evil plague" (*wa-'eyn saṭan wa-pega' ra'*). *Jubilees* offers a similar picture: The little apocalypse in chapter 23 anticipates that in the end of days "there will be neither satan nor any evil who [or better: which] will destroy" (23:29), in which *saṭan* generically denotes someone—anyone—who destroys by cutting short the life of human beings. Less clear is *Jubilees* 10:11: The angels of the presence are made to say that "[a]ll the evil ones [i.e., the spirits from the giants] who were savage we tied up in the place of judgment, while we left a tenth of them to exercise power on the earth before the satan." Here, "the satan" refers to the chief of the evil spirits who has just previously been mentioned by name as Mastema; the expression, then, describes a function associated with Mastema.

In the one remaining occurrence, the "Prayer of Deliverance" mentioned above (see "'Angel of Darkness' *mal'āk ha-ḥošek*"), the word may function as a proper noun. The petition for divine help, in 11Q5 xix 13–16, reads,

> Forgive my sin, YHWH, and cleanse me from my iniquity.
> Bestow upon me a spirit of faithfulness and knowledge.
> Do not allow me to stumble in transgression (*ba-'awyah*).
> Do not let Satan or a spirit of uncleanness have authority over me;
> Let neither rain nor evil purpose take hold of my bones.[18]

The interpretation of "satan" in the text may be sharpened when we consider it alongside the only other occurrence of the word among the Scrolls:

the older *Aramaic Levi Document* at 4Q213a 1 i 10, which is also preserved in
a much later Greek manuscript from Mt. Athos (Athos Koutloumous no. 39)
to the *Testament of Levi* and therefore can be restored with some confidence
as follows:[19]

> And do n⌉ot let have authority over me any satan ⌈to lead me astray from
> your path.
> (*wa-'al tišlaṭ bi kol saṭan ⌈la'at'ani min 'orḥeka⌉*)

In this text, the placement of *kol* before *saṭan* leaves little doubt that a
proper name is not in view. Furthermore, both texts, as argued by Armin
Lange, show a striking affinity to Psalm 119:33b: "and do not let any iniquity
rule over me" (cf. Lange, 2003a, p. 262). If the "Prayer of Deliverance" in
11Q5 is aware of these traditions, then the absence of *kol* may suggest that
a more specific malevolent being is in view, that is, one called *Satan*. A move
in this direction, though without involving the designation *Satan*, is also at
work in Jubilees. In chapter 1:19–20 of Jubilees, Moses pleads that God not
deliver Israel "into the hand of their enemy, the gentiles, lest they rule over
them" and that God "not let the spirit of Beliar rule over them to accuse
them before you and ensnare them from every path of righteousness so that
they might be destroyed from your face." As in the petition in the "Prayer of
Deliverance" of 11Q5, this text in *Jubilees* contains no equivalent for *kol* ("any"
with the negative); perhaps by analogy, an abstract term (such as "iniquity"
from Ps 119:33b) or a generic designation (such as "satan" from *Aramaic Levi
Document*) has been replaced in *Jubilees* by "spirit of Beliar," whose activity
involves bringing accusations against God's people. For similar adaptations
of this tradition in *Jubilees*, see Noah's prayer for his grandchildren in 10:3–6
("do not let evil spirits rule over them . . . let them not rule over the spirits of
the living . . . do not let them have power over the children of the righteous
now and forever"); and Abraham's prayers in 12:19–20 ("save me from the
hands of evil spirits which rule over the thought of the heart of man"), 19:28
("may the spirits of Mastema not rule over you and your descendants"), and
15:30–32 (Israel, over whom God "made no angel or spirit rule").

"Mastema" and "Belial"

Both terms are treated together here, as the texts provide evidence that
they can be associated with one another and because neither word is necessarily a proper name. Both are only preserved among Hebrew texts of the
Scrolls. Not counting Jubilees, the Hebrew scroll fragments of which do not
preserve either word, *masṭema* occurs 18 times and *beliya'al* occurs 88 times.
Although *masṭema* as a noun or substantive can denote "enmity" or "animosity" in the abstract, *beliya'al* can represent a noun meaning "worthlessness."

Although there is little doubt that in Jubilees, "Mastema" represents a proper name for the chief demonic power that has jurisdiction over a contingent of evil spirits (see below), the function of the term in a number of the Qumran texts as well as its relation to Belial are unclear. We cannot, for example, assume that Mastema and Belial are but different names for the same figure, as the narrative world of Jubilees might lead one to infer (*Jub.* 1:19–20 and 10:5–6). For example, according to *4QBerakot* in 4Q286, a curse is pronounced against Belial "in his inimical plan" (*ba[mah]šebet mastemato*), so that *mastema* functions here as a feature of Belial's activity (see the parallel expression 1QS iii 23, where a similar phrase—"and the times of their troubles are in his inimical dominion [*ba-mamšelet mastemato*]"—applies to the "Angel of Darkness").

A couple of interesting examples illustrate how both can appear alongside each other, with some ambiguity as to whether both refer to different beings. This seems to be the case in the fragmentary text from *Pseudo-Jubilees* at 4Q225 2 ii 14:

the Prince of An[im]osity/Mastema, and Belial listened to[

The text does not preserve sufficient context for us to decide how the Prince of Animosity/Mastema and Belial are related; Belial's activity of listening does not necessarily imply subordination (as Dimant, 2010, has recently suggested). In any case, it is not even clear that we should be comparing Mastema with Belial to begin with; the text could instead be drawing a comparison between the Prince (i.e., of Animosity or Mastema)[20] and Belial.

A final example occurs in the *Serek ha-Yahad* at 1QM xiii 10–12. This text, formally part of a lengthy prayer, declares that God "made Belial for the pit, an angel of *mastema*; and in dark[ness is] his [rule] and in his counsel is to bring wickedness and guilt about; and all the spirits of his lot are angels of destruction; they walk in the statutes of darkness." Here the equation, as Dimant (2010) rightly argued, is not between Belial and Mastema, but between Belial and an "angel of mastema," where "mastema" either characterizes the kind of angel that Belial is or is the proper name of the angel with whom Belial is being identified.

It is possible that in the *Damascus Document*, in which the expression "angel of mastema" (*mal'āk ha-mastema*) occurs by itself, we may not have to do with a proper name such as "the angel of/from Mastema" (i.e., the angel under Mastema's jurisdiction) or "the angel Mastema" (so that Mastema is identified as an angel). The text in CD xvi 2–5 (pars. in 4Q270 6ii 18 and 4Q271 4 ii 6) reads.

And the precise interpretation of their ages with regard to the blindness of Israel in all these things, behold, it is defined in the book of the divisions of

the periods according to their jubilees and in their weeks. And on the day
in which a man takes upon himself to return to the Torah of Moses, the
Angel of Animosity/Mastema (*mal'āk ha-masṭema*) will turn away from
him if he sustains his words. This is why Abraham circumcised himself on
the day of his knowledge.

In this passage, the construction, in which *masṭema* is attached to the definite article as the nomen rectum, is telling; one would not expect a proper
name to require an article *the*. By analogy, in *Pseudo-Jubilees* at 4Q225 2 ii 6,
the plural expression "angels of Animosity" (*mal'āke ha-masṭema*) describes
those beings who were anticipating that Abraham would indeed sacrifice
Isaac. The episode in this incomplete text is initiated by "the Prince of A[ni]
mosity" (*sar ha-ma[s]ṭema*), with whom these "angels of Animosity" are
aligned (the same form of the expression occurs also in 4Q225 2 ii 13–14),
whereas in Jubilees itself the account mentions only the presence of the
"Prince of Mastema" (*Jub.* 18:9). Essentially, the malevolent figures are the
Prince (*sar*) and the angels (*mal'ākim*), not M/mastema him- or itself. If this
is correct, then the three occurrences of the phrase *mal'āke ha-masṭemut* in
4QPseudo-Ezekiel (4Q387 2 iii 4, 4Q390 1.11 and 2 i 7), which are "angels of
Animosity" (the form of the noun, *masṭemut*, is abstract) who rule over the
disobedient of Israel, may be a variant that makes the linguistic possibility of
an abstraction inherent in *ha-masṭema* more explicit.

Unfortunately, not a single text in *Jubilees* (in which *masṭema* occurs 12
times) is sufficiently preserved from the Scrolls for us to know whether
Mastema was affixed to a definite article. The most frequent expression is
"Prince of Mastema/Animosity" or, better translated, "Prince Mastema"
(11:5, 11; 18:9, 12; and 48:2, 9, 12, 15); as the context suggests, the Prince
is to be identified with Mastema, who is introduced as the leader of the
spirits requesting permission for a tenth of their number to carry out their
work after the Flood. In this way, "prince" seems to be a title given to
Mastema rather than the main designation itself. As such, Prince Mastema
is written into the storyline: He is the initiator of the testing of Abraham
to sacrifice Isaac (17:16; cf. 18:9, 12), he is the force behind an attempt
to kill Moses (48:2–4, where Mastema encounters Moses, *contra* Exodus
4:24–26, where it is YHWH [MT] or an "angel of the Lord" [LXX]), he
is behind the work of Pharaoh's magicians to counteract Moses (48:9, 12),
and he foments the Egyptians to pursue the Israelites in the wilderness
(48:15–18). Finally, it is "all the forces of Mastema" that are sent to kill the
firstborn in the land of Egypt (cf. Exodus 12:29, where the subject of the
verb "to strike," *hikkah*, is the Lord). In each of these passages where Prince
Mastema is mentioned, the narrative of *Jubilees* makes clear that his activities happen only under the terms of allowance granted him and his reduced
entourage in chapter 10.

As the statistics indicate, Belial is by far the most frequent designation used for an evil being in the Dead Sea Scrolls. Like Mastema, there must have been a close connection between the figure and the meaning of the name, in this case "worthlessness." However, unlike Mastema, the word *Belial* never appears in a text affixed to the definite article, even in the position of nomen rectum. Therefore, phrases such as "dominion of Belial," "lot of Belial," "army of Belial," "spirits of Belial," "congregation of Belial," and "child" or "children of Belial" and "men of Belial" all suggest that, in many cases at least, we have to do with a term that has become a proper name. On the other hand, when Belial is preceded by *kol* ("any"), then we are dealing with the same linguistic phenomenon that we have observed in relation to *satan* (see 1QH^a xi 28, which refers to "the time of anger against any *belial*").

Most of the extant occurrences of Belial are to be found among the sectarian, that is, the proto-Yahad texts (i.e., *Damascus Document*) and Yahad documents (*Serek ha-Yahad, Serek ha-Milhamah, Hodayot*, pesharic interpretations, and *4QCatena, 4QBerakot*, and *11QMelchizedek*). Belial only occurs in *Jubilees* twice (1:20 and 15:30–33), though in 1:20 it is in a prominent position as part of Moses's initial petition that future generations of Israel not be ruled by "the spirit of Beliar" (so the Eth. spelling), whereas in 15:33 it is the unfaithful of Israel who are branded "the people of Beliar" (something not said of Mastema). It is possible, however, that in both these phrases we are dealing with *beliar* (derived from Belial) as a descriptive, rather than as a proper noun. In any case, among the sectarian writings, Belial comes to be associated in the most immediate sense with faithless Jews (though it certainly would have included Gentiles as well).

The striking development here is, of course, that under the name Belial, a number of the motifs associated with other malevolent beings found in the Aramaic and Hebrew texts are brought together. There are two important examples of this. First, Belial—and those errant Jews associated with Belial (1QS ii 11–18 pars. 4Q257 ii 1–7; and 5Q11 1.2–6)—is denounced (cf. 1QS ii 4–10 par. 4Q256 ii 12–iii 4), just as other malevolent beings are directly addressed and denounced in earlier apocalyptic literature.[21] There is a difference, however: in relation to Belial the curse formula, which is more fixed and ritualized, is pronounced by a priestly figure or by the worshipping congregation. A second example that illustrates how language about Belial is indebted to earlier tradition relates to his rule or dominion in the present age (1QS i 23–24, ii 19; 1QM xiv 9–10 par. 4QM^a = 4Q491 8–10 i 6–7; cf. further 1Q177=4QCatena A iii 8). This is, of course, a motif in the Enochic tradition in which the present—that is, the time between now and the eschatological visitation of God—demonic evil appears to hold sway. Like the Enochic tradition and those traditions that took it up, the texts hold unequivocally that Belial's dominion is temporary; moreover, like the apocalyptic traditions, it is possible to manage or neutralize demonic power in anticipation of its final destruction.

Again, however, there is a difference in the Belial texts: whereas the Enochic tradition itself could be compatible inter alia with the practice of exorcism, no such measures are appropriated against Belial. During the time of
Belial's dominion, the community's curses and blessings, based on Numbers
6:24–46, which petition for protection and according to *Serek ha-Yaḥad* are
to be spoken year on year (1QS ii 19), function as the predominant means (cf.
1QS i 16–iii 11). See similarly the *Serek ha-Milḥamah* at 1QM xiv 9–10 par.
4Q491=4QMᵃ 8–10 i 6–7 and *4QCatena A* at 4Q177 iii 8. In other words, the
chief power is cursed, not exorcised.

Traditions that are pivotal in receiving Enochic tradition and paving
the way for the Yaḥad way of dealing with Belial may be seen in *Jubilees*,
on the one hand, and *Songs of the Maskil*, on the other. The *Book of Jubilees*
presents demonic activity under the leadership of Mastema as an inevitable
characteristic of this age until the final judgment (ch. 10). Thus, in *Jubilees* not only do angels reveal remedies to Noah (and his progeny) for warding off or neutralizing the effects of evil spirits (*Jub.* 10:10–13), but also the
patriarchs—Moses (1:19–20), Noah (10:1–6), and Abraham (12:19–20)—are
made to utter prayers of deliverance against them. There is no formal denunciation or curse against any of the malevolent powers. In *Songs of the Maskil*,
the language of dominion by evil powers in the present age comes closer to
later Belial texts, without actually pronouncing curses at the demonic beings
themselves (at least, this is the absence among the extant texts). In one of the
songs, the sage initially declares the splendor of God's radiance:

> [I]n order to terrify and fr[ighten] all the spirits of the angels of destruc-
> tion, and the bastard spirits, demons, Lilith, owls and [jackals . . .] and
> those who strike suddenly to lead astray the spirit of understanding and to
> cause their hearts to shudder. (4Q510 1.4–6a par. 4Q511 10.1–3a)

This proclamation of divine majesty, which Armin Lange has described as
a "hymnic exorcism,"[22] is then followed by an address to "righteous ones" in
which the sage states,

> You have been put in a time of the dominion [of] wickedness and in the
> eras of the humiliation of the sons of lig[ht] in the guilt of the times of
> those plagued by iniquities, not for an eternal destruction, [but] for the
> era of the humiliation of transgression. Rejoice, O righteous ones, in the
> God of wonder. My psalms (are) for the upright ones. (4Q510 1.6b–8; par.
> 4Q511 10.3b–6)

The Maskil's declarations about God, told in the third person (i.e., they are
not in the form of a second-person prayer addressed to God), are here presumed to be sufficiently potent to diminish or counteract demonic powers that

are at work in the present order of things ("the dominion [of] wickedness"). Although the text does not furnish a prayer for divine protection against these demons, it reflects a framework that holds two concurrent things in tension: (a) the existence of a community of those who are unambiguously "righteous" and "upright," and (b) the characterization of the present age as "a time of the dominion [of] wickedness." Analogous to the pronouncement of a benediction in the yearly covenant renewal ceremony in *Serek ha-Yaḥad*, the song addressed by the Maskil to those who are righteous functions as an expedient measure that neutralizes the threats associated with demonic powers until the present age of wickedness is brought to an end.

The pronouncements against Belial and his lot bring together and merge several evolving features that in their specificity are partly lost yet whose conceptual framework is preserved within a new form. The eschatological framework in the Enochic pronouncements of doom against the fallen angels, prayers for deliverance we have observed in other texts, exorcisms, and hymnic forms of protection, is retained in the community's treatment of Belial. However, the various means of dealing with Belial are formally replaced by curses that adapt language from the Aaronic blessing (Num. 6:24–27) and should be understood in relation to the larger context of covenant blessings and curses found in Deuteronomy (cf. Deut. 28–30).

CONCLUSION

Our survey of language used for the demonic world in the Dead Sea Scrolls yields several conclusions. First, the texts, especially the earlier ones in Aramaic, apply a wide variety of terms to designate the demonic: *demon*, *spirit*, *angel*, *watcher*, and even *holy ones*. In addition, in at least the Enochic traditions of the Book of Watchers and *Book of Giants*, a range of demonic beings—leaders and sub-leaders of the fallen angels and their giant sons—are also referred to with proper names to which, no doubt, some significance was attached.

A corollary to the diversity of terms and use of proper names is an interest in the texts in different classes of evil beings. Here, mostly in the Aramaic literature, we have early representatives of a tradition, to be more fully developed at a later period, which itemized and classified malevolent powers and dealt with them in accordance with their particular functions and characteristics (so *1 En.* 15:8–16:1; Asmodeus in Tob. 6–8; 4Q560; 11Q11 v; see the later demonic classes in *T. Sol.*; *Sefer ha-Razim*; incantation bowls; cf. already Mk. 9:29, "this kind [of demon]").

Second, this chapter has also highlighted some distinctions that can be made within the literature. An overall shift in thought and approach can be discerned if we distinguish between (a) Aramaic documents and (b) literature composed in Hebrew. Allowing for instances of occasional overlap and genetic development, this shift in language corresponds to the difference between (a) earlier "nonsectarian" and (b) later "sectarian" literature.

Third, the most important witnesses to the shifts between earlier and later trends can be found in three works: *Jubilees*, Treatise on the Two Spirits, and *Songs of the Maskil*. The authors who composed each of these writings were pivotal to developments that followed. They gathered up and reformulated ideas from the literature and traditions they inherited and recast them in ways that were eventually picked up in the liturgical life of the Qumran Community.

Fourth, "demons" and other lower-class beings tended to attract responses that regarded them as powers to be "managed" or "relocated" by various means. The afflictions, illnesses, other evils, and human sins they were thought to have caused could be effectively dealt with or at least addressed with confidence through exorcism, prayer, recitation of hymns, and other acts of piety. The matter was different for a chief of demons—for example, Mastema, Belial, Satan, the Angel of Darkness, or Melki-reša'. These demonic bosses, catapulted into a position at the top (whether they were chiefs of other demons or simply organizing principles that represented evil as a whole), are not managed or neutralized in the same way. The Qumran Community, for example, resorted to the formal reciting of curses. However, whether by small-scale activities or community liturgy, the means undertaken to deal with the demon functioned as "temporary expedients" in recognition that the evil powers that malign human dignity and distract from faithfulness to God will indeed come to an end.

Fifth and finally, the present review of demonology in the Dead Sea Scrolls lays the groundwork for drawing a series of distinctions that are crucial to understanding and interpreting the demonic world as it is dealt with in the New Testament and in early Christian literature. These are threefold and overlapping: (a) the distinction between the nature of evil (which distorts the cosmos as created by God) and humanity (whose essential dignity within the created order remains intact); (b) the distinction between the present "era of wickedness" (in which evil can never be extinguished and persists as a reality) and the eschatological annihilation of evil; and, in practical terms, (c) the distinction between matters of "salvation" (to draw on the Christian sense of the term) and "the management of evil powers." It remains for further studies to work out the theological implications coming from each of these points.

NOTES

1. This awareness is the product of numerous efforts to distinguish between "sectarian," "proto-sectarian" (e.g., the *Damascus Document*), and "nonsectarian" documents among the scrolls. The most important of these discussions include Newsom

(1990), Dimant (1995), Lange and Lichtenberger (1997), and the contributions by Lange and Hempel (2003, pp. 59–69 ["Kriterien essenischer Texte") and pp. 71–85 ["Kriterien zur Bestimmung 'essenischer Verfasserschaft' von Qumrantexten"]).

2. Some interpreters argue that the fallen angels and their gargantuan progeny simply refer to the Seleucid overlords in the wake of Alexander the Great's conquest of Judea-Palestine or to an elite priesthood that did not observe purity regulations with regard to marriage and other practices; see, e.g., Nickelsburg (1977, 2001, p. 170) and Suter (1979), who takes *1 En.* 10:9 as his point of departure (on this text, see immediately below). An oversimplified and reductionistic reading that decodes the traditions in this way is, however, misleading (see Stuckenbruck 2009b, 191–208).

3. See only, possibly, the mention in 4Q180 1.7–8 of 'Azaz'el (so, the approximate spelling of the chief angel's name in the later Ethiopic texts of *1 En.*; cf. 8:1 and Cod. Pan. to 6:7, Αζαλζηλ); and see Wright (2005, pp. 107–114).

4. So the Aramaic. See *Genesis Apocryphon* in 1Q20 ii 1 and vi 19, which is clearly influenced by the fallen angels story; *Jubilees* 5:1 (Heb.) in 11Q12 7.1 (where the Eth. text has "giants"), and 1Q36 16.3, a broken text difficult to interpret.

5. For a discussion of the etymologies and possible significance of these names as they occur in the *Book of Giants* (they include Hahyah, 'Ohyah, .hobabish, and Mahaway) see Stuckenbruck (2003, bibl. in n. 5).

6. A further reference to mamzerim in 1QHᵃ xxiv 12 is isolated and without sufficient context to determine its precise meaning (i.e., whether it is a label applied to a class of sinners or functions as a designation for demonic beings per se).

7. See 4Q510 1.6–7 ("and you [viz., the demonic beings] have been placed in the age of the dominion of wickedness and in the periods of subjugation of the sons of ligh[t]" (par. 4Q511 10.3–4). In the Ya.had texts, this era is referred to as the time of "the dominion of Belial" (e.g., 1QS i 18, 23–24; ii 19).

8. Another text in which an evil being who has entered into the human body is directly addressed and adjured is preserved in 4Q560 (two small fragments). Although the text shows no obvious influence of the Enochic tradition, its understanding of the relation of the demonic to the human body is consistent with it.

9. This may be inferred from *Jub.* 5:8–9 and 10:1–6, passages that are conceptually influenced by *1 En.* 7:4, 10:9, and 15:9. On the influence of the Enoch tradition on the understanding of evil and demonology in Jubilees, see Stuckenbruck (2009a, pp. 298–306).

10. 11Q11 i 10; ii 3, 4; v 12—the term is restored and may be an equivalent for the being who is denounced at the beginning of the song in v 6.

11. For the edition, see Collins and Flint (1996), combined text beginning on p. 132.

12. For the text, translation, critical notes, and commentary on the versions, see Stuckenbruck (2007, pp. 393–395, 399–403).

13. The English translation of Jubilees, here and throughout this chapter, is taken from VanderKam (1989).

14. The Treatise on the Two Spirits in 1QS may not be a Ya.had composition; see Jörg Frey, "Different Patterns of Dualistic Thought in the Qumran Library", in eds. M. Bernstein, F. García Martínez, J. Kampen, *Legal Texts & Legal Issues* (STDJ, 23; Leiden: Brill, 1997), pp. 275–335. Thus Belial does not occur in the Treatise, and the reference to "the spirits of his lot" in 1QS iii 24 has to do with the dominion of "the Angel of darkness". Nevertheless, the phrases "spirits of his lot", "lot of" (1QS ii

4–5), and "dominion of" (1QS i 17, 23–24; ii 19) are overwhelmingly applied to Belial in the sectarian texts.

15. Alexander, "The Demonology of the Dead Sea Scrolls", pp. 343–344.

16. For a summary of scholarship on the Treatise, see Levison (2006).

17. So e.g., Charlesworth (2006, p. 11). This assumption is rightly questioned inter alia by Lange (1995, pp. 126–130) and Frey (1997).

18. My translation.

19. For the presentation of these texts, see Drawnel (2004, esp. pp. 98–101).

20. Linguistically, a parallel problem of choosing between "Prince Mastema" and "Prince of Mastema" presents itself in *Jubilees*; cf. *Jub.* 11:5, 11; 18:9, 12; and 48:2, 9, 12, 15. However, the macro-context, in which Mastema is initially introduced as the chief of demonic beings and continues to act in the narrative, suggests that "Prince" is simply used here as a title; see below.

21. As against the fallen Watchers who have corrupted the earth, who are denounced with the formula "you will have no peace" (*1 En.* 12:5 Cod. Pan.—"there is no peace for you," with third person in Eth.; 13:1—against 'Asa'el, Cod. Pan. Azael, Eth. Azazel; and 16:4; cf. also *Book of Giants* at 1Q24 8.2 and 4Q203 13.3), which not only influences pronouncements against the human wicked in *1 En.* 5:4 and in the Epistle of Enoch (98:11, 16; 99:13; 101:3; 102:3; and 103:8), but also carries over into formulae that adapt the language of the Aaronic blessing in Numbers 6:24–26; see 4Q480 2.2 (a curse against Melki-reša'). For other denunciations of the demonic in the Scrolls, see 4Q410 1.5, 4Q511 3.5 (against demonic spirits), and 11Q11 v.

22. See Lange (1997, pp. 383, 402–403, 430–433), who also applied this classification to *Genesis Apocryphon* at 1Q20 xx 12–18, and *Jub.* 10:1–14 and 12:16–21. On the problem of categorizing the passage from *Genesis Apocryphon* in this way, see Stuckenbruck (2005, pp. 60–62).

REFERENCES

Alexander, P. A. (1997). "Wrestling against wickedness in high places": Magic in the worldview of the Qumran community. In S. E. Porter & C. A. Evans (Eds.), *The scrolls and the scriptures: Qumran fifty years after* (JSP Supplements, No. 26, pp. 318–337). Sheffield, UK: Sheffield Academic Press.

Alexander, P. A. (1999). The demonology of the Dead Sea Scrolls. In P. W. Flint & J. C. VanderKam (Eds.), *The Dead Sea Scrolls after fifty years: Vol. 2. A comprehensive assessment* (pp. 331–353). Leiden: Brill.

Charlesworth, J. H. (2006). John the Baptizer and the Dead Sea Scrolls. In J. H. Charlesworth (Ed.), *The Bible and the Dead Sea Scrolls* (3 vols., Vol. 3, pp. 1–35). Waco, TX: Baylor University Press.

Coblentz-Bautch, K. (2007). Heavenly beings brought low: A study of angels and the netherworld. In F. Reiterer, T. Nicklas, & K. Schöpflin (Eds.), *The concept of celestial beings: Origins, development and reception: Deuterocanonical and cognate literature yearbook* (pp. 59–75). Berlin: Walter de Gruyter.

Coblentz-Bautch, K. (2009). Putting angels in their place: Developments in Second Temple angelology. In M. Kőszeghy, G. Buzási, and K. Dobos (Eds.), *"With wisdom as a robe": Studies in honour of Ida Fröhlich* (pp. 174–188). Sheffield, UK: Phoenix Press.

Collins, J. J. (1997). *Seers, sibyls and sages in Hellenistic-Roman Judaism.* Leiden: Brill.

Collins, J. J., & Flint, P. W. (1996). 4Q423 (4QpsDan^a). In G. Brooke et al. (Eds.), *Qumran cave 4. XVII: Parabiblical texts, part 3* (DJD XXII, pp. 95–152). Oxford: Clarendon Press.

Dimant, D. (1995). The Qumran manuscripts: Contents and significance. In D. Dimant & L. H. Schiffman (Eds.), *Time to prepare the way in the wilderness* (STDJ, No. 26, pp. 23–58). Leiden: Brill.

Dimant, D. (2010). Between Qumran sectarian and non-sectarian texts: The case of Belial and Mastema. In A. Roitman, L. H. Schiffman, & S. Tsoref (Eds.), *The Dead Sea Scrolls and contemporary culture* (pp. 235–256). Leiden: Brill.

Drawnel, H. (2004). *An Aramaic wisdom text from Qumran* (JSJ Supp., No. 86). Leiden: Brill.

Eshel, E. (1999). Demonology in Palestine during the Second Temple period [in modern Hebrew]. Ph.D. dissertation, Hebrew University.

Eshel, E. (2003). Genres of magical texts in the Dead Sea Scrolls. In A. Lange, H. Lichtenberger, & K. F. D. Römheld (Eds.), *Die Dämonen—Demons. Die Dämonologie der israelitisch-jüdischen und frühchristlichen Literatur im Kontext ihrer Umwelt* (pp. 395–415). Tübingen: Mohr Siebeck.

Frey, J. (1997). Different patterns of dualistic thought in the Qumran library. In M. Bernstein, F. García Martínez, & J. Kampen (Eds.), *Legal texts and legal issues* (STDJ, No. 23, pp. 275–335). Leiden: Brill.

Hempel, C. (2003). Kriterien zur Bestimmung "essenischer Verfasserschaft" von Qumrantexten. In J. Frey & H. Stegemann (Eds.), *Qumran kontrovers* (Einblicke, No. 6, pp. 71–85). Paderborn: Bonifatius.

Kister, M. (1999). Demons, theology and Abraham's covenant (CD 16:4–6 and related texts). In R. A. Kugler & E. M. Schuller (Eds.), *The Dead Sea Scrolls at fifty: Proceedings of the 1997 Society of Biblical Literature Qumran Section meetings* (EJL, No. 15, pp. 167–184). Atlanta, GA: Society of Biblical Literature.

Lange, A. (1995). *Weisheit und Prädestination: Weisheitliche Urordnung und Prädestination in den Textfunden von Qumran* (STDJ, No. 15). Leiden: Brill.

Lange, A. (1997). The Essene position on magic and divination. In M. Bernstein, F. García Martínez, & J. Kampen (Eds.), *Legal texts and legal issues* (STDJ, No. 23, pp. 377–435). Leiden: Brill.

Lange, A. (2003a). Considerations concerning the "spirit of impurity" in Zech 13:2. In A. Lange, H. Lichtenberger, & K. F. Diethard Römheld (Eds.), *Die Dämonen—Demons. Die Dämonologie der israelitisch-jüdischen und frühchristlichen Literatur im Kontext ihrer Umwelt* (pp. 254–268). Tübingen: Mohr Siebeck.

Lange, A. (2003b). Kriterien essenischer Texte. In J. Frey & H. Stegemann (Eds.), *Qumran kontrovers* (Einblicke, No. 6, pp. 59–69). Paderborn: Bonifatius.

Lange, A., & Lichtenberger, H. (1997). Qumran. Die Textfunde von Qumran. In G. Müller et al. (1997), *Theologische Realienzyklopädie* (36 vols., Vol. 28, pp. 45–79). Berlin: Walter de Gruyter.

Levison, J. R. (2006). The two spirits in Qumran theology. In J. H. Charlesworth (Ed.), *The Bible and the Dead Sea Scrolls* (3 vols., Vol. 2, pp. 169–194). Waco, TX: Baylor University Press.

Lyons, W. J., & Reimer, A. M. (1998). The demonic virus and Qumran studies: Some preventative measures. *DSD, 5,* 16–32.

Newsom, C. A. (1990). "Sectually explicit" literature from Qumran. In W. Propp, B. Halpern, & D. N. Freedman (Eds.), *The Hebrew Bible and its interpreters* (pp. 167–187). Winona Lake, IN: Eisenbrauns.

Nickelsburg, G. W. E. (1977). Apocalyptic and myth in 1 Enoch 6–11. *JBL, 96,* 383–405.

Nickelsburg, G. W. E. (2001). *1 Enoch 1: Hermeneia.* Minneapolis, MN: Fortress Press.

Stuckenbruck, L. T. (2002). The Book of Tobit and the problem of "magic." In H. Lichtenberger & G. S. Oegema (Eds.), *Jüdische Schriften in ihrem antikjüdischen und urchristlichen Kontext* (JSHRZ Studien, 1, pp. 258–269). Gütersloh: Gütersloher Verlagshaus.

Stuckenbruck, L. T. (2003). Giant mythology and demonology: From the ancient Near East to the Dead Sea Scrolls. In A. Lange, H. Lichtenberger, & K. F. D. Römheld (Eds.), *Die Dämonen—Demons. Die Dämonologie der israelitisch-jüdischen und frühchristlichen Literatur im Kontext ihrer Umwelt* (pp. 318–338). Tübingen: Mohr Siebeck.

Stuckenbruck, L. T. (2004). The origins of evil in Jewish Apocalyptic tradition: The interpretation of Genesis 6:1–4 in the second and third centuries B.C.E. In C. Auffarth & L. T. Stuckenbruck (Eds.), *The Fall of the Angels* (TBN, No. 6, pp. 87–118). Leiden: Brill.

Stuckenbruck, L. T. (2005). Pleas for deliverance from the demonic in early Jewish texts. In R. Hayward & B. Embry (Eds.), *Studies in Jewish prayer* (JSS Supp. No. 17, pp. 55–73). Oxford: Oxford University Press.

Stuckenbruck, L. T. (2007). *1 Enoch 91–108* (CEJL). Berlin: Walter de Gruyter.

Stuckenbruck, L. T. (2009a). The Book of Jubilees and the origin of evil. In G. Boccaccini & G. Ibba (Eds.), *Enoch and the Mosaic Torah* (pp. 294–308). Grand Rapids, MI: Eerdmans.

Stuckenbruck, L. T. (2009b). The Eschatological Worship by the Nations: An Inquiry into the Early Enoch Tradition. In Karoly Dobos et al. (Eds.), *Wisdom as a Robe: Festschrift in Honour of Ida Fröhlich* (pp. 191–208). Sheffield: Phoenix.

Suter, D. (1979). Fallen angels, fallen priests. *HUCA, 50,* 115–135.

VanderKam, J. C. (1989). *The Book of Jubilees* (CSCO, No. 511). Leuven: Peeters.

Wright, A. T. (2005). *The origin of evil spirits* (WUNT, No. 2.198). Tübingen: Mohr Siebeck.

CHAPTER 10

Evil in the Hebrew Bible, Mishnah, and Talmud

Ilona Rashkow

INTRODUCTION

In essence, the Jewish principle of good and evil, as reflected in the Hebrew Bible, Mishnah, and Talmud, emphasizes "good" and is based on God's words in Genesis 1:10: "God called the dry land Earth, and the waters that were gathered together He called Seas. And God saw that *it was good.*" In the traditional Jewish texts, God appears to be concerned with the human ability to separate the good from the evil and act in accordance with certain guidelines. According to biblical thought, God gives us a list of 613 rules, which tell us what to do and what *not* to do (*mitzvoth*), and by following all 613 of them we can either prevent doing evil or make retribution for it.

> Evil is not man's ultimate problem. Man's ultimate problem is his relation to God. . . . The biblical answer to evil is not the good but the holy. It is an attempt to raise man to a higher level of existence, where man is not alone when confronted with evil. (Heschel, 1987, p. 376)

With regard to the concept of evil, the Torah (the first five books of the Hebrew Bible) deals primarily with broad rules and regulations for his followers to obey rather than the problem of the existence of evil in the world. Indeed, of the 389 times the words *evil* or *evildoer* are used in the entire Hebrew Bible, only 29 occur in the Torah. In comparison, of the 451 times the word *good* appears in the Hebrew Bible, 86 occur in the first five books. In the later books, however, when the focus shifts to the individual vis-à-vis God, the issue of good and evil in a world governed by a benevolent and omnipotent God becomes more evident. Jeremiah, Isaiah, Job, and the Psalms question the prosperity of the wicked and the adversity of the righteous. Various answers are given, many of which were elaborated upon by the Talmudists[1] and the philosophers, but the idea of a heavenly reward for good or eternal damnation for evil does not appear to be offered in the Bible as a possible solution.

Despite the lack of a sustained discussion of evil in the Torah, there is a biblical basis to the idea of the existence in human nature of an instinctive tendency or impulse that, left to itself, would lead to one's undoing by acting contrary to the will of God (*yezer ha-ra*, or "inclination to evil"). Gen 6:5 reads that "every inclination of the thoughts of their hearts [humankind] is only evil continually," and this is reinforced in Gen 8:21, "for the inclination of the human heart is evil from his youth." The doctrine of two inclinations (or drives) is a major feature of Jewish thought. According to the rabbis,[2] humans were created with two opposing inclinations or tendencies, one toward the good and the other toward evil, as discussed below.

To confuse matters further, according to the Talmud, despite the fact that our natural inclinations are "evil," they are given by God and thus should not be eliminated completely. These basic impulses are the impetus for marriage, procreation, and our very livelihood. However, when our thoughts turn to "evil" rather than "sanctioned" desires, the Talmud instructs that the study of the Torah is an effective antidote (Kid 30b). Again, according to the Talmud, unless the *yezer ha-ra* is checked and controlled, it will grow out of control. To quote,

> R. Simeon b. Lakish stated, "The Evil Inclination of a man grows in strength from day to day and seeks to kill him . . . and were it not that the Holy One, blessed be He, is his help, he would not be able to withstand it." (Suk 52b)

According to the rabbinic writings, the evil inclination is an entirely earthly phenomenon: "In the world to come there is no eating or drinking, procreation or barter, envy or hate" (Ber 17a). However, the *yezer ha-ra* can be considered as having originated by other than humans—in Genesis 3, the serpent seems to exhibit an evil inclination when it tempts humankind to eat the forbidden fruit.

The apparent contradiction of the existence of "evil" in a "good" world that God created poses a conundrum: attempts to reconcile belief in a deity who, after creating the world, "saw that it was good" (Gen 1:10) with the same deity who says in Isa 45:6–7, "I make peace, and create evil." Why create evil? The Talmudists begin their explanation with an analysis of the creation of evil. For example:

R. Akiba said: Four directions were created for the world, and they are east, south, west, and north. East is the direction from which light emerges for the world. South is the direction from which dews of blessing and rains of blessing emerge for the world. West (is the direction) wherein the treasuries of heat and cold are situated. North is the direction from which darkness comes forth for the world, and it is the habitation of harmful entities, spirits, and demons, and it is from that direction that evil emerges into the world, as scripture attests: "Evil will initiate from the north" (Jer 1:14). (Mann, 1971, p. 13)

Baba Bathra gives a more elaborate form of this same tradition. There God deliberately leaves the northern quadrant "unfinished" and invites all those entities who think they are "gods" to replicate his creative activities. None is able to meet this challenge, and so the "north" becomes the domicile of demons, spirits, and various natural disasters:

The northern quadrant (of the world): from there darkness issues forth onto the world, and it is there that specters, devils, demons, spirits, and horrors have their abode, and it is from there that an evil spirit comes out into the world. While the Holy One, blessed be He, was responsible for creating the northern quadrant, He did not finish it. Why did He not complete it? He reasoned: "Unless there should come some entity styling himself 'god' to the world and who claims 'I am God!!' [If that happens], then he can finish the quadrant, (and) then everyone will know that he is truly God!" (Pirqe R El §3)

Another problem for the rabbis was the issue of a lack of a just distribution of good and evil to the righteous and wicked respectively. One particularly problematic verse is Exod 33:19: "I will be gracious to whom I will be gracious, and will show mercy on whom I will show mercy." Once again, the Talmud offers possible solutions. Based on the biblical reference "Neither shall the children be put to death for the fathers" (Deut 24:16), R. Johanan stated,

A righteous man who prospers is a perfectly righteous man; the righteous man who is in adversity is not a perfectly righteous man. The wicked man who prospers is not a perfectly wicked man; the wicked man who is in adversity is a perfectly wicked man.

On the other hand, R. Meir quoted Exod. 33:19 as follows:

[O]nly two [requests] were granted to him [Moses], and one was not granted to him. For it is said: "And I will be gracious to whom I will be gracious, although he may not deserve it, And I will show mercy on whom I will show mercy." (Ber 7a)

Meir interpreted "although he may not deserve it" to mean that "God's ways therefore cannot be known" (Ber 7a).

Genesis Rabbah blames evil on Satan in a rather circuitous interpretation of why Jacob had to dwell in Egypt:

> R. Aha said: "When the righteous wish to dwell in tranquility in this world, Satan comes and accuses them: They are not content with what is in store for them in the Hereafter, but they wish to dwell at ease even in this world! The proof lies in the fact that the Patriarch Jacob wished to live at ease in this world, whereupon he was attacked by Joseph's Satan; and Jacob dwelt in the land." (Gen R 84:3)

While recognizing the ambiguities in conflicting biblical passages regarding evil and suffering, the rabbis make a concerted effort to emphasize that God and His creation are good. Ber. 60b, for example, stated, "It was taught in the name of R. Akiba: 'A man should always accustom himself to say "'Whatever the All-Merciful does is for good.'" Ber. 60b then elaborated.

> Indeed, one should "bless for the evil in the same way as for the good . . . we have learnt: for good tidings one says, who is good and bestows good: for evil tidings one says, blessed be the true judge?"—Raba said: "What it really means is that one must receive the evil with gladness" . . . Where do we find this in the Scripture? "I will sing of mercy and justice, unto Thee, O Lord, will I sing praises," (Ps 60:1) whether it is "mercy" I will sing, or whether it is "justice" I will sing. "In the Lord I will praise His word, in God I will praise His word" (Ps 61:11). "In the Lord I will praise His word": this refers to good dispensation; "In God I will praise His word": this refers to the "dispensation of suffering." R. Tanhum said: "We learn it from here: 'I will lift up the cup of salvation and call on the name of the Lord' (Ps 66:13); I found trouble and sorrow, but I called upon the name of the Lord (Job 1:21)."

Even a Jewish burial service encompasses God's perfection and the goodness of God's creations: Once the grave is completely filled with earth, the prayer of Tzidduk HaDin (צידוק הדין)—justification of the Divine decree—is recited. With this moving prayer, the mourners declare their acceptance of the Divine decree and pray to God to have mercy upon the living (Lamm 60).

SATAN

Perhaps one of the most difficult concepts in trying to understand the concept of "evil" in traditional Jewish texts is the identity and entity of Satan. English Hebrew Bible translations are not consistent in their word choice when translating שטן. Occasionally, they view שטן as a proper name; in other places, the word is translated as "adversary" and refers to either (a) a human adversary, as in 1Kings 11:14, "And the Lord raised up an adversary against Solomon, Hadad the Edomite; he was of the royal house in Edom" (Revised Standard Version); or (b) God's adversary, as in Job 2:6, where שטן is clearly a proper name: "The Lord said to Satan, 'Very well, he is in your power; only spare his life'" (New Revised Standard Version).

Although the word שטן ("Satan") appears approximately 30 times in the Hebrew Bible, used either as a proper name or as "adversary," it is not as prominent in the Mishnah or the Tosefta (a supplement to the Mishnah), and, as discussed above, they refer generally to a being who accompanies the wicked man. For example, Tosefta Sha Mas. Baba Bathra at 17 (18):3 stated, "If you see a wicked man setting out on a journey and you wish to go by the same route, anticipate your journey by three days or postpone it for three days, because Satan accompanies the wicked man."

References to Satan in the Talmud are much more numerous. There are almost 90 Talmudic references to Satan as an entity, and his identity is clearly adversarial—either as a foe of humans (where Satan upon occasion is the victor) or as God's nemesis (where Satan is always vanquished). As man's adversary and accuser, he is without independent power—Satan's power must be derived from God. In Talmudic writings, Satan is identified with the evil inclination and with the angel of death: "Resh Lakish said: Satan, the evil prompter, and the Angel of Death are all one. He is called Satan" (Mas. Baba Bathra 16a). And perhaps as a throwback to the Genesis 1 narrative, when Satan does appear to humans he is often in the form of a seductress. For example, one Talmudic text states, "One day Satan appeared to him as a woman on the top of a palm tree. Grasping the tree, he [a man] went climbing up: but when he reached half-way up the tree he [Satan] let him go, saying 'Had they not proclaimed in Heaven, "Take heed of R. Akiba and his learning," I would have valued your life at two ma'ahs'" (Mas. Kiddushin 81a). Another says, "A Tanna taught: '[Satan] comes down to earth and seduces, then ascends to heaven and awakens wrath; permission is granted to him and he takes away the soul'" (Mas. Baba Bathra 16a).

Not surprisingly, Jews make relatively few references to Satan during worship. During the evening worship service (Ma'ariv), the concluding prayer (Hashkivenu)[3] says,

> Enable us, O Lord our God, to lie down in peace . . . save us quickly for your name's sake, protect us, remove from us the adversary (שטן), the pestilence, the sword, the famine, the anxiety. . . . Blessed art thou, O Lord, who guards His nation Israel eternally.

(It should be noted, however, that Sephardic prayer books omit the Hebrew word for Satan on the Sabbath on the holidays. Otherwise, Satan is back in.)

The High Holidays prayer book (Mahzor) contains references to Satan: six Biblical verses, the initial letters of which form the acrostic "Kerah Satan" ("tear Satan") are recited; one of the purposes of the blasts of the Shofar on the High Holidays according to Rabbi Isaac is to confound and confute Satan (Mas. Baba Bathra 16a); and in the Hinneni prayer (the prayer of the Hazzan [cantor] before the Musaf Amidah), there is a sentence in which he pleads, "And rebuke Satan that he accuse me not."

ADAM'S DEMONIC FAMILY

Despite the fact that there is only one biblical reference to Lilith ("Wild-cats shall meet with hyenas, goat-demons shall call to each other; there too Lilith shall repose, and find a place to rest"; Isa 34:14), she is perhaps the most famous "evil" female in Jewish demonology. Although the biblical reference is in connection with what horrendous things will happen on the day of vengeance, Lilith's presence in later writings is more pronounced. Midrash Numbers[4] describes her as "Lilith who, when she finds nothing else, turns upon her own children" (Midrash Num 26:16). Midrash Avkir graphically describes the relationship of Adam and Lilith:

> Our teacher Asi said: Adam the protoplast was wholly righteous, and when he saw that death had been decreed [as punishment] through his fault, he gained control over himself with fasting, kept away from his wife, and slept alone. A *lilītu*-demon named *Pīznā* came across him and became enamored with his handsomeness, for his handsome appearance was comparable to [that of] the solar disc. She slept with him [and eventually] gave birth from him to demons and *lilû*-devils.
>
> The name of the first-born son of Adam the protoplast was Agarīmus. Agarīmus went and married a *lilītu*-demon [named] Imrīt, [and] she bore him 92,000 myriads of demons and *lilû*-devils. The name of the first-born son of Agarīmus was Abelmus. He went and married Gōfrīt the *lilītu*-demon, and she bore him 88,000 myriads of demons and *lilû*-devils. The name of the first-born son of Abelmus was Akrīmus, and he went and [married] Afīznā, the daughter of Pūznā the *lilītu*-demon who was dwelling ... [in] the mountain, and she bore him 3,000 myriads of demons and *lilû*-devils ... the entire universe became filled with them ... the Angel of Death, and he strikes dead anyone who encounters him. (Gaster 48–49)

The Talmud states that she is a danger to women in childbirth as well as to men who sleep alone (Shab 151b). The Testament of Solomon[5] quotes Lilith as saying,

> [B]y night I sleep not, but go my rounds over all the world, and visit women in childbirth. And divining the hour I take my stand; and if I am

lucky, I strangle the child. But if not, I retire to another place. For I cannot for a single night retire unsuccessful. For I am a fierce spirit, of myriad names and many shapes. And now hither, now thither I roam. And to westering parts I go my rounds. (Testament of Solomon 58)

Another Talmudic version is less detailed:

R. Yermiyah b. El'azar said, "All those years that Adam the protoplast spent in banishment he was engendering spirits, demons, and *lilû*-devils, for scripture states *and Adam lived for 130 years, and then he engendered one in his image and in his likeness*" (Gen 5:3). It follows that up to that point (i.e., year 130) he had not engendered any in his likeness! They (the assembly) objected: R. Meir used to say, Adam the protoplast was a great *Hasid*: when he saw that death had been decreed (as punishment) through his fault, he sat fasting for 130 years, kept away from his wife for 130 years, and wore clothes made of fig-leaves for 130 years. (b. 'Erub 18b)

The most famous tale of Lilith originates in a medieval work called The Alphabet of Ben-Sira, a work whose relationship to the conventional streams of Judaism is tenuous. Although the idea of Eve having a predecessor is also not new to Ben Sira, and can be found in Genesis Rabbah, those traditions make no mention of Lilith, and, in fact, do not mesh well with Ben Sira's version of the story:

After God created Adam, who was alone, He said, "It is not good for man to be alone" (Gen 2:18). He then created a woman for Adam, from the earth, as He had created Adam himself, and called her Lilith. Adam and Lilith began to fight. She said, "I will not lie below," and he said, "I will not lie beneath you, but only on top. For you are fit only to be in the bottom position, while I am to be in the superior one." Lilith responded, "We are equal to each other inasmuch as we were both created from the earth." But they would not listen to one another. When Lilith saw this, she pronounced the Ineffable Name and flew away into the air. Adam stood in prayer before his Creator: "Sovereign of the universe!" he said, "The woman you gave me has run away." At once, the Holy One, blessed be He, sent these three angels to bring her back.

Said the Holy One to Adam, "If she agrees to come back, fine. If not, she must permit one hundred of her children to die every day." The angels left God and pursued Lilith, whom they overtook in the midst of the sea, in the mighty waters wherein the Egyptians were destined to drown. They told her God's word, but she did not wish to return. The angels said, "We shall drown you in the sea."

"Leave me!" she said. "I was created only to cause sickness to infants. If the infant is male, I have dominion over him for eight days after his birth, and if female, for twenty days."

When the angels heard Lilith's words, they insisted she go back. But she swore to them by the name of the living and eternal God: "Whenever I see you or your names or your forms in an amulet, I will have no power over that infant." She also agreed to have one hundred of her children die every day. Accordingly, every day one hundred demons perish, and for the same reason, we write the angels' names on the amulets of young children. When Lilith sees their names, she remembers her oath, and the child recovers.

EVIL SPEECH

Generally speaking, *lashon ha-ra* (לָשׁוֹן הָרָע) is the prohibition against slandering, slurring, or defaming one's fellow Jews, even when the derogatory remarks are true (Lev 19:16). However, there is an exception: Defaming individuals who constantly cause strife and dissension is permissible (Pe 1:1, 16a). The sages constantly stressed the severity of this prohibition, asserting that slander destroys three persons: "he who relates the slander, he who accepts it, and he about whom it is told" (Ar 15b). They recognized the power of the spoken word to build or ruin human relationships, and considered the tongue the "elixir of life" (Lev R 16:2) and the primary source of good and evil (Lev R 33:1). It was even considered forbidden to spread discreditable comments that the slanderer would have told to the person himself (Tos to Ar 15b).

The Bible and the Talmud have many examples of righteous and wicked individuals who violated this rule, but this is not surprising because virtually every character in the Hebrew Bible violated rules! Sarah is accused of slandering Abraham when she spoke about his advanced age and inability to beget children (Gen 18:12–15; Pe 1:1, 16a). Joseph was punished for the "evil reports" he spread about his brothers (Gen 37:2; Pe 1:1, 15d–16a). Miriam was punished by God for slandering Moses (Num 12:1–15). The spies were punished for their reports concerning Israel (Num 14:36–37). The division of the kingdom of David is attributed to his listening to slander (Shab 56a–b). On the other hand, Jeroboam king of Israel (I Kings 12:20) was worthy of being counted together with the kings of Judah (Hos 1:1) because he did not listen to slander against Amos (Amos 7:10–11; Pes 87b). The murder of Isaiah by Manasseh was considered divine retribution for Isaiah's slurs against the Jewish people (Isa 6:5; Yev 49b). Haman was considered the most skillful of all in engaging in *Lashon ha-ra* (Meg 13b).

Indirect slander was also forbidden, and the sages cautioned against speaking in praise of a person to prevent mentioning the person's bad deeds and qualities (Mas. Baba Bathra 164b). Equally objectionable under this heading is the implicit form of slander exemplified by the statement, "Do not speak of him; I want to know nothing about him," in which one expresses a disinclination to listen, not because of a distaste for slander, but because of the implied unworthiness of the subject (see Maim. Yad, De'ot 7:4). Although the hearer was cautioned not to believe slander, he still was permitted to safeguard himself cautiously in case the reports prove true (Nid 61a).

The rabbis often emphasized the rigorous punishments for those engaging in "evil speech." They are immediately chastised by plagues (ARN 19), and rain is withheld because of them (Ta'an 7b). Croup comes to the world on account of slander (Shab 33a–b), and whoever makes derogatory remarks about deceased scholars is cast into Gehinnom (Ber 19a). Slanderers will not enjoy the Shekinah (Divine Presence; Sot 42a), and a bearer of evil tales is considered as denying God (Ar 15b).

Within this narrow concept, *slander* is used generally to describe defaming an individual by either true *or* untrue statements. *Evil speech* is generally used in the sense of defaming someone by spreading false tales. Whoever relates or accepts slander deserves to be cast to the dogs (Pes 118a) and stoned (Ar 15b). (Slander is generally an untrue statement made that is implied to be factual; *lashon ha-ra* is more general.)

The Talmud delineated the repentance for those wishing to atone for this sin. Scholars were advised to engage in Torah study, whereas simple persons were urged to humble themselves (Ar 15b). The robe of the high priest and the incense aided in achieving atonement for this sin (Zev 88b). Mar, the son of Ravina, on concluding his daily prayer added the following: "My God, keep my tongue from evil and my lips from speaking guile" (Ber 17a), a formula that has been added at the end of the *Amidah*.

EVIL EYE

According to the Mishnah, the "evil eye" (עין הרע) (*ayin ha-ra*), expresses the idea that there are some people who, merely by looking at a victim, can cause harm—both bodily and financially. Pirkei Avot (Ethics of the Fathers)[6] has three references to the "evil eye":

> He said to them: Go and see which is the evil way which a man should avoid. Rabbi Eliezer said, an evil eye. (Pirkei Avot 2:14)
> Rabbi Joshua said: The evil eye, the evil desire and hatred of his fellow creatures put a man out of the world. (Pirkei Avot 2:16)
> Whosoever possesses these three qualities belongs to the disciples of Abraham our father: a generous eye, a humble spirit, and a meek soul. But he who possesses the three opposite qualities—an evil eye, a proud spirit, and a haughty soul—is of the disciples of Balaam the wicked. (Pirkei Avot 5:22)

The Talmud has several references to the "evil eye." For example, in Gen. Rabbah 45:5 Sarah uses her evil eye on Hagar, causing her to be banished

to the wilderness; Gen. Rabbah 84:10 explains that because of the evil eye
cast upon Joseph by his brothers, Joseph was taken to Egypt; and Num. Rabbah 12:4 explains the breaking of the first tablets of the law as having been
caused by an "evil eye."

There are a number of superstitious practices to ward off the harmful effects
of the evil eye, for example, spitting out three times when a person seems to be
at risk. Even today some people, when praising others, will add, "[L]et it be
without the evil eye" (in the Yiddish form, *kenenhora*), meaning I do not intend
my praise to suggest that I am enviously casting a malevolent glance.

AMULET

An amulet is a small object that a person wears, carries, or offers to a deity
because he or she believes that it will magically bestow a particular power or
form of protection. The conviction that a symbol, form, or concept provides
protection, promotes well-being, or brings good luck is common to all societies: even today, some people carry a favorite penny or a rabbit's foot.

In 1979, two silver amulets dating to the late seventh to sixth centuries
BCE were discovered in a burial cave in Ketef Hinnom, outside of Jerusalem.
The smaller of these amulets reads, "Blessed be [he or she] by Yahweh, the
helper and dispeller of evil. May Yahweh bless you (and) protect you, and
may he cause his face to shine upon you and grant you peace." The larger
amulet mentions "the covenant" and Yahweh's "graciousness to those who
love him," refers to Yahweh as "our restorer," and concludes with the benediction "May Yahweh bless you and protect you, may he cause his face to
shine" (this blessing is a slight variant of the priestly benediction in Numbers 6:22). The tiny rolled-up scrolls were no doubt intended to be worn
as amulets to safeguard their owners. The prophylactic nature of the two
tiny scrolls to prevent sickness and disease is evident from the words *bless*
and *keep*. Apparently, all humans, whether "great" or "small," are spiteful and
vain—and, as history has demonstrated, the more "important" the individual, the greater the likely these tendencies are to manifest themselves. The
Ketef Hinnom amulets must have been regarded as having an apotropaic or
ritual observance that is intended to turn away evil effect, as is emphasized in
the smaller amulet by a reference to the deity as the "rebuker of evil": "May
he/she be blessed by YHWH, the warrior and the rebuker of Evil" (Barkay,
Vaughn, Lundberg, & Zuckerman, 2004; see also Barkay, Lundberg, Vaughn,
Zuckerman, & Zuckerman, 2003).

Although many Jewish homes have a mezuzah[7] on the doorpost, a mezuzah is not considered an amulet. Rather, it fulfills a biblical injunction to have
God's word be a sign on your doorpost (Exod 11:7,13). Similarly, Tefillin[8]
(prayer phylacteries) are not amulets; they too fulfill the commandment in
Deut 6:8 that they are to be a "sign upon the heart and upon the hand."

Many contemporary Jews wear jewelry that could be regarded as amulets. For example, a Star of David, which is worn often as a pendant on a chain, contains a six-pointed star. The six points symbolize that God rules over the universe and protects us from all six directions: north, south, east, west, up, and down. King David used this symbol in the battlefield on his shield as an omen from God.

Another piece of jewelry that can be viewed as an amulet is a hamsa (also known as the "hand of Miriam"). The hamsa serves as an ancient talismanic way of averting the evil eye and providing a "protecting hand" or "Hand of God." The hamsa often appears in stylized form, as a hand with three fingers raised, and sometimes with two thumbs arranged symmetrically.

REPENTANCE

The phrase "Repentance, prayer, and charity remove a bad decree" sets the tone to the days of Rosh Hashanah and Yom Kippur[9] more than any other in the High Holy Days prayer book. Indeed, of the three, repentance is probably the most significant because the period of time between Rosh Hashanah and Yom Kippur is called the "Ten Days of Repentance."

Within this context, repentance occurs once a person realizes that he or she has sinned, acknowledges the error, and takes a personal oath never to repeat the sin again. In this manner the person is in effect changing and becoming a new person.

In the Hebrew Bible, תשובה (teshuvah, literally "return") is the term used for repentance, and the Bible states that repentance brings pardon and forgiveness of sin. Apart from repentance, no other activities, such as sacrifices or religious ceremonies, can secure pardon and forgiveness of sin ("Let the wicked forsake his way, and the man of iniquity his thoughts; and let him return unto the Lord, and He will have compassion upon him, and to our God, for He will abundantly pardon"; Isa 55:7). The Torah (five books of Moses) distinguishes between offenses against God and offenses against another human. In the first case, the manifestation of repentance consists of confession of one's sin before God (Lev 5:5; Num 5:7), the essential part being a solemn promise and firm resolve not to commit the same sin again; and making certain prescribed offerings (Lev 5:1-20). Repentance of a sin against God generally leads to the deity's forgiveness. In some cases, individuals or nations repent of their sins and are spared God's judgment (Gen 4:7; Lev 4, 5; Deut 4:30, 30:2; I Kings 8:33, 48; Hosea 14:2; Jer 3:12, 31:18, 36:3; Ezek 18:30-32; Isa 54:22, 55:6-10; Joel 2:12; and Jonah 2:10).

Offenses against another human require, in addition to confession and sacrifice, restitution in full of whatever has been wrongfully obtained or withheld from the aggrieved, with, in effect, a 20% interest penalty (Lev 5:20–26). If the injured party has died, restitution must be made to the heir; if there is

no heir, it must be given to the priest, who officiates at the sacrifice made for
the remission of the sin (Num 5:7–9).

There are other examples of repentance mentioned in the Bible. These
include pouring out water (I Sam 7:6); prayer (II Sam 12:16); self-affliction,
such as fasting (Ezra 9:5; Neh 1:4, 9:1; Esth 4:3; Ps 35:13, 69:10, 109:24; Isa
58:4; Dan 6:18, 9:3; Joel 2:12; and Neh 9:1); wearing sackcloth (although there
are over 40 instances of wearing sackcloth in the Hebrew Bible, only one
occurs in the Torah: Gen 37:34, "Then Jacob tore his garments, and put sackcloth on his loins"); and sitting and sleeping on the ground (I Kings 21:27;
Joel 2:13; Jon 3:5). However, the prophets criticized these forms of repentance
as basically self-aggrandizing and focused on a change in the sinner's mental
and spiritual attitude ("Rend your heart, and not your garments, and turn
unto the Lord your God: for he is gracious and full of compassion, slow to
anger and plenteous in mercy, and repenteth him of the evil" (Joel 2:13).

Many rabbinic sources state that repentance is an essential aspect of the
existence of this world, and was one of the seven provisions that God made
before the Creation (Pes 54a; Ned 39b; Genesis Rabbah 1). Sincere repentance
is equivalent to the rebuilding of the Temple, the restoration of the altar, and
the offering of all the sacrifices (Midrash Leviticus Rabbah 7; Sanh 43b).

According to Jewish doctrine, repentance is the prerequisite of atonement
(Mishna Yoma Chapter 8, 8). Yom Kippur, the Day of Atonement, derives its
significance only from the fact that it is the culmination of the 10 penitential
days with which the Jewish religious year begins. It is of no consequence
without repentance. However, repentance and the Day of Atonement can
only absolve one from sins committed against God; sins against another person are absolved only when restitution has been made and the pardon of the
offended party has been obtained (Yoma 87a; Mishneh Torah Teshuva 2:9).

Jewish doctrine holds that it is never too late, even on the day of death, to
return to God with sincere repentance: "as the sea is always open for everyone who wishes to cleanse himself, so are the gates of repentance always open
to the sinner" (Midrash Deut Rabbah 2.; Midrash Psalms 43)—the hand of
God is continually stretched out to receive a sinner (BM 58:2). Indeed, one
Talmudic tractate states that one who has repented is more worthy than one
who has never sinned (Ber 34b).

CONCLUSION

Abraham J. Heschel wrote in *God in Search of Man*, "The world is in flames,
consumed by evil. Is it possible that there is no one who cares? . . . [367] . . .
What have we done to make such crimes [the Holocaust] possible? What are
we doing to make such crimes impossible?" [369].

Perhaps the Bible and the Talmudic sources provide a starting point. The
New Testament quotes Jesus giving a solution: "In everything, do to others

what you would want them to do to you. This is what is written in the Law and in the Prophets" (Matt 7:12), and "Do to others as you want them to do to you" (Luke 6:31).

The Sage Hillel, an elder contemporary of Jesus, used a negative structure to express the same basic sentiments. When asked by a potential convert to sum up the entire Torah concisely, he answered, "What is hateful to you, do not to your neighbor: that is the whole Torah, while the rest is the commentary thereof; go and learn it" (Shab 31a).

Perhaps the essence of "evil in the Hebrew Bible, Mishnah, and Talmud" is the last part of Hillel's answer to the potential proselyte: "[T]he rest is the commentary thereof; go and learn it." In other words, avoid doing evil because God said, "It is good."

Abbreviations of Tractates

Ar	Arakhin
ARN	Avot de-RaMas. Baba Bathra i Natan
Avot	Avot
AZ	Avodah Zarah
Mas. Baba Bathra	Bava Batra
Bekh	Bekhorot
Ber	Berakhot
Betz	Betzah
Bik	Bikkurim
BK	Bava Kamma
BM	Bava Metzia
De	Demai
DER	Derekh Eretz RaMas. Baba Bathra ah
DEZ	Derekh Eretz Zuta
Ed	Eduyyot
Er	Eruvin
Ger	Gerim
Git	Gittin
Hag	Hagigah
Hal	Hallah
Hor	Horayot
Hul	Hullin
Ka	Kallah

(continued)

Abbreviations of Tractates

Kel	Kelim
Ker	Keritot
Ket	KetuMas. Baba Bathra ot
Kid	Kiddushin
Kil	Kilayim
Kin	Kinnim
Kut	Kutim
Maas	Maaserot
Mak	Makkot
Makh	Makhshirin
Me	Meilah
Meg	Megillah
Men	Menahot
Mez	Mezuzah
Mid	Middot
Mik	Mikvaot
MK	Moed Katan
MSh	Maaser Sheni
Naz	Nazir
Ned	Nedarim
Neg	Negaim
Nid	Niddah
Oh	Ohalot
Or	Orlah
Par	Parah
Pe	Peah
Per Sha	Perek ha-Shalom
Pes	Pesahim
RH	Rosh ha-Shanah
Sanh	Sanhedrin
Sem	Semahot
Shab	ShaMas. Baba Bathra at
Shek	Shekalim
Shev	It
Shevu	Shevuot

Abbreviations of Tractates

Sof	Soferim
Sot	Sotah
ST	Sefer Torah
Suk	Sukkah
Ta	Taanit
Tam	Tamid
Tef	Tefillin
Tem	Temurah
Ter	Terumot
Toh	Toharot
TY	Tevul Yom
Tz	Tzitzit
Uk	Uktzin
Yad	Yadayim
Yev	Yevamot
Yoma	Yoma
Zav	Zavin
Zev	Zevahim

NOTES

1. The Talmud, a central text of mainstream Judaism, is a compilation of rabbinic discussions of Jewish law, ethics, customs, and history. It has two components: the Mishnah (c. 200 CE), the first written compendium of Judaism's Oral Law; and the Gemara (c. 500 CE), a discussion of the Mishnah and related writings that ventures often onto other subjects and expounds broadly on the Tanakh.

2. The term *rabbis* is used throughout this chapter when referring to the Talmudic writings.

3. Hashkivenu (הַשְׁכִּיבֵנוּ) ("cause us to lie down") is the initial word of the second benediction after the Shema of the daily evening prayer. This prayer for protection during the night is mentioned in the Talmud (Ber. 4b).

4. *Midrash* (literally, "to investigate" or "to study") is a Hebrew term referring to the not exact, but comparative, method of exegesis of biblical texts. The term *midrash* can also refer to a compilation of homiletic teachings on the Tanakh, in the form of legal and ritual parts (Halakhah) and legendary, moralizing, folkloristic, and anecdotal parts (Haggada), and is a valuable source of Jewish interpretations of the Bible.

5. The Testament of Solomon is a pseudepigraphical work, the authorship of which is ascribed to King Solomon. It describes how the Archangel Michael gave Solomon a magical ring that allowed him to control demons and build the Temple.

6. Pirkei Avot ("Ethics of the Fathers") is a compilation of the ethical teachings in the Mishnaic tractate of Avot ("Fathers"), the second-to-last tractate in the order of Nezikin in the Talmud.

7. A mezuzah (מְזוּזָה) is a parchment scroll attached to the doorpost of most rooms in a Jewish home (any room that has two doorposts and an overhead lintel requires a mezuzah, so bathrooms, closets, laundry rooms, boiler rooms, and so forth do not require a mezuzah). The original meaning of the word *mezuzah* is "doorpost" (cf. Ex. 12:7), but a mezuzah has come to also mean the parchment on which the verses of the Torah are inscribed: "and ye shall write them (the words of God) upon the *mezuzot* of thy house and in thy gates" (Deuteronomy 6:4–9, 11:13–21) as well as the case or container in which the parchment is enclosed. The mezuzah consists of a piece of parchment, made from the skin of a clean animal, on which Deuteronomy passages are written in square (Assyrian) characters, traditionally in 22 lines. The parchment is rolled up and inserted in a case with a small opening. On the back of the parchment is the word שַׁדַּי, which means "Almighty"; in addition, the letters stand for the initial letters of יִשְׂרָאֵלשׁוֹמֵר דְּלָתוֹת "Guardian of the doors of Israel." The parchment is so inserted that the word is visible through the opening. It is affixed to the right-hand doorpost of the room, house, or gate, where it is obligatory, in the top third of the doorpost and slanting inward.

8. Tefillin (תְּפִלִּין), usually translated as "phylacteries," are two black leather boxes containing scriptural passages that are bound by black leather straps on the left hand and on the head by men for the morning services on all days of the year except Sabbaths and scriptural holy days. Four passages of the Bible (Ex. 13:1–10 and 11–16; Deut. 6:4–9 and 11:13–21) require Jews to put "these words" (of the Law) for "a sign upon thy hand and a frontlet between thine eyes."

9. Yom Kippur, the Day of Atonement (יום הכפורים), is one of the "appointed seasons of the Lord, holy convocations," a day of fasting and atonement, occurring on the Tenth of Tishri. It is the climax of the "Ten Days of Penitence" and the most important day in the Jewish liturgical year.

REFERENCES

Barkay, G., Lundberg, M. J., Vaughn, A. G., Zuckerman, B., & Zuckerman, K. (2003). The challenges of Ketef Hinnom: Using advanced technologies to reclaim the earliest biblical texts and their context. *Near Eastern Archaeology, 66*, 162–171.

Barkay, G., Vaughn, A. G., Lundberg, M. J., & Zuckerman, B. (2004). The amulets from Ketef Hinnom: A new edition and evaluation. *Bulletin of the American Schools of Oriental Research, 334*, 41–71.

Dan, J. (1999). Samael and the problem of Jewish Gnosticism. In *Jewish mysticism* (Vol. 3, pp. 382–385). Northvale, NJ: Jason Aronson.

Ginzberg, L. J. (2003). *Legends of the Jews.* Philadelphia: Jewish Publication Society of America.

Heschel, A. J. (1987). *God in search of man: A philosophy of Judaism.* Northvale, NJ: Jason Aronson.

Lamm, M. (2000). *The Jewish way in death and mourning.* New York: Jonathan David.

Maimonides, M., Pines, S., & Strauss, L. (1974). *The guide of the perplexed* (Vol. 1). Chicago: University of Chicago Press.

Mann, J. (1971). *The Bible as read and preached in the old synagogue: Vol. 1. The Palestinian triennial cycle: Genesis and Exodus.* New York: Ktav.

Neusner, J. (2006). *The Babylonian Talmud: A translation and commentary.* Peabody, MA: Hendrickson.

CHAPTER 11

EVIL IN THE NEW TESTAMENT AND ITS GRECO-ROMAN CONTEXT

J. Harold Ellens

In the Hebrew Bible (Old Testament, or OT), there is a persistent tension between the notion that God is the source of evil (Gen 6) and that evil derives rather from human unintentional or willful dysfunction (Gen 3). In the New Testament (NT), there is virtually none of that ambivalence. In the NT, evil is a product of human misbehavior and the damage and pain it inflicts.

Paul's letters were the first NT documents to be written and are interesting especially for two reasons. First, he took the narrative of Jesus's life and ministry and fashioned from it a theology of radical, unconditional, and universal divine grace (Rom 8). The story itself was apparently communicated to him orally by Peter and James. Second, he locates the source of evil in human behavior, particularly the conduct that arises when the lower passions of humans dominate their higher passions. This is a strictly Greek idea and could not be further from the essential Hebrew model one would have expected to be Paul's normal Jewish outlook on life.

It is easy to notice in the Hebrew Bible that the ancient Israelites saw a close connection between evil, sin, sickness, suffering, and the will of Yahweh. Human pain was seen as suffering from the chastisement or punishment inflicted by God if you made him angry. This was supposed to produce growth or refinement, as gold is refined in fire. The pain–pleasure, health–illness continuum was really the simple equation of life–death. So suffering was associated with the effects of evil in a person's life.

The ancient Israelites did not understand that illness represents a temporary stage in the process of health and growth to self-actualization, and is not part of an equation of evil and its consequences. Illness, in fact, can sometimes bring a person to greater growth and spiritual maturity. Job and his book in the Hebrew Bible return ancient Israelite thought to an authentic theology about evil and about God. Job's argument with God establishes the fact that human suffering is not an element in the equation of how God and evil stand toward each other or relate.

That scripture makes it clear that we are unable to sin ourselves out of God's grace, unable to squirm out of his long embrace. In the direst of human circumstances, God is not seen as the problem but as the shepherd of human growth, the source of human survival, and the energy behind human thriving and flourishing. However, those facts of grace in God's disposition toward us do not eliminate evil or its consequences, whether that evil is personal, social, or institutional.

There is also another side to the Hebrew understanding of humans carrying on life before the face of God. Humans are not split in two, as the Greeks thought. The theological theme and pattern in the Hebrew Bible (OT) and in Jesus's ministry as reported in the NT depict human life as a dynamic line of growth. The outcome is full personhood and self-realization in interaction with God. On that growth continuum, suffering and shalom are temporary interactive states, enhancing life as a means toward eternal life. On that trajectory, growth is a total-person experience. It is not a Greek notion of the godlike higher passions of mind and psyche gaining dominance and control over the evil lower passions of the "animal appetites": sex, avarice, anger, addictions, narcissism, and gluttony. Surely that comprehensive and theologically oriented perspective or model is valuable in constructing a responsible understanding of the way evil is conceived. However, Paul's thought on evil is ambiguous because his notion of human nature is ambivalent. He sees humans caught in the struggle of the higher passions over the lower passions. At the same time, he has in the back of his mind the Hebrew notion of the unity of the human person.

Paul's manner of viewing human persons is constructed on a continuum of three states of development, as noted above: primordial persons, as in the story of paradise in Genesis 1–3; fallen persons who are alienated from God; and whole persons *in Christ*. This is a continuum of growth leading to God's ultimate destiny for us all, namely, our fulfillment as persons. This implies our self-realization and self-actualization as image bearers of God and God's compatriots in bringing in his reign of love and grace on earth.

However, Paul remained confused throughout his life and work about the relationship of his Greek tendencies as a Hellenized Jew, and the Hebrew roots of his theology. The historic Hebrew notion of a person (Hebrew = *nephesh*, or body, mind, and spirit) is that humans are unitary beings. There is no such thing as a separation between various parts or functions of a person. The ancient Israelites saw the entire person as a unity made in the image of God, genitals and all. "God made humans in God's own image, male and female" (Gen 1:27). Paul's Greek worldview shaped his theology in terms of the notion that persons are made of three or four parts. These were all in tension with each other. Paul used the four terms to speak of the four facets of human personhood. In sound Greek fashion, he spoke of the body (*soma*), our fleshly nature (*sarx*), our soul and mind (*nous*), and our spirit natures (*psyche*).

To use Freudian terms that apply here, Paul always struggled to describe how the *psyche* and *nous* (ego and superego—the higher passions) adequately disciplined the *soma* and *sarx* (id—the lower passions) to insure that the person did not do evil. In the end, the Hebrew theology of grace triumphed in his theology. We cannot sin ourselves out of God's grace (Rom 8), but the function of our lower passions is, nonetheless, what introduces evil into the world, in Paul's view.

Our bodies (*soma*) are not the whole of our fleshly nature (*sarx*), but they are the source and center of it, and the dangerous root of evil in human behavior. Paul thought our appetites were inherently evil or led us into evil. Likewise, our souls and minds (*nous*) are not the whole of our spirit (*psyche*), but they are its source and center, and thus the wellspring of *shalom* that triumphs over evil in this world.

By the time of Socrates, the Greeks differentiated markedly between the spiritual and psychological issues, on the one hand, and the physiological matters, on the other. This was a corollary of their perception that human physical nature and drives were essentially animalistic and subhuman. These lower passions were to be subdued and held in check by the higher passions in so far as possible, namely, by the intellectual and psychological powers. They were sure that ideal humanness resided essentially in the *psyche* and the *nous*.

The Hebrew outlook was different in the very revealing ways just suggested. By viewing human nature in a thoroughly unified manner, they perceived the whole person as made in the image of God's ethereal and mundane characteristics. Our spiritual and physiological functions equally reflect the divine imprint upon us. The Hebrews discerned no inherent tension between the physiological and the psychological, no conflict between body and soul. There was little compartmentalization of the various facets and functions of persons until the debate between the Pharisees and Sadducees about the resurrection of the soul and its survival after death. Prior to that, a human being was discerned to be inherently unitary, rendering absurd the Greek idea of a division between *soma* and *psyche*.

These two traditions are the primary roots of our present Western Judeo-Christian view of the human sources of evil. The Greeks thought evil comes from the uncontrolled and often unconscious function of the lower passions of humans, whereas the Hebrews thought that evil comes from a willful choice by humans to act contrary to the will of God. Both contribute important elements to our present way of viewing the question.

In the Synoptic Gospels, Mark, Matthew, and Luke-Acts, the picture of evil in the world is a derivative of the various apocalyptic forms of Judaism that were afloat in Jesus's world at the time of the writing of the NT documents. The type of apocalyptic Judaism that influenced the NT was one that held evil to be a result of human misbehavior prompted by evil powers from a realm outside of this world. These gospels present a worldview in which the devil and demons exist in the form of agents who have rebelled against God and are busy trying to wreck God's world and God's intentions for this world.

In this model, Jesus is opposed by the devil and his angels, who cause suffering and evil throughout the human race and human world. Jesus's avowed objective in those stories is to put down these evil powers, overcome the evil forces at work in this world, and ultimately triumph over them and exterminate them. According to the first three gospels, this will be a work completed when he returns on the clouds of heaven with all the *holy* angels, in the power and glory of God the Father. When he returns in that dramatic *parousia*, he will set in motion a cataclysmic judgment day, a termination of history, and an end of all evil. The Synoptic Gospels are a form of apocalyptic Judaism that explains the source of evil by deriving it from a rebellion of the wicked angels in heaven. Those demons invaded God's world here on earth to corrupt it. They did so by tempting humans to behave contrary to God's law, word, and will. Evil comes from the other world, according to the Synoptic Gospels, but is implemented in the world by humans who allow themselves to be agents of the devil and his minions.

John's Gospel is very different from the Synoptic Gospels, in virtually every way. In this fourth gospel there is no end to history, there is no judgment day, there is no extermination of the wicked or eternal punishment of evildoers. There is also no second coming in John. Jesus, the Christ, is in John the carrier of the *Logos* from heaven. He came down to reveal the divine mysteries of the salvation of the whole world by God's grace (Jn 3:13–18, esp. 16–17). He then returned to heaven, his true home, to stay there for all eternity.

In John the judgment took place before the world was created. God was the judge, and he judged in that pre-creation act that he would create this world and that he would utterly save it. Evil in John is only the actions of human beings who do not identify with and commit themselves to Jesus as the Christ, the Son of Man, as Jesus called himself. Such persons judge themselves in the sense that light has come into the world and they have preferred the darkness. That darkness comes from ignoring the divine mysteries of grace in Christ. Nonetheless, in the end all evil will be removed from the world progressively in each generation by the fact that God absolutely forgives it all in advance. John's Gospel was the last item in the NT to be written, so we ought to take seriously this final word from God, so to speak. The evil perpetrated in the world is always caused by humans, according to John's Gospel, either by not being adequately conformed as yet to the ways of God revealed in Jesus the Christ, or by willful rejection of God's way for humans.

John's Gospel is universalistic in its view of the ultimate elimination of evil (e.g. 3:16–17), just as is Paul's theology of divine triumph over all evil in the world (e.g., Rom 8). For both of these authors, evil is produced by humans rejecting God's will and way for his world. Both also assert that in the end, God will triumph over evil by forgiving it in God's radical, unconditional, and universal grace. The difference between John and Paul lies in the fact that in the fourth gospel, the model of human beings is the Hebrew model of persons as unified in nature, so choosing evil is a choice made by the whole person, whereas in the Pauline epistles the choice to do evil is the influence of the bodily and animal instincts and not of the spiritual side of the person.

This model leaves room for believing that I did not really intend to do evil, but my God-given lower passions made me do it. The "devil in me" made me do it. It is interesting that Paul actually says of himself, "The good that I would do, I do not, and the evil that I would not, that I do." Here we see not only the tension in Paul between his Hebrew and Greek worldviews but also the tension between the notions of evil as caused by *God* and evil derived from *human* disorder, dysfunction, and disobedience. Even so, at one place in Romans 1:18–32 Paul says that people had an evil mind (*nous*). However, even there he declares that "God gave them over to an evil mind." The Greek model removes the cause of evil one step of abstraction from the center of responsibility of the person's self. Paul declares in that passage,

> The wrath of God is revealed from heaven against all ungodliness and wickedness of men who by their wickedness suppress the truth. For what can be known about God is plain to them, because God has shown it to them. Ever since the creation of the world his invisible nature, namely, his eternal power and deity, has been clearly perceived in the things that have been made. So they are without excuse, for although they knew God they did not honor him as God or give thanks to him, but they became futile in their thinking and their senseless minds were darkened. . . . Therefore, God gave them up to the lusts of their hearts, to impurity, to the dishonoring of their bodies among themselves, because they exchanged the truth about God for a lie. . . . For this reason God gave them up to dishonorable passions . . . since they did not see fit to acknowledge God, God gave them up to a base mind and improper conduct. They were filled with all manner of wickedness, evil, covetousness, malice. Though they know God's decree . . . they not only do them [evil things] but approve those who practice them.

It is interesting that Paul clearly sees humans as divided between the "lusts of their hearts" (*nous and psyche*); the lusts of "their bodies" (*soma and sarx*); "dishonorable passions"—presumably, lower passions or animal instincts (*soma and sarx*); and "base minds" (*nous and psyche*) that lead to "improper conduct" (i.e., doing evil). This is a Greek model of how humans are constructed and function. Nonetheless, all the way through this passage Paul gets his categories mixed up. One has *lust* or *animal passions* not only of the body (*soma and sarx*) but also of the mind (*nous and psyche*). Evil conduct comes not only from the *soma* and *sarx* but also from "base minds" (*nous*, at least, and probably *psyche* [spirit] as well). So all through Paul's Greek model, there is a stream of Hebrew ideology that tries to get the whole person, not just the lower passions, involved in the production of evil.

He had his own struggle to do the good his real self (*nous* and *psyche*—mind and spirit) wants to do, and against doing the evil the "devil" (*soma* and *sarx*—fleshly passions) in him does. Paul has this to say in Romans 7:13–25:

> Sin was working death in me . . . so that sin might be shown to be sin. . . .
> We know that the law is spiritual (of the *nous* and *psyche*); but I am carnal
> (*soma* and *sarx*), enslaved under sin. I do not understand my own actions.
> For what I (*nous* and *psyche*—the real me) want to do, I do not, but I do
> the very thing I hate. Now if I do what I do not want, I agree that the law
> is good. So then it is no longer I (*nous* and *psyche*—the real me) that do it,
> but sin which dwells within me (*soma* and *sarx*—that opposing force). For
> I know that nothing good dwells within me, that is, in my flesh (*soma* and
> *sarx*—the enemy). I can will what is right, but I cannot do it. For the good
> that I would, I do not, and the evil that I would not, that I do. Now if I do
> what I do not want, it is no longer I (*nous* and *psyche*—mind and spirit) that
> does it, but sin which dwells within me (*soma* and *sarx*—the enemy opposed
> to the real me). So I find it to be a law that when I want to do right, evil
> lies close at hand. For I delight in the law of God, in my inmost self (*nous*
> and *psyche*—mind and spirit), but I see in my members (penis—*soma* and
> *sarx*) another law that is at war with the law of my mind (*nous*) and making
> me captive to the law of sin which dwells in my members (*soma* and *sarx*—
> genitals?). Wretched man that I am! Who will deliver me from this body
> (*soma and sarx*) of deadliness? Thanks be to God through Jesus Christ our
> Lord! So then, I of myself (*nous* and *psyche*—my real self) serve the law of
> God with my mind, but with my flesh (*soma* and *sarx*—that thing out there
> that stands over against my real self) I serve the law of sin.

It is amazing to what extent Paul is willing to cut himself up into pieces in order to get himself off the hook for being responsible for evil. He affirms that his higher passions are really him, but that his lower passions are not him. He has separated himself from everything below the belt. What was the evil that he was having such a hard time dealing with, acknowledging, and accepting responsibility for? Was his "thorn in the flesh" the fact that he was an obsessive masturbator and his mother had caught him at it as a pubescent boy, shamed him unmercifully, and so left him with a permanently negative view of the sexual appetite?

Paul prided himself in being a Hebrew of the Hebrews, and, as touching the law, a Pharisee. So it is not surprising that his Hebrew traditions and mind-set kept breaking through his learned Hellenistic Judaism. However, when we consider the context in which he was working, it is not surprising that he was constantly thinking in terms of the model and language of his Greek or Hellenistic perspective. Paul lived at the time of Philo and the Hellenization of the Jewish world. It was the time that Middle Platonism was sliding into Neo-Platonism. Platonism held that a radical divide existed between the ethereal or heavenly world and the mundane or earthly sphere of existence, and thus between the world of the spirit (*psyche*) and the material or physical world (*soma* and *sarx*). This cosmic split also split humans at the beltline.

Neo-Platonism developed this idea further and created an ideology in which a hierarchy of God and the lesser gods was devised. It was designed to explain the distance between the flawed material or physical world and the pure and ineffable world of the spirit and the divine. God is pure spirit, transcendent and ineffable. Therefore, God could not have created the flawed world in which evil exists. Hence, one of the demigods must have done it. The big problem for Neo-Platonism was to discern how far down the ladder from the high God of pure spirit the evil creator god needed to be in order to protect God from culpability for the evil in this world. These were the kinds of issues with which Paul was already struggling, though Neo-Platonism would not become fully formed for a couple more centuries, with the rise of Plotinus and Porphyry.

As we saw in previous chapters, Zoroastrianism had heavily influenced the apocalyptic Judaisms of Paul's time. That ideology taught that there was a radical split between the kingdoms of light and darkness. The soul of humans was considered an element of the light but entangled in the roots and tentacles of the darkness. Manichaeanism was a second-century form of Christianity that taught this Zoroastrian model, claiming that Jesus Christ was the redeemer who enabled the particles of light to escape from the darkness and return to their ethereal realm. This was, for most Christian thinkers who followed Pauline thought, an inadequate explanation of the problem of evil. Nonetheless, it combined with the Greek model of human nature to influence the Church's interpretation of the NT.

The Platonist and eventually the Neo-Platonist perspective seemed to line up with Pauline NT theology much more precisely than Zoroastrian Manichaeanism. In Neo-Platonism, there is only one reality (i.e., God), from whom the material world came forth as a series of emanations. So from absolute unity came multiplicity, the many aspects of the material world. Also from the transcendent God arises self-conscious mind (*nous*) and spirit (*psyche*). Soul and life derive from the universal mind, and soul is the bridge between the two spheres of our spirituality and physicality.

The material world is the most degraded of the reality encompassed in the supreme unity. Within the unity of all reality in God, the material and fleshly world is the farthest distant from God's pure spirit. Universal soul provides the structure to the material world and rules it from above, much like the function of the divine *Logos* in Philo's thought. The immanence of soul within the universe, Plotinus thought of as nature—the indwelling principle of life and growth. It produces all material bodies. This makes the material world, and our fleshly existence, the source and ground of evil—the world of darkness.

Plotinus thought, in keeping with Plato, that the material world is not inherently evil:

> He strongly maintained its goodness and beauty as the best possible work of Soul [at the material level of existence]. It is a living organic whole, and its wholeness is the best possible (though very imperfect) reflection on the space-time level of the living unity [divine] in [the] diversity of the world of forms in Intellect [*nous*]. It is held together in every part by a universal sympathy and harmony. In this harmony external evil and suffering take their place as necessary elements in the great pattern, the great dance of the universe. Evil and suffering can affect men's lower selves [*soma* and *sarx*] but cannot touch their true, higher selves [*nous* and *psyche*] and so cannot interfere with the real well-being of the philosopher [who ignores his or her body and lives in his or her mind]. (Armstrong, 1974, p. 541)

According to Neo-Platonism, as humans we can choose to place ourselves on any level of the universal soul. We can ascend in the spiritual realm to universal soul itself and so become the complete entity we always have the potential of being. In doing this, we participate in the perfect realm of the mind (intellect) and spirit. On the other hand, we may choose to place ourselves on the lower level, imprisoning ourselves in the lusts, longings, tastes, concerns, and experiences of the lower level of mere material existence and animal appetites. The body and material existence weigh a person down; but conversion empowers one by a concerted act of intellect, will, and moral effort to rise above the life of the body and awake to the spiritual way of seeing. All of us have the potential, but few use it. This is the mystical union with God that is the ideal of experience and existence.

It is readily apparent how extensively the Pauline writings, and the NT in general, were shaped by the early stages of this kind of Middle Platonist and Neo-Platonist ideology. The NT never really gets back to its Hebrew roots, but reflects a world that has moved on into the Hellenistic perspective that spread over the whole world after the conquests of Alexander the Great four centuries before Paul. Woven through this as well was the Zoroastrian apocalypticism that came back from Babylon with the returning Jewish exiles. Thus, except for the Gospel of John, the NT is largely caught up in a mind-set in which evil is the product of the flawed or inferior nature of the material world. This is reflected in the physical nature of the human body with its fleshly drives. Thus evil is some other force than the real human person, but it works within the person, causing wreckage within that person and in society. Humans can rise above this by sheer force of will, but cannot eliminate evil. Only the radical act of divine grace can do so. In the NT, only Paul in his better moments (Rom 8) and the author of the Gospel of John really saw this clearly. Even so, Paul remained enmeshed in the unresolvable perplexities of his psychological, theological, and spiritual splitting. John transcends this perplexity.

One of the large background problems regarding how the entire Bible handles the problem of evil is the frequent temptation to link and confuse suffering with evil. This has been the human proclivity throughout history. However, to identify human suffering as evil is to resort to a kind of human imperialism that assumes that human life is supposed to be comfortable and if it is not, that raises a question about God's goodness. This is absurd. Obviously this world is created as a matrix of total freedom with the specific purpose that everything is designed for growth. Growth inevitably brings change. Change inevitably brings the pain of loss of the old and adjustment to the new. This pain inevitably brings suffering.

Additionally, freedom means experimentation, chance, errors, accidents, and bad choices. This is true on the cellular level, and so cancers arise. It is true on the genetic level, so some of us are born with a proclivity to heart disease. It is true on the level of life forms everywhere in the food chain of existence. It is true on the level of humans in relationship to our selves and each other. In a free world of individuals questing for growth and meaning, interests on the part of each will not always be mutual interests. Thus conflict is built into creation, and how we resolve it is dependent upon how well we are motivated to care about *shalom* (Feikens, 2001).

The Bible, in neither the OT nor the NT, has a satisfactory biblical theological resolution of the problem of evil or the problem of pain. In the end, Paul gasps that he is persuaded in the face of everything that neither evil derived from some rebellion in heaven, nor evil derived from the unresolvable problem within our own natures, nor evil as the product of willful destructive choices can stand against God's ultimate triumph of grace. He declares in Romans 8:37–39,

> In all these things we are more than conquerors through him who loved us. For I am persuaded that neither death nor life, neither angels nor constituent structures of the creation nor divine decrees, neither things present nor things to come, nor things from above [bad angels] nor things from below [demons or the devil within us], nor anything else in all creation will be able to separate us from the love of God that is in Jesus Christ our Lord.

The author of John's Gospel would resoundingly agree. They never quite got the problem figured out, but they surely found the solution.

REFERENCES

Armstrong, A. H. (1974). Plotinus and Neo-Platonism. S.v. in *Encyclopaedia Britannica, Macropaedia* (Vol. 14, p. 541). Chicago: Helen Hemingway Benton.

Feikens, J. (2001). Conflict: Its resolution and the completion of creation. In *Seeking understanding: The Stob lectures 1986–1998* (pp. 343–372). Grand Rapids, MI: Eerdmans.

CHAPTER 12

THE THEOLOGIAN AS DIAGNOSTICIAN: JEFFREY DAHMER AND (D)EVIL AS A THEOLOGICAL DIAGNOSIS

Nathan Carlin

Nevertheless, in some of these perversions the quality of the new sexual aim is of a kind to demand special examination. Certain of them are so far removed from the normal in their content that we cannot avoid pronouncing them "pathological." This is especially so where (as, for instance, in cases of licking excrement or of intercourse with dead bodies) the sexual instinct goes to astonishing lengths in successfully overriding the resistances of shame, disgust, horror or pain. But even in such cases we should not be too ready to assume that people who act in this way will necessarily turn out to be insane.

—Sigmund Freud, (1905, p. 161)

INTRODUCTION

There are certain persons whom one must deal with when defining evil, or when giving an account of the history and development of evil—what, in other words, volume 1 of this work sets out to do. One historically recent example would be Jeffrey Dahmer. According to his lawyer, Dahmer believed that he was the devil (Boyle, 2003). And there is reason to believe Dahmer. Indeed, he was one of the most brutal serial killers in history, admitting to murdering 17 boys and men. Although there are others on record as having committed more actual murders (Donald Leroy Evans, for example, claims to have murdered some 60 people), it is not so much the number of Dahmer's victims that lends credence to his claims of devilry (Davis, 1991, p. 169), but, rather, it is the graphic nature in which Dahmer described his sexuality, his necrophilia (which involved having anal intercourse and engaging in fellatio with dead bodies), his cannibalism, his enjoyment of ritually dismembering human corpses, and his masturbation on severed heads and with internal organs that confirms for most everyone that Dahmer was in fact evil.

If all of these heinous acts were not enough, the fact that he would call the families of his victims—announcing to them that he had killed their loved ones or pretending to be their loved ones, saying things like "Help me, Help me, Help me!" (Davis, 1991, pp. 111–112, 120)—should convince any doubters, as should the fact that he would perform a number of lobotomies on his unconscious victims in an attempt to create human zombies so that he could have a permanent sexual partner whom he could completely control. There is also the firsthand experience of Tracy Edwards, the man who escaped and brought Dahmer to the attention of the police, who said, "It was like I was confronting Satan himself" (quoted in Ratcliff, 2006, p. 41). And then, too, there was the fact that Dahmer had plans to build a "power center" in his apartment out of human skeletons (O'Meara, 2009, p. 47). There is indeed reason to believe Dahmer's claims to be the devil, and I suggest that we take the claims of this expert witness—that is, Dahmer's own testimony—seriously.

THE ARGUMENT AND LAYOUT OF THIS CHAPTER

In *The Minister as Diagnostician*, Paul Pruyser (1976) argued that pastors have a special body of knowledge, just like every other profession, and that pastors ought not to give up their tradition and their language when they are dealing with cases and problems that, in recent years, have been taken up by other professions, such as psychiatry. In this book, Pruyser did not attempt to integrate pastoral theology and clinical psychiatry, but, rather, he wanted to bring them into "thoughtful apposition" (p. 17). This chapter, as the title suggests, follows in Pruyser's tradition, and I suggest that the theologian, like the minister, has diagnostic tools as well. Recently I have used psychology to diagnose God both with melancholia and with gender confusion (Carlin, 2009, 2010); here I use theology—specifically, Origen's (1973) *On First Principles* and a contemporary interpretation of the deadly sins tradition (Capps, 2000)—to diagnose Dahmer as a devil.

No theologian, as far as I am aware, has addressed the topic of evil as it might apply to Dahmer. This is curious because virtually every commentator raises the issue of evil when discussing Dahmer (see, e.g., Bauman, 1991; Davis, 1991; Jaeger & Balousek, 1991; Schwartz, 1992; Tithecott, 1997). I argue that a theological diagnosis deepens the psychological diagnosis of Dahmer, though I am not suggesting that theology ought to replace psychology—the task is, as Pruyser put it, apposition, not integration.

This chapter is divided into three basic parts. The first part provides the reader with an overview of the life and crimes of Dahmer, and I draw on the major journalistic accounts about Dahmer, Lionel Dahmer's account of his son's life, and scholarly literature on Dahmer. The second part of this chapter deals with the clinical literature on Dahmer, and the third part offers my theological diagnosis of Dahmer.

BACKGROUND INFORMATION

Jeffrey Dahmer was born on May 21, 1960, to Lionel and Joyce Dahmer. He grew up in Bath Township, Ohio. Dahmer seems to have had a relatively normal childhood—nothing to suggest that this boy would become a mass murderer. Indeed, Richard Tithecott (1997) described Dahmer as a "white boy with a privileged background, from an industrious, well-educated family" (p. 69). "So many of us wanted to believe that something had traumatized little Jeffrey Dahmer," Schwartz (1992) wrote, "otherwise we must believe that some of us give birth to monsters" (p. 39).

Yet, in retrospect, there has been some material for journalists and psychologists to contemplate. Ann Schwartz (1992) noted that Dahmer's first grade teacher wrote on his report card that he seemed to feel "neglected" (p. 38). This was just months after his younger brother, David, was born. Dahmer's father also claimed that Dahmer was sexually abused by a neighbor at the age of 8, though Dahmer denied this, and the claim was never substantiated. In elementary school, Dahmer became interested in chemistry—his father was a chemist—and he played with chemistry sets. As a boy, he began experimenting on insects, and, when he got older, he began experimenting on dead animals. Lionel also remembers a time when Dahmer played "fiddle sticks" with the bones of a dead animal. His father wrote,

> In the last few years, I have often thought of my son as he looked that afternoon, his small hands dug deep into a pile of bones. I can no longer view it simply as a childish episode, a passing fascination. It may have been nothing more than that, but now I have to see it in a different way, in a more sinister and macabre light. (Dahmer, 1995, p. 53)

In retrospect, one can impose impending doom, and perhaps we are compelled to do so, despite the fact that many children go through similar experiences and have similar fascinations but do not grow up to be mass murderers.

Dahmer's father, as a chemist, was somewhat distant from the family. Dahmer's mother suffered from anxiety and depression. And they did not have a loving marriage. In the second half of the 1970s, things became very heated between them, and they divorced in 1978. Lionel Dahmer remarried the same year on Christmas Eve to Shari Shinn Jordan. All of this, to be sure, was very hard on young Dahmer, and, as a teenager, he would often go out into the woods hitting trees to express his anger. He also became an alcoholic.

Dahmer attended Revere High School. He took up a number of extra-curricular activities: He played the clarinet for a year, he played tennis for a few years, and he worked on the school newspaper for a year. Most of his high school friends noticed that something was off about Dahmer—that he liked dead animals, that he was a loner, and that he drank heavily—but, in any case, he seemed to be well liked because of his humor and pranks. In the 1978 Revere High School yearbook, for example, Schwartz (1992) noted that "Dahmer showed up for the National Honors Society photo even though he was not a member. His face was blocked out before the books went to press" (p. 41). One day Dahmer would have his revenge: His face would appear in hundreds of newspapers, which could not be blotted out because of his own literal blotting out of faces.

Dahmer bounced around a bit after he graduated from high school in 1978. He attended Ohio State University for one semester the following fall. But he dropped out after one semester because of poor grades, which were likely the result of his heavy drinking. On December 29, 1978, Dahmer joined the U.S. Army. He signed up for 3 years. He trained as a medical specialist, and he held a post in Baumholder, Germany. In 1981, just months before fulfilling his contract, he was discharged from the army on account of his drinking. He moved to Florida for a little while, but he eventually moved in with his paternal grandmother, Catherine Dahmer, in West Allis, Wisconsin.

Once Dahmer moved to Wisconsin, his life slowly came apart over the period of a decade. Although Dahmer committed his first murder in 1978—shortly after his high school graduation and shortly before his parents' divorce became final—he did not kill again until 1987. He would kill two times in 1988, one time in 1989, four times in 1990, and eight times in 1991. His killing became considerably more frequent after 1988 because he moved into his own apartment then: in the now infamous Oxford Apartments, formerly on 924 North Twenty-Fifth Street in Milwaukee.

One exception to this downward spiral is the fact that, in 1985, Dahmer took a job at Ambrosia Chocolate Company in Milwaukee. Although Dahmer was not able to stay in school or in the army, or to hold down any other job, he was able to work at the chocolate factory. He made a considerable amount of money for a bachelor, and he received a number of raises over the years. His former boss noted,

[H]e had no problems with Dahmer whom he described as "polite." "He was quiet. He had no problems reacting with others." Further, his boss thought Dahmer did "a satisfactory job." One of the facts that came out at trial was that Dahmer was able to mix almost five hundred distinct choco-late recipes during his time there, indicating his ability to perform and be paid for complex tasks. (O'Meara, 2009, p. 50)

This success at the chocolate factory enabled Dahmer to buy drinks for men on the weekends and to offer boys money for posing nude in his apartment. The expendable income also enabled him to buy tools to dismember bodies—saws to cut up bones and drums of acid to take flesh off of bodies.

Dahmer had a couple of run-ins with the police—both involving sexual behavior with minors. In 1982, Dahmer was charged with indecent exposure at the Wisconsin State Fair. In 1988, he was arrested for molesting a 13-year-old boy. He was sentenced to 5 years probation and 1 year in work-release program, though he was released 2 months early from work release program on account of good behavior. His next major interaction with the police occurred on May 27, 1991, involving yet another minor. This episode will be discussed in detail below. Dahmer was finally arrested for murder on July 22, 1991—he had lost his job at the chocolate factory about a week before this—and his trial began in Milwaukee on January 22, 1992.

THE MURDERS

There are two murders, and an attempted murder, that are most commonly discussed with regard to the 17 murders that Dahmer committed. They include his first murder; a murder in which Dahmer should have been caught; and the attempted murder in which Dahmer was caught.

He committed his first murder in 1978, shortly after his high school graduation. He picked up 18-year-old Steven Hicks, who was hitchhiking his way back from a music concert. Dahmer suggested that they go back to his parents' house to party, and Hicks agreed. Dahmer said that they had an enjoyable evening, but when Hicks said that he wanted to go—he was trying to make it back home for his father's birthday—Dahmer struck Hicks on the head with a barbell and strangled him to death in front of the bookshelves in the den. He dismembered the body with a large knife, peeled the flesh off of the bones, and smashed the skeleton into pieces with a sledgehammer. He eventually scattered the parts around town, leaving some parts in his own backyard (Davis, 1991, pp. 37–43). Hicks's parents filed a missing persons report, but the case went unsolved until Dahmer confessed to the murder years later. The forensic evidence matched Dahmer's story, despite the fact that the details of Dahmer's story changed a number of times (O'Meara, 2009).

On May 27, 1991, a 14-year-old boy, Konerak Sinthasomphone, lost his life at the hands of Dahmer. This murder constitutes the second murder that is universally discussed when talking about Dahmer's murders. Ironically and tragically, Sinthasomphone's older brother also suffered at the hands of Dahmer a few years earlier. In 1988, Dahmer lured this boy into his apartment by offering him $50 to take nude pictures of the then 13-year-old boy. The boy ran away and told the police, and Dahmer was arrested.

In 1991, Dahmer lured Sinthasomphone into his apartment, apparently with the same kind of technique that he used on his older brother. He drugged the boy, as he normally did to his victims. Sinthasomphone passed out, and, while he was unconscious, Dahmer raped him. Afterward, Dahmer went out to buy some beer. While he was away, Sinthasomphone, naked and traumatized, escaped from the apartment. Because he was drugged and traumatized, Sinthasomphone was having trouble walking and talking. But he eventually stumbled upon two young women: Nicole Childress and Sandra Smith. Dahmer was only a little ways behind, and he spotted the three and attempted to take back the boy.

The young women would not let him take Sinthasomphone, and they called 911. Within minutes, police officers and firefighters were there. They covered Sinthasomphone, who was bleeding from the rape, with a blanket. The police wanted this situation to be handled quietly, so they escorted Dahmer and Sinthasomphone back to Dahmer's apartment, against the wishes of the young women. Dahmer, being calm and respectful, convinced the police officers that he and Sinthasomphone were lovers, that Sinthasomphone is much older than he looks, that they had had drunken fights like this before, that they were sorry, and that this would never happen again. Sinthasomphone surely was horrified about what was transpiring before his eyes, but he was unable to speak because of the trauma and the drugs. The police left the boy with Dahmer, and Dahmer strangled him. Dahmer would kill five more times after this.

When these details about the case came out after the fact, tensions rose in Milwaukee concerning racism and homophobia. If, many citizens reasoned, a *black* man were trying to take a *white* boy back to his apartment after the police were called, the police would have been much more thorough. They would have run background checks. If they had, they would have discovered that Sinthasomphone was only 14 and that Dahmer had been convicted of second-degree sexual assault on a minor. Put simply, Sinthasomphone's life would have been spared.

Two other factors about this incident made the Milwaukee Police Department look very unprofessional and incompetent. The first was that, after returning Sinthasomphone to Dahmer, the police made jokes on the radio about the affair. Davis (1991) relayed the recording:

"Intoxicated Asian, naked male, was returned to his boyfriend." On a tape recording of the call, laughter was audible. "My partner is going to get deloused at the station," the reporting officer said. There was more laughter. (p. 12)

Another embarrassing incident for the police involved Glenda Cleveland, the mother of Sandra Smith and aunt of Nicole Childress—the two young women who found Sinthasomphone naked. After Sinthasomphone was returned to

Dahmer, the young women went to Cleveland's house and told her what had happened. Cleveland then called 911 to find out what was going on. She was eventually transferred to the Milwaukee Police Department. She even spoke with a police officer who was at the scene. The phone call was recorded:

Officer:	It was an intoxicated boyfriend of another boyfriend.
Cleveland:	Well, how old was this child?
Officer:	It wasn't a child. It was an adult.
Cleveland:	Are you sure?
Officer:	Yup.
Cleveland:	Are you positive? Because this child doesn't even speak English. My daughter has dealt with him before, seen him on the street, you know.
Officer:	Yeah. No, uh, he's uh, he's. . . [i]t's all taken care of, Ma'am.
Cleveland:	Isn't this . . . I mean, what if he's a child and not an adult? I mean, are you positive this is an adult?
Officer:	Ma'am. Ma'am. Like I explained to you, it's as positive as I can be.
Cleveland:	Oh. I see.
Officer:	I can't do anything about someone's sexual preferences in life, and if . . .
Cleveland:	Well, no, I'm not saying anything about that, but it appeared to have been a child, this is why. . .
Officer:	No.
Cleveland:	No?
Officer:	No, he's not. (Davis, 1991, pp. 50–51)

A few days later, a missing persons report appeared in the newspaper regarding Sinthasomphone. Cleveland next phoned the FBI. The FBI got in touch with the Milwaukee Police Department, and Davis wrote that "since no evidence existed that a federal crime had been committed, [they decided] the local authorities should handle the matter" (p. 51).

As it turned out, Cleveland's efforts, as noble as they were, still would not have made a difference. Davis wrote, "Dahmer, in discussing the matter, told investigators that as soon as the door closed and the three police officers walked back downstairs, he had strangled the drugged Laotian boy until he was dead" (p. 52). Davis continued, "Dahmer said he then had sex with the corpse, took some photographs to add to his horrible collection, and began the long process of dismembering the body. As a trophy, he chose to keep the teenager's skull" (p. 52).

The only man to have escaped Dahmer is Tracy Edwards. Edwards offered, then, the only firsthand account of what Dahmer was like in his murderous rage. Richard Jaeger and William Balousek (1991) offered a summary of Edwards's account. They noted that Dahmer approached Edwards and Edwards's friend—Jeffrey Stevens—in the Grand Avenue Mall, asking them if they wanted to come over to party. Stevens actually recognized Dahmer because they lived in the same neighborhood. Edwards went back to Dahmer's apartment. Dahmer gave Stevens, who was going to pick up some other people for the party, the wrong address—one of Dahmer's standard tricks. Edwards had no idea he was walking into a trap.

When they got back to Dahmer's apartment, Edwards said, "It smells like somebody died in here" (Jaeger & Balousek, 1991, p. 110). Dahmer chuckled and explained, "It's a problem with the sewer" (p. 110). They went into the living room, which was spotless, and they had a few beers. They talked for a while, mostly about Chicago. But then the smell was really getting to Edwards, and he began to wonder where the others were. He said to Dahmer that they should leave and find out what happened to the others. Dahmer instead made him another drink, this one with his special potion, and he told him to take a look at the fish tank. Dahmer said he liked the fish because one of them would eat the others. As Edwards was looking at the tank, Dahmer placed a handcuff on Edwards, and he pulled out a knife, saying, "Do exactly what I tell you" (p. 111).

Dahmer took Edwards back to his bedroom and turned on the movie *The Exorcist III*—Dahmer's favorite movie (Dahmer also liked the *Star Wars* movies, as he identified with the evil Emperor in the movie and even purchased yellow contact lenses to have the same eye color as the Emperor for his nights out on the town). Dahmer made Edwards sit on the bed, and he pulled out a human head from a filing cabinet, saying, "This is how I get people to stay with me. . . . You'll stay with me" (p. 111). Edwards was shocked and horrified, and he was very drowsy, struggling to stay awake, but he knew that he had to or else he would die. Dahmer also taunted Edwards by showing him a pair of human hands hanging in the closet. Dahmer eventually tried to get the other handcuff on Edwards, but he was unable to do so. After some wrestling, Edwards managed to overpower Dahmer—Dahmer was going in and out of trance states every fifteen minutes or so, Edwards testified, and Edwards punched Dahmer when he was in one of these odd states, enabling him to escape. Edwards stumbled out into the street to search for the police. He found them, led the police to Dahmer's apartment, and Dahmer was arrested. It was finally over; Dahmer would never murder again.

WAS DAHMER SICK OR EVIL—OR BOTH?

In the literature on Dahmer, there has been a considerable amount of discussion over whether Dahmer was sick or evil—or both. This framing of the discussion derives from Dahmer's own words. At the close of the trial, he said,

> Your honor, it is over now. This has never been a case of trying to get free. I didn't ever want freedom. Frankly, I wanted death for myself. This was a

case to tell the world that I did what I did not for reasons of hate. I hated no one. I knew I was sick or evil or both. Now I believe I was sick. The doctors told me about my sickness, and now I have some peace. (Quoted in Schwartz, 1992, pp. 216–217)

Before the trial, it seems that Dahmer was leaning toward being evil, rather than being sick. In a statement to the police, Dahmer said that "I have to question whether there is an evil force in the world and whether or not I have been influenced by it" (quoted in Tithecott, 1997, p. 20). He went on, "Although I am not sure if there is a God, or if there is a devil, I know as of lately I've been doing a lot of thinking about both, and I have to wonder what has influenced me in my life" (p. 20). What is interesting is that Dahmer is offering two kinds of subtle rationalizations for his crimes here: If he were sick, then, in some sense, he is not fully accountable for his crimes, and if he were evil, this would have been on account of the fact that some evil force (perhaps the devil himself) made him do it—or at least considerably influenced him and, therefore, deserves at least some of the blame.

After the trial, and after he was baptized in prison, Dahmer retrospectively interpreted his crimes in a religious light:

If a person doesn't think that there is a God to be accountable to, then what's the point of trying to modify your behavior to keep it within acceptable ranges? That's how I thought anyway. I always believed the theory of evolution as truth, that we all just came from the slime. When we died, you know, that was it, there is nothing, and I've since come to believe that the Lord Jesus Christ is truly God, and I believe that I, as well as everyone else, will be accountable to Him. (Quoted in Ratcliff, 2006, p. 55)

Here Dahmer shifts some of the blame to evolution—what Dahmer came to see as a faulty worldview. This subtle rationalization is not so much about being sick or evil, but simply about being mistaken. It is as though Dahmer accounted for his actions by saying to himself, "If I had only known that evolution was incorrect, then I would not have committed these crimes." Roy Ratcliff, Dahmer's pastor, seemed to agree with this interpretation, and he may have encouraged Dahmer in this regard. Ratcliff (2006) wrote,

I think it is faith in God that makes us care about others. When God is ignored, and we live our lives as if He doesn't exist, there is a profound effect on our actions and psyche. This is not to say that all atheists become murderers, but it is to say that not believing in God allows us to justify the most evil treatment of other people. (pp. 157–158)

This, of course, has a ring of truth to it, but *believing* in God *also* allows many to justify the most evil treatment of other people (cf. Pagels, 1996).

Dahmer, then, offered three subtle defenses or rationalizations of his crimes: (a) He was sick (mentally ill), (b) he was influenced by evil forces, and (c) he held a mistaken worldview (evolution). I will focus on the question of evil in this chapter, but first I want to focus on the issue of mental illness.

PSYCHOLOGICAL DIAGNOSIS

Dahmer has been given a number of psychiatric diagnoses. George Palermo, a psychiatrist who worked on Dahmer's trial, diagnosed Dahmer for the court as "having a mixed personality disorder with sadistic, obsessive, fetishistic, anti-social, necrophilic features, typical of what has been called the organized, nonsocial, lust murderer" (Jentzen et al., 1994, p. 291). Martens and Palermo (2005) later stressed that loneliness contributed to Dahmer's antisocial personality disorder; however, Silva, Ferrari, and Leong (2002) noted that, although many clinical experts agree that Dahmer had antisocial tendencies, there is widespread agreement that he did not have a full-blown disorder (p. 1355). Silva et al. (2002) argued that Dahmer suffered from Asperger's syndrome. These authors also noted that a case could be made for Dahmer as having schizoid personality disorder or a personality disorder not otherwise specified with schizoid and schizotypal traits (Silva et al., 2002, p. 1355).

Dahmer's father thought that he suffered from shyness or social phobia (Silva et al., 2002, p. 1348). Jeffrey Jentzen, George Palermo, Thomas Johnson, Khang-Cheng Ho, Alan Stormo, and John Teggatz (1994), forensic experts involved with the Dahmer case, characterized Dahmer's psychiatric problems as "destructive hostility." Judith Becker suggested that Dahmer's necrophilia was the central issue that led him to kill as he did (O'Meara, 2009, p. 45). Others, however, have doubted Becker's argument because Dahmer seemed to have preferred live sexual partners—he was, after all, trying to create a zombie (O'Meara, 2009). Dahmer also had severe drinking problems, and he was treated for depression (Davis, 1991).

Here I want to present two of these diagnoses; there is simply not space to review all of these arguments. The first that I want to present is the diagnosis of the forensic team, because these experts had the most and closest access to Dahmer. I also want to present Silva et al.'s (2002) diagnosis because it is the most recent clinical article, and, furthermore, these articles contrast quite nicely in terms of methodological approach.

Jentzen et al. (1994) offered a psychoanalytic explanation for Dahmer's behavior. The bulk of the article discusses the forensic evidence of the case, but the article also discusses the emotion of hostility. The authors suggested that hostility is "the common emotion behind any violent criminal act," and that, among those who commit violent criminal acts, "one may find feelings of dependence, passivity, helplessness, a need to be loved frustrated in childhood, or a wish to control or dominate—a reaction formation against dependency and passivity" (p. 283). They also noted that one may find the fear of abandonment, avoidance of close relationships, and sudden bursts of aggression toward persons for whom they feel ambivalence. "Some hostile, aggressive people," they wrote, "go through a life of neurotic, repetitive behavior, trying to avoid fantasized or real injuries to the ego" (p. 283).

Jentzen et al. (1994) suggested that "[a]ggressive, violent individuals may feel engulfed by a world that they sense to be hostile," and "[t]herefore, their hostile conduct *has a primary unconscious aim[:] the end of any possible fusion with people* around them and the reaffirmation of a distinction between the self and others" (p. 284, italics in original). These persons hate their loneliness but nevertheless engineer it themselves. "Their explosive or often programmed methodical, violent conduct," they wrote,

> could be seen as a recurrent, neurotic, repetitive behavior that channeled into what can be thought of as a primary instinct of aggression, and short of incorporating and fusing with the loved person, destroys it on the altar of ambivalence, driven by repressed hostility accumulated through years of injury to the ego. (p. 284)

These authors suggested that Dahmer's ambivalent sexuality expressed itself in sadism because he expected to be rejected (p. 288). They wrote,

> His destructive behavior and his fetishistic memorabilia are an obvious expression of his deep ambivalence about his own homosexual behavior, and his profound mixed hostility and love toward the objects of his interest. Regardless of his expressed loving feelings for them, his victims were not treated as persons but as objects that he disposed of as a child does with his toys, taking them apart to see what makes them the way they are, taking them apart to show who was in power and in control, and possibly unconsciously that he was not always the passive, dependent individual he feared himself to be. (p. 289)

They argued that "[o]ne explanation for his abhorrent conduct is that he was driven by a compulsive hostile aggressivity and that his violence was so profound as to cause him to kill, cut, dismember, and dissect in an obsessive, sadistic way" (p. 290). He did this, perhaps, "to get rid of his inner emotional torture and unwanted attraction" (p. 290). These actions, they suggested, actually could have prevented Dahmer from committing suicide: "His sadism could be viewed as the exercising of power and violence upon another for self-assertion and self-preservation" (p. 291).

The upshot of this article, then, is that these authors believed that Dahmer's basic problem was primary unconscious feelings of hate that were channeled into sadistic sexuality. There are, however, a couple of problems with this interpretation. The first is that this view does not square with Dahmer's own self-understanding, as Dahmer said in his closing statement to the court: "This was a case to tell the world that I did what I did, not for reasons of hate. I hated no one" (quoted in Schwartz, 1992, pp. 216–217). It is possible, of course, that Dahmer simply was not conscious of his feelings of hate—the authors, after all, argued for primary *unconscious* feelings of hate—but this nevertheless remains a problem, leaving the interpretation to seem forced. Another problem with the interpretation is that Dahmer's sexuality seemed to have less to do with violence or aggression than it did with control. He was, after all, trying to create a zombie so that he would not have to go through the violent act of killing again, and, as he stated numerous times, he disliked killing and needed to be drunk in order to do so (cf. Phillips, 2006). The chief contribution of this article, which I take to be accurate and insightful, is that Dahmer craved intimacy but nevertheless found it threatening and therefore engineered his own loneliness—a genuine expression of ambivalence.

In "The Case of Jeffrey Dahmer: Sexual Serial Homicide From a Neuropsychiatric Developmental Perspective," J. Arturo Silva, Michelle Ferrari, and Gregory Leong (2002) took another approach, one rooted in *The Diagnostic and Statistical Manual of Mental Disorders* (DSM-IV-TR). They argued that Dahmer suffered from Asperger's disorder. They listed the criteria for Asperger's disorder from the DSM-IV-TR, and they offered the following evidence from Dahmer's life, all of which is congruent with the DSM-IV-TR criteria for the Asperger's diagnosis:

- Dahmer, from an early age and throughout his life, had troubled social interactions.
- Dahmer demonstrated awkward body kinetics.
- Dahmer demonstrated repetitive and eccentric interests.
- These characteristics presented themselves from about age 3.

The authors also noted some exclusionary criteria for Asperger's disorder as well, criteria that also apply to Dahmer—namely, he did not have any language problems or delays; he had an average or even a high IQ; and he did not seem to have any pervasive developmental disorders, including schizophrenia.

Silva et al. (2002) were attempting to provide a general theory of sexual serial killing—they believed Asperger's disorder is often a common denominator—and they used Dahmer as a single case study to support this thesis. They suggested that the strength of their thesis—namely, that there is a connection between Asperger's disorder and sexual serial killing—is that it "provides a better explanation regarding the origin of sexual fantasy as an antecedent in serial killing behavior," and "that intrinsically [Asperger's disorder] tends to promote isolation, resulting in a relative inability to test fantasy formation against the backdrop of the surrounding social world" (p. 1351). They continued, "Arguably, the foremost advantage of the proposed pervasive developmental disorder paradigm for serial sexual killing behavior is that it may provide a central insight into the specific psychological causes for serial killing in association with specific underlying neurobiological events" (p. 1351).

In any case, whatever one makes of the thesis suggesting a correlation between Asperger's disorder and sexual serial killing, the diagnosis of Asperger's disorder does provide a compelling explanation for Dahmer's fetishistic sexuality. Silva et al. (2002) noted that one can often observe in persons with Asperger's disorder fetishistic behavior such as stamp collecting or eccentric interests like memorizing the names of persons who died on the *Titanic*. With Dahmer, this fetishistic behavior manifested itself in collecting animal bodies and, later, human cadavers. The upshot here is that Dahmer's problem was not fundamentally sexual, nor was it aggression or "destructive hostility." The fundamental issue, rather, was Asperger's disorder, which created for him certain social problems in life and also contributed to his need for control and his obsessive collecting.

Other developmental factors contributed to his sexuality, which merged with his Asperger's disorder tendencies. That is to say, his needs for control and collecting, which themselves were eccentric (e.g., a fascination with dead animals), became sexualized, and, further, because he was not able to form friendships or relationships, also on account of his Asperger's disorder, he turned to killing to satisfy both his sexual needs and his needs for control and collecting.

THEOLOGICAL DIAGNOSIS

Although I neither want to dispute the many psychological and psychiatric diagnoses listed in this chapter, nor do I want to weigh in on which diagnosis fits Dahmer the best, I do, however, want to offer a theological diagnosis. My theological diagnosis draws, as noted, from two sources: Origen's (1973) ontology and a contemporary interpretation of the deadly sins tradition (Capps, 2000). Although the deadly sins tradition continues to be seen as relevant—books continually are written about them (see, e.g., DeYoung, 2009)—Origen's ontology is something that has fallen by the wayside, as many of his ideas were disavowed by orthodox Christianity (cf. Pagels, 1996).

Recently, Donald Capps and I have rescued the concept of limbo from being left behind in the scrapheap of theological ideas (cf. Capps & Carlin, 2010), and here I do the same with regard to Origen. Origen's ontology provides a general framework for understanding evil, and the deadly sins tradition provides a contextual understanding of sin—taken together, these theological tools offer a compelling interpretation of Dahmer that deepens the psychological diagnoses.

ORIGEN'S ONTOLOGY

In the introduction to Origen's *On First Principles*, G. W. Butterworth (1973) noted that, despite the fact that many of Origen's (b. circa 185 CE) ideas have been discarded as heretical and misguided, "It never occurred to him that he was anything but an orthodox defender of the faith" (p. liii). Origen was simply marching into uncharted territory, asking questions that no one else had yet dealt with in a systematic way: How can suffering be accounted for, or evil? Why does the world exist? How are we saved? Will everyone be saved? Do human beings have free will?

Origen's system can be described as follows. In the beginning, there was God. God created a number of souls in a condition where they had free will— they could either travel closer to God or move away from God. All souls were equal, Butterworth noted, "and apparently identical" (p. lv). But some souls fell away, and, as they fell, they became heavier. Some souls became bright stars; other souls were not so bright. Some souls became even heavier and therefore required bodies so as to not fall into nonbeing. Butterworth wrote,

> In this way the various orders of angelic beings arose and below them the daemons; for all are of one original nature and ascend or descend in accordance with their own wills. From one class of these spirits the human race was constituted, and the qualities of each human soul and the environment into which it is born are due to its merits or demerits in previous existences. (p. lv)

This might be described as a Christian form of reincarnation. The value of this system is that it explains (a) the creation of the world, (b) the cause of suffering, and (c) how suffering might be overcome. The system is very dynamic, so much so that Jerome criticized it by stating that "according to Origen angels might become devils and the devil an archangel" (p. lvi).

Butterworth noted that this process could, logically speaking, continue indefinitely. However, Origen argued that eventually God would overcome the fall and that one day God would bring all souls back to Godself—Origen's system, then, was universalistic. And the means by which God the Father would accomplish this is through God the Son, who suffers for all. This system, though highly creative and rooted in scripture, came to be rejected by orthodox Christianity because it was highly pessimistic: Creation exists only because of the fall, and all of human history is, in some fundamental way, a mistake. It would be hard in this system to affirm the Jewish and Christian notion of the good creation (cf. Genesis 1). Other Christian traditions, such as those of Augustine and Calvin, also would have a problem with Origen's emphasis on free will. And, further, Origen's theology is fundamentally anti-body. As Origen (1973) himself wrote, "[F]or wherever bodies are, corruption follows immediately" (p. 247).

Despite fundamental flaws in Origen's theology, theologians, like scavengers, should nevertheless feel free to hunt and peck through his theology to grab and apply what seems to be useful and life giving. As Robert Dykstra (2005) put it, "[T]he pastoral theologian . . . must scavenge unapologetically, rummaging about resolutely in what others individually or collectively discard" (p. 9). And, in this case, this means scavenging through Origen's theology.

DAHMER AS FALLING AWAY

Despite the many possible critiques of Origen, I suggest that one of Origen's ideas is nevertheless still particularly useful—namely, his idea of the falling away of souls. If we take this idea out of context—both out of historical context and out of the original Christian context—we can apply it to life on this side of the grave and in our own culture. Origen described how souls fall away by means of an analogy. He noted that men who become skilled in certain areas, such as geometry or medicine, gain their skills over time with much practice. When they go to sleep at night, and afterward in the morning, they still have the same skills. "If, however, he loses interest in these exercises and neglects to work," Origen writes, "then through this negligence his knowledge is gradually lost, a few details at first, then more, and so on until after a long time the whole vanishes into oblivion and is utterly erased from his memory" (p. 40). This, too, is how souls fall away from God, Origen suggested: "All rational creatures who are incorporeal and invisible, if they become negligent, gradually sink to a lower level and take to themselves bodies suitable to the regions into which they descend" (pp. 40–41).

Origen, then, described a *process* of descending into evil: Some souls can fall so far that they can become devils or demons. This, I suggest as a theological diagnosis, is what happened to Dahmer—that is, he gradually descended during his life to become a devil. I do not mean this literally but, rather, existentially. The fact that he recognized himself as the devil is not a delusion but, rather, an expression of his existential condition. He gradually became more selfish, more disregarding of others, and, finally, more evil, as his world became increasingly more destructive, hostile, full of lies, and lonely. A biblical example of this can be observed in Jesus's own words, where he described Judas as a devil (John 6:70).

An unlikely place where one can observe Dahmer's progressive falling away involves, interestingly, his discomfort with passive anal intercourse. He reported that he had had passive anal intercourse only once or twice in his life, and that he experienced it as very uncomfortable. He preferred what he called "light sex," such as oral sex and mutual masturbation. When engaging in anal intercourse, what he called "heavy sex," he preferred to be active, that is, the one penetrating. His anxiety around "heavy sex," apparently because he was afraid of being expected to be on the receiving end of anal inter-course, seemed to have led him to have problems achieving erections in such situations. He needed his partner to be unconscious the vast majority of the time in order to achieve orgasm (cf. Dahmer, 1995, p. 220). Initially, Dahmer seemed to be satisfied masturbating with a male mannequin that he kept in his closet while he was living with his grandmother. But when his grandmother found the mannequin, she told his father, and he forced him to get rid of it. Dahmer's next solution to his anxiety concerning passive anal intercourse was to drug men in bathhouses, ensuring that sex would happen on his terms in the ways that he preferred. When the owner of a given bathhouse fig-ured out that Dahmer was drugging men, he was banned from the bathhouse (Davis, 1995, pp. 81–82). What he wanted was a body that he could control. So his next step, because he was no longer allowed in the bathhouse, was to take a man to a hotel room so that he could have more privacy. He did this, but he "accidentally" killed a man while doing this, and so, from this point on, he decided to take men back to his apartment, because it was too difficult and too risky to remove dead bodies from hotel rooms (Phillips, 2006).

One wonders if Dahmer's deviant behavior was directly connected to his anxiety concerning passive anal intercourse—if, in other words, he were able to be comfortable with passive anal intercourse, or if he were able to communicate his anxiety about this sexual act to other men, would he have needed unconscious or dead bodies in order to ejaculate? In any case, Dahmer's vari-ous strategies to avoid passive anal intercourse and his efforts to maintain control over his sexual interactions all failed: his masturbation with a man-nequin, his drugging of men in bathhouses, his drugging of men in hotel rooms, his murdering of boys and men in his apartment, and his attempts at creating a zombie.

My main point here is that Dahmer's killing over the years became more frequent—and, if Dahmer's account of his own deviance is to be believed (cf. O'Meara, 2009), he became more deviant in order to satisfy his sexual urges (he went from necrophilia to cannibalism to experimental lobotomies)—and that one can thus observe Dahmer falling away. It is not, however, that Dah-mer's urges became more deviant and that this deviance marks his falling away. It is, rather, his growing disregard for others—his objectification of the human body—and his need to have greater and greater control over others that mark his falling away. Perhaps an early step of his objectification of the human body was indicated by his choice of playing the clarinet as a boy, if the clarinet is viewed as a phallic symbol and if playing the instrument is viewed as a substitutionary form of fellatio. In any case, at some point it wasn't enough for him to have control of an unconscious body; he had to have a part of the body to keep forever. Next, it wasn't enough for him to just have a part of a body; it had to become a part of him by means of ingestion. And, finally, it wasn't enough to consume another; he had to have permanent control of a living human being in the form of a passive zombie. It was his lust for sexual control and literal objectification and complete disregard for others, I suggest, that led to his becoming a devil.

DAHMER'S DEADLY SIN: LUST FOR SEXUAL CONTROL

So far, I have used Origen to provide a theological framework for understanding how Dahmer fell and for how one might think about evil as a theological diagnosis with regard to Dahmer, and I have suggested that Dahmer's lust for sexual control contributed to his becoming a devil. I now want to turn to a contemporary discussion of the deadly sins tradition for insight into the particular nature of Dahmer's sin.

In *Deadly Sins and Saving Virtues*, Donald Capps (2000) defined sin as an orientation that is harmful in several ways: (a) to the human community, (b) to God's intentions for the world, and (c) to the individual (pp. 1–2). Capps wrote,

> By emphasizing that sin is an orientation to life, we avoid the suggestion that sin is purely a matter of action or behavior. Any orientation to life may range from a relatively permanent *disposition* to life, to an *attitude* that is relatively amenable to change, to a transitory *impulse*, which is the most unstable orientation of all. Actions issue from all three sorts of orientation. (p. 2)

Capps's main point of the book is to show that "the basic forms of the disposition to sin are directly related to the stages of the life cycle," and "thus, that dispositions to sin follow a developmental pattern or sequence" (pp. 2–3). The developmental theory that guides Capps's work is Erik Erikson's life cycle stages. Although Erikson's life cycle stages do seem to be relevant to Dahmer—the fact that Capps links lust to Erikson's intimacy versus isolation stage seems especially fruitful—I do not want to explore this theme here. Rather, what I want to convey here is Capps's analysis of sin, as this analysis can shed more light on the nature of Dahmer's fall.

Capps noted that the traditional deadly sins are pride, envy, anger, sloth, greed, gluttony, and lust. He also noted that other lists had eight deadly sins, with pride being the root of all sin, and that the logic was that the seven deadly sins followed from pride (melancholy, Capps pointed out, is the major sin that has been omitted from the traditional list of seven). Capps suggested that there may have been a couple of reasons that the list contained seven sins. One is that seven is a sacred number. Another reason is that there are seven days of the week, meaning that one could focus on resisting a particular sin each day. This means that lust, the seventh sin, would be Saturday's sin—the sin of the weekend. This seems strangely appropriate for Dahmer, as he committed his murders on the weekend because this was when he could pick up his victims in malls, bars, and bathhouses.

Capps located the deadly sin of lust in young adulthood, in Erikson's stage of intimacy versus isolation. This, too, fits with Dahmer, as he committed all of his murders during these years of his life. Capps described lust as "1) a desire to gratify the senses; 2) a sexual desire, often implying the desire for unrestrained gratification; or 3) an overmastering desire, as a lust for power" (p. 53). Dahmer's lust had all three of these qualities, especially as his lust manifested itself in rape. A major problem with lust is that often it becomes all consuming in terms of one's interests and activities, and, as Dahmer said himself in interviews, his life became obsessed with and ordered around his sexual killing—everything was done for the sake of lust (Phillips, 2006).

Capps described several major ways in which lust is particularly destructive. One is that, as Capps wrote, "Lust is an enemy of intimacy and is also a very destructive form of isolation" (p. 55). In lust, although one might be with another physically or sexually, one still remains separate emotionally and relationally, and, in this sense, *lust is a form of self-subjugation*, as one is all consumed with bodily pleasure but remains emotionally isolated. Dahmer's life was one of isolation without intimacy: He never had a romantic relationship, and he had no close friendships. He replaced love with lust and intimacy with isolation—he was self-subjugated by his desires. Another major way that lust is destructive is that, as Capps pointed out, *lust disregards others* (p. 56). This disregard for others can easily and disturbingly be observed in Dahmer's exploitation of and cruelty toward others, as he literally reduced others to objects such as food and decorations. Still another way that lust is destructive is that *lust is socially irresponsible*. Capps wrote, "The major difficulty with lust from the social point of view is that it inhibits our capacity to perform our social roles and to carry out our social responsibilities" (p. 54). Dahmer, of course, was extremely socially destructive, neglecting virtually all of his social responsibilities. Indeed, he was able to perform only one socially responsible activity—namely, his work at the chocolate factory. But even here, this social task was carried out for the sake of enabling his lust; that is, he maintained a job so that he could afford rent (so as to have a place to commit his murders and have sex) and so that he could have expendable income (so as to have a means to lure boys and men into his apartment by, for example, offering them money to pose nude for cash).

Origen's notion of falling away provides a framework for understanding how Dahmer could become evil, and even how he could become a devil, and

Capps's articulation of the deadly sins tradition provides insight into the particular way that Dahmer fell away: lust. Capps, as noted, described sin as an orientation to life, not merely as an action or a behavior. Impulses can become attitudes, attitudes can become dispositions, and actions and behaviors derive from all three of these orientations (Capps, 2000, p. 2). Combining Origen's and Capps's perspectives, then, Dahmer can be seen as first acting on an impulse, but, over time, he began to act out of an evil attitude, which justified his actions, and then an evil disposition, which consumed his life, and this disposition toward a lust for sexual control marked his falling away.

TWO CRITIQUES OF EVIL DISCOURSE

Some intellectuals are resistant to calling Dahmer evil, and for good reasons. Maier (1991), for example, was critical of the fact that someone such as "Dahmer can be perceived as Satan, or a devil, and left at that, be cast out of humanity as bad, or worse, mad and bad" (p. 204). He suggested that this tendency derives from what he considers to be a mistake in Western theology—namely, the separation of good and evil in God. Maier wrote that "the satanic side of God has been cast into the shadow of the unconscious where it erupts into existence randomly because we do not know how to celebrate the two sides of God" (p. 206). He continued, "For me, Dahmer has been a reminder that I need to become more responsible for the parts of myself that live in my shadow, waiting for the right external circumstances to emerge" (p. 206). "[T]he criminal mind," he suggested, "is not some exotic distortion, but my everyday mind and your everyday mind. It is this identification that can help prevent the doubling process from taking grotesque proportions" (p. 206). Maier's point, then, is that we ought not to separate Dahmer from ourselves, and that we, too, are like Dahmer or could become Dahmer. This perspective is grounded in psychiatry and psychoanalysis, particularly in the thought of Carl G. Jung (1969).

Tithecott (1997), too, was critical of the rhetoric of evil surrounding Dahmer, though his critique was grounded in a Foucauldian perspective. The discourse of evil, Tithecott suggested, surrounds Dahmer because "[t]he horror evoked is beyond the reach of psychiatry, [and] is indicative of a madness which cannot be treated, and consequently imprisonment or execution (as opposed to hospitalization) are perceived as the state's only suitable response" (p. 15). Dahmer or other such serial killers, courts so often conclude, may have this or that psychological disorder, but, whatever the diagnosis, the perpetrator is still figured as evil, because not everyone with the given disorder has committed such brutal actions. Tithecott continued, "Central to such discourses is the idea of evil, the widespread acceptance of which, I suggest, allows those who protect society from its monsters to once again assume an aura of priestly authority" (p. 15). Tithecott wanted to challenge the discourse of evil because, as Maier suggested, it tends to separate Dahmer from us, but Tithecott went further to point out that this separation often provides grounds for disciplining those whom we construct as serial killers. If they were merely "sick," they might be treatable, but if they are "evil," then they can be imprisoned or executed.

WHAT DOES A THEOLOGICAL DIAGNOSIS ADD?

These critiques of the discourse of evil are valuable, especially as they challenge the distinction between normal and abnormal. However, I think that we ought not to give up the theological category of evil, because without a theological diagnosis, our interpretations of Dahmer and other such individuals would remain too shallow. Psychological or other contextual interpretations never seem quite satisfying enough; the existential questions of why such evil exists and how any person could do such a thing still remain, because these are ultimately theological questions. It is as though we need the power of the language of myth and of religion to come to terms with such questions. As Pruyser (1976) wrote, "I believe that problem-laden persons who seek help from a pastor do so for very deep reasons—from the desire to look at themselves in a theological perspective" (p. 43). Dahmer himself raised the issue of theological diagnosis when he wondered if he were sick or evil or both, and, as noted, virtually every commentator has done so as well. Such horrible acts require us to ask theological questions—what do these acts *mean*, and where is *God* in all of this? And theologians, especially pastoral theologians, should not be afraid to offer these diagnoses, especially when society seems to be crying out for them, not unlike the problem-laden person who goes to see a pastor for help. And if theologians—those who are professionally trained to speak about God—do not offer such diagnoses, others in our society—most likely journalists—surely will offer such commentary to fill this collective need.

A theological diagnosis, I suggest, can add to various psychological or other diagnoses by helping to account for a wider range of data that are usually overlooked or regarded as unimportant. Dahmer, for example, believed that he was the devil. It is unclear whether he believed this literally, but, in any case, this point is rarely, if ever, taken seriously. Origen's thought would suggest that we take Dahmer's experience seriously, especially because he did not seem to be psychotic or delusional. Furthermore, the only eye-witness account that we have of Dahmer in the act of murdering comes from, as noted, Edwards, and he described Dahmer as "the devil" and as "a madman who intended 'to cut my heart out and eat it'" (Jaeger & Balousek, 1991, p. 17). This, perhaps, was a glimpse of Dahmer at his worst—at his "farthest" point away from God—after he had murdered 17 people and was attempting to murder Edwards.

Dahmer, as noted, has been widely regarded as evil by the general public and has been often described as Satan or the devil. This rhetoric describing Dahmer—and other serial killers—has been criticized, rightly, by some on the grounds that it separates the serial killer from normalcy. Origen's thought, however, would serve as a corrective here, placing Dahmer on a continuum—any one of us could become a devil. And Origen's thought would also contest the idea that Dahmer was evil "by nature" and would further suggest that there was and is hope for Dahmer—any one of us can rise again. That is, even when one becomes a devil, one is not condemned to being a devil forever, and, indeed, even the devil will be saved, according to Origen. Origen's thought, finally, allows us to take seriously the possibility of Dahmer's rehabilitation and his subsequent religious conversion in prison, though one cannot help but wonder if this conversion was Dahmer's final prank, a prank against God, a way to sneak into heaven like he snuck into the yearbook picture of the National Honors Society.

CONCLUSION

In the movie *Silence of the Lambs*, which was playing in theaters for the first time while Dahmer was on his killing spree, Hannibal Lecter, the serial killer and cannibal, reflected on his own violent behavior:

> Nothing happened to me, Officer Starling. *I* happened. You can't reduce me to a set of influences. You've given up good and evil for behaviorism, Officer Starling. You've got everybody in moral dignity pants—nothing is ever anybody's fault. Look at me, Officer Starling. Can you stand to say that I am evil? (Quoted in Tithecott, 1997, p. 136)

Interestingly, Dahmer made a similar claim in an interview: "The person to blame is the person sitting across from you. Not parents, not society, not pornography. These are just excuses" (Tithecott, 1997, p. 136).

In this chapter, I have made the case that we should in fact say that Dahmer was evil. I have argued for evil—specifically, Origen's conceptualization of falling away—as a category of theological diagnosis, and that the deadly sin of lust was the primary contributor to Dahmer's falling away. This theological diagnosis, following Pruyser (1976), is not meant to replace psychological diagnosis, but to deepen it. It does so by helping to answer Dahmer's own question of whether he was sick, evil, or both: The answer, I suggest, is *both.* Dahmer did have mental and emotional problems, but the court was right to give a ruling of sane to this man who would wear condoms when having sex with lifeless bodies and body parts, who would only pick up boys and men on the weekends so he had time to dismember them, and who would only target boys and men who did not have cars because it was hard enough to get rid of bodies, let alone cars. Freud, as the epigram for this chapter suggests, would have likely ruled the same as the court did in fact rule: sane, but obviously perverted.

Although, as I suggested above, there are good reasons for critiquing evil discourse, Origen's theology goes beyond these critiques by maintaining that Dahmer is not fundamentally different from us, even though he happened to become a devil and experienced himself as such. We should not let go of evil discourse, because these metaphors seem to be necessary to make sense of malevolence in more satisfying ways than psychology or other social sciences can offer. Indeed, as Carl Goldberg (1996) noted, "[T]he public tries to come to terms with malevolence through the media and popular books, perhaps because psychiatry and the behavioral sciences have failed to do so" (p. 2). It is as though the public needs to be able to say that Dahmer was evil so that the depth of underserved suffering can be recognized. The language of evil, which is theological, provides a framework for speaking about such suffering.

Lecter and Dahmer were evil. But, following Origen, this does not mean that they were *essentially* evil, only *accidentally* evil. And this does not mean that they were evil once and for all. What I am suggesting, following Origen and Capps, is that sins, particularly the deadly sins, can lead to a disposition toward evil, so much so that one can even become a devil. But there still is always hope for the devil and the worst of fallen souls. As Dahmer said in his closing statement to the court, quoting the Bible:

Christ Jesus came into the world to save sinners—of whom I am the worst. But for that very reason I was shown mercy so that in me, the worst of sinners, Christ Jesus might display his unlimited patience as an example for those who would believe on him and receive eternal life. (1 Timothy 1:15–16)

Perhaps Dahmer was genuine in this statement. Or perhaps, as a devil, he meant to taunt Christians with their own scriptures. Or maybe he had some other motive. In any case, this fallen soul never had the chance to commit his favorite deadly sins again, and, perhaps for this reason, one hopes that his soul traveled a little closer back to God.

ACKNOWLEDGMENTS

I would like to thank Kattie Basnett and Donald Capps for reading and commenting on previous drafts of this chapter, as well as Ryan White, who got me interested in the topic.

REFERENCES

Baumann, E. (1991). *Step into my parlor: The chilling story of serial killer Jeffrey Dahmer.* Chicago: Bonus.

Boyle, G. (2003, December 23). Interview with Court TV. Retrieved from http://
    news.findlaw.com/court_tv/s/20031223/23dec2003164734.html.

Butterworth, G. W. (1973) Introduction. In *On first principles* (pp. xxiii–lxi). New
    York: Peter Smith.

Capps, D. (2000). *Deadly sins and saving virtues.* Eugene, OR: Wipf & Stock.

Capps, D., & Carlin, N. (2010). *Living in limbo.* Eugene, OR: Cascade Books.

Carlin, N. (2009). God's melancholia. *Pastoral Psychology, 58* (2), 207–221.

Carlin, N. (2010). God's gender confusion: Some polymorphously perverse pastoral
    theology. *Pastoral Psychology, 59* (1), 101–124.

Dahmer, L. (1995). *A father's story: One man's anguish at confronting the evil in his son.*
    New York: Time Warner.

Davis, D. (1991). *The Jeffrey Dahmer story: An American nightmare.* New York: St.
    Martin's.

DeYoung, R. (2009). *Glittering vices: A new look at the seven deadly sins and their rem-
    edies.* Grand Rapids, MI: Brazos Press.

Dykstra, R. (2005). *Images of pastoral care: Classic readings.* St. Louis, MO: Chalice.

Freud, S. (2001). *Three essays on the theory of sexuality.* In J. Strachey, *The standard
    edition of the complete psychological works of Sigmund Freud* (Vol. 7, pp. 123–245).
    London: Vintage. (Original work published in 1905.)

Goldenberg, C. (1996). *Speaking with the devil: Exploring senseless acts of evil.* New
    York: Penguin.

Jaeger, R. W., & Balousek, M. W. (1991). *Massacre in Milwaukee: The macabre case of
    Jeffrey Dahmer.* Middleton: Waubesa Press.

Jentzen, J., Palermo, G., Johnson, L. T., Ho, K. C., Stormo, K. A., & Teggatz, J. (1994).
    Destructive hostility: The Jeffrey Dahmer case: A psychiatric and forensic study
    of a serial killer. *American Journal of Forensic Medical Pathology, 15* (4), 283–294.

Jung, C. G. (1969). *Answer to Job* (Trans. R. Hull). Princeton, NJ: Princeton Univer-
    sity Press. (Original work published in 1951)

Maier, G. (1991). Afterword. In R. Jaeger & W. Balousek (Eds.), *Massacre in Mil-
    waukee: The macabre case of Jeffrey Dahmer* (pp. 203–206). Middleton: Waubesa
    Press.

Martens, W. H. J., & Palermo, G. B. (2005). Loneliness and associated violent and
    antisocial behavior: Analysis of the case reports of Jeffrey Dahmer and Denis
    Nilsen. *International Journal of Offender Therapy and Comparative Criminology,
    49*(3), 289–307.

O'Meara, G. (2009). "He speaks not, yet he says everything; what of that?" Text, context,
    and pretext in *State v. Jeffrey Dahmer. Berkley Electronic Press.* Retrieved from http://
    works.bepress.com/cgi/viewcontent.cgi?article=1001&context=greg_omeara.

Origen. (1973). *On first principles.* New York: Peter Smith.

Pagels, E. (1996). *The origin of Satan.* New York: Vintage.

Phillips, S. (2006). Inside evil: Jeffrey Dahmer [Interview]. MSNBC. Retrieved from
    http://www.itunes.com.

Pruyser, P. W. (1976). *The minister as diagnostician: Personal problems in pastoral perspec-
    tive.* Louisville, KY: Westminster John Knox Press.

Ratcliff, R. (2006). *Dark journey, deep grace: Jeffrey Dahmer's story of faith.* Siloam
    Springs, AR: Leafwood.

Schwartz, A. E. (1992). *The man who could not kill enough: The secret murders of Milwaukee's Jeffrey Dahmer.* New York: Citadel.

Silva, J. A., Ferrari, M. M., & Leong, G. B. (2002). The case of Jeffrey Dahmer: Sexual serial homicide from a neuropsychiatric developmental perspective. *Journal of Forensic Sciences, 47* (6), 1347–1359.

Tithecott, R. (1997). *Of men and monsters: Jeffrey Dahmer and the construction of the serial killer.* Madison: University of Wisconsin Press.

CHAPTER 13

GNOSTICISM AND EVIL

Ronald Reese Ruark

One encounters few religious movements as fascinating as Gnosticism, a movement that flourished in the ancient Mediterranean in the second and third centuries CE. Gnosticism is a fascinating phenomenon because it illustrates the nature and dynamics of religion.[1] It is the quintessential religious movement, using god-talk to define itself, to locate itself in the world, to distinguish itself from competing religious movements, to assert itself socially, and to create new worlds.[2] The concept of evil that is so basic to Gnostic thought illustrates how socially expedient theology can be.

This chapter will concentrate on one particular Gnostic text, the Secret Gospel According to John (SBJ), also known as the Apocryphon of John. It is not dependent upon any theory of Gnostic organization, though it does assume that a social reality of some kind exists behind this particular religious text, as difficult as it might be to define it.[3] A conception of evil lurks in the background of many Gnostic texts, including SBJ. SBJ was a widely used Gnostic text that reflects a Gnostic worldview; it is therefore characterized as a "classic" Gnostic text.[4] As much as any other Gnostic text, it comprises a handbook of Gnostic theology. This makes it an ideal text for examining the Gnostic idea of evil, or at least one Gnostic idea of evil.

Our task is not simple, because any discussion of the concept of evil in ancient Gnosticism immediately presents three problems. First, Gnosticism is difficult to define, not only because it is a diverse movement[5] but also because the definition of Gnosticism usually depends upon a definition of "normative"[6] Christianity in the first 3 centuries (see the discussion in King, 2003, pp. 5–19). Gnosticism flourished[7] in the second and third centuries CE, establishing itself as a competing ecclesiastical movement. Eventually it attracted the attention of ecclesiastical competitors, most notably Irenaeus, bishop of Lyons, but it remains an elusive social movement, at least to the modern interpreter.[8]

Harnack considered Gnosticism the Hellenization of Christianity. Even though Harnack wrote in the 19th century, when scholars were perhaps overly enthusiastic about Greek influences on Christianity, his emphasis upon the secularization of Christianity is not far off the mark.[9] In the second and third centuries, many Christian traditions were distancing themselves from Judaism. Nonetheless, Gnosticism has both Jewish and Christian features, and Gnostic theologians gleaned their truth wherever they happened to find it—Persian dualism, Platonic philosophy, Hellenistic mystery cults, Babylonian astrology, as well as Judaism and Christianity. It was syncretistic, opportunistic, and elitist. It was also a broad historical phenomenon, existing in most of the major cities of the Roman Empire and throughout the ancient Mediterranean, from Rome to Mesopotamia, from Anatolia to Egypt, and exercising a substantial influence on many streams of early Christianity. It reflects secret traditions of the church, which Gnostic theologians used to their own aggrandizement.[10]

The historian does not consider Gnosticism a heresy, because the concept of heresy, like the concept of canon, is a theological creation, used by a religious person or group to condemn rival groups with whom they are competing. Social condemnation is the task of religionists, not historians, and anytime a historian resorts to terms such as *mainline* or *heretical*, a nonhistorical agenda emerges.[11] The writings of the heresiologists[12] as well as the Nag Hammadi texts demonstrate that Gnosticism was a diverse movement in the early centuries of the Christian era that generally interpreted religious texts from a Platonic perspective.

That may be as specific as the historian can get. For just as there were many Judaism*s* at the turn of the era, and many Christianit*ies* in the first few centuries, so there existed several streams of Gnosticism. Because of its alleged lack of uniformity, Gnosticism is in danger of becoming an overgeneralized and overused historical category, and at least one scholar rejected it as a "dubious category."[13] Admittedly, it is difficult to lump together all so-called Gnostics in the first three centuries CE into one theological stream or homogeneous social group. Perhaps it's impossible to posit a social reality behind Gnostic texts at all.[14]

The second problem is that the Gnostics (so called) spent little time overtly philosophizing about evil, at least in any direct way, though they were clearly concerned about it and they were willing to exploit it for its social utility. Like many religionists, the Gnostics believed that they were good, and their ecclesiastical adversaries evil. Writing in the second century and addressing matters of life and death, heaven and hell, in the context of fierce ecclesiastical disputes, they lacked the detached flexibility that modern scholars usually appreciate but often fail to emulate. The author of SBJ offers neither a consistent theological evaluation of evil nor an apologetic that will satisfy the minds of his readers. The concept of evil is rather an underlying assumption upon which the author bases a theological understanding. But the world he creates[15] reflects his preoccupation with evil and the need to protect his community and theology from it, and ultimately to escape it.[16] To the extent that a major goal of SBJ is defending the integrity of "the God and Father of all," the author is engaged in theodicy.

A third problem involves the concept of evil itself. Defining evil is as slippery as defining Gnosticism. Evil appears to have a social component, but it is an ambiguous one. The large majority of modern people believe that the Holocaust was evil, probably the greatest social evil in the last 100 years. They're more evenly divided on contemporary social issues such as capital punishment, human genetic engineering, health care disparities, and abortion. From the social standpoint, evil is closely connected to not just social values but also social perspectives. The Gnostics considered themselves aliens in an evil world. "I hid from them because of their evil and they did not recognize me" (SBJ 30.20–21).[17] This is more than just theological speculation on the incarnation; it reveals as much about the situation and mentality of the Gnostics as it does about any divine being. The incarnation suggests that the Gnostics considered their environment hostile.

> I entered the midst of the darkness and the interior of Hades, striving for my governance.
>   And the foundations of chaos moved, as though to fall down upon those who dwelt in chaos and destroy them. (SBJ 30.25–29)

The Savior doesn't merely provide a social model for the Gnostics to emulate; their theology of the incarnation reflects an essential Gnostic orientation. Like their Savior, the Gnostics dwelt in the midst of evil, and considered their opponents as evil. "Be on your guard against the angels of poverty and the demons of chaos and all those who are entwined with you" (SBJ 31.16–19).

If knowledge (*gnosis*) is redemptive in Gnostic thought, those lacking *gnosis* lack redemption. In the end, those who end up communing with God are good, and those who end up elsewhere are evil. They dwell in darkness and chaos, and their ultimate end is destruction. The primary orientation of Gnosticism is social. The study of Gnosticism begins with the social reality that the Gnostics were outsiders looking into the ecclesiastical edifice. It is this social reality that moves Gnostic theology along.[18] The Gnostics concluded that their social environment was evil because they didn't fit into their world. So they dubbed it evil and moved along, forming their own communities along the way.

When we talk about the origin of evil in Gnosticism, we must keep this social orientation in mind. From the theoretical standpoint, evil may derive from a supernatural being, the inherent depravity of people, a catastrophic event, or a combination of them. In the Secret Book According to John, the world was evil because a rupture existed between it and the divine gnosis. But theory does not exist in a theological vacuum. Our theories invariably conceal our social situations. If our environment is hostile to our social agenda, an easy way to approach the problem is to call it evil.[19] A primary theological burden of SBJ is to demonstrate how "the God and Father of all" remains pure in spite of rampant evil in the physical world.[20] That's an overt agenda. The covert agenda of rationalizing the Gnostic place in the world is much more subtle but much more fascinating from religious and historical perspectives.

GNOSTICISM IN GENERAL

Gnosticism is the marriage of Platonism and the Judeo-Christian tradition. "The formulation of the gnostic myth ultimately drew on Platonist interpretations of the myth of creation in Plato's *Timaeus*, as combined with the book of Genesis" (Layton, 1987, pp. 5ff.). Teachers such as Basilides, Valentinus, and Heracleon led the movement, which was sufficiently influential to attract the attention of ecclesiastical opponents who viewed it as a theological and social threat. The widespread written attacks that the Gnostic threat generated, not to mention these attacks' vitriolic nature, are cogent proof of the ubiquity of the Gnostic movement.

The writings of Christian teachers such as Irenaeus, Clement of Alexandria, and Tertullian, who considered Gnosticism a perversion of the truth, contain summaries of Gnostic theology from a hostile point of view. Until the discovery of the Nag Hammadi texts in 1945, scholars were almost exclusively dependent upon the heresiologists for information about Gnosticism.[21] The Nag Hammadi discovery revolutionized the academic discussion. Today we have the advantage of possessing actual Gnostic texts that can be mined for firsthand information about the movement.

As far as describing Gnosticism is concerned, we begin with the general observation that Gnosticism, being Platonic in orientation, is dualistic. This is a basic insight that binds together all Gnostic groups, though perhaps no more so than it binds together other religious movements. The Gnostics viewed reality in polarities: Everything is black and white, darkness and light, flesh and spirit, order and chaos, life and death.[22] "The cardinal feature of gnostic thought is the radical dualism that governs the relation of God and the world, and correspondingly that of humanity and its world" (Jonas, 1958, p. 42).[23] This Gnostic dualism is grounded, as mentioned, in Platonic philosophical speculation, which was rampant in the second and third centuries CE.[24] The dualistic orientation of Gnosticism lent itself to sharply defined conceptions of good and evil.

Judaic religious traditions influenced the Gnostics as well, in spite of the
fact that the author of SBJ was actively distancing himself from Judaism.[25]
Theological antagonists invariably leave their fingerprints on their adversaries. The great monotheistic traditions of the sixth century BCE were well
known to Gnostic authors. Second Isaiah, the great progenitor of monotheism, is radically dualistic in orientation. Once the theologian adopts a
universe controlled by one omnipotent being, radical dualism becomes a
foregone conclusion, given the human need to identify with a Supreme Being
that validates human existence. Indeed, dualism is so endemic to the human
conceptual universe that it would be mistaken to assume that it originates in
any one source.

Dualistic ideas are rampant in other Judaic traditions that predate Platonic philosophy. Within the Pentateuch itself, complete by the sixth century BCE, we can discern several groups—Yahwist, Elohist, Priestly, and
Deuteronomic—all of them approaching reality from a dualistic orientation.
The Deuteronomic perspective especially was socially grounded in temple
elitism; the elite who controlled society were blessed by God, leaving the
rabble under a curse. The Judaic creation myth in Genesis 1 is based upon
fundamental dualities such as light–darkness, good–evil, order–chaos, and
life–death. The New Testament is largely Judaic and monotheistic in orientation, and reflects the same dualistic approach to religion.

Therefore, when the Gnostic author of SBJ sat down to write, there was
no shortage of theological and philosophical traditions, all of them dualistic
in orientation, which could have influenced the author. But there is a basic
distinction between the dualism of Gnosticism and the dualism of many other
religious traditions. Gnosticism creates a radical bifurcation between two
overarching worlds—an essentially evil material universe and a good divine
realm. It is this radical dualism that marks off Gnosticism as a Platonic sect.[26]

This pervasive dualism in Gnostic texts probably reflects a strong sense
of group identity. The Gnostics were composed of groups, disjointed groups
perhaps, but groups nonetheless. Layton considered this group identity one
of the cardinal features of classic Gnostic texts. Referring to the Gnostic
creation myth of origins, Layton (1987) stated that it "expresses a *strong sense
of group identity*, which is backed up both by genealogies and by psychological analyses of humanity, with the conclusion that there are two essential
types of human being, gnostic and non-gnostic" (p. 9). An "us-versus-them"
mentality characterized much of Gnosticism, just as surely as it characterized much of the broader ecclesiastical world. Gnosticism was the product of
ecclesiastical and social conflict as well as philosophical speculation.

Recognizing a group of some sort behind the Gnostic texts reflects a basic
insight into how religion works. Religious ideas emerge out of intense social
conflict. Religious insight and religious creeds are not so much the product of individual creative geniuses but the result of social tensions. Even an

innovative religious thinker like the apostle Paul was influenced by group dynamics. He grew up in the context of groups. Paul's Pharisaism, apocalypticism, ideas about redemption, and theology of the cross and resurrection and justification emerged in the context of infighting and social conflict. He learned these ideas at the feet of teachers who were representatives of Jewish groups in the early first century. Likewise, the author of SBJ articulated religious ideas in the context of groups competing for ecclesiastical authority and dominance. Religious authors are fighting not just for their religious ideas but also for social position, social control, social influence, and social resources.

The existence of a group behind SBJ is most evident in the ritual of baptism, a technique used by Gnostics and other religious groups to solidify group identity and to remove their converts from active participation (spiritual, mental, physical, and financial) in the society at large, whether that society is ecclesiastical or imperial. The religious impulse is usually exclusive, rejecting large segments of society. In SBJ John, having heard the criticisms of the Pharisee Arimanios, "turned away from the temple and went to a mountainous and barren place" (SBJ 1.17–20). The language indicates a conscious rejection of a Jewish way of life for what the author considers a more satisfying path. The practice of baptism reinforces the break with competing religious groups. Having penetrated the veil that separates the perfect world from the imperfect one below, the Savior sealed human recipients of gnosis in the baptismal waters.

The language of baptism in SBJ is evocative: "I raised and sealed the person in luminous water with five seals, that death might not prevail over the person from that moment on" (SBJ 31.22–23). The word *raised* suggests more than a social elevation. As the officiant raised the person out of the water, a fundamental break with competing social groups and their social ideas, all of which are viewed as evil, occurred. The symbolism of Romans 6 may provide part of the conceptual background of the religious significance of baptism, and in that text we sense a fundamental break with the outside world. The word *sealed* also has social ramifications, reinforcing the break with the outside world, which is identified with death. The word *luminous* suggests illumination. Therefore, prior to the baptismal moment, the convert was mired in darkness, chaos, death, and evil.

Another basic characteristic of this Gnostic group(s) is their idea of salvation acquired via knowledge. Gnosticism by definition is *gnosis*, an esoteric knowledge available to an elite group that identified the group as "elect." The Gnostics craved gnosis of the way things really were, not only on this earth but also beyond it. They wanted divine knowledge so that they might participate in divine realms. Gnosis is a body of knowledge and an orientation. The Gnostics wanted to know the nature of metaphysical reality, but they also wanted to know how the individual fit into the overall scheme of things. Clement of Alexandria (c. 200 CE) has left behind a text (*Excerpta ex Theodoto*) outlining some of the major inquiries of the Gnostics.

> Who were we?
> What have we become?
> Where were we?
> Whither have we been thrown?
> Where are we going?
> Whence have we been set free?
> What is birth? What is rebirth? (Cited in Klauck, 2003, p. 431)

As Klauck (2003) pointed out, the questions are thoroughly modern inquiries (p. 431), but they are thoroughly mundane as well, the basic stuff of religious questing. Similar questions are outlined in SBJ, though from a Christian perspective:

> How indeed was the savior chosen?
> Why was he sent into the world by his parent who sent him?
> Who is his parent who sent him?
> What is that realm like, to which we shall go? (SBJ 1.21–26)

The Gnostics were obsessed with these ideas, especially the relationship between the "parent" and the "savior" because its theological and practical implications were enormous. The Gnostics wanted to know what every other religionist wants to know, and they needed to know what every other human being needs to know—where they fit into the world, where they were going, and why they were superior to competing social groups. The final question concerning a divine realm occupies much of SBJ. This divine realm, as we shall see, is metaphysically superior to the earthly realm below, characterized as it is by such pervasive evil.

A final observation that we can make about Gnosticism is that it possessed a generally pessimistic outlook toward earthly life and the physical world as a whole. This was a necessary implication of its world-negation. Unlike many streams of the Judeo-Christian tradition that view the world as harmonious and "good," Gnosticism contains within itself an essentially pessimistic outlook on the world. This made denunciation and contempt—not just for the world itself but also for those who inhabit the world outside of the Gnostic sphere of influence—hallmarks of Gnostic teaching. The Gnostics' creation of a new world necessarily involved rejection of the old physical world.

EVIL IN THE SECRET BOOK ACCORDING TO JOHN

The Secret Book According to John is a classic Gnostic text containing a myth of creation as well as good and evil.[27] Its notions of good and evil flow naturally from its idea of creation. Because Irenaeus was intimately aware of SBJ, it dates no later than 180 CE. Several copies of it were found at Nag Hammadi in various versions, always prominently placed in the codex, suggesting that it was a favorite text of many Gnostics.[28] The frame story of SBJ, containing a refutation of Judaism and explicit mention of the "Nazarene," marks it off as a Christian text, although the text itself contains few explicitly Christian features (Pearson, 2007, p. 11).

SBJ contains secret teachings revealed by Jesus to John of Zebedee. It has been viewed as an epilogue to the Gospel of John because in it Jesus reveals heavenly mysteries after his ascension into heaven. SBJ is grounded in the Platonic philosophy of the Timaeus. In Platonic philosophy the physical world, the habitation of flesh-and-blood human beings, is evil, and the spiritual world, the world of ideas, good. These are the philosophical ideas that motivate the Gnostic author of SBJ. It will be no surprise, then, to find a preoccupation with evil at the center of Gnostic thought.

Gnostic cosmology in SBJ begins with the First Principle, a Being of inexpressible light and perfection.[29] SBJ describes God the Father in the following way:

> The One is a sovereign that has nothing over it.
> It is God and Father of all,
> the Invisible One that is over all,
> that is imperishable,
> that is pure light no eye can see. (SBJ 2.26–32)

From the onset of the text, the author of SBJ protects God from human contamination. SBJ continues with a lengthy description of this ineffable God, the product of extensive theological speculation. He is remote and hidden. He does not interact with his creation; he is transcendent (beyond creation—not equal to creation) but not immanent (participating in creation). He is insulated from everything that might corrupt him. A majority of the theological energy in SBJ is devoted to preserving the integrity of this First Principle. The author is adamant that "the God and Father of all" is unconnected with the world of human habitation. SBJ illustrates the principle that absolute gods tend to become more and more remote from the world below.

From a traditional theistic perspective God, a perfect being, is both *transcendent* and *immanent*. Unlike the creation account in Genesis, where the Creator interacts with his creation, and the line between creator and creature is razor thin, the author of SBJ constructs an impenetrable wall between the First Principle and the creation. The god of this Gnostic text does not walk in the garden in the cool of the day (Gen 3:8). He does not even thunder from heaven (John 12:28). The author of SBJ rejects these ideas. "The God and Father of all" is concealed behind a curtain like the great and powerful

Wizard of Oz. The remoteness of the Gnostic god disturbed their opponents. Tertullian complained that the Valentinians concealed their god in the attics of a high-rise apartment.[30] Although this theological move protects the First Principle from the accusation that he is influenced by evil, it does so at the risk of sacrificing God's sovereignty and love. In SBJ, God is absolute—he does not connect with anyone. He is called sovereign, but in reality he is not. A sovereign controls something; in SBJ God does not connect with anything.

It is the primary task of the theologian(s) behind SBJ to protect "the God and Father of all" from any insinuation that he is responsible for this present evil world. That responsibility is reserved for the God of the Jews and Christians. The thought of the Perfect One becomes active and produces a "First Power," called Barbelo,[31] whom the Father impregnates "with a gaze, with the pure, shining light surrounding the invisible Spirit" (SBJ 6.10ff.). This is as active as "the God and Father of all" gets in SBJ. "Barbelo conceived . . . a ray of light that was similar to the blessed light but not as bright" (SBJ 6.12–13).

This ray of light is the Christ, the product of Barbelo and the Father, and it is altogether good. "The Father anointed it with goodness until it was perfectly and completely good, for the Father anointed it with the goodness of the Invisible Spirit" (SBJ 6.23–24). The author reiterates the essential goodness of the Christ:

> The holy Spirit brought the self-produced divine Child of the Spirit and Barbelo to perfection. Then the Child could stand before the powerful and invisible virgin Spirit as the self-produced God, Christ, whom the Spirit had honored with divine acclaim. (SBJ 6.23ff.)

This is a Christology created for a Platonic universe. In general, the docetic tendencies of Gnostic theologians had devastating consequences for Christology from the point of view of the church of Irenaeus and Tertullian (Gonzalez, 1970, pp. 132–133). There is no theology of physical incarnation in SBJ, such as we find in the Gospel of John, where Jesus "tabernacles" in the midst of people. The anthropology of the Gnostics condemned such notions. The author of SBJ is distancing his movement from the church centered at Rome, rejecting the material Christology eventually reflected in the Nicene and Chalcedonian creeds where Jesus Christ is the eternal second person of the Trinity (Nicea in 325), fully God and fully human (Chalcedon in 451). The Gnostics could not tolerate a physical Christ. The docetic tendencies of the Gnostics, designed to preserve Christ from an evil physical nature, were considered heretical at both Nicea and Chalcedon.

Eventually Sophia appears, several emanations later, in the fourth eternal realm (SBJ 8.16ff.). She is the mother of Yaldaboath, the evil creator of the world. The author carefully explains that Sophia gave birth to Yaldaboath without the permission of "the God and Father of all." This is a prophylactic move. The author of SBJ emphasizes that "the God and Father of all" has no responsibility for Yaldaboath. Not only did the conception of Yaldaboath occur four emanations from "the God and Father of all," but also it was parthenogenetic. "She produced it without her lover" (SBJ 10.2–4). Sophia was deeply ashamed of her creation, and she named it Yaldaboath. There is a radical contrast here between the Christ, the consensual child of Barbelo and the Father, and Yaldaboath, an essentially bastard "misshapen" child, conceived without the participation and blessing of the Father. Social realities lurk menacingly in the background of this text.

The text is implicitly misogynist, reflecting the Jewish tradition in Genesis 3 where the woman is responsible for evil. "In the Secret Book of John all the evils and misfortunes of this world derive from Sophia's blunder" (Meyer, 2007, p. 114). In SBJ, a female figure creates evil by conceiving Yaldaboath without the participation of a male figure. The product is thoroughly ugly, and the world is doomed. "And out of her was shown forth an imperfect product that was different from her manner of appearance, for she had made it without her consort. And compared to the image of its mother it was misshapen, having a different form" (SBJ 10.2–5).[32] Such is the awesome power of myth! With a simple dual allusion to Genesis and Greek mythology, the author of SBJ condemns women and Judaism in a single stroke of world creation.

A wholesale rejection of Judaism characterizes the text as a whole.[33] Yaldaboath is not just any evil being; in the Gnostic worldview, he is the god of the Old Testament, the creator of the evil world. The framing story of SBJ suggests that the text was written in the context of social tension between a Christian group and a Jewish group. A Pharisee named Arimanios[34] warns John that Jesus the Nazarene "has deceived you, filled your ears with lies, closed [your minds], *and turned you from the traditions of your ancestors*" (SBJ 1.12–13, emphasis added). The final italicized clause suggests that the group behind SBJ had Jewish roots but was distancing themselves from them. This is the social context in which the Gnostics denounced their opponents. Particularly in his account of the creation of the world and Adam and Eve, the author of SBJ distances his own theological viewpoints from the book of Genesis, frequently reminding the reader that "it is not as Moses taught" (SBJ 22.22–23, among others). In this way, theology sprouts from the soil of social tension.

Yaldaboath is the creator of our present material world, the physical habitation of humanity. But Yaldaboath is an evil being, unlike the creator in Genesis who is undeniably a good being. "He (Yaldaboath) is wicked because of the Mindlessness that is in him." This is a severe indictment of Judaism. The author's implication is that the Jewish people are characterized by "mindlessness" or lack of gnosis, which for Gnostics was the cornerstone of every evil.

Yaldaboath is a suitable scapegoat for the creation of an evil world. In this way, SBJ posits a gulf between the perfect Being, "the God and Father of all," and the world of human habitation, the realm of Yaldaboath and other evil beings who eke out their existence in a physical environment. The underlying assumption is that the present world of flesh-and-blood human beings is thoroughly corrupt, too corrupt and evil to be the habitation or product of the "God and Father of all." This "web of highly structured emanations . . . forms a thick and almost inscrutable barrier between the human world and god" (Layton, 1987, p. 23). Not just *inscrutable* but also *insurmountable*. It is an impenetrable brick wall that cannot be breached.

Like many religions, Gnosticism promised salvation from the present evil physical world. In Gnostic thought, the physical world of humanity was oppressive and stifling, and people on this physical planet walked around in a cloud of confusion without knowing the ultimate nature of reality. The creation of Adam reflects an essentially Gnostic orientation. Although Adam enjoyed enlightenment, he was also fallen: "Adam became a mortal person, the first to ascend and the first to become estranged" (SBJ 22.12–13). The human race from the beginning was destined to devolve into periods of diminishing enlightenment. From this basic ignorance of the masses of humanity, the Gnostics sought liberation. Psychologically it allowed them to master fear and anxiety. They told themselves that they were the chosen elite, the favorites of the divine realms, and one day they would return there, no matter what kind of rejection they had to endure on earth from their ecclesiastical opponents or their imperial masters.

Socially it reflects basic tension between Gnostic groups and competing groups. The Gnostics found themselves out of favor with surrounding political and religious structures. The Gnostic myth reflects intense social alienation. Whether the originating impetus came from Judaism or Christianity we cannot say.[35] What we do know is that the Gnostics used religion and theology as a form of social condemnation. The Gnostic Scriptures, which have been called "a supplementary body that constituted a challenge to the proto-orthodox canon" (Layton, 1987, p. xxiii), are evidence of this social tension. It is difficult to say what constituted the "proto-orthodox canon" in the second and third centuries, but presumably it included many texts that eventually were included in the Roman Christian canon, including several texts refuting proto-Gnostic ideas.[36]

For this reason, evil is a necessary constituent of the Gnostic orientation. Any religion offering redemption necessarily recognizes the existence and pernicious influence of evil. If a person needs redemption, that person must be redeemed from something, usually some kind of evil. Either the person contains the seeds of damnation within, or the person is being influenced by some exterior evil agency, either an evil person or an evil environment or a combination of the two. Evil and redemption are inextricably connected.

Even if evil does not exist as an ontological reality, it can always be created, and Gnosticism didn't hesitate to condemn the material world as irredeemably evil and in need of redemption. In other words, the Gnostic purveyors of religion sold the idea of evil as part of the soteriological package, working from the alienation that characterizes humanity to the solution found in divine gnosis.[37]

In Gnostic thought material reality is especially marked out as evil, and the Gnostics viewed the material world and material bodies as prisons. This view of reality is evident in SBJ's description of the incarnation contained in the "Hymn of the Savior" at the end of the text:[38] "I traveled in the realm of great *darkness*, and continued until I entered the midst of their *prison*" (SBJ 30.17). The Gnostics above all else sought liberation from this imprisonment. The appeal to the concept of travel suggests a radical spatial differentiation between themselves and their ecclesiastical opponents. No doubt the Gnostics found their competitive assemblies less and less tolerable. Jesus, the "abundance of light" and the "memory of fullness," leaves his perfect habitation of light and glory and enters a habitation marked by darkness and servitude. "And I entered the midst of their prison, which is the prison of the body" (SBJ 31.3–4). This is how the Gnostics viewed their physical environment. To descend into the material world was to descend into darkness and chaos. The Savior entered "the midst of the darkness and the interior of Hades" (SBJ 30.35). SBJ views the incarnation as a descent into chaos: "And the foundations of chaos moved, as though to fall down upon those who dwell in chaos and destroy them" (SBJ 30.27).

SBJ views the incarnation differently than the canonical gospels, particularly the Gospel of John. In SBJ there is no validation of physical existence on earth. The incarnation functions to confirm the evil nature of the physical world and especially to confirm the inhabitants of the physical world in their evil. Those who reject gnosis are doomed to an existence of darkness and chaos. Again, we see the creative power of myth. One simply condemns as evil what one dislikes.

The evil of the material world originates in the work of Sophia, who produced Yaldaboath, but it exists practically and principally as the work of four demonic powers: Ephememphi (associated with pleasure), Ioko (desire), Nenentophni (grief), and Blaomen (fear) (SBJ 18.14–19). Like many other religious texts containing laundry lists of various "passions" (of the flesh), the author of SBJ expends significant energy outlining the evils resulting from these demonic powers: envy, fanaticism, pain, distress, contention for victory, lack of repentance, anxiety, mourning, imperfections, vain boasting, anger, wrath, bitterness, bitter lust, insatiableness, terror, entreaty, anguish, and shame (SBJ 18.20–30). Although these are far too general to shed much light on the Gnostic group behind the text, they reflect the religious tendency to separate the human world into good and evil, one of the key functions of myth, whether or not the Gnostics participated actively in the evil they condemned.

Thus, the radical dualism of Gnosticism created a consistent view of evil among Gnostic thinkers, resulting from a world-negating myth. The description of human life in the "Hymn of the Savior" is bleak. A strong contrast exists in the Hymn between the divine habitation of light and the dungeon of darkness. The author uses terms such as *darkness, chaos,* and *sleep* to describe life on earth. The world itself is evil, the product of an evil creator, the realm of evil beings. The Gnostic treated the mundane (and evil) realities of this present world with contempt or indifference. One approach led to asceticism, and the other led to libertinism. Their view of evil gave the Gnostics a handy tool to denounce their theological opponents as well as their religious institutions such as temples and churches.

One naturally wonders how much of Gnostic speculation concerning evil was socially based. References to chaos, darkness, and prisons were not merely conceptual ideas; they reflect the way that the Gnostics viewed their competitors. The Gnostics were social beings, and they had ecclesiastical opponents, people who blocked their access to power structures, their right to ecclesiastical posts, their reputation in ecclesiastical communities, and their possession of all of the accouterments of ecclesiastical power, including its financial benefits. The same could be said for the author of the canonical Gospel of John, the self-acclaimed "beloved disciple," and the author of any other religious text. The concept of evil is a weapon that is quickly brandished against one's opponents. Note how effectively Paul uses it in the Epistle to the Philippians: "Beware of the dogs, *beware of the evil workers,* beware of those who mutilate the flesh!" (Philippians 3:2, NRSV). He could just as easily have said, "Now there are some people who look at the issue differently, but I don't think they're right," but it wouldn't be nearly as effective.

In addition to a social dimension, the concept of evil is psychologically useful to people. We utilize it to make sense of our worlds, to justify our place in the world, to enhance our reputations with colleagues and friends, and to compete with opponents. The radical denial of the present world not only reflects a group challenging the powers that be but also suggests people struggling to make sense of where they are in the world. I do not like to admit that I'm not what I'm supposed to be, that the fundamental currents of my life are flowing against the current of the universe, that I'm out of sync with the cosmic rhythms. So we tell ourselves that we are fundamentally good and others are fundamentally evil. It's this kind of self-delusion that helps us sleep through the night.

Evil also has theological implications, and in the Gnostic religion these are blatant. In SBJ, evil distances God from his creation. God becomes an alien creature, in the words of Hans Jonas (1958) "absolutely transmundane" (p. 42). The social ramifications of this theological idea are enormous. The world is left to itself, usually to rot of its own corruption. The Gnostics had little use for this present evil world. For them the world was a harsh reality, filled with ubiquitous evil, capable of great destruction, and beyond redemption.

SBJ concludes with a beautiful poem of deliverance, but it provides no redemption for this world (SBJ 30:11–31:27). Pervasive and persistent evil renders it irredeemable. The poem limits redemption from evil to individuals and perhaps groups of individuals. The physical environment is left to rot of its evil disease. In the radical dualistic world of the Gnostics, it was inconceivable that redemption would occur in a physical environment. The Gnostic approach is not unlike the traditional approach of fundamentalist Christians who have abandoned society to rot of its own evil nature, eschewing social reform. Neither contains a theology that supports social involvement.[39]

Kurt Rudolph, another pioneer in the study of Gnosticism, suggests that the Gnostics followed one of two basic approaches to the concept of evil. The Iranian system (Mandeism and Manichaeism) posited a radical dualism between a kingdom of light and a kingdom of darkness. These two kingdoms existed from the beginning of creation. But the majority of Nag Hammadi texts, including *The Secret Book According to John*, followed the Syrian-Egyptian system, where evil results from a gradual decline from the divine realm. Evil is not a preexistent principle but a "darkened level of being" (Rudolph, 1983, pp. 65–66). The more removed I am from the First Principle, the darker my experience. That's a basic corollary of Gnostic theology. On the other hand, the more removed I am from my physical environment, the more enlightened my experience. Hence the need for a radical rejection of material culture.

Religions have a tendency to withdraw from human society, a tendency usually resulting from a radical distinction between the sphere or realm of God and the sphere or realm of humanity.[40] This tendency is apparent in Gnosticism. Sometimes, as in the Gospel of Luke, human government and divine government are fundamentally opposed to each other. Jesus, the agent of divine government, appears "in the days of Caesar Augustus," the agent of human government. Many early Christians met together in assemblies for prayer and *koinonia* (fellowship). The little Christian text of 1 John, perhaps written to refute a primitive form of Gnosticism, extols life apart from the world of evil people. "But our fellowship (*koinonia*) is with the Father and with his son, Jesus Christ" (1 John 1:7). [41] No matter how one interprets these texts theologically, from the social standpoint they all suggest a reluctance on the part of some religious people to fully participate in human life, which they view in some sense as evil. Churches, synagogues, and mosques are designed as sanctuaries from the harsh realities of a hostile world. The Gnostic approach to life reflects the same tension between a religious group and the outside world.

Finally, the Gnostic creation myth as it appears in SBJ solves at least two theological problems relating to evil. First, by insulating God with successive walls of emanations, the Gnostics preserved God from the criticism that He created evil and thus is responsible for it. Instead, the reader can blame the Jews. Yaldaboath created evil, and he is responsible for it; therefore, one cannot blame "the God and Father of all" for the presence of evil in the world. That much is clear. "The God and Father of all" didn't consent to Yaldaboath's birth, a further indictment of the Jewish god because he has no divine life in him. Neither does "the God and Father of all" participate in the creative act. Theodicy is a primary motivating factor of the Gnostic author, but so is the condemnation of Judaism.

Second, the Gnostic theologians preserved God from the criticism that evil influences him. In SBJ, God is absolute; he does not participate in any way with his creation. He dwells in unapproachable light, totally walled off from anything or anyone that might corrupt him. At least four emanations separate God from the evil world. The Gnostic author of SBJ could not conceive of a god who could participate in a presumably evil creation and still remain essentially good. His Platonic tendencies refused to entertain the idea. One detects here the theological seeds of asceticism, or at least a theological rationale for an ascetic lifestyle. To drink deeply from divine gnosis, one must withdraw from an evil world.

But the preservation of God and his reputation is only one motivation of the Gnostic theologian. Theology is more than ideas; it organizes heaven and earth. It creates bold new worlds that help us cope with the darker realities of our present world. Gnostic theology has a utilitarian purpose. By removing God to an isolated room, he becomes more and more unknowable, more and more inscrutable, and more and more in need of interpreters. Like many religious specialists,[42] the Gnostics were involved in a sophisticated form of job security. They created a God who was shrouded in secrecy, and then they proclaimed themselves the chief revealers, or interpreters, of his mysteries.

Knowledge was the key to the divine world, and the religious specialists who were the Gnostic theologians jealously guarded those keys. In effect, they held the keys to the kingdom and salvation, providing them with tremendous social power. They were the sole possessors of truth about God; their theological opponents in Rome and elsewhere lacked real gnosis. This is the common assumption that justifies the need for all professional religious specialists, not just the Gnostics. In many ways, and particularly in this final way, Gnosticism was a thoroughly modern phenomenon.

CONCLUSION

The idea that evil is a pervasive presence is both an ancient idea and a contemporary one. Like Anton Chigurh in the superb film *No Country for Old*

Men, evil is a constant reality that impacts every corner of our physical environment.[43] In the film Chigurh, a relentless and sometimes arbitrary killer, symbolizes the harsh reality of evil that we all must endure. Chigurh's brand of human evil reflects the reality of physical evil in our environment. Storm clouds, thunder, and lightning appear in the background of the film, suggesting that evil is endemic to our earthly existence. Evil renders the earth hard; the viewer hears it crunch under the boots of people. Evil manifests itself acutely in human affairs, as symbolized by the unstoppable Chigurh. As Uncle Ellis says to Ed Tom, you "can't stop what's coming."

The Gnostics viewed evil in the exact same way, except with a more sophisticated ideological underpinning. The physical environment of the Gnostics was essentially evil, the creation of a lesser god, lacking the divine gnosis that originates in "the God and Father of all." The Gnostic world is permeated with evil because evil is endemic to it, a systemic problem. There is one crucial difference between Gnosticism and the film. In *No Country for Old Men*, a person can escape evil, but only by being lucky. It depends on the toss of a coin. Ed Tom sits in a dark hotel room at the end of the film, Chigurh hiding behind an open door only a few feet away. Chigurh does not kill Ed Tom, and we're not told why. Presumably he's just lucky.

The Gnostics escaped evil, too, but they relied on myth, not luck. The author of the Secret Book According to John found a solution in divine gnosis, which becomes a convenient line of demarcation between an elect group of people and the rest of lost, darkened humanity. Myth, that ineluctable creation of the human mind, made the difference.

NOTES

1. On Gnosticism in general, see King (2003), Layton (1987), and Pearson (2007). Two older texts are still helpful: Jonas (1958) and Rudolph (1983).

2. Peter Berger in *The Sacred Canopy* suggested that religion engages in the enterprise of "world building," the attempt "to impose a meaningful order upon reality." Berger, *The Sacred Canopy* (Garden City, NY: Doubleday, 1969), 22.

3. There are hints of social reality in SBJ texts such as 31:28–30 ("those who are like you in spirit") as well as the framing story involving conflict between a Jew and a Christian. This is not to suggest that a community always exists behind a text. One would be hard pressed to suggest the existence of a social group behind *The Cat in the Hat* or *Green Eggs and Ham*, though both texts may reflect widespread concerns and values in society. There is also the problem of extracting social history from myths. "Determining how to write social history from myth is surely one of the thorniest issues in ancient historiography" (King, 2003, p. 10).

4. See Layton, 1987, pp. 23*ff.*

5. The diversity of Gnosticism is seen, for instance, in a comparison of the Gospel of Thomas, a composite text that connects early Jesus-Galilean traditions to later Platonic ideas, and the Secret Book According to John, a classic Gnostic text that

reflects a more consistent Gnostic worldview. On the Gospel of Thomas, see De Conick (2005, 2006). For a more conservative approach to Thomas, see Perrin (2007).

6. The terms *normative* and *mainline* are theologically loaded terms. They are used to distinguish a more acceptable and satisfying form of Christianity from a less acceptable and satisfying form. They suggest that a tradition is not what it should be, implying that a tradition is deviant or not as pure as the "normative" tradition. As such, the terms *normative* and *mainline*, and all similar religious terms, do not belong in the discipline of history.

7. Irenaeus stated in *Against Heresies* (1.29.1) that "a multitude of gnostics have sprung up, and have been manifested like mushrooms growing out of the ground."

8. There is a possibility that gnosticism may have preceded the emergence of Christianity, and that the "orthodox" church with its doctrine of apostolic succession based on historical texts may have emerged as a response to the world-negating philosophy of gnosticism. Among many other scholars, Pagels demonstrates how politically expedient the so-called canonical gospels were. See Elaine Pagels, *The Gnostic Gospels* (1979/1989). This revisionist perspective on the history of the early church(es) lies behind much of the current "Jesus didn't exist" craze.

9. Adolf von Harnack, German church historian, was a leading member of the History of Religions school (Religionsgeschichtliche Schule) in the 19th and early 20th centuries. He argued that "Gnosticism in all its phases was the violent attempt to drag Christianity down to the level of the Greek world" (see Harnack, 1886–1890, 2:3). According to Harnack, Gnosticism "was ruled in the main by the Greek spirit, and determined by the interests and doctrines of the Greek philosophy of religion" (cited in King, 2003, p. 63). Harnack also wrote *What Is Christianity?* (1901) and *The Expansion of Christianity in the First Three Centuries* (1904–1905). King's entire discussion of Harnack and the History of Religions school is informative; see King (2003, pp. 55–109).

10. *Pseudo-Dionysius* refers to "the succession of gnostic masters or spiritual masters, separate from the succession of bishops, who transmit the faith of the Apostles ... but who continue the charismatic tradition of apostolic times and of the Apostles" (cited in Eliade, 1982/1984, p. 370). Pseudo-Dionysius was much kinder than most opponents of the Gnostics.

11. Ignoring a phenomenon is a subtle form of condemnation. For instance, Wilken (2003) appeared more religious in orientation than historical, because Wilken devoted virtually no space to the existence and presence of Gnostic teachers in the early centuries of Christianity, even though they were widespread. The reader naturally assumes that they didn't exist or didn't matter. The same could be said for Urban (1995). Both texts are slaves to canonical restrictions. The problem may also be a lack of appreciation for Gnostic influence. Robin Lane Fox also largely ignored Gnosticism in *Pagans and Christians* (1989), an otherwise valuable and interesting text.

12. Someone who hunts down and exposes heretics. Irenaeus of Lyon is probably the most famous for his five-volume *Adversus Haereses* (*Against Heresies*; Greek title: *On the Detection and Overthrow of So-Called Gnosis*), written in 180 CE, but many others existed, including Justin Martyr, Clement of Alexandria, Tertullian, Hippolytus, and Epiphanius. Irenaeus wrote *Against Heresies* "to expose and counteract" the "machinations" of the Gnostics (see Book I, Preface). All of the heresiologists considered the

Gnostics a sufficiently potent social force to require refutation. Irenaeus complained that the Gnostics were "draw(ing) away the minds of the inexperienced and tak(ing) them captive" (see Book I, Preface).

13. Williams (1996) suggested that we replace the term *Gnosticism* with "biblical demiurgical myth." Not surprisingly, he has not persuaded a large segment of historians persisting in the study of Gnosticism.

14. Wisse (1981) characterized the Gnostic writings as "frustratingly abstruse" (p. 570). On the social reality behind Gnostic texts, see also Scott (1995).

15. World creation is the heart of the religious enterprise. The religionist is a metaphysician, and metaphysics thrives on the creation of alternative realities. Religion at its core posits a metaphysical reality that helps the religious devotee cope with present realities.

16. See, for example, SBJ 31.24: "So that from henceforth death might not have power over that person. And lo, now I shall enter the perfect eternal realm." These are boilerplate Gnostic (religious) ideals.

17. The text references throughout conform to Bentley Layton's (1987) scheme in *The Gnostic Scriptures.* The translations are from both Layton (1987) and Meyer (2007, pp. 107–132). I generally use Meyer's translation because it is less technical than Layton's.

18. For an interesting study of how social reality moved the Gnostics' opponents along, see Pagels (1979/1989). Pagels's argument is strengthened if we date the canonical gospel texts another 30–40 years into the future—say, the beginning of the second century—placing them in the context of intense theological debate.

19. One immediately thinks of Ronald Reagan dismissing the Soviet Union as an "evil empire."

20. This is the great burden of all religions that claim a divine being is behind the physical world. Simply put, if God is behind it all, how did things get so crazy? The problem of evil is the greatest single obstacle to belief in God. One of the clearest and most concise discussions of evil from a staunchly theistic perspective is still Geisler (1978).

21. Many of the standard secondary texts contain helpful introductions to the writings of the heresiologists. See Pearson (2007, pp. 25–50), King (2003, pp. 20–54), and Layton (1987, pp. 159–214, 223–227, 276–302, 420–425).

22. The tendency of Gnostic authors to view reality in polarities is best evidenced in the Gnostic text "The Thunder—Perfect Intellect." See Layton (1987, pp. 77–85).

23. Eliade (1982/1984) mentioned three fundamental ideas in Gnosticism: (a) the dualism of spirit and matter, (b) the myth of the fall of the soul and its resultant incarnation into the material body or "prison," and (c) the certainty of deliverance (redemption) by virtue of gnosis (p. 372).

24. Bos (2002) suggested that Platonic dualism in Gnosticism was mediated by Aristotle. Bos conceded that the "call to awaken" is the starting point for Gnosticism (SBJ 31.4—"O listener, arise from heavy sleep"), but he suggested that Aristotle's distinction between the "sleeping soul" and the "awakened soul" also influenced Gnostic thought (2002, p. 291).

25. In the introduction to SBJ, John goes up to the temple where he meets a Pharisee, who tells John, "This Nazarene really has deceived you, filled your ears with lies,

closed [your minds], and turned you from the traditions of your ancestors" (SBJ 1.12–16). Significantly, John "turned away from the temple, and went to a mountainous and barren place," reflecting a movement away from Judaism and toward a Christian wilderness.

26. Two factors should always be kept in mind when discussing the influence of Platonism. First, the Platonic distinction between spirit and flesh, mind and body, was diffused throughout the second and third century world. It is quite possible that many theologians and philosophers did not consider themselves "Platonists"; they merely thought that way. Second, Platonism does not necessarily mean that the material world is evil. It merely subordinates the material world to the non-material world. One is more significant than the other.

27. Layton (1987) referred to SBJ as "one of the most classic narrations of the gnostic myth" (p. 23). Although Layton classified SBJ as a classic Gnostic text, other scholars of Gnosticism classify SBJ as a Sethian text.

28. SBJ exists in four separate Coptic manuscripts, three from the Nag Hammadi codices (2, 3, 4), copied prior to 350 CE, and one from a fifth-century papyrus manuscript (*Berolinensis gnosticus*). See Layton (1987, pp. 25–26) and also Meyer (2007, p. 103).

29. For an excellent introduction to Gnosticism in general, and the Secret Book According to John in particular, see especially Layton (1987).

30. Tertullian, *Against the Valentinians*, 7. The reference to *insulam feliculam* in this text is obscure. It could mean the "apartments of Felicula," or it could be "apartments in the heavens." It should be noted that the Romans commonly built apartment buildings (*insula*) several stories high.

31. The Barbelo myth is more fully explicated in the Gnostic text "The Thunder—Perfect Intellect." See Layton (1987, pp. 77–85). Unlike "the God and Father of all," Barbelo, the First Power, interacts with creation.

32. The myth that inspired the story is probably the conception of Hephaestus, the son of Zeus and Hera. Hera conceived Hephaestus parthenogenetically. Hera cast him down from Olympus, perhaps because he was ugly and lame, perhaps out of guilt for conceiving him without the aid of Zeus. The author of SBJ, by alluding to the Greek myth, suggests that Yaldaboath has no more claim to the divine realms than Hephaestus.

33. I would not go so far as to suggest the text is anti-Semitic, because the hostility is only theological. The charge of anti-Semitism is sometimes made too quickly and without support. Just because an author disagrees with the Jewish worldview or Jewish ideas does not make him or her anti-Semitic. The post-Holocaust sensitivity toward Judaism is sometimes unnecessary.

34. Meyer (2007) suggested that the name recalls the evil Zoroastrian deity Ahriman (p. 107).

35. Green (1985) argued that Gnosticism originated in Roman-occupied Jewish Alexandria in the first century. Gonzalez (1970) presented a typical Christian viewpoint that the Gnostics gleaned whatever they could use from Christianity but remained an essentially non-Christian movement, thereby subordinating Gnosticism to the "orthodox" church. Pagels (1979/1989) presented the more intriguing, and possibly more accurate, idea that the "orthodox" church fed off of Gnosticism just as much as Gnosticism fed off of it.

Gnosticism and Evil

215

36. For example, the Johannine literature, the Corinthian correspondence, and Colossians, all of them written toward the end of the first century. Bultmann argued that the Gospel of John attached a Gnostic redeemer myth to the historical Jesus. If so, the text is rather schizophrenic. The pastoral epistles as well, late and deutero-Pauline, include references to early Gnostic groups. See 1 Tim 6:20 ("falsely called gnosis").

37. Gonzalez (1970) in his treatment of Gnosticism emphasized that "Gnosticism is salvation" (pp. 1:130–131).

38. The "Hymn of the Savior" (Layton referred to it as the "Poem of Deliverance") is found at SBJ 30.11–31.25.

39. At least they did not appreciate those tenets of their theology (the incarnation) that support social reform. In the canonical stream of Christian theology, Jesus leaves a divine realm to participate in this present evil world. That would seem to support redemptive social reforms of all kinds.

40. Jesus's *kingdom of God* is an excellent example of this phenomenon.

41. On the social context of 1 John, see Brown (1982), Painter (2002), Perkins (1983, 1993), and Smalley (1984).

42. The term *religious specialists* derives from the work of Rodney Stark. See Stark and Bainbridge (1987/1996, pp. 89–96) and Stark (2007).

43. The Joel and Ethan Coen film *No Country for Old Men*, based on the Cormac McCarthy novel, deservedly won the Academy Award for Best Picture in 2007. It is a chilling reflection on the existence of evil in the United States.

REFERENCES

Bos, A. P. (2002). "Aristotelian" and "Platonic" dualism in Hellenistic and early Christian philosophy and Gnosticism. *Vigiliae Christianae, 56* (3), 273–291.
Brown, R. E. (1982). *The Epistles of John: Translated with introduction, notes, and commentary* (Anchor Bible 30). Garden City, NY: Doubleday.
De Conick, A. D. (2005). *Recovering the original Gospel of Thomas: A history of the gospel and its growth.* London: T & T Clark.
De Conick, A. D. (2006). *The original Gospel of Thomas in translation: With a commentary and new English translation of the complete gospel.* London: T & T Clark.
Eliade, M. (1984). *A history of religious ideas: Vol. 2. From Gautama Buddha to the triumph of Christianity.* Chicago: Chicago University Press. (Original work published in 1982)
Fox, R. L. (1989). *Pagans and Christians.* New York: Knopf.
Geisler, N. L. (1978). *The roots of evil.* Grand Rapids, MI: Zondervan.
Gonzalez, J. L. (1970). *A history of Christian thought: Vol. 1. From the beginnings to the Council of Chalcedon in* A.D. *451.* Nashville, TN: Abingdon.
Green, H. A. (1985). *The economic and social origins of Gnosticism* (SBL Dissertation Series 77). Atlanta, GA: Scholars Press.
Jonas, H. (1958). *The Gnostic religion: The message of the alien god and the beginnings of Christianity.* Boston: Beacon.
King, K. L. (2003). *What is Gnosticism?* Cambridge, MA: Harvard University Press/ Belknap.
Klauck, H. J. (2003). *The religious context of early Christianity.* Minneapolis, MN: Fortress.

Layton, B. (1987). *The Gnostic scriptures.* Garden City, NY: Doubleday.

Meyer, M. (Ed.). (2007). *The Nag Hammadi scriptures.* New York: HarperOne.

Pagels, E. (1989). *The Gnostic gospels.* New York: Vintage. (Original work published in 1979)

Painter, J. (2002). *1, 2, and 3 John* (Sacra Pagina 18). Collegeville, MN: Liturgical Press.

Pearson, B. A. (2007). *Ancient Gnosticism: Traditions and literature.* Minneapolis, MN: Fortress.

Perkins, P. (1983). *Koinonia* in 1 John 1:3–7: The social context of division in the Johannine letter. *Catholic Biblical Quarterly, 45,* 631–641.

Perkins, P. (1993). *Gnosticism and the New Testament.* Minneapolis, MN: Augsburg Fortress.

Perrin, N. P. (2007). *Thomas: The other gospel.* Louisville, KY: Westminster John Knox Press.

Rudolph, K. (1983). *Gnosis.* New York: Harper & Row.

Scott, A. B. (1995, Summer). Churches or books? Sethian social organization. *Journal of Early Christian Studies, 3* (2), 109–122.

Smalley, S. S. (1984). *1, 2, 3 John* (Word Biblical Commentary 51). Waco, TX: Word.

Stark, R. (2007). *Discovering God: The origins of the great religions and the evolution of belief.* New York: HarperOne.

Stark, R., & Bainbridge, W. S. (1996). *A theory of religion.* New Brunswick, NJ: Rutgers University Press.

Urban, L. (1995). *A short history of Christian thought* (rev. and expanded ed.). Oxford: Oxford University Press.

Wilken, R. L. (2003). *The spirit of early Christian thought.* New Haven, CT: Yale University Press.

Williams, M. A. (1996). *Rethinking Gnosticism: An argument for dismantling a dubious category.* Princeton, NJ: Princeton University Press.

Wisse, F. (1981). Stalking those elusive Sethians. In B. Layton (Ed.), *The rediscovery of Gnosticism: Sethian Gnosticism* (Vol. 2). Leiden: Brill.

CHAPTER 14

EVIL IN FILM: PORTRAYAL AND BIBLICAL CRITIQUE

Nicolene L. Joubert and
Zelmarie E. Joubert

INTRODUCTION

The origin, existence, and expression of moral and natural evil in the world are popular themes in literature, film, and television. *Moral evil* refers to harmful deeds performed by humans to hurt or destroy others or the environment, whereas *natural evil* refers to forces in nature that can cause destruction (Schrag, 2006, p. 149). Humans feel compelled to explain, address, and abolish both types of evils, and this drive is clearly visible in film since its birth, which happened, according to Monaco (2000, p. 572), in a brief period between the late 1800s and early 1900s.

Throughout the relatively short history of film, audiences have marveled at the extensive variety of characters employed to represent the many facets of moral evil that humans are confronted with. A few names that might come to mind include Captain Hank Quinlan (*Touch of Evil*, 1958), HAL (*2001: A Space Odyssey*, 1968), Michael Myers (*Halloween*, 1978), Freddy Krueger (*A Nightmare on Elm Street*, 1984), Hannibal Lecter (*The Silence of the Lambs*, 1991), and Samara Morgan (*The Ring*, 2002). These memorably evil characters and the films they appear in belong to a diverse variety of genres such as film noir, horror, thriller, and science fiction that deliberately explore, and often exploit, the concept of evil. The emphasis on evil in these film genres indicates how people grapple with the different facets of evil—being both drawn to evil and repulsed by it. Additionally, the emphasis and treatment of evil in film exhibit the potential utilization of film space for the purpose of considering, and also experimenting with, the concept of evil.

Norden (2000, p. 51) argued that film and television programming are a form of culture that not only reflects reality but is the reality on which many viewers base their ideas and views of the world. Hoorn and Konijn (2003, p. 250) underscored this argument, stating that the conceptual framework that serves as people's "real-world knowledge" mostly consists of information gathered through stories of people that they have never met or events that they have not experienced. A well-developed understanding of the power of story and character in the shaping of people's worlds and worldviews provides a necessary basis for the value of the type of exploration and evaluation conducted by the authors.

The purpose of this chapter is to explore and evaluate film's capacity for representing moral evil by looking at four films—*M* (1931), *The Godfather* (1972), *Nosferatu the Vampyre* (1979), and *Funny Games* (1997)—and to evaluate these efforts within a biblical philosophical framework.

EXPLORING EVIL IN FILM

Media coverage of evil, including in film, is not always viewed as having positive value. It has been frequently condemned in the past as only imitating evil, thus offering no in-depth insight or strategies for addressing and containing evil (Alfred cited in Norden, 2000, p. 51). Such a superficial, sensationalist treatment of evil results in desensitizing society to evil, and it lessens the ability of viewers to distinguish between reality and fiction. Grace (2000, p. 58) reported with concern on the reactions of adolescents watching the re-release of the film *The Exorcist*, and pointed out that these reactions were to convulse with laughter at the portrayal of a demon-possessed child rather than the expected shock reaction. Grace (2000, p. 58) was furthermore of the opinion that our culture has lost its sense of the numinous and that the portrayal of evil in film may have contributed to this. The critique against depiction of evil in mass media has to be taken seriously and considered in any investigation into the use of film as a tool to develop and test our understanding of evil.

THE VALUE OF FILM AS A MEDIUM IN PORTRAYING EVIL

In defense of media coverage of evil, Freeland (cited in Norden, 2000, p. 51) argued that horror films can and do "offer a rich, varied, subtle and complex view on the nature of evil." Freeland (cited in Norden, 2000, p. 51) is of the opinion that films depicting evil elicit a variety of responses in their viewers ranging from emotional responses such as fear, anxiety, dread, and sympathy to cognitive responses such as contemplating the degrees of evil, internal versus external evil, and natural versus supernatural evil. This argument implies that the media coverage of evil can serve a good purpose by helping people to understand the "banality of evil," a phrase coined by Hannah Arendt (cited in Norden, 2000, p. 51) in her analysis of the crimes committed by Adolf Eichmann during the Nazi regime.

Considering both sides of the argument, the hypothesis that film as medium can be effectively used to increase our understanding of the complexity of evil as expressed in society, tested in this chapter, has to be clarified. Not all films utilize film space in a responsible manner, and these films are thus rendered less useful and less effective in dealing with the topic of evil. In response to a question about the 2008 remake of his 1997 experimental film *Funny Games*, Austrian director Michael Haneke said,

> I wanted to show the audience how much they can be manipulated. First they think it's all an illusion, just a film, then I do this rewinding and suddenly you go back. . . . In view of this overriding illusion in movies, it's a good idea to create a little bit of mistrust in the *verité*, in the truth of moving pictures. (Quoted in Rich, 2008)

The answer might not lie in the reactionary response of disallowing the making of films with gratuitous violence, even though that might be the ideal, but in educating the audience (ourselves) to be alert and discriminating.

The classical German drama-thriller *M*, released in 1931 and directed by Fritz Lang, was chosen as the central film for this chapter. The selection of *M* is significant because it was made early in the history of film, and despite being made almost 80 years ago it remains remarkably relevant today in respect to its complex portrayal of the evil at work in society. The story of *M* revolves around a serial killer of children. According to Lang, Germany was plagued by a few serial killers at the time when he drew on this subject matter (Morris, 2010). The subject matter of this film is thus based on a real-life situation.

In Lang's film, *M*, the principal character, who is a murderer, embodies both compulsive evil and the self-awareness of evil. The audience first meets this character as an ominous shadow cast against a pillar, talking to a little girl about her ball. Even though the audience has no confirmation of the shadow's identity at this point, they are aware of a mother anxiously waiting for her child to come home and of a monster preying on kids. Lang sets up this awareness during the opening scenes of the film. The first scene is of little children playing a game and singing a song about a "nasty man" who will chop them up (Lang, 1931). This scene is significant for two reasons, one of which is the establishment of the film's tone and the other one being the introduction of evil stalking innocence, and eventually destroying it. The children in this scene, as well as every young girl out in the street, are continual reminders to the audience and also to the people in the film world of how fragile and fleeting human innocence is. The opening sequence of *M*

220 Explaining Evil

illustrates how effective film as a medium can be applied to portray some of the most enthralling facets of evil, *id est* evil lurking around the corner, stalking the innocent, and creating a silent pervasive fear.

Film reflects what humans perceive evil to be, which is undoubtedly that evil is pervasive as well as continuous. These two characteristics of evil are primary themes in *M*, together with the recurring contemplation of the awareness and recognition of evil, response to evil, and lack of a satisfactory answer to evil.

THE PERVASIVE AND UNDYING NATURE OF EVIL

Hans Beckert is the serial killer in the film who hunts and kills little girls. He is portrayed as haunted by himself—his evil self. Sometimes the voice of evil becomes so strong, so unrelenting that he has seemingly little choice but to feed the starving and desperate mouth of evil by killing a young girl, thus temporarily stilling the hunger. In Beckert's own words, "This evil thing inside me, the fire, the voices, and the torment!" (Lang, 1931). In *M*, the persistent and endless hunger of evil, which can only be sated momentarily with the shedding of innocent blood, is powerfully captured in the face of the protagonist. When the "thing" in him demands satisfaction, we see his eyes bulging from terror and recognition, and after he has killed his face changes and reflects an inner peacefulness.

The audience never actually see the evil operating in *M*, but in Werner Herzog's *Nosferatu the Vampyre* (1979) evil is externalized in the form of Count Dracula, who has the spirit of Nosferatu—the undead. This film opens with a shot of a monstrous figure whose face is dominated by a dark open mouth. The open-mouthed figure symbolizes the nature of Nosferatu, who is of an ancient family that feeds on humankind's blood. In one particular scene, the viewer sees Nosferatu entering Lucy's bedroom as a shadow whose hunger is reflected in the restless moving of his fingers, and later, when they converse, in his perpetually open mouth that is a powerful recurring sign of his barely controlled, unending appetite. The image of Nosferatu's hunger can be seen as a dramatic visualization of Beckert's (serial killer in *M*) internal evil self.

The film figure of Nosferatu is a notable attempt at testing the concept of evil as spirit, who is able to move freely, sometimes operating as a force external to humans and sometimes, frighteningly, entering into humans. Evil in the form of Count Dracula tells of evil's experience of living without life. Nosferatu is forever trapped in a futile existence in which he longs for death but cannot die. He perceives such an existence as cruel and laments that he must endure the "most abject pain" when he is denied the experience of true love again and again (Herzog, 1979). Nosferatu's thoughts may be taken as evil's stream of consciousness and reminds the viewer of the character of Satan in Milton's *Paradise Lost* when he says,

. . . aside the Devil turned for envy, yet with jealous leer malign
Eyed them askance, and to himself thus plained.
Sight hateful, sight tormenting! Thus these two
Imparadised in one another's arms
The happier Eden, shall enjoy their fill
Of bliss on bliss, while I to Hell am thrust,
Where neither joy nor love, but fierce desire,
Among our other torments not the least,
Still unfulfilled with pain of longing pines. (2000, IV, 502–511)

Nosferatu, like Satan in *Paradise Lost*, realizes that he will always remain an outsider and unable to partake of the good things that human beings are able to enjoy. He is also doomed, like Satan, to do the only thing he can do, and that is to destroy these good things and bring death.

Viewers of *Nosferatu the Vampyre* come to fear the sound of creaking doors in the night, but the audience watching *M* comes to dread the sight of a young girl walking alone and the whistled tune of Edvard Grieg's *In the Hall of the Mountain King*. They know that those elements together signal yet another possible abduction and killing. It is for this reason that one expects to feel relief at the end of *M*, when Beckert is captured first by underworld leaders and later by police. Strangely, though, the relief never comes and for one very good reason, which is that by now the audience has witnessed a much more subtle and hidden evil than the one raging in Beckert. The double shock of the evil operating in and through Beckert and the evil operating in societal structures keeps the audience from relaxing at the end and instead aligns audience members more with the mourning mothers in the final scene, feeling that what has been lost can never be regained again—the children and, by implication, humankind's innocence.

M, *Nosferatu the Vampyre*, and many other films seem to repeatedly return to the theme of loss of innocence and purity. Through these films, viewers often become newly aware of this mysterious loss, and our attempts to fix its origin. Mirror images in *M* play a major role in highlighting the question of evil, as well as the related question of why it is ours to battle with. In *Nosferatu the Vampyre*, an ancient unseen predator is put forth as the cause. Just as we are bound to continue our search for the origin of individual and social chaos, so also will we continue to ponder and construct a variety of versions of the Fall and the serpent based on a biblical view of evil (Genesis 3). Nosferatu is a representation of the serpent, contaminating our life blood with the poison of death. The fact that he so readily enters bedrooms at night is symbolic of the fateful decision of Adam and Eve to succumb to temptation.

The continuation of evil through generations is often a motif in film. In *Nosferatu the Vampyre*, Nosferatu is placed within an ancient family reflecting evil as embedded in a transgenerational family context. Likewise, in Francis

Ford Coppola's *The Godfather* (1972), the perpetuation of evil is placed within a family context confirming the perception of the transgenerational character of evil. Similarly, the presentation of the corrupt societal structures in *M* reflects the undying and pervasive nature of evil.

Toward the end of *M*, Beckert is caught by a group of criminals and beggars and put on trial in a kangaroo court (a court consisting of the people affected by Beckert's deeds). Beckert is framed as the evil figure standing trial in a kangaroo court that is an illegal court, thus making the court guilty of committing evil. Schränker, the underworld leader, acts as prosecutor and judge but has himself murdered three people. The complexity of evil as it presents itself in society is clearly portrayed through the staging of this pseudo-trial.

When the prosecutor and judge put the following question to Beckert, "Do you say that you have to murder?" he answers with a passionate speech, telling those present of being trapped in his own evil behavior against his will:

> It is there all the time, driving me out to wander the streets following me silently but I can feel it there. It's me pursuing myself. I want to escape, escape from myself! But it's impossible. I can't escape. I have to obey. I have to run . . . endless streets. I want to escape, to get away. And I am pursued by ghosts. Ghosts of mothers. And of those children. They never leave me. They are always there, always there. Always, except when I do it. When I . . . Then I can't remember anything. Afterwards I see those posters and read what I have done. Did I do that? But I can't remember anything about it. But who will believe me? Who knows what it's like to be me? How I am forced to act. . . . How I must. . . . Must. . . . Don't want to. Must! Don't want to, but must! And then . . . a voice screams. I can't bear to hear it. I can't go on. (Lang, 1931)

Beckert presents his intrapsychic process of compulsion to murder as a self-defense. His speech describes how he cannot resist this inner driving force and how he is compelled to murder. Thus, *M* portrays the driving force behind the evil deeds committed by the evil figure of Beckert as an internal force. The interpretation and explanation of moral evil as a result of an intrapsychic weakness or illness are frequently encountered in psychological theories, and although this approach is valuable to some extent, it unfortunately fails to offer any real hope or solution to the presence of evil that affects society.

Beckert enhances his self-defense by contrasting his compulsive behavior with the crimes chosen and committed by Schränker and his group. The question of free will is indubitably addressed in this film. On the one hand, a psychologically imbalanced serial killer is portrayed as a huge threat to the security and happiness of the city's people. On the other hand, a variety of freely chosen illegal actions active in the same society is portrayed, *id est* falsified identity documentation, theft, murder, and so forth. Through this film, viewers are made aware of the evil inherently part of all humans that persistently undermines the safety and happiness of a society.

Film successfully represents the complexity of the pervasiveness of moral evil as it stems from the evil inherent in humankind, fostering an undying cycle of evil. This leads to a heightened awareness of the difficulty to conquer or eradicate evil, which in turn highlights the importance of finding solutions for evil.

AWARENESS AND RECOGNITION OF EVIL

Upon viewing films that deal with the topic of evil in one way or another, it emerges that humankind must have knowledge of evil, and can therefore recognize it and portray it in opposition to good. So, we are not ignorant and can distinguish between good and evil—a point that is portrayed with great cinematic flair in *M*. After all, in Milton's *Paradise Lost*, Satan's strategy to destroy creation is revealed to involve corruption of the mind: "Yet let me not forget what I have gained/From their own mouths; all is not theirs it seems:/ One fatal Tree there stands of Knowledge called,/Forbidden them to taste: knowledge forbidd'n?" (2000, IV, 512–515). In relation to film, it is important for us to examine the depiction of awareness and recognition of evil, but additionally we should ask how films have represented the usefulness of our knowledge in devising effective strategies to eradicate evil.

During the trial of Beckert staged by the underworld, it materializes that Beckert is fully aware of the evil that drives him to murder. At first he denies everything, but after he realizes that he has been unmistakably identified as the murderer, he admits to his impulse to kill. He speaks of the torment of having to contend with this evil and its haunting consequences. The verbal admission of awareness is prefigured in the film through striking scenes involving Beckert and mirrors. The first scene of this kind occurs after Beckert has murdered Elsie Beckmann and while the graphologist provides an analysis of the murderer's personality. In this scene, Beckert is half-smiling and examining his face, first pulling down the corners of his mouth, signaling that he should feel remorse for what he has done, and secondly widening his eyes in mock horror at what he sees reflected. He knows who he is and what he is doing, but feels no real remorse or repulsion, although he tries to simulate it in front of the mirror because he also knows that is what he should feel. Evidently, Beckert knows not only that he has evil inside him but also that evil feels no remorse and will continue.

In a later scene, Beckert's awareness of his evil persona is brought to the surface when he is confronted with his reflection in a mirror and sees that he has been branded with a "M" on his shoulder. The fake horror of the earlier mirror scene is replaced by the real horror of coming face-to-face with a murderer, caught in the act of prepping his next victim. The painful self-awareness of Beckert gives him a haunted, stalked air that is as tragic as the similar awareness expressed by Nosferatu as he tells of being a prisoner to evil, doomed to drain life to sustain his undead state and to be forever unable to enjoy good things, like love.

Examining viewers' relationship to film and specifically to film portrayals of evil further elucidates the role of film in exploring evil. In *M*, one poignant scene involves the viewer in a more provocative way than most others, and like with the mirror scenes, this scene involves reflection. The viewers watch Beckert as he walks through the streets, an ordinary man buying and eating an apple. Then, he stops and looks into the glass of a shop's window, which brings him almost face-to-face with the audience. The scene seems to say that Beckert is just a human being like all the members of the audience. However, Lang uses the frame-within-a-frame technique to frame Beckert's face in a diamond-shaped reflection of knives for sale in the shop (Corrigan, 2001, p. 108).

The effect is twofold as viewers are once again reminded of Beckert's evil self but also of the evil self that might be in each audience member, or in each member of society. This scene is thus designed to reflect, and enhance the awareness of, the evil that permeates society. It furthermore reveals that by involving the audience, one moves closer to the discovery and utilization of the progressive potential of film to deal with the issue of evil, not just as a fictional reality but also as a fiction that is reality.

Haneke's film *Funny Games* (1997) centers on the sadistic and fatal games that two young men play with a wealthy family, the Schobers, for no apparent reason. One of these men, Paul, is a self-aware character that breaks the fourth wall several times to speak to the audience directly, thereby actively involving them in the action that takes place in the film space. This technique allows the director to close the gap between himself, his work, and the audience. In doing so he gains the opportunity to ask questions of his audience, to encourage them not only to think about the topic of the film but also to become aware of how they would like the film to proceed. The effect of this level of observer involvement is to shatter the illusion that there is a definite, unbreakable line between reality and fiction. An idea tested by *Funny Games* is film's potential to reach us and moreover to teach us about ourselves and our paradoxical relationship with evil. Mr. Schober asks Paul twice why they are doing this; he responds the first time with a brief "Why not?" and later he responds by providing many versions of the same sympathetic story, for example, he cites divorce, abuse, poverty, drug addiction, and boredom as reasons (Haneke, 1997).

Not one of these stories is true, and through this "game" Paul unmistakably demonstrates an important point about audience expectation—that it requires a neat and acceptable explanation for the occurrence of the evil deeds. Haneke believed that one cannot imagine a worse fictional event than what occurs in reality (Rich, 2008). Through the figure of Paul, he illustrates that film can also be employed to confront audience expectations and sources of pleasure that will ultimately discourage blind and complacent viewership. Our paradoxical relationship with evil is similarly portrayed in *M*, when Beckert points out that although he does not have a choice but to murder, the criminals who are participating in the kangaroo court and prosecuting him commit evil by choice. This brings us again to the question of free will and whether humans are truly able to make morally good choices.

The decision made by the group of criminals to hunt down the murderer seems like a morally good choice but is motivated by the losses they have suffered as a result of intensified police raids to hunt down the murderer. Although the motive is wrong, the decision to assist in finding the serial killer and putting a stop to his evil deeds seems right. Subsequently, the question arises whether this choice is morally right and the deed truly good. The complexity that is irrevocably part of good and evil as they manifest in the motives, thoughts, emotions, and behavior of humans is portrayed in a thought-provoking way. The difficulty of defining the root of evil is illustrated as the root is shown to be inherently part of the human psyche, expressed in selfish motives to make a morally correct choice.

Thus, we assert that film portrays evil not only as recognizable but also as inherently part of humans, resulting in the double bind of being simultaneously drawn to, and repulsed by, evil. This implies a full awareness and self-awareness of evil, and additionally the ability to distinguish right from wrong and take responsibility for wrong choices.

RESPONSE TO EVIL

The exploration of evil in film up to this point has revealed that evil permeates all levels of society, and this naturally leads to the consideration of how the various sections of society are depicted as they respond to evil. In *M*, society looks upon the tragic evil figure of Beckert as lost and doomed. Upon closer investigation of society's position, we learn much more about the insidious nature of evil than we would have had we only investigated Beckert himself. Lang includes the actions of three large groups in society—the public, legitimate law-and-order institutions, and the underworld. The general populace in *M* vacillates between complacency and chaos, which hardly assists with the tracking down of a serial killer. Lang points out in an early scene that there might be something amiss in ordinary people's ability to distinguish between good and evil that is most visible when they are threatened by external evil, like a serial killer. This societal disorder and confusion are not surprising considering that you are asking people, who each have their own individual conflict between good and evil, to identify evil and rid themselves of it.

Lang portrayed this very well in a scene where members of the public accuse an innocent man of wrongdoing. An old man is talking to a little girl, which leads to suspicion on the part of several people in the vicinity, who then accuse the man of being a killer of children although he is completely innocent of that charge. As the innocent man is stared down by a larger accuser, Lang shows him using an exaggerated high-angled shot that highlights the fragility of innocence. He then switches to a shot of the accuser employing an exaggerated low-angled shot that makes the accuser, a self-designated protector of the innocent, seem menacing. It interestingly opens the way for a further layer of complexity to our understanding of the nature of human recognition and awareness of evil. It seems as if an obviously, compulsively evil character like Beckert is more fully aware of the evil lurking in him than the ordinary man who covers his own with a thin layer of civility and good intentions, thereby repressing any surface awareness of own evil tendencies.

Lang further delves into this issue with his treatment of two opposing forces in society—the legitimate and the illegitimate. Frequent police raids designed to flush out the killer have a crippling effect on the city's organized crime system. Criminal leaders meet to discuss the "evil" that has brought the law to their doorstep almost permanently. While underworld lords meet, their counterparts in government and law enforcement also meet to report on progress and devise new plans to catch the killer. Beckert and the hunt for him function like a mirror in which society is reflected, specifically the motives at the heart of society's protectors and its criminal element. In effect, Beckert has threatened the status quo of life in the city, and the audience witnesses a frantic rush to restore the balance, which can be summarized as government and police being able to go quietly about their business of governing and policing without undue scrutiny and pressure, and the underworld bosses making money without undue disturbances. Thus, these two forces react to the serial killer situation in such a way as to protect their own interests first and foremost.

The criminals' response is probably the more provocative of the two and enjoys a large amount of screen time. The underworld leader, Schränker, suggests that the criminals form an alliance with the beggars' union in order to catch the killer. The inherent contradiction of criminals setting out to rid society of an evil element makes the audience sit up and pay attention. Schränker, a murderer himself, believes that Beckert is giving the criminal world a bad name and that he should be eliminated without pity as he has no right to live—a belief shared by many in the underworld. This puzzling distinction made in the underworld between acceptable illegitimate acts and those that go too far is treated at length in Coppola's film, *The Godfather*. In a perplexing scene, audiences witness a discussion between the heads of the families about whether or not to venture into the drug business. Some bosses are agreeable, but others, including Don Vito Corleone, object but later agree that it would be acceptable as long as it is kept out of schools. This is a remarkable discussion that is not far removed from typical discussions between ordinary people about which evil is the lesser evil; for example, should the audience consider Beckert's evil impulses to be greater than Schränker's?

Lang masterfully links Schränker with Beckert when he films the shadow Schränker and his fellow criminal leaders cast against the wall after they have successfully hatched their master plan to capture Beckert. Lang seems to pose the question of what the difference really is between those who serve the master of shadows. Indeed, Nosferatu himself tells Harker that he has long since lost interest in the light and now keeps to the shadows, where he can be alone with his thoughts—in the context of *M*, these "thoughts" can translate as "evil plans" to either kill little girls or kill killers.

When Beckert is tried by these crooks, he makes the point that they, the criminals, have no right to condemn him to death and asks to be handed over to the police. The assembly of murderers, thieves, prostitutes, and con artists laughs at him in response because they, of all people, know how hard it is to cure or rehabilitate evil tendencies. Lang goes to great length to show the police and government at work to capture the murderer—a meticulous, systematic, and scientific methodology is employed to ensnare the serial killer. Ironically, it is quite by accident that the police are able to apprehend Beckert in the middle of his "trial." By implication, it seems that no matter how advanced the science or how thorough the method, evil still eludes capture and continues to roam the city streets looking for its next victim.

Spinelli (2000, p. 564) hypothesized that the reaction of society to the media coverage of evil, picking at every morsel to dish it up to a very receptive audience, is indicative of the kinship with those committing the crimes rather than alienation. In support of his hypothesis, Spinelli referred to a quote from Mantel (cited in Spinelli, 2000, p. 564) in a review of Gitta Sereny's biography of the child-killer Mary Bell:

> But part of us wants more information . . . to feed our fascination and fear. What is it that we fear? Not the loss to the victim, but the loss of innocence in ourselves; . . . not her loss of control, but the fragility of it in ourselves. We can, as Gitta Sereny suggests[,] "use" Mary, less to confirm our faith in society than to confirm the daily wonder that we believe in society at all. We can, with effort, see Mary not as an alien, but Mary as kin, as a stained and transgressive being like us: with the malady of being human and with no hope of a cure.

The response of society to evil as illustrated in *M* highlights the eagerness to blame somebody else for the evil. It illustrates the human tendency to recognize evil in somebody else rather than the self. Concurrent with this tendency is the tendency to pass the responsibility for dealing with evil to somebody else. In *M*, this is realized in Inspector Lohmann's response to the murders that a mother should guard her children—directing blame to the mothers for the disappearance of their little girls.

M furthermore expresses the recognition of evil in somebody else. The group of criminals is able to recognize the "evil" in the murderer and take responsibility to rid society of him. Although this decision is largely motivated by the predicament of their illegal activities being curbed by extended police raids, many in the group appear outraged by the pain the murders have caused the mothers of the children. Society is called upon to take responsibility for the disappearance of the children. Thus, it is everybody's responsibility to address evil and participate in devising strategies to contain societal evil. People's inherent mixture of good and evil is potently depicted in this film.

NO ANSWER TO EVIL

A lone voice, Beckert's pretend defense "attorney" calls out that the sick cannot be held responsible for their deeds. Beckert is both a symbol of the persistence of evil and a sympathetic figure because he clearly needs help. He needs to be saved, and none of society's remedies can succeed: Neither killing nor asylums or prisons can truly cure evil or rid humankind of evil. Herzog's Nosferatu represents both of these elements as well, and we can thus conclude that these are indeed perceived properties of evil. Nosferatu exhibits both the never-ending hunger and also the pitifulness, and the people in *Nosferatu the Vampyre* react in the same way toward the evil that is affecting them as those in *M*. They are afraid, suspicious, and unable to propose an adequate solution.

The lone voice of Lucy in *Nosferatu the Vampyre* is just as ineffective as the one in *M* but arguably more accurate in content. She has researched the evil, and its accompanying death, that has come upon her city and has discovered that sacrifice with a pure heart is one way to vanquish it. She fails to convince the character of Dr. von Hellsing, who insists that the phenomenon must be investigated scientifically. Finally, she goes ahead with the plan by herself—a plan that involves her sacrificing herself to overcome Nosferatu.

Lucy is seen running through a square in the city asking those carrying coffins why they do not listen to her as she knows what is plaguing them and how to be victorious over it. In Lucy we have a figure that brings hope, although nobody hears it and we see that ultimately her sacrifice is not enough as evil has already acquired a fresh vehicle in Harker, her husband. Looking at the outcomes of both *M* and *Nosferatu the Vampyre*, the viewer is left with as little hope that evil can be overcome as the societies in both films are. The law, prisons, capital punishment, insane asylums, an eye for an eye, and human sacrifice are all proposed, considered, and found wanting in dealing with evil in its many varied forms. Still, it is the character of Lucy, who reminds one of John the Baptist, who also called to the people to listen to his message.

Matthew 3:1 states that "John the Baptist came, preaching in the Desert of Judea and saying, 'Repent, for the kingdom of heaven is near'" (NIV, 1999). Lucy's plan that involves pure-heartedness and sacrifice is also reminiscent of Jesus Christ, the one John the Baptist spoke of in Matthew 3:11: "But after me will come one who is more powerful than I" (NIV, 1999). Jesus Christ indeed was pure of heart and died on the cross—a sacrifice that could overcome evil, something no amount of human sacrifice or intelligence can achieve. It is remarkable that we can, through the medium of film, explore not only our notions of evil and its consequences but also our notions of what can save us from its perpetual presence and onslaught.

The persistent existence of evil and its consequences in society lead to attempts to rescue victims of evil one way or another. In *M*, the rescue attempt is made by a group of shady characters displaying rescuer traits although they themselves are perpetrators. The rescuer trait present in humans is referred to by one of the characters in *M* who says, "In every person there is a mother at heart" (Lang, 1931). This quote indicates that humans, even criminals, possess an internal ability to care about pain, loss, and injustice. It also illustrates the need for a savior that can eradicate or conquer evil.

This need is best illustrated in the final scene of the film, when three real judges enter to judge Beckert. The mothers of the murdered children are shown in their state of bereavement. Elsie Beckman's mother states that no outcome to the trial could bring any of the children back. Her statement elucidates another facet of evil, *id est* the consequences of evil in society often cannot be rectified, or in reality one does not have the option of rewinding the action and acquiring a more favorable outcome, as demonstrated by *Funny Games*. Film has the compelling ability to represent how intricate and elusive moral evil can be and how difficult it is for humans to find an effective strategy to eradicate or contain societal evil.

A BIBLICAL PHILOSOPHICAL FRAMEWORK

As portrayed in film, the complexity and depth of evil in its different forms—moral, societal, natural, and supernatural—are encountered by humans daily. The feebleness of human attempts to conquer or contain evil is similarly portrayed. Although film may deepen our understanding of evil as presented in society, it falls short of providing a meaningful explanation of, or strategy to conquer, evil.

In philosophy, theology, and anthropology, discourses on the origin and nature of evil have been elicited over decades. These discourses aim at deepening our understanding of evil and debate possible solutions for evil.

Psychological theories, on the other hand, tend to shy away from using the term *evil* in their explanation of behavior that may be viewed as evil. Spinelli (2000, p. 562) pointed out that it is rare to find in the psychotherapeutic literature any in-depth analysis of the notion of evil. *Evil* is defined by Spinelli (2000, p. 561) as "the notion of deliberate, thoughtful yet morally indefensible acts of violence towards others." According to Spinelli (2000, p. 561), the moral and existential dimensions of evil are avoided in psychotherapy by transforming possible evil behavior into psychopathological language. The explanation for evil behavior involves a disease or dysfunction on a physical or psychic level. However, this intrapsychic view on evil fails to explain and address in an adequate fashion interrelational factors of evil (Spinelli, 2000, pp. 564–566).

A biblical philosophical framework, based on creation theory rooted in a literal Genesis, provides an explanation of the origin of evil, depicts the inherent moral abilities that humans possess, and portrays a human existence in which the power of evil is broken (Chinitz, 2005, p. 153; Calvin cited in Collins, 1999, pp. 65–70; Purdom & Lisle, 2009, p. 8).

Thus, a biblical philosophical framework of evil, rather than a psychological theory, provides us with an interpretative framework suitable for the evaluation of the portrayal of evil presented in film. Consequently, a biblical philosophical framework is applied in this section, with the aim to evaluate the moral and existential dimensions of evil as portrayed in film and discussed in this chapter.

The Pervasive and Undying Nature of Evil

The two characteristics of evil focused on in the portrayal of evil in film and discussed in this chapter are the pervasiveness of evil and the undying nature of evil.

A biblical philosophical framework explains the origin of evil as embedded in a heavenly being, Satan embodied in the serpent tempting Eve in the Garden of Eden (Genesis 3). Satan is described as a fallen angel, without any hope of redemption and only one agenda, which is to oppose God and damage His Kingdom. This explains the undying nature of evil, as Satan is immortal and can be destroyed only by God Himself. The pervasiveness of evil inherently part of humankind and well portrayed in film in its complexity is untangled in the biblical narration of the creation of humans and Adam and Eve's Fall into sin (Calvin cited in Collins, 1999, pp. 65–66). Humans were created in the image of God, which is reflected in their moral, mental, and social capacities (Farnsworth, 1985, pp. 134–135; Purdom & Lisle, 2009, p. 8). This implies that humans were created with the ability to make moral choices. Adam and Eve's wrong moral choice (disobeying God's instruction) to eat the fruit from the tree of Knowledge of good and evil opened their souls to accepting evil and marred the image of God (all Good) in them. This resulted in the paradoxical relationship that humans have with evil and explains the pervasiveness of evil as it is transferred from generation to generation.

Chinitz (2005, p. 153), a Jewish scholar, outlined the sinful nature of man, with the consequent inability to choose what is good, as one of four options regarding moral choice based on biblical texts from the Old Testament. The first option is based on Gen 8:21, Ps 51:7, and Job 5:5, which project the sinful nature of man, and states that man is inherently evil and therefore finds it impossible to choose good.

Gen 8:21: And when the LORD smelled the pleasing aroma, the LORD said in his heart, "I will never again curse the ground because of man, *for the intention of man's heart is evil from his youth*" (English Standard Version, 2001, italics added).

Calvin (cited in Collins, 1999, p. 65) concurred with this option in his argument that man in his fallen condition is deprived of free will and "miserably enslaved" to his corrupt nature. Calvin (cited in Collins, 1999, p. 65) elaborated on this stance by adding that man's soul consisting of intellect and will and by which he discerns good and evil is only partially destroyed by Adam's fall into sin and is therefore not in complete darkness. The implication is that man desires to seek the truth.

In Mark 10:18, Jesus Christ states clearly that no one is good but God, indicating that man is not inherently good: "And Jesus said to him, 'Why do you call me good? No one is good except God alone'" (English Standard Version, 2001).

The second option discussed by Chinitz (2005, p. 153) presents a theory opposite to the first option. This is based on Gen 4:7 and states that man is inherently good, but it is possible for an outside force to tempt man to do evil. Gen 4:7: "If you do well, will you not be accepted? And if you do not do well, sin is crouching at the door. Its desire is for you, but you must rule over it" (English Standard Version, 2001). This option includes the stance that it is possible for a human to have victory over evil by making the right moral choice.

Calvin (cited in Collins, 1999, p. 65) viewed this option as part of the human's position prior to Adam's fall into sin. In his original state, man was created good and had the ability to discern between right and wrong.

According to Calvin (cited in Collins, 1999, p. 65) man in his fallen state does not possess a free will and is incapable of making a righteous choice. Regeneration of the soul by Christ is a prerequisite for the restoration of man's capability to fully discern between good and evil and to make the right choices. Humans have been given the ability through the indwelling of the Holy Spirit to discern between good and evil. Likewise, humans have been given the responsibility to exercise discernment and to make right moral choices. This does not indicate that humans are purely good, as it is clearly stated in Mark 10:18 that only God is good.

Both options as discussed explain the complexity and pervasiveness of evil internally present in humans creating a double bind, as well as evil experienced as an external force tempting humans to make morally wrong choices. These factors contribute to the undying nature of evil.

AWARENESS AND RECOGNITION OF EVIL

Film, as discussed in this chapter, portrays evil as something that humans can become aware of and can recognize. Thus, evil has a recognizable face and presents in ways known to humans. This aspect raises the question of the effective implementation of this knowledge in order to freely choose to eradicate evil.

The third option for moral choice, outlined by Chinitz (2005, p. 153) and based on Deuteronomy 30, includes the view that the human is a free agent with no inherent tendencies toward good or evil. As a neutral entity, man can choose between good and evil.

Consider Deuteronomy 30:15: "See, I have set before you today life and good, and death and evil"; and verses 19–20:

> I call heaven and earth to witness against you today, that I have set before you life and death, blessing and curse. Therefore choose life, which you and your offspring may live, loving the LORD your God, obeying his voice and holding fast to him, for he is your life and length of days. (English Standard Version, 2001)

The fourth option obtained from Talmudic liturgical language indicates the soul of man as pure and not involved in moral choices (Chinitz, 2005, p. 155). The body chooses between good and evil. This view is clarified by Chinitz (2005, p. 155), who explained that although the soul is pure before entering the body, it becomes contaminated when entering the body and thus the soul–body entity sins.

Chinitz (2005, p. 155) concluded that man does have a free will and is responsible for his choices despite the fact that he has a sinful nature and may be tempted by an outside force. God's command to man is to choose life—to make the right moral choice. This indicates the availability of two or more moral choices and the ability man has to make the right choice.

Notwithstanding the fact that these options highlight free will and the responsibility of man for his choices, they do not explain the experience of evil as an inherent drive as expressed by Beckert in *M* and Nosferatu in *Nosferatu the Vampyre*. God commands humans to choose life and not death. The question remains whether humans truly have the inherent ability to make the right choice. As depicted in film, humans often make the wrong choices or a seemingly right choice but for the wrong reasons, which underscores the realization that although humans have the ability to recognize evil, they do not have the power to rid themselves or society of evil.

Calvin (cited in Collins, 1999, pp. 27–29) asserted that knowledge of God and faith in Christ allow for self-knowledge and an understanding and appreciation of the world. The fallen nature of man represents weaknesses in the psyche of man and leads to sinful or evil behavior. It is only through faith in Christ that true self-knowledge can be experienced and evil inherent to the self can be fully recognized.

RESPONSE TO EVIL

Film is effective in the portrayal of the response of society to evil as inappropriate and bizarre from a distance, as illustrated by *M*. It is hypothesized that this kind of response is triggered by our own inherent alignment with evil (Spinelli, 2000, p. 564). This kind of portrayal, though valuable, is limited because it encourages the idea that reality and fiction are separate and therefore that observers may enjoy and indulge their evil fantasies without repercussions. A film such as *Funny Games* draws attention to this illusion and therein suggests a redefinition of the relationship between the audience and the film, and in turn an increased ability of film to be of value in our common struggle against evil. Humankind's alignment with evil as depicted in both *M* and *Funny Games* implies the lack of pure societal criteria to guide our response to evil, resulting in inappropriate and displaced reactions.

Biblical philosophy proposes the exclusion of spiritual and moral relativism and serves as a framework for meaningful responses to evil. Creation theory derived from a literal Genesis provides a foundation for morality and a standard for what is defined as good and what is defined as evil (Bahnsen, cited in Purdom & Lisle, 2009, p. 8).

God is not the inventor of evil as He is all good. He created humans with a free will and the option of making the wrong moral choice by disobeying Him. In the creation of a free will and the option of a choice between right and wrong is embedded the possibility of evil. The origin of evil is placed in the fall of one of the holy angels created by God as described in the Bible. The Bible (Job 38:4–7) places the creation of angels before the creation of the earth. One of these angels desired to be like God and rebelled against God. This angel fell from heaven and is referred to as Satan or the devil. Satan personifies evil as an external force tempting humans to go against God's will.

Calvin (cited in Collins, 1999, pp. 27–29) was of the opinion that there is no knowledge without belief, and according to him any mistaken representation of the truth is either a direct result of sin or from not knowing God at all. Truth in self-knowledge and knowledge of God comes only through belief in God. Farnsworth (1985, pp. 115–117) supported this idea by stating that the Bible and the person are related to God by their very nature, and to fully know the truth involves all three. Only from a position of knowing the truth about our own sinful nature and knowing God through faith can we truly discern how to respond to evil.

NO ANSWER TO EVIL

The feebleness of the human attempt to conquer evil is certainly portrayed in film. No amount of human goodness or innocence seems to achieve the desired results, and society is time and again thrown back into the grip of evil.

A biblical philosophical framework interprets this phenomenon in light of the inability of humans to be purely good. Thus, no amount of good deeds can overcome evil. The answer to evil from a biblical philosophical point of view is faith. Faith is defined as trust in God and through Christ by which humans are saved from eternal death as a consequence of their evil nature. It is by faith alone that humans can be saved. The character of Lucy in *Nosferatu the Vampyre* correctly identifies faith as the faculty that gives humans the ability to believe things not based on scientific proof that can aid in our common struggle against evil.

Faith in God and Christ Jesus leads to the regeneration of the soul and enables humans to choose what is right (Calvin cited in Collins, 1999, p. 95). Good deeds performed without faith are still contaminated and cannot abolish evil. Faith provides hope and a way out of evil. The value of applying this framework to the portrayal of evil in film lies in the hope and solution it presents.

SUMMARY

The biblical philosophical framework indicates the following important aspects regarding the origin and expression of evil in the world and man's response to it in film.

The experience and expression of evil indicate that it is inherently part of humans as the result of a spontaneous choice by Adam and leads to the realization that evil perpetuates as an internal condition and as part of the fallen state of man. Evil likewise exists interrelationally as it is inextricably part of all humans and expresses itself in relational situations. Evil can be discerned by man in his fallen state because his original pure state reflecting the image of God in him has not been completely destroyed by his sinful nature. Humans hold two opposite poles in their nature—good and evil—and therefore are both the victim and the villain. Human attempts to curb or overcome evil are ineffectual, and internal evil can be overcome only when the fallen nature of humans is regenerated by Christ. Further to this evil exists externally from humans in the form of a supernatural force, Satan that can tempt man to commit evil or sinful deeds. A fear of evil overcoming good exists and perpetuates constant attempts to overcome evil. A need for a savior is apparent.

CONCLUSION

Media coverage of evil is rightfully critiqued when it portrays evil in a superficial and sensationalist manner that serves to desensitize viewers. Withstanding this usage of film, film as a medium can be effectively applied to portray the complexity and pervasiveness of evil as encountered by humans on a daily basis. Some films have the capacity to educate us about internal and external evil from a largely safe distance. Others have the capacity to open viewers' eyes to their own relationship with evil, specifically as it is reflected in their expectations of films that include the topic of evil and, moreover, in the pleasure they experience from viewing such films. Thus, film as a medium can be incorporated in our resistance against evil and search for effective strategies to contain evil in society.

The application of the biblical philosophical framework in the interpretation of evil as portrayed in film supports film's capacity to effectively increase our understanding of the origin, existence, and expression of evil and also points out the limitations of this medium thus far. It is not implausible to consider that film may address these limitations in future with a reasonable degree of success.

REFERENCES

Chinitz, J. (2005). Four biblical options in moral choice. *Jewish Bible Quarterly, 33* (3), 153–156.

Collins, O. (Ed.). (1999). *Complete Christian classics* (Vol. 1). London: HarperCollins.

Coppola, F. F. (Dir.). (1972). *The godfather* [Motion picture]. Los Angeles: Columbia Pictures.

Corrigan, T. (2001). *A short guide to writing about film* (4th ed.). New York: Pearson Education.

Farnsworth, K. (1985). *Whole-hearted integration: Harmonizing psychology and Christianity through word and deed.* Grand Rapids, MI: Baker Book House.

Grace, K. M. (2000). Satan on the silver screen. *The Report,* 58–59.

Haneke, M. (Dir.). (1997). *Funny games* [Motion picture]. New York: Kino Video.

Herzog, W. (Dir.). (1979). *Nosferatu the vampyre* [Motion picture]. Michigan: Starz/Anchor Bay.

Holy Bible: English Standard Version. (2001). Crossways Bibles, a division of the Good News Publishers.

Holy Bible: NIV. (1999). Seoul, Korea: Christian Publishing.

Hoorn, J. F., & Konijn, E. A. (2003). Perceiving and experiencing fictional characters: An integrative account. *Japanese Psychological Research, 45* (4), 250–268.

Lang, F. (Dir.). (1931). *M* [Motion picture]. New York: Criterion.

Milton, J. (2000). *Paradise lost.* London: Penguin.

Monaco, J. (2000). *How to read a film* (3rd ed.). New York: Oxford University Press.

Morris, G. (2010). Fritz Lang's *M. Bright Lights Film Journal.* Retrieved from http://www.brightlightsfilm.com/29/m.html.

Norden, M. F. (Guest ed.). (2000). Introduction: The changing face of evil in film and television. *Journal of Popular Film and Television, 50–53.*

Purdom, G., & Lisle, J. (2009, Spring). Morality and the irrationality of an evolutionary worldview. *Phi Kappa Phi Forum,* 8–11.

Rich, K. (2008, March 12). *Interview:* Funny Games *director Michael Haneke.* Retrieved from http://www.cinemablend.com/new/Interview-Funny-Games-Director-Michael-Haneke-8141.html.

Schrag, C. O. (2006). Otherness and the problem of evil: How does that which is other become evil? *International Journal for Philosophy of Religion, 60,* 149–156.

Spinelli, E. (2000). Therapy and the challenge of evil. *British Journal of Guidance & Counselling, 28* (4), 561–567.

CHAPTER 15

Narcissism as Evil

Deb Brock and Ron Johnson

The essence of evil is narcissism. We further propose that the essence of narcissism is a lack of self, and that the lack of self is due to a lack of proper early life attachment. In this chapter, we will focus predominantly on psychological and behavioral symptoms of narcissism and the psychological and behavioral symptoms of inadequate attachment, and propose a means for a restoration of self and reduction of narcissism in individuals, relationships, and society at large. In refraining from a concrete definition of evil, we propose that evil surfaces out of the phenomenon of narcissism as a detriment to personal growth and, consequently, relational growth. This lack of growth is, then, a reflection of a lack of goodness, or an inclination toward evil.

The term *narcissism* was coined in the field of psychology as an outgrowth of the Greek mythological figure Narcissus, who was transfixed by his reflection in a pool of water, and as a result failed to move beyond this fascination. As a result of this origin of the term *narcissism*, the term has come to mean undue self-focus and has become a central concept in the field of psychology. Simply understood, narcissism is selfishness. Narcissistic people are particularly self-oriented and self-inflating. They spend an inordinate amount of time thinking about themselves, as well as a fair bit of time concerned about what other people might think of them. Interestingly, narcissistic people can be quite attractive due to an ability to impress people with an ingratiating nature, or they can be quite the opposite, namely, challenging, angry, and generally quite difficult to live with because of their tendency to express absolute demands. These two extremes of social engagement reflect the two sides that actually exist in narcissism: undue self-absorption and undue awareness of others. Their awareness of others, however, is actually a concern for others' rejection of them, rather than concern for others.

The popular understanding of narcissism is that it roughly equates to selfishness. At a deeper level, however, narcissism is selflessness. In other words, when an individual is acting in a "narcissistic" manner or may have a narcissistic personality disorder, this individual acts selfish but, in fact, does not have a good sense of self. It is essential to have this sense of self for adequate emotional and interpersonal functioning. We propose in this chapter that narcissism needs to be distinguished from evil, but that narcissism can lead to, cause, or aggravate evil or evils. We will discuss the possibilities that narcissism is evil, that narcissistic behavior is evil, and that narcissistic individuals are evil.

Narcissism is a central figure in understanding humankind. In childhood, particularly in early childhood, it is natural and necessary for the child to be self-oriented and "narcissistic" (if we use that term). There are some natural elements of what we might call *positive narcissism* in adolescence, but in adulthood narcissism is largely pathological, harmful to oneself and to others. We shall begin our study of narcissism with an examination of natural childlike narcissism.

NATURAL AND HEALTHY NARCISSISM

Narcissism can be thought of as a predominately self-oriented means of engaging life. Due to the nature of childhood and the requirement that a child develop both a sense of self and a sense of other people, it is natural and necessary that children be predominantly self-focused, or narcissistic. This means that children of this young age see the world as serving them, and do not particularly worry about serving the world. Furthermore, this self-oriented view of life is extremely important for a child to have so that she may develop a solid sense of self from which she can eventually engage the world. The delicate task of transitioning from childhood through adolescence into the adult world may be thought of as a transition from a self-oriented perspective to an other-oriented perspective of life. This is no easy transition to make, and it is possible only if a child is given sufficient time and experience to be naturally narcissistic.

Consider what it must be like for an infant, especially a newborn, to enter into life and (ideally) be completely cared for by the external world. Although we cannot attribute too much cognition to an infant, this infant believes that her needs are not only central but also, in fact, the only needs of the world. If she is hungry or in any discomfort, she naturally cries, and this cry generally leads to a mother-figure meeting her wants and needs. In fact, at this time of life the infant does not distinguish between her wants and needs. For the most part, her wants are, in fact, needs. She needs to be fed when hungry, cared for when she is in some kind of discomfort, and comforted when she is distressed. And she needs to be nurtured with physical presence a sufficient amount of time in order to feel secure in life. Importantly, these needs are not perfectly met, nor are they met within the time span (immediately) that the infant wants them to be met. The not meeting of human needs could be considered to be the human condition, that is, we all experience attachment difficulties to some degree. When the above-mentioned imperfect meeting of needs is severe, regardless of the intention of the caregiver, the resulting adult narcissistic condition is primed.

A second important understanding of infancy is that the infant does not distinguish between her caregiver and herself. In fact, she does not distinguish herself from much of her environment as least for the first months of life. This lack of distinction leads to what we, as psychologists, consider to be an "unconscious" acceptance of total dependency on the external world as natural. The infant generally does not want to be separated from the caregiver or from the world at large. Psychologists identify this early time of connection as symbiotic; in other words, the infant feels a primary symbiosis with the mother figure and a secondary symbiosis with the world around her. There is no separation; there is no self apart from others; and there is no "other." The infant, of course, has come from a uterine environment where she was, in fact, unified with her mother physically and symbolically unified with the world. This unification is essential in order for other-orientation to evolve. Any disturbance in this natural symbiosis universally causes profound distortion of self, distortion of the world, and distortion of the self in relation to the world.

The term *narcissism* in reference to infancy and early childhood is used as a positive characteristic because it denotes proper attachment. It is healthy because the child should be self-focused for survival. Survival can occur only if there is proper attachment both physically and emotionally as one with the mother figure. This attachment is foundational for self-development, which then leads to relational development. Attachment to the mother figure gives the infant a sense of safety and completeness. When her needs are met, the infant feels safe and complete. The infant must be complete with her maternal figure before she can become complete with herself in order to eventually become complete with the world. Any inadequacy in this early symbiosis between infant and mother figure causes profound damage in an individual's sense of safety, which ultimately leads to further damage in life, particularly in relationships. In contrast, if attachment is appropriate, then by the age of 6 the child is safely prepared for and desirous of separation leading to self-identity and interpersonal activity.

The ages of approximately 6 to 12 serve as a transition from natural narcissism to a time when an understanding of other people and relationships become a central operation. These years, generally called *latency*, are hallmarked predominantly by entry and completion of elementary school as well as a departure from home as one's central field of operation. Children during these ages potentially learn more about the world around them than at any other time in life as their level of knowledge doubles every year. Most of this knowledge has to do with the existence of other people and the larger world. The primary component of this knowledge is that other people have needs and wants, which means that the individual is no longer the primary occupant of the universe. This knowledge of the real existence and significance of other people brings about much joy and grief. It is joyful to learn that there are other people to play with, learn from, and love with. The latency child learns that he is not alone. But it is also sad that the individual needs to come to some understanding that he can't have all that he wants. This same child can rejoice at learning of the existence of a playmate but not like the sharing of toys and time. He might discover the excitement of the difference in appearance and language of his Chinese neighbors but soon thereafter be disappointed that he is unable to speak Chinese. The world becomes both enlarged and limited at seemingly every juncture.

The successful completion of latency brings the child into early adulthood, ideally prepared to relate to other people from a basis of appropriate attachment, appropriate separation, and further development of self and others. In our Western culture, we have added a notion of adolescence to what is, in fact, early adulthood, at least as we understand it in primitive cultures. Unfortunately, there is often an unnecessary exacerbation of natural childhood narcissism during adolescence because the adolescent has not adequately been attached, separated, and developed during his childhood years and is unequipped to begin adult relational activity.

A major cause of what we shall now call *adult narcissism*, perhaps the basis of evil in our conception, is inadequate attachment and detachment in childhood, which limits the individual's perception of himself in relationship to others. There is a strong tendency for parents who attach well to children to have difficulty detaching from them. These children, as a result, are indulged with too much freedom and insufficient limitation, leading to parental dissatisfaction and consequent shaming. There are also a number of parents who neglect their infants and children, which leads these children to never having a sense of security that evolves from normal attachment. Additionally, there is the unfortunate phenomenon of neglect followed by indulgence followed by shame. This unholy combination is certainly fertile ground for the development of adult narcissism, which we propose to be a mannerism of evil.

We, the authors, have the privilege of frequent contact with a naturally narcissistic individual in the form of our 5-year-old grandson. It has been a "grand" opportunity to see narcissism at work. Simply put, grandson Gavin is happy when he gets what he wants and profoundly unhappy when he doesn't. We can see now, perhaps better than we did when raising our daughters, the necessity for attachment, limitation, and detachment. Although we may indeed be some of Gavin's favorite people, at least by his mother's report, we are persona non grata when Gavin doesn't get what he wants or when, for instance, we insist that his beans be eaten at the dinner table. We are absolutely hated in the bean moments. Interestingly, in these moments Gavin wants no connection with us and insists on complete detachment in his hatred. However, when we limit Gavin's verbal explosions at the dinner table and ask him to depart into the living room, he does so with profound terror associated with this other-imposed separation. It must seem to our little fellow in these moments that there is an irresolvable conflict in both his need and desire for simultaneous detachment and connection. He wants the separation from us that is caused by his refusing to eat his beans while simultaneously wanting the connection to us as loved ones. To us, however, we just want him to eat vegetables. In these significant moments of childhood, Gavin wants two things that are incompatible with each other: He wants his way, that is, separation (from the beans) and connection (with his grandparents). We might say he wants the bean counters but not the beans.

It is our contention that the evil that erupts from adult narcissism has its taproot in these formative and profound years, when both child and parents must negotiate these exchanges of connection and limitation (detachment). Simply put, some parents are not able to say "yes" to their children and encourage them in life, but many more parents are not able to say "no" and limit their children. This parental limitation is likely due to the parents' own inability to attach and detach, which is the result of indulgence and neglect in their own childhood. This lack of parental limitation keeps children in a pseudo-infantile state where they believe that they should have everything they want and also have constant connection when these two phenomena are not compatible. This basic element of adult narcissism shows itself in either grandiosity or dependency based on this early life experience. It is in these years that the psyche comes to believe it must either be connected and totally cared for, or be separated and feel permanently abandoned. Later infancy and early childhood give increasing opportunity to understand the difference between separation and abandonment. Furthermore, a young child begins to grasp the concept of delayed gratification as separate from abandonment. The resolution of adult narcissism is the re-creation of the childhood dilemma of wanting attachment and detachment simultaneously. This re-creation of the original loss of proper attachment and the subsequent losses of repeated failures in connection and detachment must become conscious and realistically grieved. To realistically grieve is for the individual to recognize the unavoidable imperfection of life (parents and the environment in which he was raised), and begin the therapeutic task of contending with real-life limitations of both others and himself. Adult narcissism can be resolved singularly through a profound grief that ideally would have occurred during the natural narcissistic years in which the child grieves either the loss of his desire for something or the loss of connection.

SYMPTOMS OF ADULT NARCISSISM

The current *Diagnostic and Statistical Manual of Mental Disorders,* 4th edition (DSM-IV), identifies a narcissistic personality disorder (NPD) as one of several personality disorders. Other such disorders include borderline personality disorder (BPD) and antisocial personality disorder (APD). DSM-IV identifies NPD as an individual displaying grandiosity, needing excessive admiration, having a sense of entitlement, being interpersonally exploitative, and lacking in empathy, among other secondary symptoms. A cursory review of DSM-IV definitions and descriptions of the various personality disorders will show, however, that there is a common thread of narcissism in them all. In fact, it is likely that most or all the disorders in the DSM-IV have a narcissistic element at their base. For instance, a case can be made for a strong narcissistic element in the diagnosis of depression, anxiety, addictions, obsessive-compulsiveness, psychosomatic illness, and possibly thought disorders.

Our experience of 70 collective years of clinical experience confirms that a strong element of narcissism exists in individuals displaying the symptoms of most, if not all, of the illnesses described in the DSM-IV. We contend that many of the features of NPD identified in the DSM-IV are also present in all psychiatric disorders, albeit often in subtle forms. There is, for instance, a strong narcissistic element in BPD, which is, in fact, much more common than NPD and encompasses the large plurality of humankind, at least in North American society. Certainly, the psychogenesis of BPD is an attachment disorder. What happens in the BPD childhood is a failure to attach to a mother figure and subsequent hunger for that attachment. This hunger ultimately leads to various symptoms and pathologies, including addictions of various sorts, depression, anxiety, and certainly interpersonal failures. In the adult form of BPD, there exists an individual who displays a subtle desperation for attachment even though such attachment is usually quite temporary. This attachment can be to a person, persons, property, an organization, an addictive substance and/or behaviors, or even excessive dreaming or excessive doing. What happens in such individuals is that they attach pathologically to one of the aforementioned elements but are unable to detach unless forced to do so, at which point they subsequently attach to another element. Borderlines never learn how to properly attach and detach, thus never getting what they ultimately need. The basic flaw in the makeup of the borderline individual is that he has not moved successfully away from childlike narcissism. They are, as a result, at least as narcissistic as individuals diagnosed as NPD.

We would challenge some of the typical symptoms identified in the DSM-IV about NPD, which asserts that narcissists are singularly self-inflating and unduly independent. We suggest that an individual can be narcissistic in undue dependence or undue independence. In other words, adult narcissism shows itself in inappropriate attachment or inappropriate detachment. The problem that exists in adult-form narcissism is an inadequate attachment, which can lead to either inadequate attachment or inadequate detachment.

It is important to note that there is a spectrum of narcissism that exists in all of humankind. Individuals, such as borderlines and those with other personality disorders, generally display deeper and more profound narcissistic traits than most other people. Other psychiatric conditions, however, always have a narcissistic element in them. Furthermore, adults without a clinically diagnosed condition may suffer to some degree or another from an element of narcissism. This narcissism in the general population shows itself in less dramatic and pathological ways, although it is still based in undue independence or undue dependency.

REVIEW OF THE LITERATURE

There are several arenas of literature that we need to examine to do even minimal justice to the matter of narcissism. We want to examine literature related to human development, classical and contemporary psychoanalytic literature, and theological and philosophical literature, as these areas all contribute to a fuller understanding of the concept of narcissism

Developmental Literature

Clearly, we are presenting a format of understanding narcissism that is developmental, namely, understanding this phenomenon as a result of inadequate or arrested development. The primary developmental theorists in the field of psychology are Maslow, Piaget, Erikson, and Adler. Although making valuable contributions to developmental psychology, these theorists do not examine the matter of narcissism with any depth, nor do they examine the intrapsychic mechanisms of infancy. Piaget viewed the early life of the infant as one of "sensory motor" behavior to the large extent, but he did not elaborate on how the young infant feels or perceives the world beyond some cursory observations and examination. Maslow's understanding of infancy is that it is a time of "physiological existence" and perhaps not particularly psychologically relevant. Erikson (1950) added somewhat to an understanding of the psychological functioning of the infant, describing this time of life as one of "trust or mistrust." Adler did good work on the matter of community (i.e., how an individual must relate to other people to be successful and happy in life), but his work is largely in relation to adult functioning, with but little reference to early childhood or infancy.

Bowlby (1969, 1973, 1980) provided for us the first thorough examination beyond that of Freud of the developmental process in infants and young children. His work on attachment, separation, and loss has served as a basis for many more attachment theorists and researchers, perhaps best represented by Ainsworth and colleagues (1978). Bowlby's contention is that the infant needs a secure attachment to the mother figure to develop a sense of self, a lack of which contributes to lifelong and chronic insecurity and relationship difficulties. Ainsworth and colleagues developed a paradigm, somewhat abridged by several other authors, identifying secure attachment in infancy and ultimately in adulthood in comparison with two or more other forms of insecure attachment. These authors do not deal with the personality disorders and other narcissism-based phenomena and diagnoses, but provide fertile ground for an understanding of the centrality of attachment in infancy and ultimately in adult life.

Classic Psychoanalytic Theory

Classical understanding of narcissism is best represented by Fenichel (1945). Fenichel and other classical psychoanalysts referred to "primary" and "secondary" narcissism. Primary narcissism is, as indicated above, a condition where the infant does not distinguish himself from the world, nor from objects in the world, nor is there a distinction between his ego and feelings. Freud (1924) would suggest that the infant does not have a sense of ego until the resolution of the Oedipus complex, occurring about age 6. This classical understanding of infant psychology suggests that the infant is not capable of loving because he does not distinguish himself from objects. There is, however, what psychoanalysts call *infantile omnipotence*. This phenomenon is also called an *oceanic feeling of primary narcissism*, which simply means a state of calm based on a fluid connection the infant feels with the world.

A secondary feature of primary narcissism in psychoanalytic thought is a phenomenon that occurs in later infancy in which the infant projects his omnipotence to parents (parental figures). This projection occurs because within a few months of life, the infant comes to realize, albeit with primitive cognition, that he cannot have all that he wants immediately. Psychoanalytic thought suggests that the infant projects his omnipotence from himself to his parental figures. This projection suggests that if I am incapable of taking care of myself, someone else must be capable; otherwise, I will die. This conclusion creates the infantile illusion that the parental figure must be perfect. The infant's "love" consists singularly of taking; he acknowledges objects insofar as he needs them for his satisfaction. He does not have a capacity to give (although some analysts, e.g. Mahler, would suggest otherwise).

Klein added an interesting twist to this understanding of infantile primary narcissism as it relates to love. In her classical work (1975), Klein suggested that the feeling of envy is intrinsically entwined with gratitude and is the basis for mature love. Thus, when an individual envies something, she is actually appreciating it, albeit with a subsequent desire to have the object. In infancy the individual can only fuse with objects (people), at least during most of this time of primary narcissism, rather than truly love them.

Fenichel (1945) described secondary narcissism as the adult narcissism that we have described above. The essence of secondary narcissism is alternating between a feeling of personal omnipotence, on the one hand, and projected omnipotence to other people, on the other hand. In other words, secondary narcissism vacillates between believing that one can have everything she wants and believing that someone external to her can give her everything she wants (i.e., be perfect). Fenichel and others suggested that all forms of mental illness, including depression, addictions, and thought disorders, are flawed attempts by individuals to return to the "oceanic feeling" of primary narcissism. Further understanding of secondary narcissism has to do with self-esteem. The proposal is that secondary narcissism is a faulty or flawed self-esteem based on a flawed understanding of personal omnipotence. Alternatively, narcissism can take the form of equally flawed low self-esteem based on the belief that other people possess the omnipotence to give them what they want.

Contemporary Psychoanalytic Theory

As there are many additional classical psychoanalytic authors, there are even more contemporary theorists in this realm. Among the predominant figures are Kernberg (1975), who wrote about the condition he called *borderline personality organization*, which we should understand as borderline personality disorder (BPD), which we have noted to be narcissistic at its basis. Kernberg's understanding of this condition or diagnosis is that it is a regressive phenomenon in which the adult operates at the stage between early infancy and toddlerhood, a stage described above as one of alternating omnipotence and projected omnipotence. Symptoms of borderlines include anxiety, "polysymptomatic neurosis," sexual aberrations, some quasi-psychotic features, lack of impulse control, and addictions. Polysymptomatic neuroses include multiple phobias, obsessive-compulsive disorder (OCD) symptoms, psychosomatic illnesses, and paranoid-like symptoms. Kernberg suggested that the underlying feature of BPDs is narcissism, namely, the regression to omnipotence and projected omnipotence. He further suggested that the treatment of borderlines encompasses profound elements of transference and countertransference, or what we might consider to be a patient loving the therapist and the therapist loving the patient. This "love" is perceived by Kernberg as being an infantile or primitive experience of fusion between the omnipotent patient and omnipotent therapist.

A contemporary of Kernberg with a profound impact on psychoanalysis and psychology is Heinz Kohut. He followed much of classical psychoanalytic thought (1971) in suggesting that there is a normal infantile narcissistic state that ideally is negotiated carefully so that "narcissistic needs" are properly met. He saw the adult form of narcissism in personality disorders as a bridge between psychotic disorders and normal development. Normal development is hallmarked by positive self-esteem and self-confidence compared to the delusional grandiosity displayed in psychotic disorders. Narcissistic (personality) disorders have primarily two forms: an excessive need for attention, which is closer to normalcy, and depression and psychosomatic illness, which are closer to psychosis. Under optimal developmental conditions, the infant moves from a grandiose self through a grandiose (maternal) object to a place of understanding personal limits and limits of the maternal figure. Under the same optimal circumstances, the child experiences gradual disappointment in the maternal figure and simultaneously becomes more realistic in his expectations of her. The desired end product of this normal narcissistic stage is for the infant and young child to withdraw unrealistic expectations of the world around him, thus preparing him for the joys and sorrows of adult life.

Kohut (1971) discussed what he referred to a "narcissistic wound," which is the result of a failure of the maternal figure to provide an adequate balance of nurturance and limitation. This wound causes retention of the grandiose self or the "idealized parent or imago": "Narcissism, in my general outlook, is defined not by the target of the instinctual investment (i.e., whether it is the subject himself or other people) but by the nature or quality of the instinctual charge" (Kohut, 1971, p. 26).

If the child experiences traumatic disappointments in the admired adult, the idealized parent imago is retained in its unaltered form and not transformed into a realistic individual who has limits as well as personal desires. Kohut believed that this narcissistic wound occurs between the ages of 1 and 3, or what Freud has called the anal stage of development. Finally, he suggested that these narcissistic wounds lead to a "general structural weakness" in one's capacity to feel personally safe and to relate adequately to other people.

Lowen (1983) gave a welcome addition to contemporary psychoanalytic understanding of narcissism. He noted, for instance, that narcissism is an "exaggerated investment in one's image at the expense of the self," which suggests that narcissistic feelings, desires, and behaviors are antithetical to real self-esteem or what psychologists generally refer to as the "self." Furthermore, he suggested that contrary to their appearance, narcissists are not actually aware of their deepest feelings. Rather, they are inclined toward explosions of rage on the one hand, or strong declarations of "love" on the other. Lowen's theme in understanding narcissism is that there is a degree of "unreality" in the individual, probably exacerbated by elements of narcissism in the culture.

Perhaps Lowen's best-known contribution to psychology is his belief that there is a physiological substrate to all aspects of emotional disturbances. Specifically, he suggested a paradigm of physical representation in the body of arrested psychological development. His belief is that the narcissist has a body structure that is "upward displaced." This body structure is typified by the masculine ideal of Western culture, namely, a muscular upper body out of proportion with the mid- and lower-body structure. Lowen's belief about body structure in relation to psychological development has to do with body "energy," work developed by Wilhelm Reich (1959). Lowen's suggestion is that the narcissist holds this energy "up" in his body, thus increasing his capacity to meet his wants, but decreasing his capacity to meet his emotional needs. In contrast to classical psychoanalytic thought, Lowen did not discuss or believe in primary narcissism. Rather, he believed that narcissism stems from a disturbance in the parent–child relationship where the child has been indulged or neglected. He does, however, agree with the classicists in their understanding that all people with personality disorders, including border- lines and others, have a basic element of narcissism. Lowen's contribution to an understanding of narcissism includes his body representation of the experience and his belief that "the more narcissistic one is, the less one is identified with one's feelings."

Theological Analogy of Narcissism as Separation From God

In this discussion, we wish to offer a cursory review of literature regard- ing matters that fall into the categories of theology, philosophy, and sociol- ogy. This will encompass examination of the theological concepts of God, sin, grace, forgiveness, and so on. Philosophical constructs include love, understanding, intellectual and emotional development, and interpersonal development. Societal constructs include individuals' impact on society and society's impact on individuals. It is obvious that we cannot do justice to any, let alone all, of these concepts in a few pages. Rather, let us briefly examine some literature, primarily from certain Christian writers, followed by a dis- cussion of the matter of evil.

There is a paucity of adequate theological work in understanding narcis- sism. Extant literature includes Johnson (1980), Hood and associates (1990), Watson and associates (1990), and Torrance (1987). Johnson (1980) exam- ined the correlation and similarity between narcissism and a biblical concept of sin. He found that the concept of sin in the scriptures is by no means uni- versal but may be summarized in a Kierkegaardian definition, namely, that sin is the opposite of faith. Other definitions of sin include breaking of the law, alienation (Tillich), and immorality (Niebuhr). Johnson suggested that there is a weak correlation between sin and narcissism in that sin, as faith-lessness, would naturally lead to personal insecurity, which would lead to undo selfishness or selflessness (i.e., narcissism).

Hood and colleagues (1990) and Watson and colleagues (1990) examined "pathological narcissism" finding elements of undo independence and undo independency. They found that both of these conditions are antithetical to biblical Christianity. These authors have provided a fair amount of research into the narcissistic character, especially as it relates to various forms of religiosity. One of their findings is that individuals with an extrinsic religiosity are more narcissistic (Watson et al., 1990).

Torrance (1987) represented a Reformed examination of what is currently called a culture and time of narcissism. Torrance argued that Western culture has moved away from a Christian understanding of community to an undo focus on the individual. He collapsed contemporary psychology into what he called an "awareness movement," where the individual is taught to be self-assertive. Torrance followed Christopher Lasch's "Culture of Narcissism" in challenging this undo individualism and self-assertion. Torrance proposed that narcissism does not, in fact, develop a genuine self-esteem, but an artificial self-enhancement due to indulgence. He concluded by suggesting that koinonia (community) provides a true context of self-discovery that can free Christians from pride and isolation of self.

Our proposition is that when people are in a state of narcissism, they have separated from their (true) selves and are unable to contribute fully to their environment due to either their grandiose perceptions or their projected blame on the environment. As noted above, most classical and contemporary psychologists suggest that there is an inherent factor of narcissism in all personality disorders. We add to those suggestions that all personality disorders are the outgrowth of improper attachment. In considering the lack of proper attachment as the basis for narcissism, we look at how an individual who is in a state of poor attachment of self is unable to properly attach to society as a whole and consequently is unattached to the nature of goodness and maturity, that is, contributing to society in a meaningful and lasting way.

We suggest that a gross definition of evil is separation from God, or not being attached to God. We further suggest that "God" is a heavenly or universal maternal figure. If an individual fails to mature, he will subsequently fail to contribute to the environment and remain stagnated at a level of undo self-focus, or narcissism. In a broad sense, *development* implies maturation that should lead eventually to a more God-like persona. This lack of contribution is, in essence, a separation from God and consequently a separation from doing the work of God, or goodness. Noting that proper attachment leads to individualization, we suggest that maturity occurs when one maintains a cycle of attaching and detaching in conscious awareness of the necessity and value of both of these operations. The mature person becomes increasingly aware of the value of any relationship as well as the need to detach from every relationship for a time. It is in this cycle that relationships are solidified. We suggest that this full cycle of personal development is true maturity, the antithesis of evil.

If people are immature—that is, narcissistic—they will then lack a basic sense of security from which they make contributions to the world. As noted above in the psychoanalytic understanding of narcissism, an individual will either project a false sense of personal grandiosity or project this grandiosity to the outer world and eventually thrust his infantile anger in the form of external blaming. Both of these projections are functionally dishonest. Theologically and scripturally, God is personified as truth. Therefore, the state of narcissism is a state of dishonesty, or ungodlike behavior. As the infant projects a necessary perfection on the maternal figure, the adult narcissist projects "necessary perfection" on the environment. The difference between the infant and the adult is that the infant has no choice but to believe her caretaker is perfect. The adult narcissistic maintains the infantile projection as a fantasy over the disappointing truths of limitation and imperfection instead of experiencing her true feelings of disappointment and sadness. Scripture instructs that there is freedom in truth. The therapeutic task for the narcissistic is to trust the truth of her feelings. Truth is what matures her, broadens her interpersonal views, and develops a more solid character base.

Narcissism can also be considered to be evil by recognizing that a narcissistic individual is functionally greedy, asking or demanding more from the environment than she needs or more than the environment can provide. An individual in this state of demand for care is unable to make contributions to the world. This neediness or greed is anti-good or unlike God—it is the antithesis of God. Again, the correlation is that adult narcissists insist that their world accommodate the infantile fantasy need for total care (i.e., dependency). This infantile dependency in adulthood can result only in greed at best, and paranoia at worst.

RESOLUTION OF NARCISSISM

We propose that the resolution of narcissism is grief. Further, we propose that grief, which we identify with uncomplicated sadness, is the central ingredient for success in relationships, success in life, and general maturity. We distinguish grief (or sadness) from depression, the former being a natural state of coping with the necessary losses of life, and the latter a clinical condition that is essentially narcissistic. This statement is a departure from the current understanding that depression is biogenic in origin and biological in its basic form. Thus, we agree with Fenichel and other classic psychoanalysts in the suggestion that depression is to some degree a choice, and to a larger degree a result of failing to grieve.

There is continual grief in the entirety of life beginning in infancy and continuing through adult life. Certainly, the neonate grieves the loss of a largely perfect uterine environment. The developing infant grieves the loss of nearly constant comfort and nurturance. The toddler grieves the limitations and loss of freedom to go where he wants and do what he wants to do. The preschool child grieves in his transition into the oedipal stage of life, and soon thereafter grieves the loss of oedipal feelings. The school-aged child grieves the loss of regular comfort and nurturance that are largely replaced by cognitive learning and social learning. Furthermore, the school-aged child (age 6–12) certainly has daily grief over mild or major failures in school, social disappointments, and loneliness. Adolescents have complicated grief because of the lack of freedom and responsibility that they have in Western society, and they experience artificial grief associated with trivial social disappointments. Grief continues through early adulthood in many forms, including academic failure or disappointment, failure in intimate relationships, and failures in entry and maintenance into the world of work. Adults have regular grief over the challenges presented in parenting young children and nurturing them into childhood and adolescence. There are no marriages or relationships that are without relatively regular grief as couples strive to understand themselves and relate to one another. As adults mature into later years, and often beforehand, they experience the loss of loved ones, loss of property, loss of ideas, and loss of ideals. Eventually they face the grief of the loss of their own health or lives.

The aforementioned statements of grief that occur over the life span could sound depressing and lead to despair. We would contend, however, that grief is neither despair nor depression, but rather a natural part of life, and something to be enhanced, experienced, and completed. We further propose that much of the distress of life is unnecessary and ultimately narcissistic because individuals and society fail to accept the necessity and ultimate value of sadness and grief. The central notion of this proposal is that grief ends, whereas despair and depression do not. Despair is the failure to accept the truth of life, and it is the maintenance of a childlike (narcissistic) view that "I should get and keep everything that I want." We can easily see that it is unwise for our children to have everything that they want, and can generally see that our acquaintances don't need everything that they want. It is much harder, however, to genuinely understand that it is not good for us to have what we want. This kind of understanding can come only with maturity, and maturity comes only by facing the routine and necessary nature of grief.

The root of narcissism is that I am perfect or you are perfect. In other words, I can have all I want by my own hand, or someone else can provide me all that I want. The primary narcissism of infancy creates and reinforces this view of life. But it takes at least another 12 years of childhood to transition out of this belief that I will continue to get everything I want. The key difference between primary narcissism and the adult form of secondary narcissism is the distinction of wants and needs. Infants do not distinguish between wants and needs. A primary purpose of the extended childhood that humans have, as compared to all other animals, is to experience life and make this distinction. This distinction can be made only by grieving that I don't get all that I want.

True grief is short lived for the most part. Indeed, it may take a year or more to grieve the loss of a loved one, during which time a person recalls the months or years of joy with the person she has lost. But for all other losses of less magnitude, grief should last something between minutes and hours. In fact, the most important losses and subsequent griefs are those of short duration and trivial matters. I can't find a parking space close to the concert hall. I drop my fork on the floor. My newspaper rips when I open it up. My computer locks up on me. More significant losses and subsequent griefs include misunderstandings among friends, loss of employment, major loss of property, loss of investment, and the like. If we are mature and become true to ourselves and to life, and particularly true to the normal period of sadness, our grief will be short lived. Furthermore, and more importantly, we will come to realize that losses are not generally as significant as we hold them to be. Mature individuals realize that losses are necessary and generally good even though they are always sad and painful. Sadly, there is a convoluted condition that is related to the understanding of the value of loss, namely, masochism. Sadly, masochists seek pain as a way of enhancing loss, probably reflecting early childhood loss that has not been properly grieved.

There is a beauty to grieving and sadness that is often overlooked. Shakespeare used the term "sweet sorrow" to capture the essence of this concept. One cannot feel grief or sorrow without first loving something. The infant feels a loss as separation, but not particularly out of love except in a primitive form because an infant does not distinguish himself from his environment. Early forms of love in preschool years are largely those of attachment, need, and pleasure. The grief that we see in infancy and early childhood is complicated predominately by fear in infancy and predominantly by anger in early childhood. Genuine sadness, which is based on love, probably does not occur frequently until the child is beyond the oedipal stage, or at about the age of 6.

Ideally, the mature adult loves much. She loves people, property, and ideas with various forms of love. This same mature loving adult will then unavoidably experience frequent sorrow. The hallmark of a mature adult is to be able to face loss and grief honestly and profit from the loss, at least in most situations. We frequently tell our patients, "If you love much, you will grieve much." The mature or maturing adult becomes familiar and friendly with the experience of sorrow as it increasingly reminds her of the depth and breadth of her love. Furthermore, where there is loss, there is always some kind of gain. The fall and winter of the year include the loss of billions of life forms, but then even more billions generate in the following spring. Likewise, in human life, where there is loss, there is always some kind of gain, usually more than the loss.

Narcissism in any form is an impediment to grief, which itself then impedes a greater love. Our proposition is that the resolution and possibly cure of narcissism are in the increased awareness of necessary grief: that our parents failed us, that not everyone likes us or approves of us, that choices have to be made, that we have to choose between eating our vegetables or leaving the dinner table, that we try our best but still fail in competition or relationships, that war happens, and that the polar ice cap melts. Our focus has been primarily on individual maturity through grief, but we might suggest that a group or society at large could profit from appropriate grief to cure narcissistic elements that exist within the group or society. Evil, as we conceive of it, is the maintenance of narcissism, to one degree or another, rather than the enhancement of love.

REFERENCES

Ainsworth, M. D. S., Blehar, M. C., Waters, E., & Wall, S. (1978). *Patterns of attachment: A psychological study of the strange situation.* Hillsdale, NJ: Erlbaum.

Bowlby, J. (1969). *Attachment and loss: Attachment.* New York: Basic Books.

Bowlby, J. (1973). *Attachment and loss: Separation.* New York: Basic Books.

Bowlby, J. (1980). *Attachment and loss: Loss.* New York: Basic Books.

Erikson, E. (1950). *Childhood and society.* New York: Norton.

Fenichel, O. (1945). *The psychoanalytic theory of neurosis.* New York: Norton.

Freud, S. (1914). On narcissism: An introduction. In *The collected papers.* London: Hogarth Press.

Freud, S. (1924). *The collected papers.* London: Hogarth Press.

Fromm, E. (1939). Selfishness and self-love. *Psychoanalytic Quarterly, 7,* 54

Hood, R. W., Morris, R. J., and Watson, P. J. (1990). Quasi-experimental elicitation of a differential report of religious experience among intrinsic and indiscriminately pro religious types. *Journal of the Scientific Study of Religion, 29,* 417–431.

Johnson, R. (1980). Narcissism and sin. Paper delivered at the Christian Association for Psychological Studies, Toronto.

Kernberg, O. F. (1975). *Borderline conditions and pathological narcissism.* New York: Jason Aronson.

Klein, M. (1975). *Envy and gratitude.* New York: Delacorte Press.

Kohut, H. (1971). *The analysis of the self: A systematic approach to the psychoanalytic treatment of narcissistic personality disorders.* New York: International Universities Press.

Lowen, A. (1983). *Narcissism.* New York: Macmillan.

Mahler, M., Pine, F., & Bergman, A. (1975). *The psychological birth of the human infant: Symbiosis and Individuation.* New York: Basic Books.

Maslow, A. (1954). *Motivation and personality.* New York: Harper.

Piaget, J. (1954). *The construction of reality in the child.* New York: Basic Books.

Raskin, R. N., & Hall, C. S. (1979). A narcissistic personality inventory. *Psychological Reports, 45,* 590.

Reich, W. (1959). *Character analysis.* New York: Orgon Institute Press.

Torrance, A. J. (1987). The self-relation, narcissism, and the gospel of grace. *Scottish Journal of Theology, 40,* 481–510.

Watson, P. J, Morris, R. J., Hood, R. W., & Biderman, M. D. (1990). Religious orientation types and narcissism. *Journal of Psychology and Christianity, 9,* 40–46.

CHAPTER 16

EXPERIENCE OF EVIL IN EVERYDAY LIVES

Suzanne M. Coyle

News of disasters bombards us from every possible venue—phone calls, the Internet, newspapers, TV, and radio. The list seems endless. At some point, we simply absorb too much information and switch off our receivers. Yet, nagging questions come at us. Is there evil in our everyday lives? Are we immersed in a quagmire of relativity? Is evil personified as a being in the devil or Satan? Are we responsible for evil? Is society the ultimately responsible party? And where is God in all of the evil?

The exploration of many of these questions will be explored in other parts of these edited volumes of *Explaining Evil.* My purpose in this chapter is to explore a basic phenomenological query. This query is that, however theoretical or abstract examining evil may remain, the personal effects of evil and our responses to evil are experienced in our everyday lives.

While recognizing that evil exists in daily life, our human natures sometimes entice us to push away any possibility of evil in our personal lives. It is more comfortable for us to believe that evil is with someone else or some other place. A haunting memory comes to me of a comment made by one of my supervisors as I traveled the journey toward licensure as a therapist. He said, "Suzanne, your problem is that you do not believe that someone you like is capable of evil."

So any of us may, as I have done, push away evil.

The title "Experience of Evil in Everyday Lives" sounds too dramatic to be true. My purpose in this chapter is not to focus on whether evil does or does not exist but how to enable people to identify evil when it occurs in their lives and respond powerfully to it.

To accomplish this task, I will first offer some definitions of evil. After then determining a useful definition of evil for this chapter, I will present two case studies of people's experience of evil in everyday life. The first case study is focused on a personal experience and personification of the devil. The second case study is a counselee's experience of evil in a vague everyday sense that even he did not always recognize as evil. These two case studies will be changed so that no identifying information is given. After a discussion of these two case studies of evil, the chapter will close with a challenge of how most helpfully to address evil in everyday life, with special attention to those of us who are professional caregivers—the clergy and mental health professionals.

DEFINING EVIL

Defining *evil* is a difficult challenge at best. Much of the endeavor traditionally has fallen into distinguishing between two categories of evil—moral evil and natural evil. *Moral evil* is essentially understood as evil that has malevolent intent with disastrous consequences. Intrinsically, moral evil has at its core ethically reprehensible actions that often have long-reaching societal effects. The Holocaust in Germany is a clear example of this kind of evil. Moral evil can also occur on a familial level such as physical abuse in a family. *Natural evil* comprises those "naturally" occurring events with bad or painful consequences that do not have a responsible agent who directs the evil. Examples of natural evil include natural disasters such as tornadoes and hurricanes, and catastrophic illnesses such as cancer. Natural evil has only victims or survivors, whereas moral evil has perpetrators.

The defining of evil when put in these two categories can often fall into a philosophical debate with little concern for the experience of the evil by humans. Because the purpose of this chapter is to focus on the experience of people's everyday lives, I am not using these two traditional categories to define evil. Instead, I am focusing on the *experience* of evil in a phenomenological sense. This approach has several advantages to a more traditional approach of moral and natural evil, which can be limited to a philosophical or even purely religious discussion.

The discussion on experiencing evil in everyday life in my viewpoint can be best explored through a phenomenological view when trying to explain the experience of evil in daily lives. In this way, daily life experience can be seen through the disciplines of psychology and religion to get a fuller understanding of what makes the core of evil palpable in everyday life. From these perspectives, evil can be understood most fully in the perception of people as they experience it and name it in their own lives as evil.

Evil, then, in this chapter, is thus understood as being both individual and systemic in its origin and effects. This means that evil can originate from an individual, a system, or both. The origin of the evil does not need to be an intentional act. It can be passive as well. An illustration of this paradox can be seen in the person who physically abuses a child. Although the abuser acts with intent, it is also true that many times the abuser was abused, which illustrates both individual and systemic acts of evil.

In this illustration of individual and systemic evil, the effects also are both individual and systemic. The abuser suffers with the effect of the evil act, as certainly the abused suffers physical, emotional, and spiritual pain. As a result, the effects for both the perpetrator and the victims form a cycle that is repeated until some action from an individual in a system that can effect change intervenes. This example, I believe, shows that at its core, evil is relational. If we understand evil as relational, then evil also speaks to us, particularly in everyday life, about not only that which "others" do but also the potential in all of us to perform evil acts (Swinton, 2007).

In deeply understanding evil, it is not only the actual consequences of the evil act but also the victim's belief that something redemptive can emerge from the evil that gives an adequate picture of how evil affects people in daily life. Daniel Day Williams (1990) wrote, "The power to resist the demonic is not simply a human power but one that grasps us from beyond ourselves so that the experience of being set free from bondage is our experience of power greater than ourselves" (p. 15). Although it is true that the victim and the perpetrator cannot escape the grasp of evil immediately, it is also true that only by anticipating a life that is different in its freedom from bondage, as Williams asserted, can the victim and perpetrator have any realistic hope of living outside the grasp of evil.

Thus, evil becomes relational out of necessity. In everyday life, evil is not experienced in the abstract. It is experienced in the here and now with intense emotion and feeling of abandonment. So, although the instinct is to flee when one meets evil, it is only in meeting and knowing evil that it can be overcome (Williams, 1990). How does one "meet and know" evil, then? Do we even want to encounter evil?

For most of us, the answer would be a resounding "no." However, it is at this point in our discussion of defining evil that the very act of defining evil also becomes a way of knowing evil. As we envision past or present struggles with evil, Jacob's wrestling with the angel evokes the kind of visceral struggle we may have with evil. Granted, the angel is better known as God, not evil. However, Jacob's palpable fear when he was wrestling is the kind of struggle that we must engage in with evil if the results are to be as redemptive as Jacob's struggle. We may limp. But, we will be better able to identify evil if we have touched it.

So, in this discussion, we come to the point of defining evil from our previous discussion and then sharing case studies that will illustrate essential aspects of evil. Evil understood in this chapter are those acts—whether active or passive—that cause destructive consequences for both individuals and the larger systems in which they live. A helpful experiential way of defining evil is not to be fully concerned with every characteristic and category of evil but, rather, to understand the inevitable way in which evil connects people in a systemic web of destruction. Evil's relational definition can be defined as "that which destroys hope in and love for God" (Swinton, 2007, p. 59).

Evil encompasses the effective blocking of any future experience for both the victim and the perpetrator, although their experiences are quite different. For the victim, it is only when that person is able to look forward to future life that the movement from victim to survivor is affected. For the perpetrator, evil blocks the future, and it is only by remaining in the throes of destructive actions that the perpetrator can live. To move into the future would necessitate facing one's actions.

This definition of evil focuses primarily on individuals. A systemic definition of evil also must be articulated. To use our earlier example, the evil of abuse that results in disastrous consequences can clearly be understood in that context. However, a systemic definition of evil (which would include the traditional concept of natural evil) can include those responses to destructive acts that are evil from those who are in society or even a passive response to a disaster. When people do not respond to a natural disaster, it then becomes systemic evil as well, despite no one individual being able to be named as the perpetrator. The definition of systemic evil involves all those people who actively participate in its acts as well as passively ignore the systemic evil. Racism is a clear example of systemic evil. Everyone thinks of the other person as being the one who should act. Also, it is common for people to not see themselves as being a participant in systemic evil. Part of the passive response to evil may lie in our very human nature. We are natural beings and subject to the "wear and tear of matter" (Adams & Adams, 1990, p. 194). So, evil is that which not only causes painful responses but also permeates our very being and wears us down to the point that we are unable to respond.

Evil, thus, as defined in this chapter is the *individual and systemic perpetration of destructive acts that result in the disconnection of both individuals and systems of relationships between humans and humans with God. Its result is a spiritual barrenness that blocks envisioning the future and finding meaning in life with God.*

Our definition of evil is thus not concerned with the abstract or theoretical definitions or the fine tuning of methodology in defining a moral concept. All these approaches, of course, contribute to more fully explaining evil in other chapters of this anthology. The definition offered here focuses on how people *experience* evil and their perceptions of it. So, in explaining evil, I will present two case studies that illustrate the experience of evil. Addie and her personal, family, and community experiences will offer an illustration of how people experience evil as personified by the devil or Satan. Juan and his personal, family, and community experiences will offer an illustration of how people experience a more ambiguous sense of evil.

ADDIE

Addie was a single White woman in her early 40s who lived in a rural area outside an Appalachian county seat. I was offering pastoral counseling in a local church and often met with area ministers. Addie was referred to me by the pastor of a local church that a friend of hers attended. This congregation offered to pay for her counseling sessions because she was not working to due to her emotional and mental distress. Addie did not attend this church. She did attend a neighboring Pentecostal congregation.

When I first met with Addie, she presented as anxious and was alarmed at the slightest disturbance. As we first met, I shared some information about my background and how long I had been doing counseling in the area. As a person who did not live in this Appalachian region, I discovered soon that it was important to let counselees know something about me in order to establish trust with them. My self-disclosure seemed to put her more at ease.

Addie, in turn, told me that she was tormented by the devil. She said that she found out about me from her friend who attended a non-Pentecostal evangelical church. Addie said that she had attended a revival at the friend's church. She had responded to the invitation hymn at the end of the service. Everyone in the church prayed that the devil would leave her. Addie said that their concern touched her deeply. At the same time, she still struggled with fighting the devil. Addie said that she had been in counseling at the community mental health center. However, she had stopped going there, she said, because the counselor told her that the devil was not real. Addie frowned deeply and said that she knew he was real.

As we talked, Addie described where she lived and how life was difficult for her. She said that she was not able to keep a public job because she had a hard time concentrating. I tried to explore what prevented her from concentrating, but she deferred. My stance changed from questioning to an attentive and affirming mode. As she shared information about everyday life, I affirmed those experiences and emphasized her strengths. Those strengths included the ability to appreciate the world around her as she described the beautiful scenes of the mountains and their creatures.

After two sessions, Addie seemed more relaxed. She began to talk about her years of growing up in an abusive family. As she described her family, tears flowed down her cheeks. She talked about how her mother physically abused her and made her do all the housework—even scrubbing the floors on her knees. Sometimes her mother made her stay under the high, open porch where the dogs stayed. Finally, after some difficulty, Addie tearfully recounted a time when her mother sexually abused her with a broom handle while telling her that she was "no good."

The next session, I experienced Addie as more trusting of me. She then told me about the many years of sexual abuse suffered at the hands of her father and brother. Addie said that the abuse occurred on a regular basis beginning when she was 8 years old and continuing until she moved out of the house at 16 years old. She then lived with her boyfriend for several years. He, in turn, physically abused her. She then moved out on her own and had not been sexually involved for years.

At the next session, Addie talked more about being tormented by the devil. I asked her to say more about her turmoil. As the words tumbled out, she described voices from the devil asking her to doubt her faith and telling her that she was going to hell. She cried for a while, indicating that the devil convinced her to doubt her salvation and tempted her to curse. Addie did not report any temptations to harm or kill herself or anyone else.

Through the next few weeks, Addie talked much about hearing the devil trying to lead her into temptation—some temptations being renouncing her faith, and other things being sexual temptations. Mainly, she reported the daily anguish of having the devil talk to her. She added that she had visual images of him but had never seen him in person. To combat the devil, Addie described lengthy prayer sessions.

Addie further described her encounters with the devil to have occurred for years. She then talked about the many Pentecostal services that she attended—a church that was close to her trailer in the hollow. Then she attended her friend's church, whose pastor had referred her to me. She described further her experience at that church. Addie said that she repented of her sins that night because she had "backslid" or not honored her original Christian commitment. Since that night, she said that she continued her battle against the devil. She attended the Pentecostal church and said that she was afraid not to attend that church lest the devil get her. She continued to talk with her friend as well as the pastor at her friend's church. Still, the devil tempted Addie.

After several weeks of counseling sessions, I took a different counseling job. After talking with Addie for several weeks about my upcoming change, I referred her to another pastoral counselor in the area. Months passed, I heard from the counselor who had accepted Addie as a counselee. After months of counseling, Addie no longer reported that she was tempted by the devil. And in her counseling sessions with her counselor, Addie expressed that she wanted to give me a gift in thanks for my support of her.

On my next visit to the area, I dropped by the counseling office, where I found a wrapped box for me. I opened a gift box. Inside it were two pillow-cases embroidered with the words "Our Father who art in heaven, hallowed be thy name . . . Give us this day." A written note inside the gift said that now she could sleep at night—not being tormented by the devil, thanking me, and saying that she prays daily for me.

ADDIE'S EXPERIENCE

Addie's powerful experience is a reminder of the palpable presence of the devil for many Christians for centuries. Believers still report experiencing a personal entity of the devil. However, many times today mental health professionals challenge their clients' experience of the devil. Instead of focusing upon their *experience*, the counseling process often focuses on whether the devil is a real entity or not. Such was Addie's experience. By accepting her experience of the devil as acceptable, I believe I was able to accept both Addie *and* her experience.

Essential in Addie's steady progress was her being able to experience a counselor who valued her experience rather than criticizing it. Her belief in the devil was consistent with her Pentecostal beliefs as well as consistent with her experience of her family. She was physically and sexually abused by everyone in her family of origin. Addie experienced the personification of evil in her everyday family life.

One also finds an interesting parallel in Addie's experience in terms of the redemptive response of two systems to her battling the devil. Addie was raised in a Pentecostal church and visited her friend's non-Pentecostal evangelical church. Even though Addie did not attend her friend's church but remained at her home church, the friend's church offered to pay for Addie's counseling session. I find this spirit of support powerful because these two churches often compete for the same pool of church members. Addie, however, had the support of both churches.

Intertwined with these parallels between individuals and community systems, the process of referral is a critical part of combating Addie's experience of the devil. The referral from the pastor to me and from me to another counselor represents the power of faith communities. Despite some differences in beliefs, the overlapping common beliefs enabled the referral process to provide tremendous support for Addie.

JUAN

Juan is a married Latino man in his early 30s with no children. He was raised in a modest but honest home with parents who moved to the United States as young children from a Caribbean country. Juan reports that his parents and three siblings did not have much money as he grew up. However, his parents stressed the importance of hard work, and soon they had a small, family-run restaurant.

Juan met his wife at the restaurant when she stopped to dine there. His wife, Heather, was the only daughter of a wealthy businessman in a metro area on the east coast. They dated for 2 years and then were married. Heather said she was willing to live on Juan's modest income from working in the family restaurant.

Slowly, through the years, Juan and Heather began taking more and more money from her family. Their standard of living was raised. Juan became suspicious of how Heather's family made millions of dollars in their business, but everything seemed to be in order.

Juan was also raised in a Catholic family. Heather's family did not attend any church when she was growing up. Juan's beliefs focused on responsible work, family, and church. Slowly, he became accustomed to material advantages through Heather's family as well as social prominence through their community influence. It seemed like a good life to Juan. All his friends agreed.

At our first counseling session, Juan shared all these things with me. When asked what prompted him to come to counseling, he replied that he was feeling that he was drowning in all the affluence of Heather's family. Clearly flustered, Juan said that he just could not understand why he felt this way. Heather's father was a well-known philanthropist to worthy organizations. Buildings had his name on them. He helped people. Juan queried about what made him feel so uneasy with their affluence.

As we worked through several sessions, Juan questioned his intense uneasiness with the lifestyle he had now embraced since marrying Heather. He now believed that his early suspicions about his father-in-law's business not being above board were groundless. Yet, his uneasiness about the family lifestyle permeated his being and seemed to cast pallor over everything.

Then, during one session, Juan plaintively inquired, "Am I crazy? What's wrong with me? I should be thankful that things are easier for me now." We then began to explore what comprised being "crazy" and how that impacted his life. Several stories came together as Juan reflected. Then he said that he remembered how he was impressed growing up about the sacrifices that Jesus made for us.

As the stories rolled out during the next few sessions, Juan finally said he realized that for him, work is important to honor the sacrifice that Jesus made for humanity. Further, he said that work was also part of his faith growing up. Juan went on to say that he believed the ease with which he could now live actually raised questions about the faith values he believed in. The emphasis on being successful in Heather's family, Juan concluded, was "just wrong." It failed to look at the way you live each day. The value was on the end product—the outcome of secular society, not what was intrinsically spiritual. After naming his struggle, Juan decided to quit counseling.

JUAN'S EXPERIENCE

Upon first reading, Juan's experience of uneasiness may seem mild and even rather petulant. Who could complain about living in the lap of luxury?

Juan is able to work less. He experiences the American dream of being important through his family affiliation. What is the problem?

Looking again at Juan's dilemma, one could argue that the problem exists
in a cultural difference or some underlying couple conflict. And both of these
scenarios may be possibilities. Yet, Juan's description of his uneasiness actually
describes well a "gnawing" that will not go away. It is something he cannot
quite shake, something that is a mist that hangs over everything in his life.

I would describe Juan's experience as evil despite its evasive quality. Our
definition of evil contends that evil is that which contributes to "spiritual
barrenness," which is what Juan describes. It permeates his existence and is
something that he cannot shake.

Juan's dilemma illustrates clearly the effects of systemic evil upon an
individual. Systemic evil is that evil that permeates the culture and makes
not participating in it difficult, if not impossible. Some examples of systemic
evil can be injustice that most people will condemn, such as racism. The
kind of systemic evil that Juan is facing is, however, described by this culture
as desirable. This systemic evil can be identified as the American dream of
success—financial and influential.

Nothing is "wrong" with success on the surface. Some theologies laud
material prospering as blessings from God for our faithfulness. Yet, the process of becoming successful in Juan's description robbed him of experiencing
the pleasures of small things in life, such as not appreciating the common-
ness of God's creation. Juan experiences the nagging existential dilemma of
the evil of success.

In his experience of evil, Juan has had the deep meaning of faith and life
with which he grew up stripped from him. Yet, because the cultural conversation lauds success as almost always good, Juan finds himself doubting his
own spiritual values. As a result, he struggles with what gives his life meaning. Further, he struggles with how he is able to counter a powerful cultural
conversation that names success as good and sheds doubt on those who challenge that belief.

In many ways, Juan will have a more difficult time than did Addie in confronting his demons. Whereas Addie was able to name and wrestle with a
palpable entity of the devil, Juan is left with sand running through his fingers. He is unable to grasp what is a film of deception over the entire culture.
Further, it is difficult to have allies in the battle against systemic evil when it
has many supporters.

SPIRITUAL AND THEOLOGICAL RESPONSES TO EVIL

In reflecting upon Addie's and Juan's experiences of evil in their daily lives,
it will be helpful to further reflect on the spiritual and theological responses
to evil. By basing our reflections on these two case studies, it will be possible

to understand more fully how evil is actually experienced and how the believers' responses and their supporters can craft a powerful response to evil. First, let us turn to Addie's experience.

Addie is so worn down and humbled that her position enables her to look to God. Her position is reminiscent of Job's experience where he exclaims, "Although He slays me, yet will I praise him." Addie's position of humbleness has great spiritual significance. Diogenes Allen concurred that "in the very act of being humbled, we can recognize that we are spiritual beings" (quoted in Adams & Adams, 1990, p. 194). As Addie moves toward a sense of being unburdened, she is able to claim an individual triumph as she defeated the devil. This kind of witness is powerful because modern psychotherapy has largely sought to explain the why of behavior with little recognition of the responsibility of the individual (Cooper, 2007). I believe it is Addie's belief of confessing her sins that enables her to battle the devil, who she believes tempts her.

Thus, where some understandings of evil emphasize individual responsibility over and above systems that produce evil, some other understandings of evil emphasize an understanding of systemic evil over and above individual evil. Both individual and systemic understandings of responses to evil interrelating and affecting each other are necessary, as Addie's progress illustrates. She is able to use the systems in her community to garner support and is able to recognize when one church or system such as her home church is not enough to support her. She accepts the support offered by another community of faith—her friend's church. In a Pentecostal faith that is often maligned by our culture as well as other churches, Addie skillfully balances individual and systemic responses to the evil personified by her battle with the devil.

Juan's struggle with evil poses a different theological dilemma than does Addie's struggle. Whereas Addie is able to grapple with a palpable devil, Juan has difficulty even being able to take the essential step of naming the evil he experiences. Jesus named the demonic as he performed miracles. And we must be able to meet and know the evil if we are to overcome evil (Williams, 1990).

Juan's experience of evil in his everyday life on the surface seems less challenging than Addie's visceral encounter with the devil. However, the amorphous quality of evil in Juan's world poses formidable challenges. Williams (1990) offered several descriptions of the faces of the demonic in our contemporary world, which are as follows: (a) fascination, (b) distortion, (c) aggrandizement, (d) inertia of established systems of control, and (e) ontological depth (p. 7).

Juan's conversations about his dis-ease follow these theological typologies of how humans often experience evil today. Heather's family's familiarity with the success and ease of the world seemed initially like a welcome gift. One can imagine Juan relaxing to think that finally he would not need to work so hard. An image of an idyllic Garden of Eden comes to mind. Like Eve, Juan becomes enticed by what material pleasures he gains by inclusion in Heather's family. And as he becomes more involved in the enjoyment of the material goods, his perception of his original beliefs becomes a little hazy.

Gradually values become larger than life, and he feels overwhelmed. He is unable to find a way through the maze of the cultural web of values that threaten to smother him. And whereas the world seems to enjoy all these benefits, Juan's daily life is impacted by the evil, which causes him to experience an existential anxiety about what is really "real" for him. Further, he struggles to know how he can confront this evil and find a meaningful faith in his life.

Although Williams's typologies should not be understood as sequential, it is instructive to see the incremental progress of evil in Juan's daily life. As Keller observed, it is in human experience that good and evil are relative (in Bracken, 2005). Whereas Addie's experience with evil may seem "worse" than Juan's, is there a true comparison?

Juan's experience with evil pushes him to seek meaning that is counter to what culture prescribes as best for him. It is hard to push back on something that is soft. And culture has made evil soft. Ultimately, Juan's task is to find a supportive system that can take some of the burden of pushing against evil from him.

IMPLICATIONS FOR SPIRITUAL RESISTANCE

As we have visited the daily experiences of evil for Addie and Juan, we are now challenged to respond to evil as people experience it in life. Our definition of *evil* as encompassing both individual and systemic evil's impact of spiritual barrenness is critical to our response. As spiritual people encounter evil, we must be quick to understand that the initial appearance of evil often skillfully masks its underbelly. Individual evil can have systemic origins. Conversely, systemic evil can be affected by even one individual.

The challenge for us is to be courageous in the face as well as absence of evil. It is only by recognizing our own capacity for evil as well as our friends' capacity that we are able to not be ambushed by evil. Resistance to evil implies that we fill our lives with the presence of God. Where God is, evil cannot exist.

So as we resist evil, we need to pay attention to *both* individual and systemic evil. We need to realize that any evil is to be resisted. We need to recognize that good overcomes evil. We need to understand the ease of our culture in accepting evil. We need to be validating different experiences of evil—personified or amorphous.

Resisting evil can be part of our spiritual growth. By experiencing God as present with us, we can experience a fuller presence of the Spirit that gives us hope in the face of despair. Evil triumphs when we are hopeless. But, we triumph when we carry the hope of Christ with us.

REFERENCES

Adams, M., & Adams, R. (Eds.). (1990). *The problem of evil*. Oxford: Oxford University Press.

Bracken, J. (Ed.). (2005). *World without end: Christian eschatology from a process perspective*. Grand Rapids, MI: Eerdmans.

Cooper, T. (2007). *Dimension of evil: Contemporary perspectives*. Minneapolis, MN: Fortress Press.

Swinton, J. (2007). *Raging with compassion: Pastoral responses to the problem of evil*. Grand Rapids, MI: Eerdmans.

Williams, D. (1990). *The demonic and the divine*. Minneapolis, MN: Fortress Press.

CHAPTER 17

ROOTS OF HUMAN VIOLENCE AND GREED: A PSYCHOSPIRITUAL PERSPECTIVE

Stanislav Grof

The study of holotropic states of consciousness has amassed a rich array of observations that have revolutionized understanding of the human psyche in health and disease. The importance of many of these findings transcends the framework of individual psychology; they seem to offer deep insights into the dimensions of the current global crisis, which have so far been neglected, and suggest strategies that might be useful for its alleviation. In this chapter, I will explore these new perspectives with special emphasis on two elemental forces that have driven human history since time immemorial to the present time—the proclivity to unbridled violence and to insatiable greed. Because of the development of weapons of mass destruction, relentless population explosion, escalating plundering of natural resources, and increase of industrial pollution, these two scourges now threaten survival of the human species and other forms of life on this planet.

VIOLENCE AND GREED IN HUMAN HISTORY

The number and degree of atrocities that have been committed throughout the ages in various countries of the world, many of them in the name of God, are truly unimaginable and indescribable. Millions of soldiers and civilians have been killed in wars and revolutions of all types or in other forms of atrocities. During his unparalleled military campaign, Alexander the Great destroyed the Persian empire and conquered all the countries between Macedonia and India. Secular and religious ambitions—from the expansion of the Roman Empire to the spread of Islam and the Christian Crusades—found their expression in the merciless use of sword and fire. In ancient Rome, countless Christians were sacrificed in the arenas to provide a highly sought-after spectacle for the masses.

Hundreds of thousands of innocent victims were tortured, killed, or burned alive in the autos-da-fé by the medieval Inquisition. In Mesoamerica, countless soldiers of the tribes defeated by the Aztecs, who had not died in the battle, were slaughtered on sacrificial altars. The Aztec cruelty found its match in the bloody ventures of the Spanish conquistadores. Genghis Khan's and Tamerlane's Mongolian hordes swept through Asia, killing, pillaging, and burning towns and villages. The colonialism of Great Britain and other European countries and the Napoleonic wars were additional examples of violence and relentless greed.

This trend has continued in an unmitigated fashion in the 20th century. The loss of life in World War I was estimated at 10 million soldiers and 20 million civilians. Additional millions died from war-spread epidemics and famine. In World War II, approximately twice as many lives were lost. The 20th century saw the expansionism of Nazi Germany and the horrors of the Holocaust, Stalin's reckless domination of Eastern Europe and his Gulag Archipelago, and the civil terror in Communist China. We can add to it the victims of South American dictatorships, the atrocities and genocide committed by the Chinese in Tibet, and the cruelties of South Africa's apartheid. The wars in Korea and Vietnam, the wars in the Middle East, and the slaughter in Yugoslavia and Rwanda are some more examples of the senseless bloodshed we have witnessed during the last hundred years.

Human greed has also found new, less violent forms of expression in the philosophy and strategy of capitalist economies emphasizing increase of the gross national product, "unlimited growth," reckless plundering of nonrenewable natural resources, conspicuous consumption, and "planned obsolescence." Moreover, much of this wasteful economic policy that has disastrous ecological consequences has been oriented toward production of weapons of increasing destructive power.

DOOMSDAY SCENARIOS THREATENING LIFE ON OUR PLANET

In the past, violence and greed had tragic consequences for the individuals involved in the internecine encounters and for their immediate families. However, they did not threaten the evolution of the human species as a whole and certainly did not represent a danger for the ecosystem and for the biosphere of the planet. Even after the most violent wars, nature was able to recycle all the aftermath and completely recover within a few decades. This situation has changed very radically in the course of the 20th century. Rapid technological progress, exponential growth of industrial production, massive population explosion, and particularly the discovery of atomic energy have forever changed the equations involved.

In the course of the 20th century, we have witnessed more major scientific and technological breakthroughs within a single decade, or even a single year, than people in earlier historical periods experienced in an entire century. However, these astonishing intellectual successes have brought modern humanity to the brink of a global catastrophe, because they were not matched by a comparable growth of emotional and moral maturity. We have the dubious privilege of being the first species in natural history that has achieved the capacity to eradicate itself and destroy in the process all life on this planet.

The intellectual history of humanity is one of its incredible triumphs. We have been able to learn the secrets of nuclear energy, send spaceships to the moon and all the planets of the solar system, transmit sound and color pictures all around the globe and across cosmic space, crack the DNA code, and begin experimenting with cloning and genetic engineering. At the same time, these superior technologies are being used in the service of primitive emotions and instinctual impulses that are not very different from those that drove the behavior of the people in the Stone Age.

Unimaginable sums of money have been wasted in the insanity of the arms race, and the use of even a miniscule fraction of the existing arsenal of atomic weapons would destroy all life on earth. Tens of millions of people have been killed in the two world wars and in countless other violent confrontations occurring for ideological, racial, religious, or economic reasons. Hundreds of thousands have been bestially tortured by the secret police of various totalitarian systems. Insatiable greed is driving people to hectic pursuit of profit and acquisition of personal property beyond any reasonable limits. This strategy has resulted in a situation where, besides the specter of a nuclear war, humanity is threatened by several less spectacular, but insidious and more predictable, doomsday scenarios.

Among these are industrial pollution of soil, water, and air; the threat of nuclear waste and accidents; the destruction of the ozone layer; the greenhouse effect and global warming; possible loss of planetary oxygen through reckless deforestation and poisoning of the ocean plankton; and the dangers of toxic additives in our food and drinks. To this, we can add a number of developments that are of less apocalyptic nature but equally disturbing, such as species extinction proceeding at an astronomical rate, homelessness and starvation of a significant percentage of the world's population, deterioration of family and crisis of parenthood, disappearance of spiritual values, absence of hope and positive perspective, loss of meaningful connection with nature, and general alienation. As a result of all the above factors, humanity now lives in chronic anguish, on the verge of a nuclear and ecological catastrophe, while in possession of fabulous technology approaching that of the world of science fiction.

Modern science has developed effective means that could solve most of the urgent problems in today's world—combat the majority of diseases, eliminate hunger and poverty, reduce the amount of industrial waste, and replace destructive fossil fuels by renewable sources of clean energy. The problems that stand in the way are not of economical or technological nature; their deepest sources lie inside the human personality. Because of them, unimaginable resources have been wasted in the absurdity of the arms race, power struggles, and pursuit of "unlimited growth." They also prevent a more appropriate distribution of wealth among individuals and nations, as well as a reorientation from purely economic and political concerns to ecological priorities that are critical for survival of life on this planet.

PSYCHOSPIRITUAL ROOTS OF THE GLOBAL CRISIS

Diplomatic negotiations, administrative and legal measures, economic and social sanctions, military interventions, and other similar efforts have had very little success; as a matter of fact, they have often produced more problems than they solved. It is becoming increasingly clear why they had to fail. The strategies used to alleviate this crisis are rooted in the same ideology that created it in the first place. In the last analysis, the current global crisis is basically a psychospiritual crisis; it reflects the level of consciousness evolution of the human species. It is, therefore, hard to imagine that it could be resolved without a radical inner transformation of humanity on a large scale and its rise to a higher level of emotional maturity and spiritual awareness.

The task of imbuing humanity with an entirely different set of values and goals might appear too unrealistic and utopian to offer any real hope. Considering the paramount roles of violence and greed in human history, the possibility of transforming modern humanity into a species of individuals capable of peaceful coexistence with their fellow men and women regardless of race, color, and religious or political conviction, let alone with other species, certainly does not seem very plausible. We are facing the necessity to instill humanity with profound ethical values, sensitivity to the needs of others, acceptance of voluntary simplicity, and a sharp awareness of ecological imperatives. At first glance, such a task appears too fantastic even for a science fiction movie.

However, although serious and critical, the situation might not be as hopeless as it appears. After more than 40 years of intensive study of holotropic states of consciousness, I have come to the conclusion that the theoretical concepts and practical approaches developed by transpersonal psychology, a discipline that is trying to integrate spirituality with the new paradigm emerging in Western science, could help alleviate the crisis we are all facing. These observations suggest that the radical psychospiritual transformation of humanity is not only possible but also already underway. The question is only whether it can be sufficiently fast and extensive to reverse the current self-destructive trend of modern humanity.

THREE POISONS OF TIBETAN BUDDHISM

Let us take a look at the theoretical insights from the research of holotropic states and their practical implications for our everyday life. Can the new knowledge be used in a way that would make our life more fulfilling and rewarding? How could systematic self-exploration using holotropic states improve our emotional and physical well-being and bring about positive personality transformation and beneficial changes of the worldview and system of values? And, more specifically, how could this strategy contribute to alleviation of the global crisis and survival of life on this planet?

Spiritual teachers of all ages seem to agree that pursuit of material goals, in and of itself, cannot bring us fulfillment, happiness, and inner peace. The rapidly escalating global crisis, moral deterioration, and growing discontent accompanying the increase of material affluence in the industrial societies bear witness to this ancient truth. There seems to be general agreement in the mystical literature that the remedy for the existential malaise that besets humanity is to turn inside, look for the answers in our own psyche, and undergo a deep psychospiritual transformation.

It is not difficult to understand that an important prerequisite for successful existence is general intelligence—the ability to learn and recall, think and reason, and adequately respond to our material environment. More recent research emphasized the importance of "emotional intelligence," the capacity to adequately respond to our human environment and skillfully handle our interpersonal relationships (Goleman, 1996). Observations from the study of holotropic states confirm the basic tenet of perennial philosophy that the quality of our life ultimately depends on what can be called *spiritual intelligence*.

Spiritual intelligence is the capacity to conduct our life in such a way that it reflects deep philosophical and metaphysical understanding of reality and of ourselves. This, of course, brings questions about the nature of the psychospiritual transformation that is necessary to achieve this form of intelligence, the direction of the changes that we have to undergo, and the means that can facilitate such development. A very clear and specific answer to these questions can be found in different schools of Mahayana Buddhism.

We can use here as the basis for our discussion the famous Tibetan screen painting (*thangka*) portraying the cycle of life, death, and reincarnation. It depicts the Wheel of Life held in the grip of the horrifying Lord of Death. The wheel is divided into six segments representing the different *lokas*, or realms into which we can be reborn. The celestial domain of gods (*devaloka*) is shown as being challenged from the adjacent segment (*asuraloka*) by the jealous warrior gods. The region of hungry ghosts (*pretaloka*) is inhabited by pitiful creatures representing insatiable greed. They have giant bellies, enormous appetites, and mouths the size of a pinhole. The remaining sections of the wheel depict the world of human beings (*manakaloka*), the realm of the wild beasts (*tiryakaloka*), and hell (*narakaloka*). Inside the wheel are two concentric circles. The outer one shows the ascending and descending paths along which souls travel. The innermost circle contains three animals—a pig, a snake, and a rooster.

The animals in the center of the wheel represent the "three poisons," or forces that, according to the Buddhist teachings, perpetuate the cycles of birth and death and are responsible for all the suffering in our life. The pig symbolizes *ignorance* concerning the nature of reality and our own nature, the snake stands for *anger and aggression*, and the rooster depicts *desire and lust* leading to attachment. The quality of our life and our ability to cope with the challenges of existence depend critically on the degree to which we are able to eliminate or transform these forces that run the world of sentient beings. Let us now look from this perspective at the process of systematic self-exploration involving holotropic states of consciousness.

PRACTICAL KNOWLEDGE AND TRANSCENDENTAL WISDOM

The most obvious benefit that we can obtain from deep experiential work is access to extraordinary knowledge about ourselves, other people, nature, and the cosmos. In holotropic states, we can reach deep understanding of the unconscious dynamics of our psyche. We can discover how our perception of ourselves and of the world is influenced by forgotten or repressed memories from childhood, infancy, birth, and prenatal existence. In addition, in transpersonal experiences we can identify with other people, various animals, plants, and elements of the inorganic world. Experiences of this kind represent an extremely rich source of unique insights about the world we live in and can radically transform our worldview.

In recent years, many authors have pointed out that a significant factor in the development of the global crisis has been the Newtonian-Cartesian paradigm and monistic materialism that have dominated Western science for the last 300 years. This way of thinking involves a sharp dichotomy between mind and nature and portrays the universe as a giant, fully deterministic supermachine governed by mechanical laws. The image of the cosmos as a mechanical system has led to the erroneous belief that it can be adequately understood by dissecting it and studying all its parts. This has been a serious obstacle for viewing problems in terms of their complex interactions and from a holistic perspective.

In addition, by elevating matter to the most important principle in the cosmos, Western science reduces life, consciousness, and intelligence to accidental by-products of material processes. In this context, humans appear to be nothing more than highly developed animals. This led to the acceptance of antagonism, competition, and the Darwinian "survival of the fittest" as the leading principles of human society. In addition, the description of nature as unconscious provided the justification for its exploitation by humans, following the program very eloquently formulated by Francis Bacon (1870).

Psychoanalysis has painted a pessimistic picture of human beings as creatures whose primary motivating forces are bestial instincts. According to Freud, if we were not afraid of societal repercussions and controlled by the superego (internalized parental prohibitions and injunctions), we would kill and steal indiscriminately, commit incest, and be involved in unbridled promiscuous sex. This image of human nature relegated such concepts as complementarity, synergy, mutual respect, and peaceful cooperation into the domain of temporary opportunistic strategies or naïve utopian fantasies. It is not difficult to see how these concepts and the system of values associated with them have helped to create the crisis we are facing.

Insights from holotropic states have brought convincing support for a radically different understanding of the cosmos, nature, and human beings. They brought experiential confirmation for the concepts formulated by pioneers of information theory and the theory of systems, which have shown that our planet and the entire cosmos represent a unified and interconnected web of which each of us is an integral part (Bateson, 1979; Capra, 1996). In holotropic states, we can gain deep experiential knowledge of various aspects of material reality, of its interconnectedness, and of the unity underlying the world of seeming separation. However, the ignorance symbolized in the Tibetan thangkas by the pig is not the absence or lack of knowledge in the ordinary sense. It does not mean simply inadequate information about various aspects of the material world, but ignorance of a much deeper and more fundamental kind.

The form of ignorance that is meant here (*avidya*) is a fundamental misunderstanding and confusion concerning the nature of reality and our own nature. The only remedy for this kind of ignorance is transcendental wisdom (*prajña paramita*). From this point of view, it is essential that the inner work involving holotropic states offers more than just increasing, deepening, and correcting our knowledge concerning the material universe. It is also a unique way of gaining insights about issues of transcendental relevance.

In the light of this evidence, consciousness is not a product of the physiological processes in the brain, but a primary attribute of existence. The deepest nature of humanity is not bestial, but divine. The universe is imbued with creative intelligence, and consciousness is inextricably woven into its fabric. Our identification with the separate body–ego is an illusion, and our true identity is the totality of existence. This understanding provides a natural basis for reverence for life, cooperation and synergy, concerns for humanity and the planet as a whole, and deep ecological awareness.

ANATOMY OF HUMAN DESTRUCTIVENESS

Let us now look from the same perspective at the second "poison," human propensity to aggression. Modern study of aggressive behavior started with Charles Darwin's epoch-making discoveries in the field of evolution in the middle of the 19th century (Darwin, 1952). The attempts to explain human aggression from our animal origin generated such theoretical concepts as Desmond Morris's image of the "naked ape" (Morris, 1967), Robert Ardrey's idea of the "territorial imperative" (Ardrey, 1961), Paul MacLean's "triune brain" (MacLean, 1973), and Richard Dawkins's sociobiological explanations interpreting aggression in terms of genetic strategies of the "selfish genes" (Dawkins, 1976). More refined models of behavior developed by pioneers in ethology, such as Konrad Lorenz, Nikolaas Tinbergen, and others, complemented mechanical emphasis on instincts by the study of ritualistic and motivational elements (Lorenz, 1963; Tinbergen, 1965).

Any theories suggesting that the human tendency to violence simply reflects our animal origin are inadequate and unconvincing. With rare exceptions, such as the occasional violent group raids of chimpanzees against neighboring groups (Wrangham & Peterson, 1996), animals do not prey on their own kind. They exhibit aggression when they are hungry, defend their territory, or compete for sex. The nature and scope of human violence—Erich Fromm's "malignant aggression"—have no parallels in the animal kingdom (Fromm, 1973). The realization that human aggression cannot be adequately explained as a result of phylogenetic evolution led to the formulation of psychodynamic and psychosocial theories that consider a significant part of human aggression to be learned phenomena. This trend began in the late 1930s and was initiated by the work of Dollard and Miller.

BIOGRAPHICAL SOURCES OF AGGRESSION

Psychodynamic theories attempt to explain the specifically human aggression as a reaction to frustration, abuse, and lack of love in infancy and childhood. However, explanations of this kind fall painfully short of accounting for extreme forms of individual violence, such as the serial murders of the Boston Strangler and Jeffrey Dahmer or indiscriminate multiple killings of the "running amok" type. Current psychodynamic and psychosocial theories are even less convincing when it comes to bestial acts committed by entire groups, like the Sharon Tate murders by the Manson family or atrocities that occur during prison uprisings. They fail completely when it comes to mass

societal phenomena that involve entire nations, such as Nazism, Communism, bloody wars, revolutions, genocide, and concentration camps.

In the last several decades, psychedelic research and deep experiential psy-
chotherapies have been able to throw much light on the problem of human
aggression. This work has revealed that the roots of this problematic and
dangerous aspect of human nature are much deeper and more formidable
than traditional psychology ever imagined. However, this work has also discovered extremely effective approaches that have the potential to neutralize and transform these violent elements in human personality. In addition,
these observations indicate that malignant aggression does not reflect true
human nature. It is connected with a domain of unconscious dynamics that
separates us from our deeper identity. When we reach the transpersonal
realms that lie beyond this screen, we realize that our true nature is divine
rather than bestial.

PERINATAL ROOTS OF VIOLENCE

There is no doubt that "malignant aggression" is connected with traumas and frustrations in childhood and infancy. However, modern consciousness research has revealed additional significant roots of violence in deep
recesses of the psyche that lie beyond postnatal biography and are related
to the trauma of biological birth. The vital emergency, pain, and suffocation experienced for many hours during biological delivery generate enormous amounts of anxiety and murderous aggression that remain stored in
the organism. The reliving of birth in various forms of experiential psychotherapy not only involves concrete replay of the original emotions and sensations but also is typically associated with a variety of experiences from the
collective unconscious portraying scenes of unimaginable violence. Among
these are often powerful sequences depicting wars, revolutions, racial riots,
concentration camps, totalitarianism, and genocide.

The spontaneous emergence of this imagery during the reliving of birth is
often associated with convincing insights concerning the perinatal origin of
such extreme forms of human violence. Naturally, wars and revolutions are
extremely complex phenomena that have historical, economic, political, religious, and other dimensions. The intention here is not to offer a reductionistic explanation replacing all the other causes, but to add some new insights
concerning the psychological and spiritual dimensions of these forms of
social psychopathology that have been neglected or received only superficial
treatment in earlier theories.

The images of violent sociopolitical events accompanying the reliving
of biological birth tend to appear in very specific connection with the four
basic perinatal matrices (BPMs), which is my name for complex experiential
patterns associated with the consecutive stages of the birth process. While

reliving episodes of undisturbed intrauterine existence (BPM I), we typically experience images from human societies with an ideal social structure, from cultures that live in complete harmony with nature, or from future utopian societies where all major conflicts have been resolved.

Disturbing intrauterine memories, such as those of a toxic womb, imminent miscarriage, or attempted abortion, are accompanied by images of human groups living in industrial areas where nature is polluted and spoiled, or in societies with an insidious social order and all-pervading paranoia.

Regressive experiences related to the first clinical stage of birth (BPM II), during which the uterus periodically contracts but the cervix is not yet open, present a diametrically different picture. They portray oppressive and abusive totalitarian societies that have closed borders, victimize their populations, and "choke" personal freedom, such as Czarist or Communist Russia, Hitler's Third Reich, Eastern European Soviet satellites, South American dictatorships, and South African apartheid; or bring specific images of the inmates in Nazi concentration camps and Stalin's Gulag Archipelago. While experiencing these scenes of living hell, we identify exclusively with the victims and feel deep sympathy for the downtrodden and the underdog.

The experiences accompanying reliving the second clinical stage of delivery (BPM III), when the cervix is dilated and continued contractions propel the fetus through the narrow passage of the birth canal, feature a rich panoply of violent scenes—bloody wars and revolutions, human or animal slaughter, mutilation, sexual abuse, and murder. These scenes often contain demonic elements and repulsive scatological motifs. Additional frequent concomitants of BPM III are visions of burning cities, the launching of rockets, and explosions of nuclear bombs. Here we are not limited to the role of victims, but can participate in three roles—that of the victim, of the aggressor, and of an emotionally involved observer.

The events characterizing the third clinical stage of delivery (BPM IV), the actual moment of birth and the separation from the mother, are typically associated with images of victory in wars and revolutions, the liberation of prisoners, and the success of collective efforts, such as patriotic or nationalistic movements. At this point, we can also experience visions of triumphant celebrations and parades or of exciting postwar reconstruction.

In 1975, I described these observations, linking sociopolitical upheavals to stages of biological birth, in my book *Realms of the Human Unconscious* (Grof, 1975). Shortly after its publication, I received an enthusiastic letter from Lloyd de Mause, a New York psychoanalyst and journalist. De Mause is one of the founders of psychohistory, a discipline that applies the findings of depth psychology to the study of history and political science. Psychohistorians explore such issues as the relationship between the childhood of political leaders and their system of values and process of decision making, or the influence of child-rearing practices on the nature of revolutions of that particular historical period. Lloyd de Mause was very interested in my findings concerning the trauma of birth and its possible sociopolitical implications, because they provided independent support for his own research.

For some time, de Mause had been studying the psychodynamics of the periods immediately preceding wars and revolutions. It interested him how military leaders succeed in mobilizing masses of peaceful civilians and transforming them practically overnight into killing machines. His approach to this problem was very original and creative. In addition to analysis of traditional historical sources, he drew data of great psychological importance from caricatures, jokes, dreams, personal imagery, slips of the tongue, side comments of speakers, and even doodles and scribbles on the edge of the rough drafts of political documents. By the time he contacted me, he had analyzed in this way 17 situations preceding the outbreak of wars and revolutionary upheavals, spanning many centuries from antiquity to most recent times (de Mause, 1975).

He was struck by the extraordinary abundance of figures of speech, metaphors, and images related to biological birth that he found in this material. Military leaders and politicians of all ages describing a critical situation or declaring war typically used terms that equally applied to perinatal distress. They accused the enemy of choking and strangling their people, squeezing the last breath out of their lungs, or constricting them and not giving them enough space to live (e.g., Hitler's *Lebensraum*).

Equally frequent were allusions to dark caves, tunnels, and confusing labyrinths; dangerous abysses into which one might be pushed; and the threat of engulfment by treacherous quicksand or a terrifying whirlpool. Similarly, the offer of the resolution of the crisis had the form of perinatal images. The leader promised to rescue his nation from an ominous labyrinth, to lead it to the light on the other side of the tunnel, and to create a situation where the dangerous aggressor and oppressor will be overcome and everybody will again breathe freely.

Lloyd de Mause's historical examples at the time included such famous personages as Alexander the Great, Napoleon, Samuel Adams, Kaiser Wilhelm II, Hitler, Khrushchev, and Kennedy. Samuel Adams, when talking about the American Revolution, referred to "the child of Independence now struggling for birth" (de Mause, 1975). In 1914, Kaiser Wilhelm stated that "the Monarchy has been seized by the throat and forced to choose between letting itself be strangled and making a last ditch effort to defend itself against attack" (quoted in de Mause, 1975).

During the Cuban missile crisis, Khrushchev wrote to Kennedy, pleading that the two nations not "come to a clash, like blind moles battling to death in a tunnel." Even more explicit was the coded message used by Japanese ambassador Kurusu when he phoned Tokyo to signal that negotiations with Roosevelt had broken down and that it was all right to go ahead with the bombing of Pearl Harbor. He announced that the "birth of the child was imminent" and asked how things were in Japan: "Does it seem as if the child might be born?" The reply was "Yes, the birth of the child seems imminent." Interestingly, the American intelligence listening in recognized the meaning of the "war-as-birth" code. The most recent examples can be found in Osama bin Laden's videotape, where he threatens to turn the United States into a "choking hell," and in the speech of U.S. Secretary of State Condoleezza Rice, who described the acute crisis in Iraq as "birth pangs of New Middle East."

Particularly chilling was the use of perinatal language in connection with the explosion of the atomic bomb in Hiroshima. The airplane was given the name of the pilot's mother, Enola Gay; the atomic bomb itself carried a painted nickname, "The Little Boy"; and the agreed-upon message sent to Washington as a signal of successful detonation was "The baby was born." It would not be too far-fetched to see the image of a newborn also behind the nickname of the Nagasaki bomb, Fat Man. Since the time of our correspondence, Lloyd de Mause collected many additional historical examples and refined his thesis that the memory of the birth trauma plays an important role as a source of motivation for violent social activity.

The relationship between nuclear warfare and birth is of such relevance that I would like to explore it further using the material from a fascinating paper by Carol Cohn entitled "Sex and Death in the Rational World of the Defense Intellectuals" (1987). The defense intellectuals (DIs) are civilians who move in and out of government, working sometimes as administrative officials or consultants, sometimes at universities and think tanks. They create the theory that informs and legitimates U.S. nuclear strategic practice—how to manage the arms race, how to deter the use of nuclear weapons, how to fight a nuclear war if the deterrence fails, and how to explain why it is not safe to live without nuclear weapons.

Carol Cohn had attended a two-week summer seminar on nuclear weapons, nuclear strategic doctrine, and arms control. She was so fascinated by what had transpired there that she spent the following year immersed in the almost entirely male world (except for secretaries) of defense intellectuals. She collected some extremely interesting facts confirming the perinatal dimension in nuclear warfare. In her own terminology, this material confirms the importance of the motif of "male birth" and "male creation" as important psychological forces underlying the psychology of nuclear warfare. She used the following historical examples to illustrate her point of view:

> In 1942, Ernest Lawrence sent a telegram to a Chicago group of physicists developing the nuclear bomb that read, "Congratulations to the new parents. Can hardly wait to see the new arrival." At Los Alamos, the atom bomb was referred to as *Oppenheimer's baby*. Richard Feynman wrote in his article "Los Alamos From Below" that when he was

temporarily on leave after his wife's death, he received a telegram that
read, "The baby is expected on such and such a day."

At Lawrence Livermore laboratories, the hydrogen bomb was referred to
as *Teller's baby*, although those who wanted to disparage Edward Teller's contribution claimed he was not the bomb's father, but its mother.
They claimed that Stanislaw Ulam was the real father, who had all
the important ideas and "conceived it"; Teller only "carried it" after
that. Terms related to motherhood were also used to the provision of
"nurturance"—the maintenance of the missiles.

General Grove sent a triumphant coded cable to Secretary of War Henry
Stimson at the Potsdam conference reporting the success of the first
atomic test: "Doctor has just returned most enthusiastic and confident
that the little boy is as husky as his big brother. The light in his eyes
discernible from here to Highhold [Stimson's country home,] and I
could have heard his screams from here to my farm." Stimson, in turn,
informed Churchill by writing him a note that read, "Babies satisfacto-
rily born."

William L. Laurence witnessed the test of the first atomic bomb and wrote,
"The big boom came about a hundred seconds after the great flash—
the first cry of a new-born world." Edward Teller's exultant telegram
to Los Alamos, announcing the successful test of the hydrogen bomb
"Mike" at the Eniwetok atoll in Marshall Islands, read, "It's a boy." The
Enola Gay, "Little Boy," and "The baby was born" symbolism of the
Hiroshima bomb, and the "Fat Man" symbolism of the Nagasaki bomb,
were already mentioned earlier. According to Carol Cohn (1987), "[M]
ale scientists gave birth to a progeny with the ultimate power of domination over female Nature."

Carol Cohn also mentions in her paper an abundance of overtly sexual
symbolism in the language of defense intellectuals. The nature of this material, linking sex to aggression, domination, and scatology, shows a deep similarity to the imagery occurring in the context of birth experiences (BPM III).
Cohn used the following examples: American dependence on nuclear weapons was explained as irresistible, because "you get more bang for the buck."
A professor's explanation of why the MX missiles should be placed in the
silos of the newest Minuteman missiles, instead of replacing the older, less
accurate ones, was "You are not going to take the nicest missile you have and
put it into a crummy hole." At one point, there was a serious concern that
"we have to harden our missiles, because the Russians are a little harder than
we are." One military adviser to the National Security Council referred to
"releasing 70 to 80 percent of our megatonnage in one orgasmic whump."

Lectures were filled with terms like *vertical erector launchers, thrust-to-
weight ratios, soft lay-downs, deep penetration,* and the comparative advantages
of *protracted versus spasm attacks.* Another example was the popular and widespread custom of patting the missiles practiced by the visitors to nuclear

submarines, which Carol Cohn saw as an expression of phallic supremacy and also homoerotic tendencies. In view of this material, it clearly is quite appropriate for feminist critics of nuclear policies to refer to "missile envy" and "phallic worship."

Further support for the pivotal role of the perinatal domain of the unconscious in war psychology can be found in Sam Keen's excellent book *The Faces of the Enemy* (1988). Keen brought together an outstanding collection of war posters, propaganda cartoons, and caricatures from many historical periods and countries. He demonstrated that the way the enemy is described and portrayed during a war or revolution is a stereotype that shows only minimal variations and has very little to do with the actual characteristics of the country and its inhabitants. This material also typically disregards the diversity and heterogeneity characterizing the population of each country and makes blatant generalizations: "This is what the Germans, Americans, Japanese, Russians, etc. are like!"

Keen was able to divide these images into several archetypal categories according to the prevailing characteristics (e.g., Stranger, Aggressor, Worthy Opponent, Faceless, Enemy of God, Barbarian, Greedy, Criminal, Torturer, Rapist, and Death). According to him, the alleged images of the enemy are essentially projections of the repressed and unacknowledged shadow aspects of our own unconscious. Although we would certainly find in human history instances of just wars, those who initiate war activities are typically substituting external targets for elements in their own psyches that should be properly faced in personal self-exploration.

Sam Keen's theoretical framework does not specifically include the perinatal domain of the unconscious. However, the analysis of his picture material reveals a preponderance of symbolic images that are characteristic of BPM II and BPM III. The enemy is typically depicted as a dangerous octopus, a vicious dragon, a multiheaded hydra, a giant venomous tarantula, or an engulfing Leviathan. Other frequently used symbols include vicious predatory felines or birds, monstrous sharks, and ominous snakes, particularly vipers and boa constrictors. Scenes depicting strangulation or crushing, ominous whirlpools, and treacherous quicksands also abound in pictures from the time of wars, revolutions, and political crises. Juxtaposition of pictures from holotropic states of consciousness that focus on reliving birth with the historical pictorial documentation collected by Lloyd de Mause and Sam Keen represents strong evidence for the perinatal roots of human violence.

According to the new insights, provided jointly by observations from consciousness research and by the findings of psychohistory, we all carry in our deep unconscious powerful energies and emotions associated with the trauma of birth that we have not adequately processed and assimilated. For some of us, this aspect of our psyche can be completely unconscious, until and unless we embark on some in-depth self-exploration with the use of psychedelics or some powerful experiential techniques of psychotherapy, such as holotropic breathwork or rebirthing. Others can have varying degrees of awareness of the emotions and physical sensations stored on the perinatal level of the unconscious.

Activation of this material can lead to serious individual psychopathology, including unmotivated violence. Lloyd de Mause (1975) suggested that, for unknown reasons, the awareness of the perinatal elements can increase simultaneously in a large number of people. This creates an atmosphere of general tension, anxiety, and anticipation. The leader is an individual who is under a stronger influence of the perinatal energies than the average person. He also has the ability to disown his unacceptable feelings (the *shadow* in Jung's terminology) and to project them on the external situation. The collective discomfort is blamed on the enemy, and a military intervention is offered as a solution. Richard Tarnas's extraordinary book *Cosmos and Psyche: Intimations of a New Worldview* (2006) added an interesting dimension to de Mause's thesis. In this meticulously researched study, Tarnas was able to show that throughout history, the times of wars and revolutions have been correlated with specific astrological transits, suggesting the participation of archetypal forces in these phenomena.

War and revolution provide an opportunity to disregard the psychological defenses that ordinarily keep the dangerous perinatal forces in check. Freud's superego, a psychological force that demands restraint and civilized behavior, is replaced by the *war superego*. We receive praise and medals for murder, indiscriminate destruction, and pillaging, the same behaviors that in peacetime are unacceptable and would land us in prison or worse. Similarly, sexual violence has been a common practice during wartime and has been generally tolerated. As a matter of fact, military leaders have often promised their soldiers unlimited access to women in the conquered territory to motivate them for battle.

Once the war erupts, the destructive and self-destructive perinatal impulses are freely acted out. The themes that we normally encounter in a certain stage of the process of inner exploration and transformation (BPM II and III) now become parts of our everyday life, either directly or in the form of TV news. Various no-exit situations, sadomasochistic orgies, sexual violence, bestial and demonic behavior, the unleashing of enormous explosive energies, and scatology, which belong to standard perinatal imagery, are all enacted in wars and revolutions with extraordinary vividness and power.

Witnessing scenes of destruction and the acting out of violent unconscious impulses, whether it occurs on the individual scale or collectively in wars and revolutions, does not result in healing and transformation as would an inner confrontation with these elements in a therapeutic context. The experience is not generated by our own unconscious, lacks the element of deep introspection, and does not lead to insights. The situation is fully externalized, and connection with the deep dynamics of the psyche is missing. And, naturally, there is no therapeutic intention and motivation for change and transformation. Thus the goal of the underlying birth fantasy, which represents the deepest driving force of such violent events, is not achieved, even if the war or revolution has been brought to a successful closure. The most triumphant external victory does not deliver what was expected and hoped for: an inner sense of emotional liberation and psychospiritual rebirth.

After the initial intoxicating feelings of triumph come at first a sober awakening and later bitter disappointment. And it usually does not take a long time before a facsimile of the old oppressive system starts emerging from the ruins of the dead dream, because the same unconscious forces continue to operate in the deep unconscious of everybody involved. This seems to happen again and again in human history, whether the event involved is the French Revolution, the Bolshevik Revolution in Russia, the Communist Revolution in China, or any of the other violent upheavals associated with great hopes and expectations.

Because I conducted for many years deep experiential work in Prague at the time when Czechoslovakia had a Marxist regime, I was able to collect some fascinating material concerning the psychological dynamics of Communism. The issues related to Communist ideology typically emerged in the treatment of my clients at the time when they were struggling with perinatal energies and emotions. It soon became obvious that the passion the revolutionaries feel toward the oppressors and their regimes receives a powerful reinforcement from their revolt against the inner prison of their perinatal memories. And, conversely, the need to coerce and dominate others is an external displacement of the need to overcome the fear of being overwhelmed by one's own unconscious. The murderous entanglement of the oppressor and the revolutionary is thus an externalized replica of the situation experienced in the birth canal.

The Communist vision contains an element of psychological truth that has made it appealing to large numbers of people. The basic notion that a violent experience of a revolutionary nature is necessary to terminate suffering and oppression and institute a situation of greater harmony is correct when understood as related to the process of inner transformation. However, it is dangerously false when it is projected on the external world as a political ideology of violent revolutions. The fallacy lies in the fact that what on a deeper level is essentially an archetypal pattern of spiritual death and rebirth takes the form of an atheistic and antispiritual program. Paradoxically, Communism has many features in common with organized religion and exploits people's spiritual needs, while not only failing to satisfy them but also actively suppressing any genuine spiritual search. The parallel of Communism with organized religion goes so far that Stalin at the height of his power was declared infallible.

Communist revolutions have been extremely successful in their destructive phase, but, instead of the promised brotherhood and harmony, their victories have bred regimes where oppression, cruelty, and injustice ruled supreme. Today, when the economically ruined and politically corrupt Soviet Union has collapsed and the Communist world has fallen apart, it is obvious to all people with sane judgment that this gigantic historical experiment, conducted at the cost of millions of human lives and unimaginable human suffering, has been a colossal failure. If the above observations are correct, no external interventions have a chance to create a better world unless they are associated with a profound transformation of human consciousness.

The observations from the study of holotropic states also throw some important light on the psychology of concentration camps. Over a number of years, Professor Bastiaans in Leyden, Holland, conducted LSD therapy with people suffering from *concentration camp syndrome*, a condition that develops in former inmates of these camps many years after the incarceration. Bastiaans has also worked with former *kapos* on their issues of profound guilt. An artistic description of this work can be found in the book *Shivitti*, written by a former inmate, Ka-Tzetnik 135633, who underwent a series of therapeutic sessions with Bastiaans (Ka-Tzetnik 135633, 1989).

Bastiaans himself wrote a paper describing his work entitled "Man in the Concentration Camp and Concentration Camp in Man" (1955). There he pointed out, without specifying it, that the concentration camps are a projection of a certain domain that exists in the human unconscious: "Before there was a man in the concentration camp, there was a concentration camp in man" (Bastiaans, 1955). Study of holotropic states of consciousness makes it possible to identify the realm of the psyche that Bastiaans was talking about. Closer examination of the general and specific conditions in the Nazi concentration camps reveals that they are a diabolical and realistic enactment of the nightmarish atmosphere that characterizes the reliving of biological birth.

The barbed-wire barriers, high-voltage fences, watch towers with submachine guns, minefields, and packs of trained dogs certainly created a hellish and almost archetypal image of an utterly hopeless and oppressive no-exit situation that is so characteristic of the first clinical stage of birth (BPM II). At the same time, the elements of violence, bestiality, scatology, and sexual abuse of women and men, including rape and sadistic practices, all belong to the phenomenology of the second stage of birth (BPM III), familiar to people who have relived their birth. In the concentration camps, the sexual abuse existed on a random individual level, as well as in the context of the "houses of dolls," institutions providing "entertainment" for the officers. The only escape out of this hell was death—by a bullet, hunger, disease, or suffocation in the gas chambers. Two other books by Ka-Tzetnik 135633, *House of Dolls* and *Sunrise Over Hell* (Ka-Tzetnik, 1955, 1977), offer a shattering description of life in the concentration camps.

The bestiality of the SS seemed to be focused particularly on pregnant women and little children, which brings further support for the perinatal hypothesis. The most powerful passage from Terence des Près's book *The Survivor* (1976) is, without a doubt, the description of a truck full of babies dumped into fire, followed by a scene in which pregnant women are beaten with clubs and whips, torn by dogs, dragged around by the hair, kicked into the stomach, and then thrown into the crematorium while still alive (des Près, 1976).

The perinatal nature of the irrational impulses manifesting in the camps is evident also in the scatological behavior of the *kapos*. Throwing eating bowls into the latrines and asking the inmates for their retrieval, and forcing the inmates to urinate into each other's mouths, were practices that besides their bestiality brought the danger of epidemics. Had the concentration camps been simply institutions providing isolation of political enemies and cheap slave labor, maintenance of hygienic rules would have been a primary concern of the organizers, as it is the case in any facility accommodating large numbers of people. In Buchenwald alone, as a result of these perverted practices, 27 inmates drowned in feces in the course of a single month.

The intensity, depth, and convincing nature of all the experiences of collective violence associated with the perinatal process suggest that they are not individually fabricated from such sources as adventure books, movies, and TV shows, but originate in the deep unconscious. When our experiential self-exploration reaches the memory of the birth trauma, we also connect to an immense pool of painful memories of the human species and gain access to experiences of other people who once were in a similar predicament. It is not hard to imagine that the perinatal level of our unconscious that "knows" so intimately the history of human violence is actually partially responsible for wars, revolutions, and similar atrocities.

The intensity and quantity of the perinatal experiences portraying various brutalities of human history are truly astonishing. Christopher Bache, after having carefully analyzed various aspects of this phenomenon, made an interesting conclusion. He suggested that the memories of the violence perpetrated throughout ages in human history contaminated the collective unconscious in the same way in which the traumas from our infancy and childhood polluted our individual unconscious. According to Bache, it might then be possible that when we start experiencing these collective memories, our inner process transcends the framework of personal therapy and we participate in the healing of the field of species consciousness.

The role of the birth trauma as a source of violence and self-destructive tendencies has been confirmed by clinical studies. For example, there seems to be an important correlation between difficult birth and criminality (Kandel & Mednick, 1991; Litt, 1974; Raine, Brennan, & Mednick, 1995). In a similar way, aggression directed inward, particularly suicide, seems to be psychogenetically linked to difficult birth (Appleby, 1998). The Scandinavian researcher Bertil Jacobson (Jacobsen et al., 1987) found a close correlation between the form of self-destructive behavior and the nature of birth. Suicides involving asphyxiation were associated with suffocation at birth, violent suicides with mechanical birth trauma, and drug addiction leading to suicide with opiate and/or barbiturate administration during labor.

The circumstances of birth play an important role in creating a disposition to violence and self-destructive tendencies or, conversely, to loving behavior and healthy interpersonal relationships. French obstetrician Michel Odent (1995) has shown how the hormones involved in the birth process and in nursing and maternal behavior participate in this imprinting. The catecholamines (adrenaline and noradrenaline) play an important role in evolution as mediators of the aggressive-protective instinct of the mother at the time when birth was occurring in unprotected natural environments. Oxytocin, prolactin, and endorphins are known to induce maternal behavior in animals and foster dependency and attachment. The busy, noisy, and chaotic milieu of many hospitals induces anxiety, engages unnecessarily the adrenaline system, and imprints the picture of a world that is potentially dangerous and requires aggressive responses. This interferes with the hormones that mediate positive interpersonal imprinting. It is, therefore, essential to provide for birthing in a quiet, safe, and private environment (Odent, 1995).

TRANSPERSONAL ORIGINS OF VIOLENCE

The above material shows that a conceptual framework limited to postnatal biography and the Freudian unconscious does not adequately explain extreme forms of human aggression on the individual and collective scale. However, it seems that the roots of human violence reach even deeper than to the perinatal level of the psyche. Consciousness research has revealed significant additional sources of aggression in the transpersonal domain, such as archetypal figures of demons and wrathful deities, complex destructive mythological themes, and past-life memories of physical and emotional abuse.

C. G. Jung (1964) believed that the archetypes of the collective unconscious have a powerful influence not only on the behavior of individuals but also on the events of human history. From this point of view, entire nations and cultural groups might be enacting in their behavior important mythological themes. In the decade preceding the outbreak of World War II, Jung found in the dreams of his German patients many elements from the Nordic myth of Ragnarok, or the Twilight of the Gods. On the basis of these observations, he concluded that this archetype was emerging in the collective psyche of the German nation and that it would lead to a major catastrophe, which would ultimately turn out to be self-destructive. James Hillman amassed in his brilliant book *A Terrible Love of War* (2004) convincing evidence that war is a powerful archetypal force that has irresistible power over individuals and nations.

In many instances, leaders of nations specifically use not only perinatal but also archetypal images and spiritual symbolism to achieve their political goals. The medieval crusaders were asked to sacrifice their lives for Jesus in a war that would recover the Holy Land from the Mohammedans. Adolf Hitler exploited the mythological motifs of the supremacy of the Nordic race and of the millennial empire, as well as the ancient Vedic symbols of the swastika and the solar eagle. Ayatollah Khomeini and Saddam Hussein ignited the imagination of their Muslim followers by references to *jihad*, the holy war against the infidels. American president Ronald Reagan referred to the Soviet Union as the "evil empire," and George W. Bush in his political speeches referred to the "axis of evil" and Armageddon.

Carol Cohn discussed in her paper not only the perinatal but also the spiritual symbolism associated with the language used in relation to nuclear weaponry and doctrine. The authors of the strategic doctrine refer to members of their community as the "nuclear priesthood." The first atomic test was called Trinity—the unity of Father, Son, and Holy Ghost, the male forces of creation. From her feminist perspective, Cohn (1987) saw this as an effort of male scientists to appropriate and claim ultimate creative power. The scientists who worked on the atomic bomb and witnessed the test described it in the following way: "It was as though we stood at the first day of creation"; and Robert Oppenheimer thought of Krishna's words to Arjuna in the *Bhagavad Gita*: "I am become Death, the Shatterer of Worlds."

BIOGRAPHICAL DETERMINANTS OF INSATIABLE GREED

This brings us to the third poison of Tibetan Buddhism, a powerful psychospiritual force that combines the qualities of lust, desire, and insatiable greed. Together with "malignant aggression," these qualities are certainly responsible for some of the darkest chapters in human history. Western psychologists link various aspects of this force to the libidinal drives described by Sigmund Freud. Psychoanalytic interpretation of the insatiable human need to achieve, to possess, and to become more than one is attributes this psychological force to the sublimation of lower instincts.

According to Freud (1955),

What appears as . . . an untiring impulse toward further perfection can easily be understood as a result of the instinctual repression upon which is based all that is most precious in human civilization. The repressed instinct never ceases to strive for complete satisfaction, which would consist in the repetition of a primary experience of satisfaction. No substitutive or reactive formations and no sublimations will suffice to remove the repressed instinct's persisting tension.

More specifically, Freud saw greed as a phenomenon related to problems during the nursing period. According to him, frustration or overindulgence during the oral phase of libidinal development can reinforce the primitive infantile need to incorporate objects to such an extent that in adulthood it is transferred in a sublimated form to a variety of other objects and situations. When the acquisitive drive focuses on money, psychoanalysts attribute it to fixation on the anal stage of libidinal development. Insatiable sexual appetite is then considered to be the result of phallic fixation. Many other unrelenting human pursuits are then interpreted in terms of sublimation of such phallic instinctual urges. Modern consciousness research has found these interpretations to be superficial and inadequate. It discovered significant additional sources of acquisitiveness and greed on the perinatal and transpersonal levels of the unconscious.

PERINATAL SOURCES OF INSATIABLE GREED

In the course of biographically oriented psychotherapy, many people discover that their life has been inauthentic in certain specific sectors of interpersonal relations. For example, problems with parental authority can lead to specific patterns of difficulties with authority figures, repeated dysfunctional patterns in sexual relationships can be traced to parents as models for sexual behavior, sibling issues can color and distort future peer relationships, and so on.

When the process of experiential self-exploration reaches the perinatal level, we typically discover that our life up to that point has been largely inauthentic in its totality, not just in certain partial segments. We find out to our surprise and astonishment that our entire life strategy has been misdirected and therefore incapable of providing genuine satisfaction. The reason for this is the fact that it was primarily motivated by the fear of death and by unconscious forces associated with biological birth, which have not been adequately processed and integrated. In other words, during biological birth, we completed the process anatomically but not emotionally.

When our field of consciousness is strongly influenced by the underlying memory of the struggle in the birth canal, it leads to a feeling of discomfort and dissatisfaction with the present situation. This discontent can focus on a large spectrum of issues—unsatisfactory physical appearance, inadequate resources and material possessions, low social position and influence, insufficient amount of power and fame, and many others. Like the child stuck in the birth canal, we feel a strong need to get to a better situation that lies somewhere in the future.

Whatever is the reality of the present circumstances, we do not find it satisfactory. Our fantasy keeps creating images of future situations that appear more fulfilling than the present one. It seems that, until we reach it, life will be only preparation for a better future, not yet "the real thing." This results in a life pattern that people involved in experiential self-exploration have described as a "treadmill" or "rat-race" type of existence. The existentialists talk about "auto-projecting" into the future. This strategy is a basic fallacy of human life. It is essentially a loser strategy, whether or not we achieve the goals that we have set for ourselves, because they do not deliver the satisfaction that we expect.

When the goal is not reached, the continuing dissatisfaction is attributed to the fact that we have failed to reach the corrective measures. When we succeed in reaching the goal of our aspirations, it typically does not have much influence on our basic life feelings. The continuing dissatisfaction is then blamed on the fact that either the choice of the goal was not correct or it was not ambitious enough. The result is either substitution of the old goal with a different one or amplification of the same type of ambitions. We cannot get enough of what we really do not want or need.

In any case, the failure is not correctly diagnosed as being an inevitable result of a fundamentally wrong strategy, which is in principle incapable of providing satisfaction. This fallacious pattern applied on a large scale is responsible for reckless irrational pursuit of various grandiose goals that result in much suffering and many problems in the world. It can be played out on any level of importance and affluence, because it never brings true satisfaction. The only strategy that can significantly reduce this irrational drive is full conscious reliving and integration of the trauma of birth in systematic inner self-exploration.

TRANSPERSONAL CAUSES OF INSATIABLE GREED

Modern consciousness research and experiential psychotherapy have discovered that the deepest source of our dissatisfaction and striving for perfection lies even beyond the perinatal domain. This insatiable craving that drives human life is ultimately transpersonal in nature. In Dante Alighieri's (1990) words, "The desire for perfection is that desire which always makes every pleasure appear incomplete, for there is no joy or pleasure so great in this life that it can quench the thirst in our soul."

In the most general sense, the deepest transpersonal roots of insatiable greed can best be understood in terms of Ken Wilber's concept of the Atman project (Wilber, 1980). Our true nature is divine—God, Cosmic Christ, Allah, Buddha, Brahma, and the Tao—and, although the process of incarnation separates and alienates us from our source, the awareness of this fact is never completely lost. The deepest motivating force in the psyche on all the levels of consciousness evolution is to return to the experience of our divinity. However, the constraining conditions of the consecutive stages of development stand in the way of this experience.

Real transcendence requires death of the separate self, dying to the exclusive subject. Because of the fear of annihilation and because of grasping onto the ego, the individual has to settle for Atman substitutes or surrogates, which are specific for each particular stage. For the fetus and the newborn, this means the satisfaction experienced in the good womb or on the good breast. For an infant, this is satisfaction of age-specific physiological needs. For the adult, the range of possible Atman projects is large; it includes, besides food and sex, money, fame, power, appearance, knowledge, and many others.

Because of our deep sense that our true identity is the totality of cosmic creation and the creative principle itself, substitutes of any degree and scope—the Atman projects—will always remain unsatisfactory. Only the experience of one's divinity in a holotropic state of consciousness can ever fulfill our deepest needs. Thus, the ultimate solution for the insatiable greed is in the inner world, not in secular pursuits of any kind or scope. The great 13th-century Persian mystic and poet Rumi made it very clear:

> All the hopes, desires, loves, and affections that people have for different things—fathers, mothers, friends, heavens, the earth, palaces, sciences, works, food, drink—the saint knows that these are desires for God and all those things are veils. When men leave this world and see the King without these veils, then they will know that all were veils and coverings, that the object of their desire was in reality that One Thing.

TECHNOLOGIES OF THE SACRED AND HUMAN SURVIVAL

The finding that the roots of human violence and insatiable greed reach far deeper than academic psychiatry ever suspected and that their reservoirs in the psyche are truly enormous could in and of itself be very discouraging. However, it is balanced by the exciting discovery of new therapeutic mechanisms and transformative potentials that become available in holotropic states on the perinatal and transpersonal levels of the psyche.

I have seen over the years profound emotional and psychosomatic healing, as well as radical personality transformation, in many people who were involved in serious and systematic inner quest. Some of them were meditators and had regular spiritual practice; others had supervised psychedelic sessions or participated in various forms of experiential psychotherapy and self-exploration. I have also witnessed profound positive changes in many people who received adequate support during spontaneous episodes of psychospiritual crises.

As the content of the perinatal level of the unconscious emerged into consciousness and was integrated, these individuals underwent radical personality changes. The level of aggression typically decreased considerably, and they became more peaceful, comfortable with themselves, and tolerant of others. The experience of psychospiritual death and rebirth and conscious connection with positive postnatal or prenatal memories reduced irrational drives and ambitions. It caused a shift of focus from the past and future to the present moment and enhanced the ability to enjoy simple circumstances of life, such as everyday activities, food, lovemaking, nature, and music. Another important result of this process was the emergence of spirituality of a universal and mystical nature that was very authentic and convincing, because it was based on deep personal experience.

The process of spiritual opening and transformation typically deepened further as a result of transpersonal experiences, such as identification with other people, entire human groups, animals, plants, and even inorganic materials and processes in nature. Other experiences provided conscious access to events occurring in other countries, cultures, and historical periods and even to the mythological realms and archetypal beings of the collective unconscious. Experiences of cosmic unity and one's own divinity led to increasing identification with all of creation and brought a sense of wonder, love, compassion, and inner peace.

What had begun as psychological probing of the unconscious psyche automatically became a philosophical quest for the meaning of life and a journey of spiritual discovery. People who connected to the transpersonal domain of their psyche tended to develop a new appreciation for existence and reverence for all life. One of the most striking consequences of various forms of transpersonal experiences was the spontaneous emergence and development of deep humanitarian and ecological concerns and the need to get involved in service for some common purpose. This was based on an almost cellular awareness that the boundaries in the universe are arbitrary and that each of us is ultimately identical with the entire web of existence.

It was suddenly clear that we cannot do anything to nature without simultaneously doing it to ourselves. Differences among people appeared to be interesting and enriching rather than threatening, whether they were related to sex, race, color, language, political conviction, or religious belief. It is obvious that a transformation of this kind would increase our chances for survival if it could occur on a sufficiently large scale.

LESSONS FROM HOLOTROPIC STATES FOR THE PSYCHOLOGY OF SURVIVAL

Some of the insights of people experiencing holotropic states of consciousness are directly related to the current global crisis and its relationship with consciousness evolution. They show that we have exteriorized in the modern world many of the essential themes of the perinatal process that a person involved in spiritual quest and deep personal transformation has to face internally. The same elements that we would encounter in the process of psychological death and rebirth in our visionary experiences make these days our evening news. This is particularly true in regard to the phenomena that characterize BPM III, such as destruction, explosions, consuming fire, scenes of violence, and satanic acts.

We certainly see the enormous unleashing of the aggressive impulse in the many wars and revolutionary upheavals in the world, in the rising criminality, escalating terrorism, and racial riots. Equally dramatic and striking is the lifting of sexual repression and freeing of the sexual impulse in both healthy and problematic ways. Sexual experiences and behaviors are taking unprecedented forms, as manifested in the sexual freedom of youngsters; gay liberation; general promiscuity; open marriages; the high divorce rate; overtly sexual books, plays, and movies; sadomasochistic experimentation; and many others.

The demonic element is also becoming increasingly manifest in the modern world. The renaissance of satanic cults and witchcraft, popularity of books and horror movies with occult themes, and crimes with satanic motivations attest to that fact. The acts of Nazis, Communists, and terrorists, including suicide bombers, resulting in the deaths of thousands of innocent civilians certainly qualify for satanic behavior. The scatological dimension is evident in the progressive industrial pollution, accumulation of waste products on a global scale, and rapidly deteriorating hygienic conditions in large cities. A more abstract form of the same trend is the escalating corruption and degradation in political and economic circles.

Many of the people with whom we have worked saw humanity at a critical crossroad facing either collective annihilation or an evolutionary jump in consciousness of unprecedented proportions. Terence McKenna (1992) put it very succinctly: "The history of the silly monkey is over, one way or another." It seems that we all are collectively involved in a process that parallels the psychological death and rebirth process that so many people have experienced internally in holotropic states of consciousness. If we continue to act out the problematic destructive and self-destructive tendencies originating in the depth of the unconscious, we will undoubtedly destroy ourselves and possibly life on this planet. However, if we succeed in internalizing this process on a large enough scale, it might result in an evolutionary progress of unprecedented proportions. As utopian as the possibility of such a development might seem, it might be our only real hope for the future.

Let us now explore how the concepts that have emerged from consciousness research, from transpersonal psychology, and from the new paradigm in science could be put into action in the world. Although revolutionary advances in many disciplines have laid foundations of a new scientific worldview, the new ideas still form a disjointed mosaic rather than a complete and comprehensive new vision of the universe. Much work has to be done in terms of accumulating more data, formulating new theories, and achieving a creative synthesis. In addition, the existing information has to reach much larger audiences before a significant impact on the world situation can be expected.

But even a radical intellectual shift to a new paradigm on a large scale would not be sufficient to alleviate the global crisis and reverse the destructive course we are on. This would require a deep emotional and spiritual transformation of humanity. Using the existing evidence, it is possible to suggest certain strategies that might facilitate and support such a process. Efforts to change humanity would have to start with psychological prevention at an early age. The data from prenatal and perinatal psychology indicate that much could be achieved by changing the conditions of pregnancy, delivery, and postnatal care. This would include improving the emotional preparation of the mother during pregnancy, practicing natural childbirth, creating a psychospiritually informed birth environment, and cultivating emotionally nourishing contact between the mother and the child in the postpartum period.

Much has been written about the importance of child rearing, as well as the disastrous emotional consequences of traumatic conditions in infancy and childhood. Certainly this is an area where continued education and guidance are necessary. However, to apply the theoretically known principles, parents themselves must reach sufficient emotional stability and maturity. It is well known that emotional problems are passed like a curse from generation to generation; it is not unlike the well-known problem of the chicken and the egg.

Humanistic and transpersonal psychologies have developed effective experiential methods of self-exploration, healing, and personality transformation. Some of these come from Western therapeutic traditions, and others represent modern adaptations of ancient and native spiritual practices. Besides offering emotional healing, these approaches have the potential to return genuine experiential spirituality into Western culture and remedy the alienation of modern humanity. There exist approaches with a very favorable ratio between professional helpers and clients and others that can be practiced in the context of self-help groups. Systematic work with them could return spiritual values into the industrial civilization and facilitate a transformation of humanity that is sorely needed for survival of our species. For this to succeed, it would be essential to involve mass media and spread the information about these possibilities to get enough people personally interested in pursuing them.

We seem to be involved in a dramatic race for time that has no precedent in the entire history of humanity. What is at stake is nothing less than the future of life on this planet. If we continue the old strategies, which in their consequences are clearly extremely destructive and self-destructive, it is unlikely that the human species will survive. However, if a sufficient number of people could undergo a process of deep inner transformation, we might reach a level of consciousness evolution where we would deserve the name we have so proudly given to our species: *Homo sapiens sapiens.*

REFERENCES

Appleby, L. (1998). Violent suicide and obstetric complications. *British Medical Journal, 14,* 1333–1334.

Ardrey, R. (1961). *African genesis.* New York: Atheneum.

Bacon, F. (1870). *De Dignitate and the Great Restauration, vol. 4 of The collected works of Francis Bacon,* eds. J. Spedding, L. Ellis, and D.D.S. Heath. London: Longmans Green.

Bastiaans, A. (1955). Man in the concentration camp and the concentration camp in man. Unpublished manuscript, Leyden, Holland.

Cohn, C. (1987). Sex and death in the rational world of the defense intellectuals. *Journal of Women in Culture and Society, 12,* 687–718.

Dante, A. (1990). *Il convivio* (Trans. R. H. Lansing, III, VI. 3). New York: Garland.

Darwin, C. (1952). The origin of species and the descent of man. In *Great books of the Western world.* Chicago: Encyclopaedia Britannica. (Original work published in 1859)

Dawkins, R. (1976). *The selfish gene.* New York: Oxford University Press.

Freud, S. (1955). Beyond the pleasure principle. In *The standard edition of the complete works of Sigmund Freud* (Ed. J. Strachey, Vol. 18). London: Hogarth Press and Institute of Psychoanalysis.

Fromm, E. (1973). *The anatomy of human destructiveness.* New York: Holt, Rinehart & Winston.

Goleman, D. (1996). *Emotional intelligence: Why it can matter more than IQ.* New York: Bantam.

Grof, S. (1975). *Realms of the human unconscious: Observations from LSD research.* New York: Viking Press.

Hillman, J. (2004). *A terrible love of war.* New York: Penguin Press.

Jacobson, B., et al. (1987). Perinatal origin of adult self-destructive behavior. *Acta psychiat. Scand., 76,* 364–371.

Jung, C. G. (1964). Wotan. In Civilization *in Transition, Collected Works,* Vol. 10. Bollingen Series XX, Princeton, NJ: Princeton University Press.

Kandel, E., & Mednick, S. A. (1991). Perinatal complications predict violent offending. *Criminology, 29* (3), 519–529.

Ka-Tzetnik 135633. (1955). *The house of dolls.* New York: Pyramid.

Ka-Tzetnik 135633. (1977). *Sunrise over hell.* London: Allen.

Ka-Tzetnik 135633. (1989). *Shivitti: A vision.* San Francisco: Harper & Row.

Keen, S. (1988). *Faces of the enemy: Reflections of the hostile imagination.* San Francisco: Harper.

Litt, S. (1974). A study of perinatal complications as a factor in criminal behavior. *Criminology, 12* (1), 125–126.

Lorenz, K. (1963). *On aggression*. New York: Harcourt, Brace.

MacLean, P. (1973). A triune concept of the brain and behavior: Lecture I. Man's reptilian and limbic inheritance; Lecture II. Man's limbic system and the psychoses; Lecture III. New trends in man's evolution. In *The Hincks memorial lectures* (Ed. T. Boag & D. Campbell). Toronto: University of Toronto Press.

Mause, L. de. (1975). The independence of psychohistory. In *The new psychohistory*. New York: Psychohistory Press.

McKenna, T. (1992). *Food of the gods: The search for the original tree of knowledge*. New York: Bantam.

Morris, D. (1967). *The naked ape*. New York: McGraw-Hill.

Odent, M. (1995, June). Prevention of violence or genesis of love? Which perspective? Paper presented at the 14th International Transpersonal Conference, Santa Clara, CA.

Raine, A., Brennan, P., & Mednick, S. A. (1995). Birth complications combined with early maternal rejection at age 1 year predispose to violent crime at age 18 years. *Obstetrical and Gynecological Survey, 50* (11), 775–776.

Tarnas, R. (2006). *Cosmos and psyche: Intimations of a new world view*. New York: Viking Press.

Tinbergen, N. (1965). *Animal behavior*. New York: Time-Life.

Wilber, K. (1980). *The Atman project: A transpersonal view of human development*. Wheaton, IL: Theosophical Publishing.

CHAPTER 18

THE THREE FACES OF EVIL IN JUNGIAN PSYCHOLOGY: THE SHADOW SIDE OF REALITY

Wayne G. Rollins

We need more psychology. We need more understanding of human nature, because the only real danger that exists is man himself. He is the great danger, and we are pitifully unaware of it. We know nothing of man, far too little. His psyche should be studied, because we are the origin of all coming evil.

—C. G. Jung (quoted in McGuire & Hull, 1977)

In the last resort there is no good that cannot produce evil and no evil that cannot produce good.

—C. G. Jung (quoted in Jacobi, 1953, p. 234)

The meeting with ourselves is one of the more unpleasant things that may be avoided as long as we possess living symbolic figures into which everything unknown to ourselves is projected. The figure of the devil . . . is a most valuable possession and a great convenience, for as long as he goes about outside in the form of a roaring lion we know where the evil lurks.

—C. G. Jung (quoted in Jacobi, 1953, p. 239)

To this day there is no definitive statement about the nature of evil in the Christian creeds, nor is there any official Christian doctrine of evil.

—John A. Sanford (1982)

INTRODUCTION

John Sanford, an Episcopal priest and Jungian analyst, tells a story in the introduction to his landmark work, *Evil: The Shadow Side of Reality* (1982):

> I once saw a film in which a disillusioned crusader has returned home and longs to know about God. He hears of a witch who is being burned at the stake and finds her just before the flames are going to engulf her. "Can you tell me where I can find the devil?" he asks. "Why do you wish to find the devil?" the doomed girl replies. The soul-sick knight answers, "Because maybe the devil can tell me about God." (p. 3)

The story illustrates a truth experienced frequently, whether as believer or militant atheist, that an indelibly wrenching experience of evil can have one of two effects: to obliterate faith and confirm radical cynicism, or give birth to insight. The Book of Job as well as the crucifixion narratives in the Gospels testify to this possibility.

The purpose of this chapter is twofold: first, to provide a vignette of Carl G. Jung's (1875–1961) personal discoveries of three faces of evil that he identified at three different stages in his life—the period from childhood to young adulthood, the period of his career as an analytic psychologist charting the anatomy of the human psyche, and the period of the advent and demise of the Third Reich in Germany in the 1930s and 1940s. The second objective is to share the light that John Sanford's book casts on the application of Jung's analytical psychology to the "vexing problem" of evil, with soundings on the symbolization of evil in world mythology, in the Old and New Testaments, and in postbiblical Christian and Jewish mythological portraits of the "devil." Though Sanford makes no claim of solving the "problem of evil," he does provide a platform for religion and psychology to get their heads together for a deeper understanding of the nature and reality of evil (Sanford, 1982, p. 3).

THE THREE FACES OF EVIL IN THE LIFE AND THOUGHT OF C. G. JUNG[1]

1.

Jung's first reflections on the face of evil occurred in his youth, when he attempted to reconcile the "evil" he knew from personal experience in the world of nature and of animals, the sun, the moon, and stars, with what he was expected to think and believe as the son of Johann Paul Achilles Jung, a Swiss Reformed pastor, and his mother, Emilie (née Preiswerk) Jung, member of an established Basel family of theologians and clergy.

Jung (1963) had once commented that "theology had alienated my father and me from one another" (p. 93). Filled with questions about traditional religion and beliefs, Jung found his father reproving him: "You always want to think. One ought not to think but believe!" But Jung had responded silently within himself, "No, one must experience and know" (1963, p. 43).

Jung began to perceive that the religion of his father and of most everyday Christians appeared to be a "theological religion," a *doctrine about God* at the expense of the *experience of God*. Even when his father would preach on such "burning questions" as grace, his sermons sounded "stale and hollow, like a tale told by someone who knows it only by hearsay and cannot quite believe it himself"(1963, p. 43). In Jung's judgment, his father "had taken the Bible's commandments as his guide; he believed in God as the Bible prescribed and as his forefathers had taught him," but he did not seem to know "the God who stands . . . above his Bible and his church, who calls upon man [*sic*] to partake of his freedom" (1963, p. 40), whose temple was the whole cosmos, ranging from the rivers and woods to "the darkness of the abyss," a God whom Jung was later to describe as an "annihilating fire and an indescribable grace" (1963, p. 56).

Shortly before his father's death in 1896, Jung discovered that his father's resolute refusal to think critically about the church's dogmas and creeds and his tendency to repeat "the same old lifeless theological answer" led him to grave inward doubts (1963, pp. 92–93).

Jung's mother, on the other hand, seemed bent on pushing Jung beyond the confines of conventional piety, introducing him as a youngster to books on the "heathen" religions of India, and as a young university student to Goethe's *Faust*, which was to feed Jung's lifelong interest in the mysterious role that evil can play "in delivering man from darkness and suffering" (1963, p. 60). It also brought to his attention the irony in the statement of Mephistopheles, who when asked by Faust who he is, replied that he is "part of that force which would do evil, yet forever works the good" (Sanford, 1982, p. 40).

In his autobiography *Memories, Dreams, Reflections*, Jung reports a lifelong sense of shuttling between "two persons" with two different ways of experiencing self and world. On the one hand, he saw himself from a "public" perspective as "the son of my parents who went to school, and was less intelligent, attentive, hard-working, decent, and clean than other boys," but who later became an excellent student, was admitted to the university, and in time made his mark in the field of analytical psychology. He called this self "personality No. 1," the objective, visible, external self known by parents, teachers, and relatives and recognized by himself as his public image.

But he had another side, a "personality No. 2." This personality was "grown-up—old in fact—skeptical mistrustful, remote from the world of people, but close to nature, the earth, sun, moon weather and living creatures." Above all it was close to the night, to dreams. "It seemed to me," he wrote,

> that the high mountains, the rivers, lakes, trees, flowers, and animals far better exemplified the essence of God than men with their ridiculous clothes, meanness, vanity, mendacity, and abhorrent egotism—all qualities with which I was only too familiar from myself, that is from "personality No. 1," the fifteen year old schoolboy. (1963, pp. 44–45)

Between his 16th and 19th years, he found "personality No. 1" emerging as his primary modus operandi, and contrary to expectations, it was "personality no. 1," the urbane, civilized, and polite one, that led him to consideration of "the problem of evil." He began reading in the history of philosophy—Pythagoras, Heraclitus, Empedocles, Aquinas, Meister Eckhardt, and Hegel. But it was in the writing of Schopenhauer that he heard the first voice that caught his whole attention, addressing the reality of "suffering of the world, which visibly and glaringly surrounds us, and of confusion, passion and evil," realities that had in the past been swept under the rug by his No. 1 personality and by conventional religion (1963, 69). Jung wrote,

> Here at last was a philosopher who had the courage to see that all was not for the best in the fundaments of the universe. He spoke neither of the all-good and all-wise providence of a creator, nor of the harmony of the cosmos, but stated bluntly that a fundamental flaw underlay the sorrowful course of human history and the cruelty of nature. . . . This was confirmed not only by the early observations I had made of diseased and dying fishes, of mangy foxes, frozen or starved birds, of the pitiless tragedies concealed in a flowery meadow: earthworms tormented to death by ants, insects that tore each other apart piece by piece, and so on. (1963, p. 69)

Though not convinced of Schopenhauer's solution for the problem of theodicy, reconciling an omnipotent, good deity with a creation riddled with evil, Jung was exhilarated by the realization that he was not alone with his questions about evil. "Whereas formerly I had been shy, timid, mistrustful, pallid, and thin . . . I now began to display a tremendous appetite on all fronts, pursuing university and medical degrees" (1963, p. 70), though he would not return to the question of evil in God's world until the publication of his "Answer to Job" in 1953 (Jung, 1953–1978, Vol. 11, pp. 355–470).

2.

Jung's discovery of a second face of evil occurred later in life with his postulation of a "shadow" personality at work in the human psyche, often

functioning as a "second personality" at odds with one's best conscious intentions. The discovery occurred in the process of his development of analytic
psychology, a field of inquiry that would never have crossed his mind as a
vocational option. But this all changed as Jung, at the age of 24, undertook
state examinations in medicine at the University of Basel.

Jung had reserved the examination in psychiatry for last. He had found
the lectures in psychiatry singularly uninspiring and was not at all convinced
this discipline did not deserve the disdain it appeared to enjoy in so much
of the medical world at the time. It was with reservation, therefore, that
Jung picked up the *Textbook on Psychiatry* by Krafft-Ebing, wondering what a
professional in the field was going to say about this controversial discipline.
What he read changed everything.

> Beginning with the preface, I read, "It is probably due to the peculiarity of
> the subject and its incomplete state of development that psychiatric text-
> books are stamped with a more or less subjective character." A few lines
> further on, the author called the psychoses "diseases of the personality."
> My heart suddenly began to pound[;] I had to stand up and draw a deep
> breath. My excitement was intense, for it had become clear to me, in a flash
> of illumination, that for me the only possible goal was psychiatry. (1963,
> p. 108)

Two streams of interest, which up to that point in Jung's life had diverged,
now seemed to be converging for him. "Here was the empirical field common
to biological and spiritual facts, which I had everywhere sought and nowhere
found," Jung stated. "Here at last was the place where the collision of nature
and spirit became a reality" (1963, p. 109).

Echoing Goethe's characterization of his epic poem *Faust* as his "main
business," Jung wrote,

> From my eleventh year I have been launched upon a single enterprise
> which is my "main business." My life has been permeated and held together
> by one idea and one goal: namely, to penetrate into the secret of the per-
> sonality. (1963, p. 206)

In 1902 Jung inaugurated his pilgrimage to chart the nature and anatomy
of the human personality. His first step, working at the Burghölzli Mental
Hospital, Zurich, was devising his famous Word Association test, news of
which brought him to Sigmund Freud's attention and in time an invitation
to travel with Freud to Clark University in Worcester, Massachusetts, in the
fall of 1909.

What did Jung learn from the Word Association tests—reading a list of
100 words, one by one, to a patient and carefully monitoring the patient's

response? He uncovered three truths that would be axiomatic for all of his future research. First, certain words or ideas become "feeling-toned" for certain individuals, conveying "an unconscious undertone that colors the idea each time it is recalled," and occasionally freighted with such profound associations for the individual that it triggers an overpowering emotional response (1971, p. 27). Second, Jung found that the "complex" of words to which a patient responded with extraordinary feeling often led the analyst to the story of the problem or crisis that had precipitated the patient's illness. And, third, Jung postulated that such "complexes" of feeling-toned words triggering anxiety in the patient's life were not the product of the patient's conscious choice, but in fact constituted an autonomous, unconscious "second personality" that welled up beyond conscious control. As Jung was wont to say, "We do not have complexes, rather complexes have us."

The momentous discovery that the Word Association test could provide data that disclosed the "cause" of a patient's illness led Jung to seek additional routes of inquiry into the unconscious. And in 1903, he returned to Freud's masterful work on *The Interpretation of Dreams* (1900), having laid it aside 3 years earlier unable to grasp its meaning. Fifty years later, he praised Freud for rediscovering "dreams as the most important source of information concerning the unconscious processes" (1963, p. 169). What also moved Jung in the direction of dreams was the hunch that hallucinatory images and the bizarre language of schizophrenia might be made of the same stuff as dreams.

Over the next 17 years, indeed the next half century, Jung examined some 80,000 dreams with his patients, searching for answers to the question of the etiology and meaning of dreams and dream images, the origin of their storyline, and the clues they might provide to the nature and functions of the human psyche.

In 1912, Jung pursued a third route into the secrets of the unconscious, namely, a personal *descensus ad inferos*, a descent into the depths of his own unconscious to discover the "myth" he was living and to understand better the fantasies that stirred within his patients as well as himself. Jung recounts that he "felt not only violent resistance to this, and a distinct fear," but he saw there was no other way to come to an understanding of these underground products of the psyche than by letting himself "plummet down, to encounter them directly" (1963, p. 178).

So it was that he left his university post to devote himself full-time "in the service of the psyche," though at the same time maintaining balance in his life with his private professional practice and with the family routine Jung deemed necessary as a "counterpoise to that strange inner world" he was exploring (1963, p. 189).

His method was the daily practice of chronicling every image he encountered in his dreams and fantasies as well as in those of his patients. His goal was to understand "every item of my psychic inventory, and to classify them

scientifically—so far as this was possible" (1963, p. 192). His research records
during these years consisted initially of "The Black Book" containing written
notes and "The Red Book" containing impressive pictorialized depictions in
paintings and sketches.

Writing some 50 years later, Jung looked back at this risk-filled period
as the most important in his life. "All my works, all my creative activity, has
come from these initial fantasies and dreams which began in 1912" (1963,
p. 174). Although it would take him 45 years to distill the meaning from the
date, he regarded all his later work as nothing more than "supplements and
clarification" of those original explorations "into the depths" that provided
him with the *"prima material* for a lifetime's work" (1963, p. 199).

The output of this period of research included a new map of the conscious
and unconscious life. He introduced the phrase *collective unconscious* to the
glossary of psychological terms, denoting the wellspring of images across
national, geographic, ethnic, and linguistic borders that populate dreams,
stories, and art around the world. He also proposed the existence of the two
fundamental attitudes of introversion and extraversion in the human psyche,
and of the fourfold "functions" of the psyche—thinking, feeling, intuiting,
and sensing—all accounting for differences in personality types.

Jung also advanced a thesis about the total goal of this psychic process. He
called it "individuation," which means the process of "becoming an 'individual,'
and, insofar as 'individuality' embraces our innermost, last and incomparable
uniqueness, it also implies become one's own self" (Jung, 1953–1978, p. 173).

He saw individuation as a process in two stages. The first stage, extend-
ing from birth to midlife, involves the psyche in its main task of forming and
consolidating the "ego," developing a personality type, gaining an identity,
choosing a vocation, and gathering a family. The second stage, commencing
in midlife, involves the troubling task of "looking under the hood" or "coming to know one's other side," which included the "shadow" personality.

Jung identified three archetypal personalities operative in the psyche, each
staking out its own functional territory: the persona, the "mask" or outer face
one adopts to portray oneself to the rest of the world; the animus or anima,
the contrasexual images adopted by the psyche; and the dark, hidden side or
"shadow" that at its lowest and most ravaging reaches can be transmogrified
into the face of evil. The "shadow" is not intrinsically evil, but stands at the
threshold, and the threshold is easily crossed when affect is high.

John Sanford offered a lucid definition of the "shadow," as a psychological concept, that refers to the dark, feared, unwanted side of our personality.
In developing a conscious personality, we all seek to embody in ourselves a
certain image of what we want to be like ("the persona"). Those qualities that
could have become part of this conscious personality, but are not in accord
with the person we want to be, are rejected and constitute the shadow personality (1982, p. 49). Sanford added Edward C. Whitmont's (1978) illuminating

addendum that "the term shadow refers to that part of the personality which has been repressed for the sake of the ego ideal" (p. 160).

How did Jung come to the notion of the shadow as a universal human psychic phenomenon? His primary sources were the dreams and analyses of his patients, as well as the rich lode of data gathered in his descent into the depths of his own psychic world from 1913 to 1917. Jung reported a dream that occurred early in the process, dated December 18, 1913. The dream finds Jung in "a lonely, rocky mountain landscape" collaborating with an "unknown, brown-skinned man, a savage," in the murder of a hero named Siegfried. Later in the dream he lays the blame on the small savage, claiming he had taken the initiative in the kill. Jung soon realized that in exculpating himself and projecting the guilt on the savage, he had come into contact with his shadow, a part of his personality repressed for the sake of his ego ideal (1963, p. 181). Jung reported that reading Goethe's *Faust* had

> struck a chord in me . . . most of all, it wakened in me the problem of opposites, of good and evil, of mind and matter, of light and darkness. Faust, the inept . . . philosopher, encounters the dark side of his being, his sinister shadow. (1963, p. 235)

Jung also found the shadow in the pages, paintings, and statuary of world religions, and in literature, the cinema, and the arts—sometimes in the forms of witches, vampires, monsters, and devils, frequently the projections "out there" of menacing possibilities that were in fact alive within one's own psychic household. John Sanford commented, "I would surmise that there are few people who at one time or another in their lives have not had the fantasy that their husbands, wives, children, or parents were dead" (1982, p. 62).

What can be said about the nature and habits of the shadow? It is an archetypal reality within the psyche and, as such, a universal or essential building block of the personality (Sanford, 1982, p. 55), appearing in dreams as the same gender as the dreamer, personifying "everything that the subject refuses to acknowledge about himself and yet is always thrusting itself upon him directly or indirectly" (Jung, 1963, p. 399). Although it is the psychic repository of qualities whose energy can be reclaimed by the ego and put to constructive use (Sanford, 1982, pp. 51, 79), it is also a constant challenge to the ego, subverting its best-laid plans and seeking domination of the psychic household.

Armed with emotion, the shadow and its repressed contents constantly attempt to challenge ego consciousness for dominance. The ego has at least four ways of coping. It can choose *repression*, keeping the contents of the shadow under lock and key, and covering the multitude of its dark wishes and fantasies with the white gloves of one's socially acceptable persona. A second strategy, tangent to the strategy of repression, is that sleight-of-hand of *projection*, turning one's own hidden inferiority into a perceived moral deficiency in someone else. As case in point, Jung cited Hitler's description of Winston Churchill during World War II, a transparent self-portrait:

> For over five years this man has been chasing around Europe like a madman in search of something he could set on fire. Unfortunately he again and again finds hirelings who open the gates of their country to this international incendiary. (1971, p. 181)

The third option is internecine warfare between the shadow and the ego, of the sort that Jung found occasionally degenerating into the gross, destructive behavior of Robert Lewis Stevenson's *Dr. Jekyll and Mr. Hyde*, in which the ego loses control, the shadow wins the day, and, in this instance, the evil deed is done.[2]

The fourth option is self-knowledge and confession, bringing the dark side to consciousness, setting up a conversation if not full-scale warfare against its intentions, and, if possible, enlisting human community support from souls dealing with analogous shadows (e.g., Alcoholics Anonymous) (Sanford, 1982, p. 109).

3.

Jung's discovery of a third face of evil is documented in a series of works he produced during the rise and fall of the Third Reich in Germany, continuing into the 1940s and 1950s with his psychological commentary on the development of thermonuclear weapons. These essays include "Wotan," an essay on the German nationalist spirit (1936); "After the Catastrophe" (1945); "The Fight With the Shadow," first presented as a BBC broadcast (1946); "The Undiscovered Self" (1957); and the closing section of his last essay, "Approaching the Unconscious" (published posthumously, 1961).

Jung identified the crisis in the modern Western world as at root a crisis in the human psyche or soul:

> The gigantic catastrophes that threaten us today are not elemental happenings of a physical or biological order, but psychic events. To a quite terrifying degree we are threatened by wars and revolution which are nothing other than psychic epidemics. . . . Instead of being at the mercy of wild beasts, earthquakes, landslides, and inundations, modern man is battered by the elemental forces of his own psyche. (Jung, 1953–1978, Vol. 10, p. 235)

The age of enlightenment taught us that reason would overcome the human tendency to destroy others and oneself; but in fact, Jung averred, this may be our "greatest and most tragic illusion" (1971, p. 101). We must ask ourselves, Jung suggested, "how it is that, for all our progress in administration of justice, in medicine and in technology, for all our concern for life and health, monstrous engines of destruction have been invented which could easily exterminate the human race" (Jung, 1953–1978, Vol. 10, p. 298). The irony, Jung added, is that these "devilish engines" are invented by "reasonable, respectable citizens" who, in many respects, are "everything we could wish."

The new dimension of the shadow that Jung became aware of before, during, and after World War II was the phenomenon of a "collective shadow," or "mass-mindedness," which at its worst and most destructive stage takes on the character of a "psychic epidemic."

Mass-mindedness is a common epiphenomenon generated in political, religious, nationalistic, and militaristic movements. As Jung commented, their common stock-in-trade is familiar: "brass bands, flags, banners, parades and monster demonstrations," combined with propaganda efforts dedicated not only to cultivating true believers but also to portraying their opponents as evil, though at the same time remaining oblivious to the evil cooking in their own psyches. Examples include Protestants versus Catholics in Northern Ireland, Palestinians and Israelis, pro-lifers versus advocates of free choice, or, in Jung's time, the standoff between the two sides of the Iron Curtain. Writing in the 1950s, Jung commented, "It is the face of his own evil shadow that grins at Western man from the other side of the Iron Curtain" (1971, p. 73).

The "success" of mass movements and the psychic epidemics they generate arise from the psychological fact that individuals who are otherwise good, gentle, intelligent citizens on their own find themselves acting in a worse manner collectively than they would as individuals, being carried by society and to that extent relieved of individual responsibility (1957, p. 56). A second psychological factor is the intrusion of the dark motives of one's unconscious in our decisions, which Jung saw at work in the case of the development of weapons of mass destruction by the physicists who produced "the bomb," which involved finding a way to give themselves permission to lend a hand in an effort that at its furthest end could result in the destruction of thousands of human beings. They were unaware that "conscious effort alone was not responsible for the outcome of their work, but that somewhere the unconscious, with its barely discernible goals and intentions, has its finger in the pie." Jung added, "If [the unconscious] puts a weapon in your hands, it is aiming at some kind of violence" (1957, pp. 99–100). The evidence of the middle years of the 20th century demonstrated visibly to Jung that "none of us stands outside his black collective shadow" (1957, p. 96).

What is the cure? Where can a change be found? Jung commented that "there are well-meaning theologians and humanitarians who want to break down the power principle—in others." But, Jung insisted, "[W]e must begin by breaking it in ourselves. Then the thing becomes credible" (1953–1978,

Vol. 10, p. 228). Jung contended that "the psychopathology of the masses is rooted in the psychology of the individual" (p. 218), and "if the individual is not truly regenerated in spirit, society cannot be either, for society is the sum total of individuals in need of redemption" (p. 276). What is required is "a complete spiritual renewal" (p. 217).

In his last essay on "Approaching the Unconscious," completed shortly before his death in 1961, Jung made this appeal:

> As any change must begin somewhere, it is the single individual who will experience it and carry it through. The change must begin with an individual; it might be any one of us. Nobody can afford to look around and to wait for somebody else to do what he is loath to do himself. But since nobody seems to know what to do, it might be worthwhile for each of us to ask himself whether by chance his or her unconscious may know something that will help us. (1971, pp. 101–102)

For Jung, the answer to "psychic epidemics," "mass-mindedness," and the collective shadow is the "individual human being . . . that infinitesimal unit on whom a world depends, and in whom, if we read the meaning of the Christian message aright, even God seeks his goal" (1953–1978, Vol. 10, p. 305).

SANFORD ON JUNG, EVIL, AND THE SHADOW SIDE OF REALITY

John Sanford, a pastoral counselor, Jungian analyst, and former Episcopal priest, is one of the premier interpreters of the life and thought of Carl Jung. He is known internationally for his 16 books that relate psychological insight (especially that of Jung's analytic psychology and Fritz Kunkel's "we-psychology"; see Sanford, 1984) to religious experience and biblical interpretation.

Though Sanford has devoted his life to counseling, he hoped in *Fritz Kunkel: Selected Writings* (1984) to take up the ambiguities and metaphysical issues raised in Jung's discourse on evil, and to focus on "the problem of evil." His goal was to provide psychological insight into evil as an absurd fact of life and also ironically as the parent of the good and as an answer to the soul-knight's question of what "the devil can tell us about God" (Sanford, 1984, p. 3).

Sanford opened his reflections on "the problem of evil" by challenging the relativist view of evil that maintains evil and good are in the eye of the beholder. For example, the gardener and the crop-destroying gopher would not see eye to eye on the value of the trap the gardener is setting to end the problem. Similarly, the 17th-century Puritan's expression of prayerful gratitude for the plague that decimated the native Indian population in the territory now called New England would be poles away from the sentiments of the victims. The conclusion to which these observations lead is, in the words of Hamlet, "There is nothing either good or bad but thinking makes it so" (Sanford, 1984, p. 7).

Sanford did not agree. In opposition to this view of relative good and relative evil, Sanford argued that not all opinions about good and evil merit equal attention. Drawing from Jung's analytical psychology, Sanford suggested a better model for evaluating what is good and what is evil, by distinguishing between two levels of maturation in the individuation process: the state of the Ego and the state of the Self.

The ego speaks from the solipsistic realm of the individual, or, as Jung put it, from the "petty, oversensitive, personal world of the ego" (Rollins, 1983, p. 38). But the Self, representing another stage of human maturation, speaks out of larger, deeper, broader experience and wisdom in the realization that one's "story" is not a solo act, but is part of a tale as wide as human and cosmic history and as deep as the memories, dreams, and reflections of the whole human race. Carl Jung defined the Self as the "complete expression" of our individuality when all its dimensions are fully considered. It is the "totality of the human psyche," the "whole circumference which embraces all the psychic phenomena" in ourselves, "our body and its workings and the unconscious," the sensate and intuitive, the intellectual and moral, the masculine and feminine, the shadow and the saint (Rollins, 1983, p. 38). In religious language, Sanford told us, it might be called "the Christ Self," or, as many cultures would describe it, the "Divine Standpoint" (1984, p. 9). A fundamental presupposition of Sanford's approach is to appeal to the opinions of the Self for insight into the nature of evil and the means of coping with its effects.

With this distinction in mind, Sanford turned to a topic fundamental to Jungian psychology, namely, the world of mythology as a seasoned expression of the Self on the nature and meaning of evil. Sanford (1984) told us that for analytical psychology, "mythology is a kind of map of the human psyche, a personification of the archetypal and eternal psychic forces that make up mankind's [sic] inner universe" (p. 23). What mythology discloses is the universal recognition of "an inevitable dark side to our nature that refuses to be assimilated into our lofty ideals of goodness, morality, and ideal human behavior." Not only that, but also it warns us that "to try to be good, and disregard one's darkness, is to fall victim to the evil in ourselves whose existence we have denied" (1984, p. 23).

Sanford found two types of mythic depictions of evil. The first is the *dualistic type of myth* that sees reality as a struggle between the forces of good and the forces of evil. He offered as examples the Norse myth of the evil god, Loki, who destroys the beautiful god Baldur with a shaft of the mistletoe plant; the Egyptian myth of treacherous Seth, who dismembers his brother Osiris; the Persian myth of the all-out warfare between Ahriman, the shadow

God, and Ahura Mazda, the enlightened; and the myth of Native American religion that pits the Great Spirit against the disturbances and devious plots of theriomorphic spirits and trickster figures.

The second is the synthetic type of myth found in classical Greek antiquity that refuses to divide the pantheon into good gods and bad goods, but instead regards each member of the pantheon as capable of turning in either direction, depending on the needs of the moment.

From his overview of mythic treatments of evil, Sanford drew two conclusions. The first is the universal recognition of evil as a standard feature of cosmic existence across the mythological spectrum. The second is a truth implicit in the synthetic approach to evil among the Greeks:

> Only among the Greeks was there no war among the gods . . . for these gods and goddesses were too wise to claim to be good. So psychology suggests that we reject any pretense of being good that forces us to keep our evil hidden from ourselves. We thus follow the example of Jesus who, when he was addressed by the rich young man as "Good Master" retorted, "Why do you call me good? No one is good but God alone." (Sanford, 1984, pp. 23–24; see Mark 10:17–18)

Sanford found further confirmation of the universal recognition of evil as an ineluctable feature of life in his overview of evil in the Old Testament and the New Testament. Casual familiarity with the two testaments might suggest that the story of evil in the Bible is essentially dualistic (i.e., a contest between God and Satan). Sanford told us that in the case of the Old Testament, nothing could be further from the truth. He found a "courageous and unflinching monotheism" implicit in all Old Testament commentary on "the problem of evil."

The most striking demonstration of the "unflinching monotheism" of the Old Testament is found in a range of statements that identify God as the one who works both good and evil. Amos 3:6 declares that evil does not befall a city unless the Lord has done it; Isaiah 45:5–7 announces that the Lord makes both weal and woe (Isa 45:7) and produces weapons of war (54:16); and I Sam 18:10 informs us that the evil spirit that rushed upon Saul was God-sent.

In the later Old Testament, however, we encounter the face of the "accuser" (Hebrew, satan). *Satan* appears in the Old Testament in two distinct roles. In his first role, occurring only four times, *satan* appears as a supernatural figure. He functions as an "accuser" in a divine court (Zechariah 3:11ff.), as a tempter who provokes David to undertake a census using a method contrary to the laws of Moses (I Chronicles 21:1), and, most astonishingly, in Job 1–2 as a quasi-divine figure in God's court on whom God projects his dark side in assigning him the task of testing Job's faith with a series of tragic assaults on his person and family. In this scenario, God gets off scot-free, with Satan left holding the bag of responsibility.

A second Old Testament portrait of *satan* plays on the secular meaning of the term, namely, "adversary," referring to someone who opposes someone else's plan of action. An example is the story of Balaam, sent on a mission by the Moabite King Balak to curse the Hebrews (Numbers 22). En route to this assignment, Balaam and his ass are confronted by Yahweh along the road, who appears as a *satan*, an "adversary," that prevents Balaam from performing a task that most certainly would have resulted in his own God-inflicted destruction. Here we learn, surprisingly, that Yahweh as *satan* has actually served to deliver Balaam from destruction, and that what appears to be evil is transformed into a good.

When we turn to the New Testament, we find a worldview informed by the ranks of demons and angels that have surfaced in later Hellenistic-Jewish mythology. The name *Satan* appears 35 times in the Gospels, the word *devil* (*diabolos*) 37 times, in addition to the title *Beelzebub* ("Lord of the flies") and in John's Gospel "the prince of this world," referring to the devil.

The meaning of the word *devil* (Greek, *diabolos*) is literally "one who throws something across your path," implying one who overrides one's best laid plans or, more seriously, introduces ruin into one's life, not unlike the trickster of Native American lore. Of what nefarious tricksterism is Satan guilty in the Gospels? The list includes inflicting a daughter of Abraham with a crippling illness for 18 years (Luke 13.16), possessing a man of Gadara with a demon and driving him out of his mind (Luke 8:28–34), entering Judas at the last supper to initiate the plan to betray Jesus (Luke 22:3), and tempting Jesus to turn away from his mission (Luke 4:1–13).

How did Jesus approach "the problem of the Devil" and the larger "problem of evil"? Sanford proposed that the parable of the Tares that Satan sows in the wheat field characterizes Jesus's acceptance of evil as native to the human condition in God's world. Evil and good grow side by side, not only because it is inevitable in the structure of things but also because it is nearly impossible to tell which of the plants are wheat and which tares (Matt 13:24–30). In the Sermon on the Mount, Jesus issues an astonishing command to love one's enemies, supporting this enjoinder with the "fact" that God sends rain and sun to both the just and the unjust. He also enjoins his followers to pray for those who persecute them (Matt 5:44–45). For Jesus in the Gospels, God does not draw an indelible line between the good and the evil. For Jesus the problem of evil is solved eschatologically, when both the righteous and the unrighteous will hear the surprising news of what the proprietor of the Last Judgment identifies as good and evil (Matt 25:31–46). For the present, however, Jesus calls his disciples to become healers and proclaimers of good news; to join in the battle against evil, its deprivations, and its wounds; and, as the Sermon on the Mount makes plain, to become conscious of the speck of evil that may be unconsciously blocking their own vision (Matt 7:1–5).

Jesus's teaching on evil no doubt inspired fourth-century church father Origen to suggest that evil in the end will be swallowed up in divine grace and that even the devil will be saved. Though Origen's notion was declared heretical at the Council of Constantinople in 553, his ideas continue to sound in the heart of the Gospel that tells us we should even love our enemies in God's world that allows good and evil to mysteriously coexist.

In time, the "monistic" perspective of Jesus that sees evil as an ineluctable part of life will succumb to the development of the radical dualism of the later New Testament, epitomized in the Book of Revelation, lining up the forces of evil against the forces of good and providing program notes for those interested in distinguishing the evil from the good. Luther and Zwingli will both denounce the Book of Revelation as un-Christian. But the continuing church in large part adopted the dualistic approach, which so easily leads to the hubris of inquisition that distinguishes so confidently the evil from the good, a project Jesus was not given to endorse.

Having discussed Satan, the devil, and the demonic in the Bible, Sanford (1984) devoted a chapter to "The Devil in Post-Biblical Mythology and Folklore," reminding us that though the devil does not seem to be alive and active in contemporary theological or cultural discourse, it still appears in plays, monster movies, songs, and cartoons. Sanford helped us understand what is going on in these postbiblical representations.

One of the earliest depictions of the devil is the figure of Lucifer, the "light-bearer," who originally dwelt in the heavens with the Almighty, but fell prey to the sin of conceit and pride, undertaking a rebellion against God, only to be driven from heaven by the Archangel Michael. The story is told in rabbinic circles and is rehearsed by the church fathers.[3]

Sanford suggested that at the core of the Lucifer–Satan archetype is the "power drive," which from the psychological point of view can be seen as a "quality of the human Ego that wants to set itself up in place of the Self," placing the ego in combat with one's higher self (Sanford, 1984, p. 114). It is precisely this split to which Satan invites Jesus in the story of the temptation in the wilderness, to subordinate the archetypal aspiration to ministry to the archetypal quest for power.

The devil comes to represent all those "disagreeable qualities of our nature that we have rejected from consciousness" (Sanford, 1984, p. 117). Accordingly he is depicted in many forms, from a human-like Mephistopheles to a man with cloven hoofs that were borrowed from the depictions of the pagan god Pan, or with a horn in the middle of his brow, borrowed from the imagery of the decadent god of wine, Dionysus. He also can appear as an ape, "a roaring lion, a ferocious dragon, a serpent, a wolf, or black dog," often accompanied by "bats, rats, mice, vermin, and flies" (Sanford, 1984, p. 116).

As such, the devil is a figure to be feared, for he has become the bearer of those qualities that a culture fears in itself. During the medieval period, the church used the figure of Satan to represent "human reason," which, with its scientific method, was challenging the authority of the church. In one instance, the devil was personified as Galileo. Later, for the Puritans, the devil represented art, music, and dancing, which remained closeted in the shadows of the Puritan unconscious (Sanford, 1984, p. 124). And in contemporary international affairs, the devil has often been projected on the enemy as the "evil empire."

The devil, therefore, does not represent "absolute evil," but a relative evil that depends for its psychological power on the fact that the qualities it represents have been repressed by the community that denounces them. From a psychological perspective, the image of the devil and the contents of one's own shadow side represent "relative evils," which in time can lose their opprobrious character and be reclaimed as less frightening than they appeared in the dimly lit cells of the unconscious. In fact, the reintegration of the shadow and of the relative evils projected on our favorite Satan images is necessary for psychological wholeness, in the admission that these are all part of "me" or "us" and on closer inspection may even prove to be the bearers of powers and gifts that can be used to fruitful ends. The anger, fear, outrage, self-indulgence, boiling resentment, vindictiveness, mendacity, arrogance, aggressiveness, fantasies, and impulses—all contain powers that can be rerouted and redeemed. As Sanford observed about the shadow figure for the individual, or about the devil image for a culture:

> The shadow personality can look like evil, it can even act evil when it is split off too far from the whole. But in itself it cannot be said to be entirely evil, for if made conscious, recognized, and accepted, the Shadow loses its seemingly Satanic character and even has the capacity to add to the stature, strength, and breadth of one's personality. (Sanford, 1984, p. 127)

CLOSING THOUGHTS ON THE ONTOLOGY OF EVIL IN SANFORD AND JUNG

One of the most surprising things we learn about the "problem of evil" from Sanford is that "to this day there is no definitive statement about the nature of evil in the Christian creeds, nor is there any official Christian doctrine of evil" (1984, p. 129). In all probability, the same void holds true for all other religious traditions.

The only point at which Christianity came to formal statements on evil is in its theories of atonement that initially relied heavily on the role of the devil. The first was the *ransom theory*, contending that God offered his son to the devil as a ransom for humankind held captive by the devil from the time of Adam and Eve, who had submitted to the devil's temptation to disobey

God. The second is the *victory theory*, which heralds Christ and his cross as victorious in a cosmic battle with the devil. It was with the third atonement theory of Anselm (1033–1109 CE), however, that the devil disappeared from the contract. Called the *satisfaction theory* or *substitutionary theory*, it held that it was not the devil who had to be satisfied, but God's justice. God offered his son as a sacrifice to satisfy divine justice that had been violated by human-kind's primordial sin.

With the disappearance of the devil from atonement theories, theologi-cal discourse turned to other theories of evil, of which there are three. The first was never formally adopted but became part of the common turf within Christendom in the form of a Latin statement: *omne bonum a Deo; omne malus ab hominem* ("All good is from God; all evil from men"). This formulation was unsatisfactory from a theological perspective in two respects. First, it "absolved God of any responsibility for evil," and detractors were quick to ask, "Who was responsible in the first place for putting the serpent in the garden of Eden?" Second, it placed the full weight of evil on the back of humanity.

A second theory, advanced by Irenaeus of Lyon in the second century and endorsed by Origen in the third, was that "God deliberately allowed evil in His creation in order to create a universe in which man's moral powers would be exercised" and in "which man's nature could be perfected" (Sanford, 1984, p. 133), reflecting the common medieval expression of *felix culpa*, or "happy sin." Thus evil, even in the Garden of Eden, is there by God's design to serve God's ultimate purpose.

A third theory, formulated in the *Clementine Homilies*—attributed to Clem-ent, bishop of Rome, in the early second century—held that God in his wis-dom is the source of both evil and good in the world, employing both to achieve his purposes. Clement illustrated this with his depiction of God rul-ing the world with a right hand and a left. The left hand rains punishment and even evil on the impious, and the right hand pours blessing on the righ-teous. Clement, convinced of the goodness of God, held that whatever evil there is in the present will be redeemed and transformed in the future at the end time.

A fourth theory defines evil as a *privatio boni*, "a privation or absence of the good," a concept derived from Aristotle and adopted by Origen, Augustine, and Aquinas. It held that the "good alone has substance, and that evil has no substance of its own, but exists by a diminution of the good" (Sanford, 1984, p. 135).

The theory of evil as the *privatio boni* became a cause célèbre in theological and analytical psychological circles, because Jung declared his opposition to it. Jung found fault with the *privatio boni* definition of evil on two counts.

The first is Christological. Jung argued that if evil is thought to be the absence of the good, then Christ, who represents the absolute good in the eyes of many Christians, must be thought of as the exemplification of the absence of the dark side, which from Jung's perspective robs Jesus of the full humanity that even the creeds assign him. Being truly human for Jung means engagement in a process of individuation that calls for the demanding integration of both the dark and light sides, a theme hinted at in the story of Jesus's temptation in the wilderness and the self-applied description of Jesus as one who came "eating and drinking" (Matt 11:19), and who drove the money changers out of the temple (Mark 11:15–19). For Jung, Christ cannot be a symbol of wholeness if the integration of the dark side is not part of the picture.

The second is ontological. To call evil simply the absence of the good is to deny evil its palpable appearance as an autonomous force in places like Rwanda or the gas chambers of Auschwitz. The word *evil*, when regarded as simply the absence of the good, would fail to capture the horrendous events it was designed to denote.

In summary, Jung and Sanford fundamentally concurred in their analysis of the "problem of evil." In the first place, both are motivated in their research by a profound dissatisfaction over the church's failure to arrive at a satisfying understanding of evil and the role it plays in the human story; nor does the church supply a psychologically satisfying understanding of the shadow side of the human psyche. Sanford expressed it as follows:

> The traditional Christian attitude as it has been mediated through the Church has rejected too much. It has refused to accept the Shadow side of the personality, and has rejected the dark side of the Self. It has insisted upon an impossible standard of perfection, and has not acknowledged the necessity, even the value, of a wholeness, that comes about through imperfection, not through perfection. (Sanford, 1984, pp. 153–154)

Second, both Jung and Sanford believed that the main tool we have to deal with, confront, and even heal the shadow and evil is to bring both into fuller *consciousness*, that part of the psyche that Jung described as our "most important weapon" (quoted in Campbell, 1971, p. 502). Jung spoke of the process of bringing things to consciousness as "integration"; Sanford described it as coming to "wholeness." In discussing the importance of integration with Mircea Eliade at a 1952 Eranos Conference, Jung commented,

> The great problem in psychology is the integration of opposites. One finds this everywhere and at every level. . . . I had occasion to interest myself in the integration of Satan. For as long as Satan is not integrated, the world is not healed and man is not saved. But Satan represents evil, and how can evil be integrated? There is only one possibility: namely to assimilate it, that is to say, raise it to the level of consciousness. (Quoted in McGuire & Hall, 1977, p. 277)

Sanford (1984) closed his book with a thoughtful and helpful description of what "wholeness" and "integration" entail and how they enable confrontation with "evil":

> When the Self is realized, there is an invulnerability to the powers of evil; the destructive powers cannot destroy the realized Self. On the human level it means that if a human being is centered, and related to the self, there is a certain protection against evil; and when the center of the personality is established, such a person is supported by a more-than-human strength to resist and overcome the evil powers. . . . We have noted that evil may be necessary if wholeness is to come about since wholeness can only occur when all creatures perform their proper function, and it would seem that human moral and psychological consciousness can only develop in the face of evil . . . yet at the same time we say this, we also say that wholeness does not include evil and that when wholeness is either established or destroyed, evil also ceases to be. (pp. 151–152)

We began our discussion of Jung and Sanford on the "problem of evil" with the story of the soul-sick knight justifying his interest in evil in the hope that "maybe the devil can tell me about God." The masterful work of Jung and Sanford maintains that bringing the devil, the shadow, and evil to fuller consciousness in effect does "tell us about God," leading us to recognize the macrocosm in which we live and the grace that enables an integrated wholeness to take place in the human psyche, fortifying it against the assaults of the dark side of the unconscious and raising its sights to the service of the self that transcends the ego, armed with an understanding of evil that, as Jung recognized, "When love stops, power begins, and violence, and terror" (1957, p. 106).

NOTES

1. Portions of this section were published originally in the second chapter of *Jung and the Bible* (Atlanta, GA: John Knox Press, 1983) by Wayne G. Rollins and are reprinted here in revised and updated form with permission.

2. See "The Problem of Shadow and Evil in *The Strange Case of Dr. Jekyll and Mr. Hyde*" (Sanford, 1982, pp. 85–111, Chap. 7), which recounts the story in detail.

3. Following the mode of apocalyptic calculations of the numbers of demons that provide the retinue of the fallen Lucifer, we hear from a theologian named Basel Barrhause that the exact figure is 2,665,866,746,664 (in Sanford, 1984, p. 114).

REFERENCES

Campbell, J. (Ed.). (1971). *The portable Jung*. New York: Viking Press.
Freud, S. (1972). *Interpretation of dreams* (Trans. J. Strachey). New York: Avon. (Original work published in 1903)

Jacobi, J. (1953). *Psychological reflections: An anthology of the writings of C. G. Jung.* New York: Pantheon.

Jung, C. G. (1953–1978). *The collected works of C. G. Jung* (Trans. R. F. C. Hull, 20 Vols.). Princeton, NJ: Princeton University Press.

Jung, C. G. (1957). *The undiscovered self* (Trans. R. F. C. Hull). Boston: Little, Brown.

Jung, C. G. (1963). *Memories, dreams, reflections* (Trans. R. Winston & C. Winston). New York: Vintage.

Jung, C. G. (1971). *Man and his symbols.* New York: Dell

McGuire, W., & Hull, R. F. C. (Eds.). (1977). *C. G. Jung speaking: Interviews and encounters* (Vol. 97). Princeton, NJ: Princeton University Press.

Philip, H. D. (1959). *Jung and the problem of evil.* New York: McBride.

Rollins, W. G. (1983). *Jung and the Bible.* Atlanta, GA: John Knox.

Sanford, J. A. (1982). *Evil: The shadow side of reality.* New York: Crossroad.

Sanford, J. (Ed.). (1984). *Fritz Kunkel: Selected writings.* Mahwah, NJ: Paulist.

Whitmont, E. C. (1978). *The symbolic quest.* Princeton, NJ: Princeton University Press.

CHAPTER 19

ARE WE BASICALLY GOOD OR EVIL, FALLEN OR UNDEREVOLVED?

J. Harold Ellens

David Frankfurter has written an impressive book on *Evil Incarnate* (2008). It deals with rumors of demonic conspiracies and satanic abuses throughout history. Periodically throughout the history of the Western world, there have arisen cults that promoted the idea that satanic forces were prominent manipulators of the human scene and even dominant controllers of government operations. Such cultic panic seems to have swept through human society periodically since the ancient world. It swept parts of the world of early Christianity, then again early modern Europe, equally postcolonial Africa, and, quite surprisingly, the American culture of both the 1730s and 1980s.

As an historian of religion, Frankfurter was particularly interested in the fact that these sinister notions show up in strikingly similar patterns and under remarkably similar circumstances, despite widely separate cultures and time frames. For example, the patterns characteristically include, as they did in the United States three decades ago, conspiracy theories about groups who were allegedly abusing children in day care centers, impregnating girls for infant sacrifice, brainwashing adults, and even controlling the government. These same aspects were present in the ancient, medieval, and early modern episodes, and cross-culturally, for example, in Africa, Europe, and the United States.

This gives rise to a number of very interesting questions. What causes people, individually and collectively, to envision evil and seek to engage with it and place themselves in league with it; or guard against it and even try to exterminate it? Why does this kind of phenomenon tend to show up in such typical, even predictable patterns? Are we inherently in touch with such imagined forces in life because we are inherently evil in ourselves, or because we are basically good and so have a built-in guardedness against evil? Are human beings inherently fallen from some ideal state, or are we flawed and inadequate because we are simply underevolved, and so still on our way to achieving our ideal potential as human organisms?

The ancient Essenes of Jesus's time, and the various types of apocalyptic Judaism that flourished then, were sure that evil was a real objective force in the world, not just a fiction of some overactive and paranoid human imaginations. They conceived the matter in one of two ways, depending upon how conservative or traditional the particular Essene group happened to be. Moreover, which of the two trajectories a person or group chose depended somewhat on whether they were following, consciously or unconsciously, the implications of Genesis 6 or Genesis 3. Genesis 6 said evil came from heaven and infected the human world from the beginning, so God, or at least heavenly forces, were to blame. Genesis 3 blamed humans for the introduction of evil into the formerly perfectly ideal world God had created.

These options worked themselves out in ancient apocalyptic Judaisms, particularly in the Essene or Enochic communities, in rather remarkable ways that have influenced Western culture ever since. As suggested in Chapter 11, some of the Enochic devotees believed that evil was pervasive in the world because a crowd of lustful angels had descended to earth in its early stages and impregnated human females, thus producing a generation of giants who taught humans to do evil. Others thought that God imposed on the earliest humans a test of obedience that those humans had failed, thus bringing about the reality of evil. Some in both categories believed that divine punishment for evil was arbitrary in that God had elected some to do evil and to be eternally damned, while electing others to be protected from doing evil and to be eternally saved. Other Enochic Essenes believed the choice was up to individual humans: whether to participate in the evil in the world and be damned eternally, or to refrain from such evil behavior and so be found among the righteous people of God (Boccaccini, 1998).

That might seem like a story from some remote and irrelevant past. Nothing could be further from the truth. When I grew up and was ordained in the Christian Reformed Church (CRC), the theological constructs that prevailed in that community were exactly those held by the conservative cloistered Essene Enochians who lived at the village of Qumran and produced the Dead Sea Scrolls. The CRC required that every official in the community, pastors, elders, deacons, and the like, had to sign what was called the *formula of subscription*. That meant that we were required to commit ourselves to believe, preach, and teach the theological framework and doctrines delineated by John Calvin as interpreted by the Canons of Dordrecht and the Belgic Confession.

These documents that we were required to endorse taught a fairly rigid form of the double predestination that prevailed at Qumran 2,200 years earlier. So a 20th-century community was promoting the notion that although evil might have a divine or human origin, either one's participation in it and its drastic eternal consequences were preset by God's eternal decree, determined before history began; or a human could choose personally to do evil. Either way, his or her eternal destiny was preset. The point here is that those ancient pagan ideas, drawn from Persian Zoroastrianism, are still influential in the world today, particularly in the traditional conservative forms of Christianity. Moreover, there are forms of Judaism and Islam today that hold to the same predestinarian doctrines.

Of course, such a mind-set is not biblical. This is readily perceived by any informed, honest, and enlightened interpreter of the Christian Scriptures. However, these ancient ideas do not continue to hang around the human race for theological reasons but for psycho-philosophical reasons. That is, as humans we long for an understanding of the meaning of things in life. So the old questions of where evil came from, what it is really like, how we are involved in it, and what the consequences will be keep coming up in our minds in virtually the same form, century after century. Most of us are quite sure that the God we wish to honor and worship cannot be the source of evil. However, that raises the problem of whether God, then, permits it and why God does not prevent it. We are sure God can prevent it if God so wishes.

In Chapters 1, 6, and 11, I argued for ruling out every notion that there exists some evil agent or force out there in the transcendent world. The only thing out there is the God of unconditional, radical, and universal grace. According to St. Paul and the Gospel of John, God has guaranteed from before the foundation of the earth that the entire world of humans, all other creatures, and this entire created cosmos will be saved in God's unconditional grace toward his whole creation. That radically reduces the urgency of the entire question of the source or origin of evil. It places the focus on the pragmatic question of where evil shows up, and in what form, and what can be done to heal and redeem it.

Because God does not cause evil, and there is no satanic force or devil out there producing it, does God somehow permit it or at least refrain from preventing it when God could, and are we then the source of it? Are we inherently evil, or good but ignorant and clumsy, thus causing evil? Are we the problem of evil? If so, is it perversity or pathology? Or is evil just a fiction of our imagination, not a reality at all? If so, where did we get the idea of evil? Moreover, what name should we then give to the intentional abuse and destruction that humans perpetrate upon each other and upon God's creation? In commenting on the more bizarre images of evil that people have conjured up repeatedly over the last 22 centuries at least, Frankfurter asked,

Where do these images of extreme evil come from? What is the relationship of such extreme images to the popular wish to expel it so violently from our midst? Why are people's larger anxieties and traumas expressed in these particular images, with rituals, perversions, cannibalism, and infant sacrifices—how do these kinds of scenarios come to represent evil? . . . What is the nature of the resemblance between this Satanic Ritual Abuse (SRA) panic, and those in history that alleged that Jews sought out Christian children for ritual sacrifice, that witches engaged in Sabbat atrocities, as well as with those I knew sprouted occasionally in the Roman Empire around Christians and other "ritual" subversives? (2008, pp. xi–xii)

In that last sentence, Frankfurter is alluding to the fact that at the rise of the Christian movement in the ancient world, Christians were often accused of cannibalism in eating the Eucharist, symbolically the body and blood of the Lord.

Nonetheless, the question remains why many humans are fascinated by the sinister, the abusive, and the violent, and seem to have an automatic inclination to project (upon the unknown other) images of the bestial, sexually perverse, demonic, and amoral. Do we have an inherent inclination toward imagining the ugly and wicked possibilities of which humans are unfortunately capable? Do we fear those evils in ourselves and therefore project them on others? Is this a form of psychopathology?

Most human beings live with the feeling that there is something flawed about us, but not all agree on whether our human frailty or dysfunction is something for which we should hold ourselves morally culpable. That is, many folks simply believe that to be human is to be limited in our capacity to know, understand, comprehend, acquire adequate data, and think things out thoroughly before we are required by life to act. Thus most humans, I suspect, do not hold themselves morally accountable for normal human shortcomings in fulfilling duties, maintaining relationships, or caring for oneself. That is, people do not generally blame themselves as guilty when they evidence normal human faults. When we encounter someone who does so blame himself or herself for normal human frailty or flaws, we sense that they are neurotic and are too hard on themselves. In severe cases in which the neurotic anxiety, fear, guilt, or shame causes significant dysfunction in a person's life, we all readily agree that such a person needs clinical treatment.

The upshot of all this is that people generally do not think of themselves as evil, and most of the time do not think of others as evil unless those others cause intolerable discomfort, danger, or damage. Even then, we consider that evil person an exception to the rule. Some faith communities, of course, have a very negatively structured theological model with an exaggerated sense of sin, and produce in their adherents an abnormal level of fear, guilt, and shame about individual persons being inherently evil. This may be found in such communions as those that emphasize that we are all infected from birth with some original sin that misshapes our humanness. That seems to have been the dominant mood and perspective in certain eras of Western history, such as the Church-dominated medieval period. However, one wonders how extensively the real people, down on the ground, actually bought into that official emphasis by the official ecclesiastical powers, particularly when they observed how obscenely the popes and church officials themselves lived, compared to what they officially preached.

That brings us back to the question of whether it is really a sensible question to ask whether humans are basically good or basically evil. Is that a necessary and practical issue to consider? A few humans do monstrously evil things. This happens too often to simply write it off as an occasional aberration or accident of personality dysfunction. Frankfurter makes two points in his book that are relevant to this issue. He says, first, that there really are awful evil acts humans do to each other and to the world God created. These are unacceptable and intolerable. We read about them in the newspapers daily: wanton murders, serial killers, child abductions and molestations, the slaughter of children, the sale of children and women as sex slaves, general slavery around the world, guerrilla warfare with its viciously murderous behavior, the abuse and exploitation of human beings by each other, and the like.

As I sit here writing this, I am being imposed upon by a news bulletin about that wretched Dutch fellow, Joran van der Sloot, who was enmeshed in the disappearance of the student Natalee Holloway in Aruba, and has been imprisoned and indicted for killing a Peruvian beauty with a baseball bat. Only God knows how many lovely young women he and his father, the late judge, sold into sex slavery to the drug cartels in Latin America; and how many Southeast Asian women they murdered or sold into slavery there. What the law enforcement network does know is that they were active in all these areas doing approximately the same demonic things, whatever those will ultimately be proven to be. Moreover, the operation of sex slavery networks based in the Netherlands has been rumored for a number of decades. As Frankfurter declares in his title, evil does seem to be *incarnate* in some human beings. The story of that van der Sloot family illustrates the extent of the depravity and wanton evil that humans can perpetrate.

Frankfurter's second point is that even when and where there are no such evils being perpetrated, there are often people, even communities of people, who project images of evil that in turn infect the cultural imagination. Throughout "history people keep conjuring horrific conspiracies at the hands of infanticidal, licentious, cannibalistic, devil-worshipping cults," for example (Frankfurter, 2008, p. xiii). Frankfurter asks where such images come from and why humans everywhere are always fascinated by such ideas. Why was Disney Enterprises in financial trouble until they began to produce children's videos that reek of violence and abusive behavior? Why do as many or more adults seek them out to watch, as children do? What can we learn from this phenomenon about the *psychological* or *cultural construction* of evil and notions of the demonic? What is the significance of the personal and cultural imagination dreamed up about supernatural and interpersonal evil? We come back to the issue. Because evil is definitively not from God or some transcendent demonic agency, is it us who are inherently infected with some original sin? Are we good or evil in nature or function, or are we ignorant and clumsy because we are underevolved?

It is time for us to turn specifically to that question in all its implications. Are we then the source or *locus* of evil? Are we inherently evil, or are we basically good but inadvertently and thoughtlessly causing evil? Are we the problem of evil, either way? If so, is our evil function perversity or pathology—that is, are those of us who do evil maliciously evil by intention, or are they sick? Or, to repeat myself, is evil just a fiction of our imagination, not a reality at all? If so, where did we get the idea, and by what name should we call the damage people do? Let us address these questions that we have raised, one at a time.

First, we get the idea of evil from a very pragmatic source. *Evil* is the name we give the painful experiences of the distance between the ideal world we can imagine and the really flawed world humans create. We expect Joran van der Sloot to behave like a responsible and godly gentleman. When he does maliciously destructive things, he falls short of our expectations and makes us feel pain. He inflicts pain upon, and terminates the lives of, his victims. That is so abnormal a behavior, and so unacceptable in terms of the societal values according to which we expect him, as well as the rest of us, to behave, that we justly call his behavior evil. We may even name him an evil man because his perversity seems so endogenous and perpetually repeated.

Second, are we humans the *locus* of evil, that is, are we the problem? Clearly it is the case that all forms of empirical, phenomenological, heuristic, and rational research and analysis return us every time to the fact that evil is what humans do to each other and to God's created world. There is reason to conclude that Mr. van der Sloot is illustrative of the paradigm in which all humans function. The spectrum of the serious flaws in our characters, of course, is very wide. It ranges all the way from (a) a thoughtless slight of attention to a tender child, to (b) infractions of thoughtlessness and carelessness like careless driving that causes an accident, to (c) the extremities of the monstrous behaviors of serial killers. Humans are the problem!

Third, are we inherently evil or just ignorant and clumsy? I think it is possible to conclude, with sensible moral judgment, that most humans perpetrate only rather ordinary evil that is not viciously intrusive or horrifically damaging to themselves or others. It is a fact that we are called upon, from youth to old age, to make significant decisions every day for which we are not given adequate information. We have a limited database, at best; and we have greater or lesser limitations of good sense, reasonableness, and appropriate feeling about things. We are all flawed in the sense of being limited humans. However, that does not mean we are inherently evil. It means we are basically good but ignorant and clumsy.

We have a divine responsibility to live ideally in God's world, but we have only human resources with which to do that. So St. Paul laments that we all fall short of the glorious destiny that God made potentially possible for us, and that most of us can imagine and seek, but never quite achieve. Life is an experiment in trial and error toward growth. That is the way God set it up. That cannot be changed. We can only try to help each other facilitate our way through it. That does not mean we are inherently evil. It only means we are limited and underevolved. So the main issue is not that we are sinners. God forgave all that before history began and decided to embrace us all in his healing grace. The main issue is undertaking to do the best we can with what we have left, at every point in life. That is the essential question from the minute we are conceived in the womb to the moment we transit the permeable screen between time and eternity. Then we shall "see reality whole and face to face, knowing God as thoroughly as God now knows us" (I Cor. 13:12).

Fourth, what about the behavior of humans that is monstrous and cannot be explained as simply caused by ignorance or clumsiness? What about serial killers and Mr. van der Sloot? Such behavior is clearly done by malicious intent and is a form of contrived damage to another human and to society. It is so aberrant in both motivation and execution, act and consequence, that there is no name to give it but willful and woeful evil—horrific destructiveness. We can call it *demonic*, if we mean that in the sense of a qualitative metaphor rather than an otherworldly agent or force. Are Joran van der Sloot and Jeffrey Dahmer inherently evil or sick? Is monstrous human evil pathology?

As a clinical psychotherapist with 55 years of experience in treating patients, I have a theory about this. Moreover, I notice that the clinical community and the perspective of the wise ones who create and constantly revise the diagnostic manual for our profession are moving progressively toward agreement with me. It is my perception that approximately 40% of every human community, cross-culturally and cross-generationally, should be diagnosed as borderline psychotic. I consider this a description of a characterological status, not just a personality disorder, as borderline patients have historically been described. Of this 40%, approximately a third are mild, a third moderate, and a third severe.

We are all acquainted with each of these categories of persons, though we do not generally have the terminology readily at hand to describe them diagnostically. Mild borderline psychotics, in my model, are those people you see in every community who seem very bright, get your attention for being particularly attractive when "on stage," and prompt you to think that they will go far in life. They may be working in restaurants to support their college degree programs, but you expect a great future no matter what course they choose. You move on in your life, and then you encounter those persons again 10 years later and are stunned by the fact that they are still spinning their wheels, have gained no ground, and are still just managing to sustain life. You wonder why all the brilliance, imagination, congeniality, and social skills have not driven the person forward to greater achievement in life. It is because their concept of reality from birth onward does not align with reality.

Borderline psychotics are born with a notion of reality in the back of their minds that is not synchronous with reality as normal people experience it. Consequently, they spend all their psychic energy coping with everyday life. This inborn characteristic can be traced back through a family history generation by generation. There is always an identifiable parent in each previous generation who stands out as the dysfunctional one. They are not brighter than the rest of us, but seem that way because their sense from childhood onward that life just never works for them puts them on full alert. They are using 90% of their gray matter, whereas the rest of us are coasting along on about 10% of our brain power. These folks get by in life so long as no major crisis arises. In crisis they tend to dysfunction overtly, often severely, flipping across the line into active psychosis and needing clinical treatment.

Moderate borderline psychotics are more noticeable as being not quite right, though they are usually not identified in society as pathological, except by the people who must live intimately with them. All borderlines consistently have five or six characteristics that cause the rest of us to notice their being a bit strange. They are very narcissistic, somewhat paranoid, generally situation inappropriate, compulsive, incapable of putting themselves into another person's feeling world, and incapable of standing outside themselves and critiquing themselves, so to speak.

Consequently, they never are able to acknowledge that they are at fault for anything and never really apologize. Moderate borderlines are generally tolerated in society but are constantly creating crises and blaming others for them. They are constantly moderately destructive people, tending to create tension and damage in their families and eventually wearing out all their friends. In crises, they are basket cases of overt dysfunction and frequently of psychotic episodes.

Severe borderline psychotics are mostly in prison or mental hospitals, or should be. They are the abusive, destructive, conscienceless epitomes of towering narcissism, chronic paranoia, constant situation inappropriateness, compulsiveness to the point of being obsessive, insensitivity to others, and exploitive behavior of everyone and everything they can touch. They really perceive, in their sick minds, that the entire world of persons and things exists for their consumption. They chew it up and spit it out, so to speak, as illustrated by serial killers, beastly persons like Adolf Hitler, and persons of either gender who chronically abuse their spouses and children in cruel ways. These severe borderline psychotics often bounce across the line, so to speak, into full-blown psychosis. This is the type of thing that may account for Mr. van der Sloot's and Mr. Dahmer's unconscionable behavior and their apparently complete lack of emotion or remorse about it.

I understand that 80% of the inmates of our prison systems are severe borderline psychotics. I suspect that is typical of prisons all over the world. That is certainly the reason that rehabilitation in our prisons has such a poor outcome record. These people cannot be changed. They can only be controlled by medication, and forced medication is not possible in our democracy. We must find a solution to that, or we will continue to have societies with monstrous evil perpetrated by the severe borderline psychotics.

Fifth, evil is not a fiction of our imagination. It is real, and we should always name it boldly for what it is. However, at least 60% of the human race, though flawed or limited, does not perpetrate what should properly be referred to as evil. Of the other 40%, at least a third do not do much evil, though they can be surprisingly thoughtless and neglectful. Evil is a distinct, identifiable, and chronically evident phenomenon in every society and is a product of a structural flaw in the genetic roots of moderate and severe borderline psychotics. It is high time that society addresses this issue and stops wasting time and treasure on the notion that evil is a product of environments.

Bad environments must be corrected. Every human has an inherent right to live decently. However, we will never get gains on the problem of evil until we face the fact that the people who do monstrous things, whether in bad environments or good ones, are sick (i.e., crazy) and must be identified early, constrained, and medicated—for their own good and the good of the rest of us. In Volume 2, Chapter 4 of this set of volumes, Cassandra Klyman, MD, addresses some of the medical and biochemical issues related to this genetically inherited problem as they show up already in children. Perpetuating dumb notions that all humans are evil or that evil derives from original sin is, in itself, a kind of sin against the human race. Let's get rid of such useless and unreal ideas.

REFERENCES

Boccaccini, G. (1998). *Beyond the Essene hypothesis: The parting of the ways between Qumran and Enochic Judaism.* Grand Rapids MI: Eerdmans.

Frankfurter, D. (2008). *Evil incarnate: Rumors of demonic conspiracy and satanic abuse in history.* Princeton, NJ: Princeton University Press.

INDEX

About the Editor and Advisers

EDITOR

J. Harold Ellens, PhD, is a research scholar, a retired Presbyterian theologian and ordained minister, a retired U.S. Army colonel, and a retired professor of philosophy, theology and psychology. He has authored, coauthored and/or edited 185 books and 167 professional journal articles. He served 15 years as executive director of the Christian Association for Psychological Studies, and as founding editor and editor-in-chief of the *Journal of Psychology and Christianity*. He holds a PhD from Wayne State University in the Psychology of Human Communication, a PhD from the University of Michigan in Biblical and Near Eastern Studies, and master's degrees from Calvin Theological Seminary, Princeton Theological Seminary, and the University of Michigan. He was born in Michigan, grew up in a Dutch-German immigrant community, and determined at age seven to enter the Christian Ministry as a means to help his people with the great amount of suffering he perceived all around him during the Great Depression and WWII. His life's work has focused on the interface of psychology and religion.

ADVISERS

Donald Capps, PhD and Psychologist of Religion, is Emeritus William Hart Felmeth Professor of Pastoral Theology at Princeton Theological Seminary. In 1989 he was awarded an honorary doctorate from the University of Uppsala, Sweden, in recognition of the importance of his publications.

He served as president of the Society for the Scientific Study of Religion from 1990 to 1992. Among his many significant books are *Men, Religion and Melancholia: James, Otto, Jung and Erikson and Freud*; also *The Freudians on Religion: A Reader*; also *Social Phobia: Alleviating Anxiety in an Age of Self-Promotion*; and *Jesus: A Psychological Biography*. He also authored *The Child's Song: The Religious Abuse of Children*, and *Jesus, the Village Psychiatrist*.

Zenon Lotufo Jr., PhD, is a Presbyterian minister (Independent Presbyterian Church of Brazil), a philosopher and a psychotherapist, specializing in Transactional Analysis. He has lectured both to undergraduate and graduate courses in universities in São Paulo, Brazil. He coordinates the course of specialization in Pastoral Psychology of the Christian Psychologists and Psychiatrists Association. He is the author of the books *Relações Humanas* [Human Relations]; *Disfunções no Comportamento Organizacional* [Dysfunctions in Organizational Behavior] and co-author of *O Potencial Humano* [Human Potential]. He has also authored numerous journal articles.

Dirk Odendaal, DLitt, is South African, born in what is now called the Province of the Eastern Cape. He spent much of his youth in the Transkei in the town of Umtata, where his parents were teachers at a seminary. He trained as a minister at the Stellenbosch Seminary for the Dutch Reformed Church and was ordained in 1983 in the Dutch Reformed Church in Southern Africa. He transferred to East London in 1988 to minister to members of the Uniting Reformed Church in Southern Africa in one of the huge suburbs for Xhosa-speaking people. He received his doctorate (D.Litt.) in 1992 at the University of Port Elizabeth in Semitic Languages and a Masters Degree in Counseling Psychology at Rhodes University.

Wayne G. Rollins, PhD, is Professor Emeritus of Biblical Studies at Assumption College, Worcester, Massachusetts, and Adjunct Professor of Scripture at Hartford Seminary, Hartford, Connecticut. His writings include *The Gospels: Portraits of Christ* (1964), *Jung and the Bible* (1983), and *Soul and Psyche, The Bible in Psychological Perspective* (1999). He received his PhD in New Testament Studies from Yale University and is the founder and chairman (1990–2000) of the Society of Biblical Literature Section on Psychology and Biblical Studies.

About the Contributors

Deb Brock, MDiv, PhD, is a clinical psychologist practicing in Madison, Wisconsin, together with her psychologist husband, Ron Johnson, a practice they have had together for 30 years. Dr. Brock's background includes both theological and psychological study in addition to advanced study in EMDR, gestalt, focusing, and other forms of therapy. Her interests center around resolution of trauma and integration of the disciplines of psychology, philosophy, and theology. She has published in the *Journal of Psychology and Christianity* and elsewhere.

Paul M. Butler, MTS, is a MD–PhD candidate completing his dissertation research under the guidance of Dr. Patrick McNamara at Boston University School of Medicine. His research covers a diverse array of topics. A recent publication assesses religious semantic network activation in patients with Parkinson's disease. The work highlights the importance of right fronto-striatal networks to sustain religious cognition. Forthcoming publications investigate the role of dopamine 4 receptor (DRD4) polymorphisms and novelty-seeking behavior in human migration patterns out of Africa in the Late Pleistocene, epigenetics and Parkinson's disease susceptibility, a genetically testable diagnosis for the philosopher Friedrich Nietzsche, a medical biography of Henry Ingersoll Bowditch, and explorations of the self in religious cognition.

Nathan Carlin, PhD, is an assistant professor in the John P. McGovern, M.D. Center for Humanities and Ethics at the University of Texas Health Science Center at Houston. He also holds an appointment in the Department

of Family Medicine in the University of Texas Medical School at Houston.
Dr. Carlin, the son of a steel mill worker, grew up in Western Pennsylvania,
some 30 miles north of Pittsburgh. He graduated with college honors in history from Westminster College in New Wilmington, PA; he holds a master
of divinity degree from Princeton Theological Seminary in Princeton, NJ,
where he concentrated on pastoral theology; and he holds master of arts and
doctor of philosophy degrees in religious studies, with a specialization in psychology of religion, from Rice University in Houston, TX. Carlin has published over 40 essays and numerous book reviews. He serves as book review
editor for *Pastoral Psychology*, a leading and historic journal in the fields of
psychology of religion and pastoral care, and he also serves as subeditor for
Religious Studies Review. He gives talks and presentations in a variety of settings and places. And he teaches at times for the Continuing Education School
at Rice University. Carlin draws on his training in psychology of religion and
pastoral theology to do work in the field of medical humanities.

Suzanne M. Coyle, PhD, is assistant professor of pastoral theology and marriage and family therapy at Christian Theological Seminary in Indianapolis,
where she also serves as the executive director of the Counseling Center and
director of the Marriage and Family Therapy Program. A diplomate in the
American Association of Pastoral Counselors and an approved supervisor in
American Association for Marriage and Family Therapy, she has many years
of experience as a pastor, therapist, consultant, and educator. Dr. Coyle holds
a MDiv and PhD from Princeton Theological Seminary.

J. Harold Ellens, PhD, is retired from his roles as professor of philosopher
and psychology, executive director of the Christian Association for Psychological Studies, founder and editor-in-chief of the *Journal of Psychology and
Christianity*, U.S. Army colonel, and Presbyterian (PCUSA) theologian and
pastor. He continues in private practice as a licensed psychotherapist and as
an international lecturer. He is the author of 180 published volumes, mainly
on the interface of psychology and spirituality, and of 167 professional journal
articles and reviews. He is the father of seven children. He and his wife have
been married for 56 years.

Richard K. Fenn, PhD, recently retired from Princeton Theological Seminary after 25 years on the faculty teaching the sociology of religion. His
interests include the sociology of time, of the sacred, and of crisis.

Stanislav Grof, MD, is a psychiatrist with more than 50 years of experience in research of nonordinary states of consciousness. He was principal
investigator in a psychedelic research program at the Psychiatric Research
Institute in Prague, Czechoslovakia; chief of Psychiatric Research at the

Maryland Psychiatric Research Center; assistant professor of psychiatry at Johns Hopkins University; and scholar-in-residence at the Esalen Institute. He is professor of psychology at the California Institute of Integral Studies (CIIS) in San Francisco. He conducts professional training programs in holotropic breathwork and transpersonal psychology, and is a founder and chief theoretician of transpersonal psychology, as well as founding president of the International Transpersonal Association (ITA). Among his publications are over 150 articles and the books *Beyond the Brain*, *LSD Psychotherapy*, *The Cosmic Game*, *Psychology of the Future*, *The Ultimate Journey*, and *When the Impossible Happens*. He is the recipient of the Vaclav Havel Prize, Vision 97.

Ralph W. Hood Jr., PhD, is professor of psychology at the University of Tennessee at Chattanooga. He is a former president of the Division of the Psychology of Religion of the American Psychological Association and a recipient of its William James Award as well as its Distinguished Service and Mentor Awards. He is a former editor of the *Journal for the Scientific Study of Religion*. He was one of the founders and coeditors of *The International Journal for the Psychology of Religion* and is a current coeditor of the *Archive for the Psychology of Religion*.

Virginia Ingram is a graduate of the SCD in Sydney, Australia, specializing in biblical Hebrew, with advanced studies in Hebrew language and literature in Rome, and at the Hebrew University of Jerusalem. She is currently studying to become an Anglican priest with the Archdiocese of Perth, Australia.

Ron Johnson, MDiv, PhD, is a clinical psychologist, therapist, and author. His interests and expertise are in the psychology of men, positive psychology, neuropsychology, and the integration of psychology with other philosophical disciplines. He has written the books *Friendly Diagnosis*, *Seen and Not Heard*, *Mantalk*, and others, as well as several journal and chapter articles. He lives and works with his psychologist wife in Madison, Wisconsin, and does specialty work in Newfoundland, Canada.

Nicolene L. Joubert, PhD, is professor of psychology at the Afrikaans Protestant Academy and founder and head of their Institute of Christian Psychology. She is a registered counseling psychologist and a trained biblical counselor with 27 years of experience. She has completed her PhD thesis on the topic of biblically based systemic therapy, and her vision is to develop the field of Christian psychology in Africa. She is founder and chairperson of the South African Society for the Study of Trauma and Dissociation. Her life's work has focused on applying biblical principles to relieve suffering in her community and country. She has authored and coauthored various publications in the field of Christian psychology.

Zelmarie E. Joubert obtained her BA honors degree in psychology from the University of South Africa and has been involved with the Institute of Christian Psychology as lecturer and course developer for the past decade. Her interests include the development of noneconomic language promotion plans and the impact of popular culture on the individual. She is currently preparing for masters degree research into language strategies for cross-cultural counseling.

Raymond J. Lawrence, DMin, is a clinical pastoral supervisor, pastoral psychotherapist, and social critic. He is the author of *The Poisoning of Eros: Sexual Values in Conflict* (1989); *Sexual Liberation: The Scandal of Christendom* (2007), also published in Vienna as *Sexualitat und Christentum: Geschichte der Irrwege und Ansatze zur Befreiung* (2010); and numerous book chapters and journal articles on subjects in the areas of pastoral counseling, supervision, and social ethics. His opinion pieces have appeared in various journals, including the *Journal of the American Medical Association, Second Opinion, Christianity and Crisis*, and many major newspapers in the United States. For 15 years until recent retirement, he directed the Pastoral Care Department and Chaplaincy Training Program at Columbia Presbyterian Medical Center in New York. He is now general secretary for the College of Pastoral Supervision and Psychotherapy.

Patrick McNamara, PhD, is the director of the Lab of Evolutionary Neurobehavior at Boston University School of Medicine and cofounder of the Institute for the Biocultural Study of Religion. His research contributes to the scientific study of religion, Parkinson's disease, the evolutionary significance of mammalian REM/NREM sleep states, language pragmatics, and historical consciousness. Recently, he has edited a three-volume series on the scientific study of religion, *Where God and Science Meet* (Praeger Press, 2006), in addition to a landmark book, *The Neuroscience of Religious Experience* (Cambridge University Press, 2009). His research pioneers the exploration of the role that human frontal lobe function serves for religiosity. Over the past 20 years, his publications have advanced our understanding of the human condition from a neuroscientific and evolutionary psychological perspective.

Ilona Rashkow, PhD, has a primary interest in psychoanalytic literary theory, particularly as applied to the Hebrew Bible. Among her publications are *Taboo or Not Taboo: The Hebrew Bible and Human Sexuality* (2000); *The Phallacy of Genesis: A Feminist-Psychoanalytic Approach* (1993); *Upon the Dark Places: Sexism and Anti-Semitism in English Renaissance Biblical Translation* (1990); and numerous chapters in books, encyclopedic articles, and journal articles. She is professor emerita at the State University of New York at Stony Brook and teaches regularly at New York University.

F. Morgan Roberts, DD, served as a pastor in the Presbyterian Church (USA) for over 50 years. Upon retirement, he was named pastor emeritus of the Shadyside Presbyterian Church of Pittsburgh. Following retirement, he served several congregations as an interim pastor, and ended his ministry as interim director of field education and adjunct professor of ministry and homiletics at Louisville Presbyterian Theological Seminary. Dr. Roberts was educated at Colgate University and Princeton Theological Seminary, and has received five honorary doctoral degrees. He is a member of the Society of Biblical Literature.

Wayne G. Rollins, PhD, is professor emeritus of biblical studies at Assumption College, Worcester, Massachusetts, and adjunct professor of scripture at Hartford Seminary, Hartford, Connecticut. He has also taught at Princeton University and Wellesley College, and served as visiting professor at Mount Holyoke College, Yale College, College of the Holy Cross, and Colgate Rochester Divinity School. His writings include *The Gospels: Portraits of Christ* (1964); *Jung and the Bible* (1983); and *Soul and Psyche, The Bible in Psychological Perspective* (1999). He coedited four volumes of essays with J. Harold Ellens, *Psychology and the Bible: A New Way to Read the Scriptures* (2004), and a volume on *Psychological Insight into the Bible: Texts and Readings* (2007) with D. Andrew Kille. He received his PhD in New Testament studies from Yale University and is the founder and chairman (1990–2000) of the Society of Biblical Literature Section on Psychology and Biblical Studies.

Ronald Reese Ruark, PhD, is a graduate student at the University of Michigan, where he studies Second Temple Judaism and Early Christianity under the supervision of Gabriele Boccaccini. He is a graduate of Bryan College (BA, 1980), Dallas Theological Seminary (ThM, 1984), and Marquette University School of Law (JD, 1991). He is a practicing attorney in Wayne, Michigan, where he resides with his wife Nancy.

Loren T. Stuckenbruck, PhD, is Richard J. Dearborn Professor of New Testament Studies at Princeton Theological Seminary, having previously held the B. F. Westcott Chair in Biblical Studies at Durham University, UK. The author of several academic monographs, he has edited a number of books and is the author of over a hundred academic articles. He is chief editor of Commentaries on *Early Jewish Literature* (Walter de Gruyter), senior editor of *Journal for the Study of the Pseudepigrapha*, and on the editorial board of *Journal of Biblical Literature, Dead Sea Discoveries*, and *Zeitschrift f. die neutestamentliche Wissenschaft*.